Singing the Crusades

Singing the Crusades
French and Occitan Lyric Responses
to the Crusading Movements, 1137–1336

Linda Paterson

in collaboration with
Luca Barbieri, Ruth Harvey and Anna Radaelli,
and with an appendix by Marjolaine Raguin

D. S. BREWER

© Linda Paterson 2018

All Rights Reserved. Except as permitted under current legislation
no part of this work may be photocopied, stored in a retrieval system,
published, performed in public, adapted, broadcast,
transmitted, recorded or reproduced in any form or by any means,
without the prior permission of the copyright owner

The right of Linda Paterson to be identified as
the author of this work has been asserted in accordance with
sections 77 and 78 of the Copyright, Designs and Patents Act 1988

First published 2018
D. S. Brewer, Cambridge
Paperback edition 2021

ISBN 978 1 84384 482 2 hardback
ISBN 978 1 84384 600 0 paperback

D. S. Brewer is an imprint of Boydell & Brewer Ltd
PO Box 9, Woodbridge, Suffolk IP12 3DF, UK
and of Boydell & Brewer Inc.
668 Mt Hope Avenue, Rochester, NY 14620–2731, USA
website: www.boydellandbrewer.com

A catalogue record for this book is available from the British Library

The publisher has no responsibility for the continued existence or accuracy of URLs
for external or third-party internet websites referred to in this book,
and does not guarantee that any content on such websites is, or will remain, accurate
or appropriate

This publication is printed on acid-free paper

Contents

List of Maps	vi
Acknowledgements	vii
Abbreviations	ix
Author's Note	xiii
Introduction	1
1. Early Expeditions	25
2. After Damascus: Reconquest, Settlement and Pilgrimage	39
3. The Third Crusade (1187–1192)	47
4. The Aftermath of the Third Crusade	76
5. The Fourth Crusade and its Aftermath	97
6. The Fifth Crusade, of Damietta, and the Albigensian Crusade	123
7. Frederick II and the Sixth Crusade	136
8. The 'False Crusade': the Albigensian war of 1224–1233	154
9. The Barons' Crusade, or the crusade of Thibaut de Champagne	167
10. The Seventh Crusade, or the First Crusade of Saint Louis	179
11. The Eighth Crusade, or the Second Crusade of Saint Louis	203
12. After Saint Louis	225
Conclusion	253
Appendix A. The Words To Say It: The Crusading Rhetoric of the Troubadours and Trouvères – Marjolaine Raguin-Barthelmebs	259
Appendix B. Chronology of events and texts	286
Appendix C. Melodies attested in the MSS	302
Bibliography	307
Index	319

List of Maps

The maps are based on the map of the Mediterranean sea (coasts, hydrography) provided on <http://www.d-maps.com/carte.php?num_car=3124>. Their content is designed as a convenient reference to places mentioned in the book.

1. France and Its Neighbours   xv
2. Occitania   xvi
3. Iberia   xvi
4. Italy and Greece   xvii
5. The Holy Land   xviii

Acknowledgements

This book is the fruit of a collaborative project, *Lyric Reponses to the Crusades in Medieval France and Occitania*, funded by research grants from the Arts and Humanities Research Council, the British Academy, the Humanities Research Fund of the University of Warwick and the Warwick Department of French Studies. I am deeply grateful to all these bodies for enabling the project. It has led to the online publication of over 200 critical editions of Old French and Occitan texts, and although I wrote the present book and take full responsibility for its defects, I drew heavily on these editions and the philological, literary and historical research involved in their establishment. In this sense the book's authorship is collaborative. Luca Barbieri and Anna Radaelli produced all but one of the Old French texts, with assistance from Stefano Asperti, the remaining song being Richard the Lionheart's *Ja nus homs pris*, edited by Charmaine Lee. I established the majority of the Occitan texts, either editing them anew or updating reliable ones. A number were also edited by Ruth Harvey, and we cross-checked each other's editions. Other scholars kindly contributed other new Occitan editions: Miriam Cabré, Sadurní Martí and Marina Navas, Walter Meliga, Lauren Mulholland, Gianfelice Peron and Giorgio Barachini who stepped in most generously at a time of crisis. I am also grateful to Stefano Asperti, Giorgio Barachini, Gilda Caïti-Russo, Gérard Gouiran, Saverio Guida, Giosuè Lachin, Monica Longobardi, Paolo di Luca, Dario Mantovani, Caterina Menichetti, Carlo Pulsoni, Paulo Squillacioti and Sergio Vatteroni for the use of their published editions. The English translations were done by me with Ruth Harvey's assistance, the Italian ones by Luca Barbieri with the help of Anna Radaelli, and Barbieri performed the technical work of putting the editions online at <http://www.rialto.unina.it/BdT.htm>, with some help from Oriana Scarpati and Paolo di Luca. Costanzo di Girolamo kindly hosted the editions in the Rialto website and gave unfailingly prompt assistance throughout the project and beyond.

I am grateful to Tom Asbridge, John Gillingham, Nick Paul, Jonathan Phillips, Isabel de Riquer and Jane Taylor for their encouragement and suggestions, and most particularly to: Simon Gaunt, who read the whole manuscript; to Jonathan Phillips and Simon Parsons, Royal Holloway University of London and the Isobel Thornley Fund for enabling us to hold a colloquium on the project in London in 2014; to Liese Perrin and Katie Klaassen for their invaluable help with grant applications and administration; to Steve Ranford who with assistance from Warwick IT Services set up the project website and gave generously of his time in contributing to its development and maintenance; and to Caroline Palmer, Rob Kinsey and the production team at Boydell & Brewer for their kind attention and hard work in bringing both *Singing the Crusades* and *Literature of the Crusades* to fruition. Francesco Carapezza and Gérard Gouiran contributed sung and spoken performances of melodies to the website, kindly recorded at short notice by Arthur Brown and Paul Savva-Andreou. Mike Paterson, unsparing as ever in his patience, inventiveness and time, took over the exacting tasks of putting the Old French texts online and producing the map outlines; he has been a boundless source of technical and moral support.

I should like to emphasise my particular gratitude to my closest collaborators over the last five years. Luca Barbieri went way beyond the call of his duties as Research Assistant, and his professional expertise, his constant and quick responsiveness and his readiness to help out in difficult circumstances have been essential to the project's success. Anna Radaelli's enthusiasm, fine scholarship and willingness to help out despite her other commitments have been of great benefit to our common endeavours and a source of keen pleasure to me personally. Ruth Harvey has done a great deal of work behind the scenes, and has been unflagging in her support and encouragement. She helps me see the wood for the trees.

Linda Paterson

Abbreviations

Text identifiers

BdT	Pillet, A. and Carstens, H., *Bibliographie der Trobadors* (Halle, 1933)
BPP	Zufferey, F., Bibliographie des poètes provençaux des XIVe et XVe siècles (Geneva, 1981)
DBT	*Dizionario biografico dei trovatori*, ed. S. Guida and G. Larghi (Modena, 2013)
GV	Geoffrey of Villehardouin, *La Conquête de Constantinople*, ed. E. Faral, 2 vols (Paris, 1938)
IDT	*L'Italia dei trovatori: repertorio dei componimenti trobadorici relativi alla storia d'Italia*, co-ordinated by P. di Luca, <http://www.idt.unina.it/index.html>
RS	Spanke, H. G., *Raynauds Bibliographie des altfranzösischen Liedes, neu bearbeitet und ergänzt* (Leiden, 1955)
SOED	*Shorter Oxford English Dictionary on Historical Principles*, ed. C. T. Onions, 2 vols (Oxford, 1933, repr. 1965)

Abbreviations for troubadours and trouvères

AimBel	Aimeric de Belenoi
AimPeg	Aimeric de Peguilhan
AudBast	Audfroi le Bastart
AustAur	Austorc d'Aorlhac
AustSegr	Austorc de Segret
BertZorzi	Bertolome Zorzi
Blacst	Blacatz
BnAlanh	Bernart Alanhan de Narbona

BnAur	Bernart d'Auriac
BnRov	Bernart de Rovenac
BtAlam	Bertran d'Alamanon
BtBorn	Bertran de Born
BtCarb	Bertran Carbonel de Marseilla
CalPanz	Calega Panzan
CavLun	Cavalier Lunel de Monteg
Cercam	Cercamon
Cerv	Cerverí de Girona
CharCrois	Chardon de Croisilles
ChArr	Châtelain d'Arras
ChCoucy	Châtelain de Coucy
CnBéth	Conon de Béthune
CtFoix	Coms de Foix
CtProv	Coms de Proensa
Dasp	Daspol
DurSartr	Duran Sartor de Paernas
ElBarj	Elias de Barjols
ElCair	Elias Cairel
ElUss	Elias d'Ussel
FqLun	Folquet de Lunel
FqMars	Folquet de Marseilla
FrRmCorn	Fr Ramon de Cornet
FqRom	Falquet de Romans
Gav	Gavaudan
GcFaid	Gaucelm Faidit
GlAdem	Guillem Ademar
GlBerg	Guillem de Berguedan
GlFabre	Guillem Fabre de Narbona
GlFig	Guillem Figueira
GlMont	Guillem Montanhagol
GlMur	Guillem de Mur
GlPeit	Guillem de Peiteu (Guillem IX)
Gorm	Gormonda
GoSoig	Gontier de Soignies

Gran	Granet
GrBorn	Giraut de Borneil
GrLuc	Guiraut de Luc
GrRiq	Guiraut Riquier
GtDarg	Gautier de Dargies
GuDij	Guiot de Dijon
HgBerzé	Hughes de Berzé
HStQuen	Huon de Saint-Quentin
HuOisy	Huon d'Oisy
JfreRud	Jaufre Rudel
JoCast	Joan de Castelnou
LanfrCig	Lanfranc Cigala
MatQuercy	Matieu de Caerci
Mbru	Marcabru
MoMont	Monge de Montaudo
OlTempl	Olivier lo Templier
PAlv	Peire d'Alvernhe
PArag	Peire III d'Arago
PaMars	Paulet de Marselha
PBrem	Peire Bremon Ricas Novas
PBremTort	Peire Bremon lo Tort
PCard	Peire Cardenal
Peirol	Peirol
Perd	Perdigon
PersDor	Perseval Doria
PhNant	Philippe de Nanteuil
PhNov	Philippe de Novare
PoCapd	Pons de Capdoill
PSalv	Peire Salvatge
PVid	Peire Vidal
PVilar	Peire del Vilar
RbVaq	Raimbaut de Vaqueiras
Renas	Renas
RlSoiss	Raoul de Soissons
RmCorn	Ramon de Cornet

RmGauc	Raimon Gaucelm de Beziers
RmMirav	Raimon de Miraval
RoiRich	Roi Richart
RostBer	Rostaing Berenguier de Marseilla
Sord	Sordel
TbChamp	Thibaut de Champagne
Templ	Ricaut Bonomel
TomPal	Tomier e Palaizi
UcPenn	Uc de Pena
UcStC	Uc de Saint Circ
VdChar	Vidame de Chartres

Other abbreviations

AAD	*Argumentation et Analyse du Discours,* http://aad.revues.org/
AdM	*Annales du Midi*
BEC	*Bibliothèque de l'École des Chartes*
CN	*Cultura Neolatina*
EHR	*English Historical Review*
JEH	*Journal of Ecclesiastical History*
JMH	*Journal of Medieval History*
Lt	*Lecturae tropatorum*
MAe	*Medium Aevum*
MR	*Medioevo Romanzo*
MS	*Mediaeval Studies*
RF	*Romanische Forschungen*
RHC	*Recueil des Historiens des Croisades*
RLM	*Revista de literatura medieval*
RMS	*Reading Medieval Studies*
RPh	*Romance Philology*
RST	*Rivista di Studi Testuali*
TSMAO	*Typologie des sources du moyen âge occidental* (Turnhout, 1972–)
ZRP	*Zeitschrift für Romanische Philologie*

Author's Note

This book is an outcome of a wish to make the lyric sources available and to diffuse the information and insights they provide. It is based on a corpus of over two hundred texts which have been placed online, half of them newly edited from the medieval manuscripts, together with translations and information about their dating and the historical circumstances of their composition.[1] References in the book are given to the trouvère (Old French) texts with the preface RS, for example RS 1125, and to troubadour (Occitan) ones with the preface BdT or BPP, for example BdT 10.1 or BPP 557.1.[2] The book is designed for a variety of readers, and to avoid overloading it with an excessive number of bibliographical references these are not given when the full background information is already provided with the online texts. The website should be consulted for these and for further discussions about dating and circumstances of composition. Such references are signalled within the book.

[1] <http://warwick.ac.uk/crusadelyrics>
[2] RS, BdT, BPP. The troubadour texts can be accessed either through our website or directly through <http://www.rialto.unina.it/BdT.htm> which hosts them as part of a larger corpus. Where texts outside our corpus are referred to in this book and are found on the Rialto site, no further references are given beyond the abbreviation BdT and the identifying number.

Map 1. France and Its Neighbours

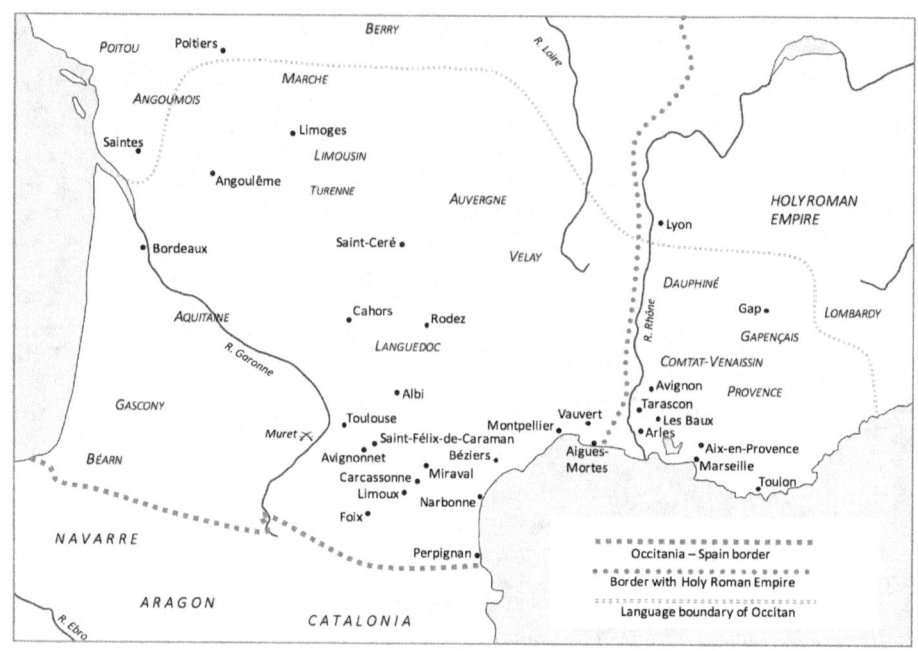

2. Occitania

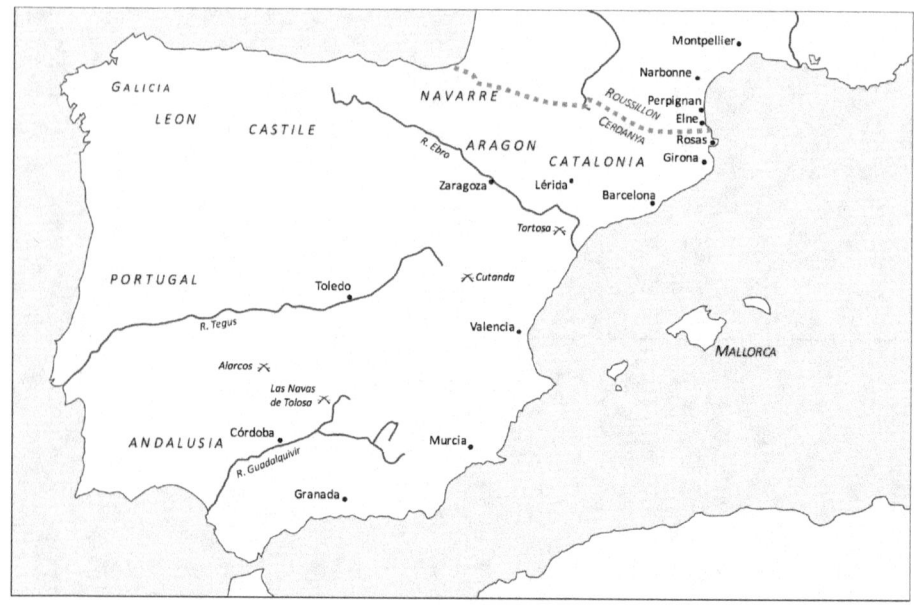

3. Iberia

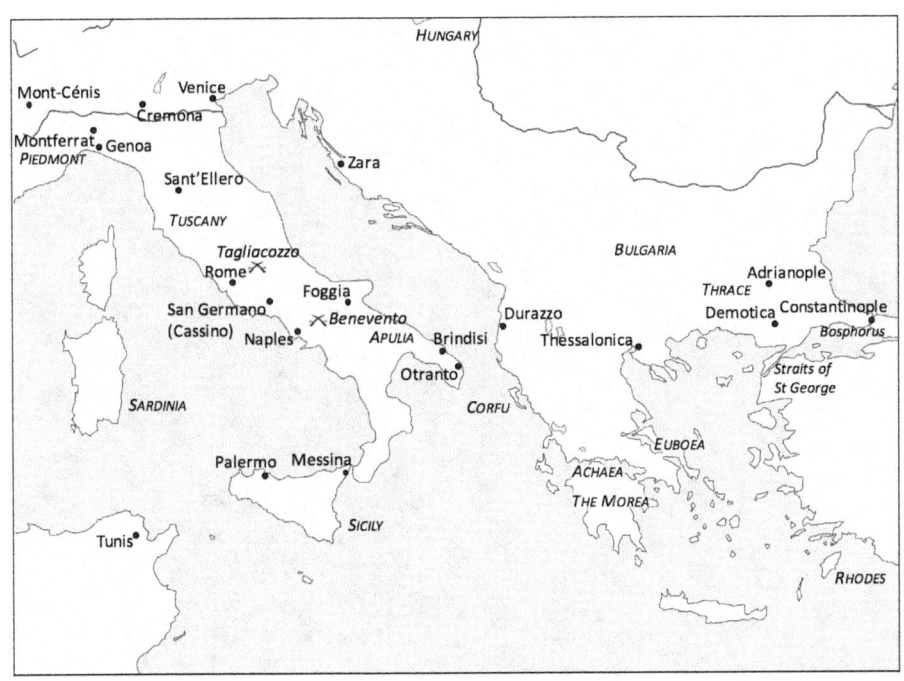

4. Italy and Greece

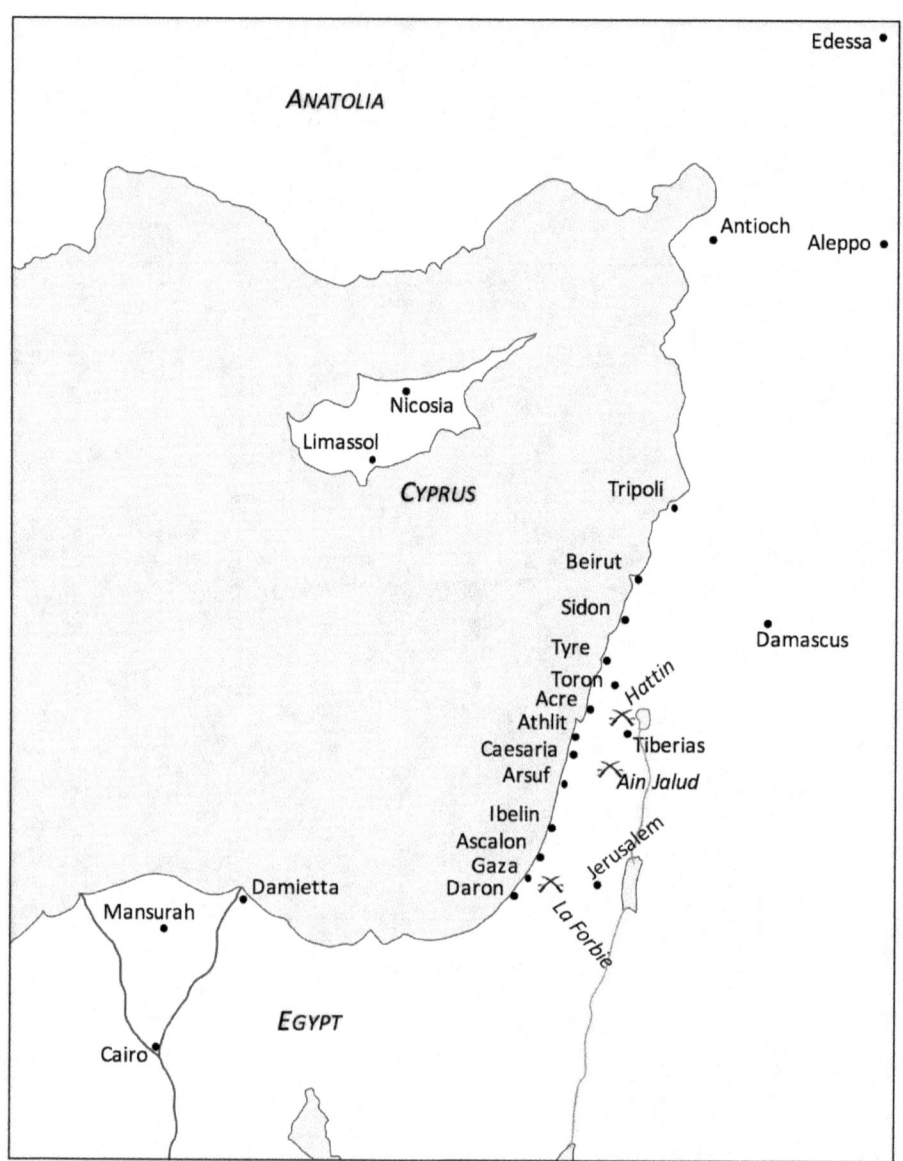

5. The Holy Land

Introduction

The crusades have left a profound and disturbing legacy in inter-cultural and interfaith relations, nationally and worldwide, not least in the continuing aftermath of the then US President George W. Bush's 2001 'crusade' against Iraq. Daily we witness the interminable ravaging of ancient Middle Eastern cities, as crusading rhetoric gushes from the global political discourse transmitted in the media. In seeking more than a simplistic view of the original, medieval crusading movement, we can draw on a wide variety of written sources. Most are in Latin. Ecclesiastical documents present official versions of the preaching, organisation and events of the medieval crusades. Narratives in both Latin and the vernacular offer a range of factual information, eye-witness or mythologised accounts of particular expeditions, the memorialisation of heroic ancestral deeds and fantasy adventures exploiting crusading themes. What the lyrics of the troubadours and trouvères[1] provide is a myriad of different secular voices – thirty-seven trouvères, seventy-five troubadours – bringing to life up-to-the-minute responses to the crusading movement, not only in France and Occitania but also in Italy, the Iberian Peninsula, Cyprus, the Holy Land and Greece. These help us to understand what the multifarious public in the Middle Ages thought of the crusades: how it responded to particular expeditions; in what ways its responses varied according to time and place; how far it was inspired by the idea of holy war; how far it envisaged crusading and secular ideals as compatible; to what extent it accepted, influenced, participated in, resisted or challenged the Church's crusading propaganda; how its attitudes were affected by the Albigensian crusade launched against troubadour lands in the South; and how it faced the repeated failures of crusading efforts, as time went on.

Crusading troubadours and trouvères

Not a few of our troubadours and trouvères went on crusade themselves. Jaufre Rudel accompanied the French on the Second Crusade. Between then and the Third Crusade Peire Bremon lo Tort was in the service of the Kingdom of Jerusalem, Giraut de Borneil made a pilgrimage to the Holy Land with Viscount Aimar V of Limoges and Peire Vidal travelled to the court of Count Raymond II of Tripoli, where he was staying when Jerusalem fell to the Muslims in 1187. During the Third

---

[1] Poet–musicians composing in medieval Occitan and Old French respectively.

Crusade Giraut returned to the Holy Land, which Peirol also visited. Crusading trouvères include Richard the Lionheart, the Châtelain de Coucy and possibly Gautier de Dargies. Conon de Béthune was supposed to go on the Third Crusade but did not. However, he played a leading rôle in the Fourth, which also saw the participation of the Châtelain de Coucy, who died at sea in June 1203, Hughes de Berzé, the Vidame de Chartres, and the Occitan poets Gaucelm Faidit, Raimbaut de Vaqueiras, Elias Cairel and Ysabella.[2] The Châtelain d'Arras took part in the Fifth Crusade; Hughes de Berzé invites Falquet de Romans in one of his songs to go with him, though there is no evidence that they went, while Pons de Capdoill announces his intention to take part (BdT 375.22, 25). His *vida* (Occitan prose 'biography') says he did so, and that he died overseas,[3] which is plausible, even if there is nothing to corroborate this. Philippe de Novare is an important source for the crusade of Frederick II Hohenstaufen. No other poets of our corpus are recorded in the context of this expedition, though Uc de Pena briefly addresses a certain Lord Guy (BdT 456.1) to say, 'May God let you return from over there where you are in order to serve Him', a nobleman probably to be identified as Count Gui IV of Forez, who accompanied Frederick on this venture; and in an exchange of *coblas* (stanzas), Peire Bremon Ricas Novas accuses Gui de Cavaillon of abandoning this same crusade.[4] Taking part in the barons' crusade of 1239 led by Thibaut de Champagne were other trouvères: Philippe de Nanteuil,[5] possibly Chardon de Croisilles (in RS 449 it would appear that he is about to leave on an expedition, though there is no historical certainty that he actually did so), Raoul de Soissons and the anonymous author of RS 1133. Raoul also went on the Seventh Crusade, as did Philippe de Nanteuil and the troubadour Austorc d'Aorlhac, who took the cross two years after King Louis IX's capture at Mansurah in 1250. During the 1260s a Templar in the East, Ricaut Bonomel, sent out a desperate appeal for help, and Louis' second crusade saw Raoul de Soissons leave for the East for a third time.

Some of our troubadours may have fought the Muslims in Spain: Marcabru supports Reconquista campaigns and may or may not have been involved in actual combat; Giraut de Borneil states his intention to participate in a Spanish campaign (BdT 242.74, 69–90), and in 1265 the troubadours Guiraut Riquier and Guillem de Mur debate whether to follow King James I of Aragon to Murcia (BdT 248.37).[6]

---

[2] Another troubadour, Imbert, may be the Count Uberto II of Biandrate who is attested in Greece at this time: see S. Guida and G. Larghi, *Dizionario biografico dei trovatori* (Modena, 2013, = DBT), s.v., and R. Harvey and L. Paterson, *The Troubadour Tensos and Partimens: A Critical Edition*, 3 vols (Cambridge, 2010), II, p. 644.
[3] *Biographies des troubadours: textes provençaux des XIIIe et XIVe siècles*, ed. J. Boutière and A. H. Schutz, second edition by J. Boutière and I.-M. Cluzel (Paris, 1973), p. 311.
[4] S. Guida, 'L'attività poetica di Gui de Cavaillon durante la crociata albigese', *CN*, 3 (1973), 235–71 (pp. 235–36).
[5] If he is indeed the author of RS 164: see Barbieri's notes to the online edition.
[6] For the possibility that Bertran Carbonel and Matieu de Caerci were rewarded after taking part in James's expedition to Murcia, see J. Anglade, 'Le troubadour Guiraut Riquier

Some of the trouvères of our corpus are known to have been in contact with their Occitan counterparts. These include: Conon de Béthune and Bertran de Born, and possibly Giraut de Borneil, at the time of the Third Crusade; Conon de Béthune, Raimbaut de Vaqueiras and Elias Cairel in Greece during the aftermath of the Fourth;[7] and Thibaut de Champagne, Falquet de Romans and possibly Peire Cardenal during the Albigensian wars of 1224–1233. During the Second Crusade Marcabru indicates his wish to send a song (BdT 293.15) overseas to the French. Gaucelm Faidit appears to have composed a song for French crusaders during a stopover as the Fourth Crusade was under way.[8]

Crusading terminology

After the First Crusade it took eighty to a hundred years before troubadours and trouvères felt the need to use specific terms for 'crusader' and 'crusade'. 'At their origins,' Benjamin Weber remarks, 'and indeed throughout the Middle Ages, crusades were usually referred to by terms, both in Latin and the vernacular, indicating movement or travel, such as *peregrinatio, iter, via, expeditio* and later *passagium*, and the corresponding verbs, often combined with a reference to Jerusalem, the Holy Land, the Holy Sepulcher, or the cross, and in the vernacular with *outre mer* or *ober meer*.'[9] Our lyric poets commonly speak of going (away, on their way,

---

de Narbonne et les Catalans', *Institut d'Estudis Catalans, Anuari*, 1–2 (1909–1910), 571–87 (p. 574).

[7] Conon and Raimbaut were both involved in the council held in Constantinople to decide on Boniface of Monferrat's claim to Thessalonica: see Chapter 5, p. 113. They may have previously known each other: see L. Barbieri, 'À mon Ynsombart part Troia: une polémique anti-courtoise dans le dialogue entre trouvères et troubadours', *MR*, 37 (2013), 264–95.

[8] See Chapters 3, 5 and 8. Walter Meliga has suggested that Jaufre Rudel's song BdT 262.5, addressed to Hugh VII le Brun of Lusignan and the people of Aquitaine, Poitou and Berry, and the count of Brittany, was intended to send greetings to various contingents of crusaders about to leave for the Holy Land under the leadership of the king of France, and that this may be the first indication of the presence of a lyric in a crusading milieu, which would be well placed to favour the diffusion of this poetry (W. Meliga, 'L'Aquitaine des premiers troubadours. Géographie et histoire des origines troubadouresques', in *L'Aquitaine des littératures médiévales (XIe–XIIIe siècle)*, ed. J.-Y. Casanova and V. Fasseur (Paris, 2011), pp. 45–58, on p. 51 and n. 26). Aimeric de Belenoi appears to have referred to Thibaut de Champagne, perhaps in the hope of patronage, in BdT 9.10, though there is no evidence that this hope was fulfilled. See S. Melani, 'Aimeric de Belenoi, Thibaut de Champage e le crociate', *RST*, 1 (1999), 137–57.

[9] B. Weber, 'Nouveau mot ou nouvelle réalité? Le terme *cruciata* et son utilisation dans les textes pontificaux', in *La papauté et les croisades / The papacy and the Crusades. Actes du VIIe congrès de la Society for the Study of the Crusades and the Latin East/ Proceedings of the VIIth conference of the Society for the Study of the Crusades and the Latin East*, ed. M. Balard (Farnham and Burlington, 1988), pp. 11–25 (p. 11).

to serve, overseas, there, on a journey), following (God) or riding.[10] If a crusade was a type of pilgrimage, up to and including the Third Crusade references in our lyrics to crusade as pilgrimage, or crusaders as pilgrims, are rare. The earliest secure examples occur in Conon de Béthune and Peire Vidal,[11] at the same time as the somewhat more specific *passar* 'to cross [to the Holy Land]', *passatge* 'the voyage [to the Holy Land]',[12] the personal nouns *crosatz* and *croisiés* (literally 'those crossed, marked by a cross') in Bertran de Born and Conon de Béthune, and the Occitan verb *crosar* ('to take the cross') in Bertran de Born and Folquet de Marselha.[13]

The vernacular term *crozada* is first recorded in a Navarrese charter of 1212 and in the Midi in 1210–1213 by Guilhem de Tudela, the Navarrese author of the first part of the *Song of the Albigensian Crusade*.[14] Marjolaine Raguin has shown that the

---

[10] *iront* CnBéth RS 1125, 32; *anava / lai* BtBorn BdT 80.3, 25–26; *irai m'en lai* Peire Vidal, 364.9, 43; *ains ke aille outremer* ChCoucy RS 985, 8; *aler en terre estraigne* ChCoucy RS 679, 12; *iront en cest voiaige* CnBéth RS 1125, 32; *s'en ala* HuOisy RS 1030, 15; *van servir* Mbru 293.1, 21; *aler Deu servir*, Anon RS 401, 23; *tenc ma via* (homewards) PBremTort BdT 361.2, 10; *siec en Belleen* JfreRud, 262.6, 37; *cavalguatz* PAlv, BdT 323.7, 18 (Spain); *chivauche sobre Serrazis* Cercam (Spain), BdT 112.2a, 42; *las ostz chevaucharan* GrBorn, 242.6, 75; also *l'anar / c'avem empres / en lai on es comunals bainz* GrBorn, BdT 242.33, 67–69. See also D. A. Trotter, *Medieval French Literature and the Crusades (1100–1300)* (Geneva, 1988), pp. 31–70, for a survey of crusading vocabulary in Old French literature as a whole.

[11] *Tous li clergiés et li home d'eaige qui ens ausmogne et ens biens fais manront partiront tot a cest pelerinaige*, CnBéth RS 1125, 25–27; *fes de mi pelegri*, PVid BdT 364.2, 40; *Puois irai pelegrins part Sur*, AimPeg and ElUss, BdT 10.37 (early 1190s?). It is uncertain whether the word *pelegris* in earlier troubadours has any crusading overtones: see GlPeit BdT 183.12, 19–20 (Guglielmo IX, *Poesie; edizione critica*, ed. N. Pasero (Modena, 1973); Cercam BdT 112.2a, 53–54; JfreRud BdT 262.2, 33). An occurrence in ChCoucy, RS 679, 36–37 (*mais ja de çou n'ere pelerins jor / ke ja vers aus boine volenté aie*) may date from either the Third or the Fourth Crusade. The earliest lyric examples of *romeria / romavia* = pilgrimage = crusade in 1201–1202 may occur in GcFaid BdT 167.9, 27 and 167.15, 53.

[12] *quan passar mi fes mar*, PVid BdT 364.2, 18; *Pour Dieu passerai mer* GoSoig RS 1404, 63; *blasmet [.l bon rey Richart] per so quar non passet dese* FqMars 155.3, 34; *pos lo reis Richartz es passatz*, GrBorn BdT 242.15, 52; *m'an mes vilan passatge*, ibid., 242.30, 65–66. P. Hölzle, *Die Kreuzzüge in der okzitanischen und deutschen Lyrik des 12. Jahrhunderts* (Göppingen, 1980), p. 33, also mentions *perdon* and *romavia / romaria*.

[13] Nouns: *mas per so·l fatz qe·ls crosatz vauc reptan / del passage q'an si mes en obli* (BdT 80.4, 24–25); *Vous ki dismés les croisiés, ne despendés mie l'avoir ensi* (CnBéth RS 1314, 17–18) and *a teus croisiés sera Dieus mout soffrans / se ne s'en venge a peu de demorance* (ibid., 31–32); past participles / adjectives: *q'als reis crozatz es amta, qar non van* (BtBorn BdT 80.17, 38), *Pos can de Deu gaban / quar son crosat e d'anar mot no fan!* (BtBorn BdT 80.4, 20–21); *mas laissei m'en qan vi qe li plus gran / si croiçavan, li rei e li primsi* (BtBorn BdT 80.17, 24–25); *Aras sai eu qu'adreitz vol esser reis / lo reis Felips, que dizen qu'es crozatz* (BtBorn BdT 80.30, 19–20); *e s'en dis ben al crozar, ieu dis ver* (FqMars BdT 155.3, 39).

[14] S. A. Garcia Larragueta, *El gran priorado de Navarra de la orden de san Juan de Jerusalen: Siglos XII–XIII*, 2 vols (Pamplona, 1957), II, pp. 148–49, no. 145: *Facta carta sub era*

Anonymous Continuator (Guilhem Anelier de Tolosa?),[15] who unlike Guilhem was profoundly hostile to the French invasion under Simon de Montfort, then used the word sarcastically to illustrate the way it was manipulated by the crusade's clergy. She notes that both authors use the term an equal number of times (five), but argues convincingly that this apparent balance needs to be considered alongside the word *guerra* (war), employed by Guilhem in five instances but omnipresent in the Continuator (forty-five occurrences). Guilhem's notion of crusade is supplanted in the Continuator's text by its insistence on the *guerra* between southerners and the French (or the foreigners), a lexical change showing how the *crozada* has become secondary for this author, and the word *crozada* only figures in the text to emphasise what the author sees as the clergy's travesty of the idea of holy war.[16] The troubadours Tomier and Palaizi echo such usage when they excoriate the *falsa croisada* of the French (BdT 442.1, 18). Raguin shows how the Continuator also exploits the term *perdon*, which can mean 'indulgence' and then the crusade that leads to it, to denounce Pope Innocent III's distortion of the idea of crusading and to set up the idea of a counter-crusade on the part of the southerners.[17]

MaCCaLa mense octobris, in anno quo rex Sancius / fuit super sarracenos cum illa crozada (referred to in G. Constable, 'The Historiography of the Crusades', in *The Crusades from the Perspective of Byzantium and the Muslim World*, ed. E. Laiou (Washington, 2001), pp. 1–22, 11–12 and n. 52). For Guilhem de Tudela see E. Martin-Chabot, ed., *Chanson de la croisade contre les Albigeois*, 3 vols (Paris, 1931–1961), I, pp. vii–xi.

[15] F. Zambon, 'Una nuova ipotesi sull'autore della seconda parte della *Canzone della Crociata Albigese*', *RPh*, 70 (2016), 267–81.

[16] M. Raguin, *Lorsque la poésie fait le souverain. Étude sur la 'Chanson de la Croisade albigeoise'* (Paris, 2015), pp. 610–12. For Innocent's introduction of the crusade in his approach to heresy in the South see N. Housley, 'Crusades against Christians: Their Origins and Early Developments, c. 1000–1216', in *Crusade and Settlement. Papers Read at the First Conference of the Society for the Study of the Crusades and the Latin East Presented to R. C. Smail*, ed. P. Edbury (Cardiff, 1985), pp. 17–36, especially pp. 28–30.

[17] Raguin, *Lorsque la poésie fait le souverain*, pp. 456–62. Trotter, *Medieval French Literature*, p. 70, concludes that the Old French authors' vocabulary is 'in general, superficial, and does not attempt to explore deeply the implications of either crusading ideology or of the juridical and technical consequences of the crusades', and that they 'are not unduly bothered about such details'. Those on the receiving end of the Albigensian Crusade, however, had good reason to be bothered.

For discussion of Innocent III's use of the term *crucesignatus* to designate a crusader, see M. Markowski, '*Crucesignatus*. Its Origins and and Early Usage', *JMH*, 10 (1984), 157–65, who argues that he 'appears to be the first pope to use the term *crucesignatus* officially and regularly in its fullest, substantive meaning of crusader', and that, although he seemed reluctant at first to used it to designate those fighting the Albigensians, 'this reluctance soon passed'. For a contrary view see W. R. Cosgrove, '*Crucesignatus*: A Refinement or Merely One More Term among Many?', in *Crusades – Medieval Worlds in Conflict*, ed. T. F. Madden, J. L. Naus and V. Ryan (Farnham, 2010), pp. 95–107.

The vernacular term *crozada* is transferred to papal usage only two centuries later, as the noun *cruciata*. Weber states that in the fifteenth century it is an Iberian word which the pope uses for the sake of convenience to designate a reality which has no name in his vocabulary.[18] It refers first of all to a letter of indulgences, and then to a crusading expedition. He argues that by introducing the word *cruciata* to designate indulgences and the warfare waged thanks to those indulgences, popes justified their action by minimising their novelty. It was a way of legitimising their wars and the way they were waged: the new word was a political act aimed at imposing the right of popes to direct war, as they understood it, against the Ottomans. Weber raises the question of how far terms specific to oriental crusading appearing in narratives of the Albigensian Crusade represented a conscious move to justify that crusade, and how far it was just a 'simple rapprochement mental'. Guilhem de Tudela's use of the word *crozada* certainly incorporated the legitimising sign of the cross into the Albigensian war. Whether or not it was a conscious move on his part, the Continuator's scathing response to it shows he was fully conscious of its political implications.[19]

Christopher Tyerman has observed that 'The inability of an otherwise articulate and categorizing intellectual elite to agree or even propose a term for the activity which later was named "crusade" has tended to be noted without too much comment by modern observers. Yet the terminological vagueness of the twelfth century may be significant. To put it crudely, *we* know there were crusaders: *they* did not; or, if they did, their perception was far from the canonically or juridically precise definition beloved of some late twentieth-century scholars.'[20] The present book is not in fact concerned with defining what was or was not a crusade, and indeed the lyric poets themselves show little interest in this beyond arguing about the legitimacy of different Church-endorsed enterprises. The book adopts an inclusive approach to the crusading movement, and takes as its starting-point what medieval lyric poets composing in Occitan and Old French said, both about wars against Muslims in Spain and the Holy Land, and about wars against Christians

---

[18] Weber, 'Nouveau mot ou nouvelle réalité?', pp. 13–17 and 25.
[19] Martin-Chabot generally translates *crozada* in Guilhem de Tudela's account simply as 'croisade' (12.19 *aisels de Proensa vengro a la crosada*; 42.5 *que tornec la crozada, co fai mantas sazos*; 72.4, *cel mante la crozada, que li presta l'argiant*; 130.5, *que sia en la crozada, ni ja no sai vendra*), but is baffled by 17.19, *Can conosc li evesque la crozada es mesclea*. Here he translates 'Quand l'évêque vit que les hostilités étaient commencées avec la croisade', commenting (III, p. 53, n. 6) 'Les derniers mots du vers restent sans traduction possible'. It is unclear exactly what Martin-Chabot thought *crozada* or 'croisade' meant, but the emphasis in all five instances is on 'war' or 'fighting' rather than 'expedition'. So in the case of 17.19, one might translate as 'when the bishop learned that the [holy] war had started up again'.
[20] C. Tyerman, 'Were There Any Crusades in the Twelfth Century?', *EHR*, 110 (1995), 553–77, p. 555.

in Greece, Occitania, Cyprus, Aragon and Italy which the Church sanctioned as holy wars.[21]

The corpus of texts

Since the focus of interest in this book is what the lyric poets say about the crusades, questions of genre are secondary. Just as it is not concerned with what was or was not a crusade, so the book does not attempt to define what was or was not a crusade song, even if it will offer some indication of the different types of text in which these responses appear.[22] Our corpus of relevant texts comprises 151 Occitan and 51 Old French songs. In the previous most complete overview of troubadour crusading songs, published in 1905, Kurt Lewent identified 33 so-called crusade songs and 30 others containing crusading elements, so 63 in all relevant to the crusades: some two-fifths of ours.[23] In her 1995 study of the Old French crusade song Cathrynke Dijkstra drew up a list of 35 texts on the basis of Bédier, Oeding and Schöber, excluding 5 of these from her own corpus; ours adds 16 more to her total.[24]

We have excluded many texts containing passing references of little historical value beyond showing that their authors and audiences were imbued with a general awareness of the crusades. So, for example, it was not thought necessary to include twelve texts mentioning cities of the East as symbols of wealth and power, of the kind 'I felt more joy than if I'd been given Corrosana', or eight where the Holy Land represents exotic places meaning 'far away', in phrases such as 'from here to Edessa'. Also excluded are fixed phrases such as *trufas de Roais* (trivial or illusory

---

[21] This approach coincides with neither the traditionalist nor the pluralist approach summed up by Giles Constable in 'The Historiography of the Crusades', pp. 12–13, the defining feature of the first said to be the the fact of it being directed towards the East, and that of the second, papal authorisation. Both groups, he observes, 'are uncertain what to do with the so-called pre- or proto-crusades, which were neither directed toward the east nor summoned by the pope'. Compare N. Housley, *The Later Crusades* (Oxford, 1992), pp. 2–6.
[22] For attempts to define 'crusade song' as a genre see J. Frappier, *La poésie lyrique française aux XIIe et XIIIe siècles: les auteurs et les genres* (Paris, 1966), pp. 79–90; P. Bec, *La lyrique française au moyen âge (XIIe–XIIIe siècles)*, 2 vols (Paris, 1977), I, pp. 150–57, and more recently C. T. J. Dijkstra, *La chanson de croisade: étude thématique d'un genre hybride* (Amsterdam, 1995), pp. 37–65.
[23] K. Lewent, 'Das altprovenzalische Kreuzlied', *RF*, 21 (1905), 321–448. In his later study of Occitan and German crusade songs, confined to the twelfth century, Hölzle (I, p. 624) adopted a narrow definition of such songs and identified only 13 Occitan ones (and 6 French ones, on p. 731).
[24] Dijkstra, *La chanson de croisade*, pp. 185–87; J. Bédier and P. Aubry, *Les chansons de croisade avec leurs mélodies* (Paris, 1909; Geneva, 2011); F. Oeding, *Das altfranzösische Kreuzlied, Inaugural-Dissertation zur Erlangung der Doctorwürde bei der hohen philosophischen Facultät der Universität Rostock* (Braunschweig, 1910); S. Schöber, *Die altfranzösische Kreuzzugslyrik des 12. Jahrhunderts*, 'Temporalibus aeterna [...] praeponenda' (Vienna, 1976).

things from Edessa), 'Saracen' used as an insult to a Christian adversary, allusions to holy places in religious songs recounting lives of Christ or the Virgin, without reference to crusading, and what are judged to be the essentially literary exploitation of crusading locations or ideas, sometimes for the sake of a rhyme, such as a troubadour joking about defeating a couple of Saracens or Christians anywhere from here to the River Jordan, or saying that it would have been better to be imprisoned by the *Masmutz* (Muslims) than by his lady. Also set aside are references of doubtful or no value, where their significance or the referent is unclear, or they add nothing to our understanding of the crusades. Brief reference is made to a number of marginal texts for which online editions are not provided, and there are inevitably some grey areas in applying our criteria.

The history of the Albigensian Crusade is well known,[25] and the lyrics that concern it have been the subject of an excellent study by Eliza Ghil which this book does not attempt to reduplicate.[26] Included in our corpus are texts which shed light on ideas of crusading through comparisons their authors make between the Albigensian Crusade and combat against Muslims in the East or in Spain, but we exclude those which essentially constitute general anticlericalism, exhortations to resistance, or reminders of specific events such as Raymond VII's humiliation at the Treaty of Paris in 1229.[27]

The trouvères' lyric treatment of the topic of crusading is different from that of the troubadours, not least because of the predominance of Old French songs of departure, which emphasise the love theme above that of crusading. We have decided whether to include a French text on the basis of two criteria: whether or not a trouvère is referring to a crusade, and whether a crusading reference is more than a passing literary exploitation of a crusading motif which adds little or nothing to our understanding of the crusades themselves. RS 768, RS 800 and RS 1157 fall

---

[25] See for example P. Belperron, *La croisade contre les Albigeois et l'union du Languedoc à la France, 1209–1249* (Paris, 1961); J. R. Strayer, *The Albigensian Crusades* (New York, 1971); J. Sumption, *The Albigensian Crusade* (London, 1978); M. Costen, *The Cathars and the Albigensian Crusade* (Manchester and New York, 1997); L. W. Marvin, *The Occitan War: A Military and Political History of the Albigensian Crusade, 1209–1218* (Cambridge, 2008); M. G. Pegg, *A Most Holy War: The Albigensian Crusade and the Battle for Christendom* (Oxford, 2008).

[26] E. M. Ghil, *L'Age de Parage: Essai sur le poétique et le politique en Occitanie au XIIIe siècle* (New York, Bern, Frankfurt am Main, Paris, 1989); see also M. Aurell, *La vielle et l'épée. Troubadours et politique en Provence au XIIIe siècle* (Montaigne, 1989).

[27] Martín Alvira identifies 31 lyrics referring to this crusade, of which BdT 406.12, 442.2, 442.1, 217.2, 177.1, 335.31, 80.42 are in our corpus, and another 16 refer to the wars of 1236 onwards, of which 126.1, 66.3, 66.2 are in our corpus. See M. Alvira Cabrer, 'Del *Sepulcro* y los *sarracenos meridionales* a los *herejes occidentales*. Apuntes sobre tres "guerras santas" en las fuentes del sur de Francia (siglos XI–XIII)', in *Regards croisés sur la guerre sainte. Guerre, idéologie et religion dans l'espace méditerranéen latin (XIe–XIIIe siècle)*, Actes du Colloque international tenu à la Casa de Velásquez (Madrid) du 11 au 13 avril 2005 (Toulouse, 2006), pp. 187–229 (pp. 216–18).

under the latter category. We have regarded RS 1404 by Gontier de Soignies, in which the speaker, in the face of failure in love, announces his determination to voyage overseas and become a Templar, as a variation of *chansons de départie* (songs of departure and separation) and a *cas limite* for inclusion. Unlike Dijkstra, who rejected pieces by Gautier de Dargies (RS 1575 and 795), the Vidame de Chartres (RS 502) and Raoul de Soissons (RS 1204), we have included them. The Vidame took part in the Fourth Crusade and refers to being overseas, and his pieces have both historical and thematic interest. Raoul de Soissons' song RS 1204 explicitly refers to crusading. It is uncertain that Gautier de Dargies went on crusade or that the two lyrics refer to this: RS 1575 states simply that he has been abroad for a long time, but it forms part of a fairly uniform group of texts on the subject of separation from the lady (see, for example, the introductory notes to RS 1204 and RS 421), some of which refer to crusading explicitly, and the piece is moreover linked to Raoul de Soissons' song RS 1204, which explicitly refers to crusading, follows it chronologically and almost certainly draws on it. His song RS 795 contains elements that suggest, albeit inconclusively, his intention to leave on crusade, and it was judged appropriate to include it alongside his other piece.

Typology and transmission

It is easier to classify, in broad terms, the types of Old French texts included in our corpus than the Occitan ones. Dijkstra and Barbieri[28] identify the former as: firstly, songs of exhortation: propaganda texts often relaunching themes expressed in preaching, papal bulls and official documents of kings and lords;[29] secondly, political *sirventes* containing references to the Holy Land; and thirdly, love songs or *chansons de départie*, with either a masculine or a feminine first-person speaker.

The more extensive Occitan corpus also includes these elements, but is more wide-ranging and varied. Its exhortations concern Spain as well as the Holy Land and the Latin empire in Greece.[30] While a few of these exhortations are addressed to an unspecified general audience,[31] in the vast majority of cases, unlike the French texts, they mention specific noblemen, named or implied; and they are often mixed in with other themes, sometimes little more than short references in love or moral-

---

[28] Dijkstra, *La chanson de croisade*, pp. 35–49, who expresses reservations about whether crusade songs can be considered a recognisable literary genre; L. Barbieri, 'Le canzoni di crociata e il canone lirico oitanico', *Medioevi*, 1 (2015), 45–74 (p. 47, n. 5).
[29] Barbieri, 'Le canzoni di crociata', n. 13 on p. 50, and Dijkstra, *La chanson de croisade*, pp. 88–90.
[30] For Spain, see L. Paterson, 'Troubadour Responses to the Reconquista', *RPh*, 70 (2016), 181–201; for Greece, see ElCair BdT 133.9 and 133.13; RbVaq BdT 392.9a and 392.24.
[31] For example, PoCapd BdT 375.2 and RmGauc BdT 401.1.

ising songs on unconnected topics.³² Occitan political *sirventes* in our corpus are often hard to differentiate from songs of exhortation: a number concern the conflict between Frederick II and the papacy;³³ not a few involve criticism of crusading,³⁴ crusaders,³⁵ or those who sabotage or abandon crusades,³⁶ and may refer to expeditions to the Holy Land as a foil for actions at home, particularly in the context of papally sanctioned crusades against Christians.³⁷ While Old French *chansons de départie*, comprising about two-fifths of the Old French corpus, lament the pain of separation from the beloved as the man leaves on crusade, Occitan songs of departure hardly ever conform to this general model. They may, for example, celebrate an imminent crusade,³⁸ announce departure in a local political context, regret departure from a specific courtly environment, emphasise the lovers' fidelity rather than the pain of separation or claim that the lady has driven him overseas. Two troubadours focus on arrival rather than departure, giving thanks for safe landfall.³⁹ The Occitan songs often contain personal elements: Raimbaut de Vaqueiras tries to come to terms with the desperate situation in Greece; Peirol thanks God for letting him visit the holy places in Jerusalem.⁴⁰ A number concern contingent issues such Frederick II's conduct towards John of Ibelin in Cyprus, or Louis IX's failure to secure the release of Venetian prisoners in Genoa as he leaves on his second crusade. Two troubadours discuss whether to join the Reconquista in hope of gain.⁴¹ Comedy and burlesque feature particularly in the Occitan texts, whether in the light-hearted (or even outrageous) presentation of the troubadour's persona or crusading themes,⁴² or in playful dialogue poems, though the Old French songs

---

32 Love: for example, GrBorn BdT 242.28 and 242.33; JfrRud BdT 262.6; PVid BdT 364.4; moralising: for example, Mbru BdT 293.12a; PAlv BdT 323.5; PCard BdT 335.62 (in a probably apocryphal stanza).
33 For example, FqRom BdT 156.11; GlFig BdT 217.1, 217.8; PCard BdT 335.31; ThChamp RS 273, 1152.
34 See P. A. Throop, *Criticism of the Crusade: A Study of Public Opinion and Crusade Propaganda* (Philadephia, 1940), and E. Siberry, *Criticism of Crusading 1095–1274* (Oxford, 1985).
35 Mbru BdT 293.7, 293.15, 293.21.
36 For example, PCard BdT 335.18, 335.31, 335.51, 335.54; PVid BdT 364.35; Perd BdT 370.5; PersDor BdT 371.1; RostBer BdT 427.4; RmCorn BPP 558.4.
37 For example, BdT BnRov BdT 66.2, 66.3; BtAlam BdT 76.16; BtBorn BdT 80.3, 80.42; CalPanz BdT 107.1; DurSartr BdT 126.1; TomPal BdT 442.1, 442.2; see Chapters 6 and 8.
38 Respectively GrRiq BdT 248.79 and RbVaq BdT 392.3 (though the *tornada* addresses separation from the lady); PVid BdT 364.9, concerning the situation of Eudoxia of Constantinople; GcFaid BdT 167.9, 167.33; PVid BdT 364.2.
39 GrBorn BdT 242.24, GcFaid BdT 167.19.
40 Mbru BdT 293.24 Peirol BdT 366.28.
41 GlFig BdT 217.8, 217.4a; BertZorzi BdT 74.12; GrRiq BdT 248.37. Some analogous pieces are also found among the Old French texts, such as Philippe of Novare's RS 184a, 190a, 1990a and Verse Letter.
42 For example, GcFaid BdT 136.3, 167.13, 136.2, 167.3a; PVid BdT 364.43; GlAdem BdT 202.9; Dasp BdT 206.4; MoMont BdT 305.12; Sord BdT 437.18.

of Philippe de Novare satirise the poet's enemies through comic allusions to the *Roman de Renart*, which itself parodies crusading themes.⁴³

The differences between our Old French and Occitan songs may have a lot to do with their respective manuscript traditions. Luca Barbieri's important research on the Old French songbooks has shown how these generally appear to be aristocratic, luxury productions, focusing primarily on an exclusive, monothematic canon of love songs, and making a more rigid distinction between genres. Their uniform and exclusive nature has probably emphasised the development of the Old French crusade lyric in the direction of the love song, and may well explain the proliferation of *chansons de départie* where crusading is largely subsumed into, and subordinate to, the theme of love. Barbieri observes that texts more closely linked to the Occitan *sirventes* tradition do exist, but these are contained in marginal manuscript traditions, or in association with chronicles, or in the exceptional *Liederbuch* (songbook) of the trouvère Thibaut de Champagne, and must in fact have been much more numerous in Old French than it would appear from the surviving material which reflects the tastes of the songbook compilers and those who commissioned them. Types of lyric composition extraneous to the courtly love song, the 'grand chant courtois', tended to be set aside and have been preserved thanks to chance circumstances or less exclusive collections.⁴⁴

The composers' social status

Barbieri's conclusions are mirrored in the social position of the known Old French and Occitan authors in our corpus. If we assume that all of the anonymous pieces were written by different authors, our corpus includes approximately twice as many Occitan composers (75) as Old French ones (37). There is a much higher proportion of anonymous texts in Old French: 18/51 of the Old French texts, only 6/151 of the Occitan ones (and only two of these are definitely without manuscript attribution).⁴⁵ There is also a higher proportion of noblemen in Old French. Of the 26 trouvères whose social status is known, half or more (14–17) are nobles.⁴⁶ The situa-

---

43 AimPeg BdT 10.37; FqLun BdT 154.2; CtProv BdT 184.1; Gran BdT 189.5; PhNov RS 190a and *Verse letter*. Compare S. Lambert, 'Translation, Citation, and Ridicule: Renart the Fox and Crusading in the Vernacular', in S. Lambert and H. Nicholson, eds, *Languages of Love and Hate. Conflict, Communication, and Identity in the Medieval Mediterranean* (Turnhout, 2012), pp. 65–84.
44 Barbieri, 'Le canzoni di crociata', pp. 1–2 and 9–10; compare his 'Note sul Liederbuch di Thibaut de Champagne', *MR*, 23 (1999), 388–416.
45 The manuscripts misattribute BdT 168.1a, 182.1, 242.77. It was thought until recently that the two manuscripts of BdT 461.112 offered no attribution, but the word 'Nompar' written above the text may be the name of the author.
46 CnBéth, ChCoucy, ChArr, GtDarg, Henry de Lacy, HgBerzé, Huon d'Oisy, PhNant, PhNov, RlSoiss, RoiRich, TbChamp, VdChar, Walter de Bibbesworth, CharCrois (probably), Anon RS 1020a (probably), Anon RS1887?

tion for the Occitan troubadours is hazier, since for those of lesser rank in particular we must rely for our information on the *vidas* or the conclusions of the *Dizionario Biografico dei Trovatori* (DBT). However, the overall picture gives a lower proportion of noblemen (23/59), with few of these belonging to the higher nobility and more being minor nobles, simple knights or stemming from knightly families.[47]

There is a correspondingly smaller range of non-noble trouvères than troubadours. The trouvères appear to include: one member of the minor bourgeoisie; two members of the upper bourgeoisie from Arras; a poor knight; a 'master'; an Anglo-Norman scribe from the Royal Chancery of Henry II; and three clerics.[48] The troubadours range more broadly over the social spectrum: 14 members of the bourgeoisie;[49] a tailor (Guillem Figueira); a gold- and silver-worker who designed armour (Elias Cairel); 2 masters and 5 other clerics including a monk;[50] a teacher (Giraut de Borneil); three high-ranking officials (a *podestà*, a judge and a magistrate);[51] a royal court poet (Cerverí de Girona); seven jongleurs; and a troubadour with outstanding musical gifts, Peirol, who may have been a servant at the court of Auvergne.

These figures seem to confirm that, as Barbieri has emphasised, the Old French manuscript tradition favours the preservation of aristocratic poetic production, while the Occitan one is more open and inclusive. When the Old French manuscripts do transmit songs which fall outside the traditions of *chansons de départie* and courtly love, they seem rather less interested in preserving the names of their authors. In a few cases[52] one may wonder whether the pieces have been commissioned for propaganda purposes and the authors, however talented, are under the

---

[47] (V) in this section indicates the *vidas* as the source of information (see *Biographies des troubadours*, ed. Boutière, Schutz and Cluzel), and (D) the DBT: higher nobility: AustAur (D), CtFoix, CtProv, PArag, PoCapd ('rics hom fo e molt gentils bars', V); minor nobility, BtBorn and ElUss, part-holders of their lordships, Blacst, DurSartr (D), GlBerg, GrLuc, JfreRud, RmMirav, Anon, *168.1a, if the author is actually Gauceran de Saint Leidier; knights or of knightly families,* AustSegr (D), BtAlam (V), GlAdem, son of a poor knight (V), PBremTort, a poor knight (V), PCard, son of a knight and a lady, who wanted him to be a canon (DV), RbVaq (knighted by Boniface of Monferrat), Sordel, son of a poor knight (V), Tomier, Palaizi.

[48] Respectively, HStQuen; AudBast and Anon, RS 1582; RS 1133; Renas; Anon, RS 401; Anon, RS 665a, 1020a, 1967.

[49] AimPeg, son of cloth merchant (V), BertZorzi, a Venetian merchant (V), BtCarb? (D), CalPanz, a Genoese merchant (D), ElBarj, a merchant's son (V), FqMars, a merchant's son (V) who became bishop of Toulouse, GcFaid, a burger's son (V), GlFabre, GlMur, GrRiq? (D), PAlv, a burgher's son, well educated (V), PVid (V), RmGauc, UcPenn, a merchant's son (V).

[50] Masters: BnAur and MatQuercy (V). Other clerics: AimBel (a cleric who became a jongleur (V), MoMont (a 'gentleman' who became a monk and then a prior (V), two Templars, OlTempl and Templ (V), and RmCorn, priest and friar.

[51] Respectively PersDor, LanfrCig (also a knight), CavLun (also a knight).

[52] RS 1738a, RS 1729, RS 1887.

direction of royal or ecclesiastical authorities. In the South, the figures may reflect the importance of towns as centres of troubadour activity, as well as the fluid border between knights and burghers, and indeed other social classes.[53]

It might be assumed that the lower down the social scale the poet–musician was, the more dependent he was likely to be on patronage. Many troubadours did, clearly, voice the views of their actual or potential patrons; but they could be very free in their expression. Bertran d'Alamanon told Charles of Anjou in diplomatic but no uncertain terms not to waste time on Louis IX's first crusade; Sordel wrote scurrilously about his alleged sexual preferences.[54]

Public opinion

How far can our lyric poetry be said to reflect public opinion of the time? This is a question that has been primarily discussed in relation to vernacular lyric expressions of dissent: some scholars, such as Palmer Throop and Saverio Guida, have claimed that these can be regarded as a reliable index of public opinion, and others (Elizabeth Siberry, David Trotter) have minimised their value in this respect, while Alessandro Barbero concludes that whether or not the poet–musicians were reflecting public opinion, they were helping to form it.[55] But the question applies not only to songs of dissent but also, more widely, to any lyrics which comment on the crusading enterprise.

The historian Nicholas Paul has recently presented a compelling example of one troubadour at least whose poetry is an excellent source for evidence of the mentality of his region. By setting Bertran de Born within the historical and cultural context of the Limousin nobility in conflict with royal authority, Paul reveals how well the troubadour's testimony concerning royal inaction in the face of repeated calls for help from the East complements that of other sources, such as the Limousin chronicler Geoffrey of Vigeois. Paul's analysis shows not only the support felt in this region for the crusading enterprise but also the role played by the memory of the crusades in contemporary regional politics. Crusading, he argues, was a key part of the strategy that Henry the Young King used against his father King Henry II of England and his brother Richard the Lionheart in the Limousin in 1182–1183. All three were under considerable pressure to take the cross and help defend the Kingdom of Jerusalem against Saladin. When the Young King heard that Henry

---

53 L. Paterson, *The World of the Troubadours* (Cambridge, 1993), pp. 153–54 and 184–85.
54 See pp. 192 and 195. For discussion of the relationship between troubadours and their patrons see *inter alia* A. Barbero, *Il mito angioino nella cultura italiana e provenzale fra Duecento e Trecento* (Turin, 1983), pp. 46–49.
55 Throop, *Criticism of the Crusade*, pp. 27–36; Barbero, *Il mito angioino*, pp. 46–49; Siberry, *Criticism of Crusading*, who draws on medieval Latin and German lyrics as well as Occitan and Old French; Trotter, *Medieval French Literature*, pp. 198–99; S. Guida, *Canzoni di crociata* (Parma, 1992), pp. 7–8.

and Richard were on their way to Limoges, he first withdrew to a nearby town, then 'suddenly returned to Limoges and seized the initiative by placing his hands over the body of Saint Martial and vowing to take the cross as a crusader'. Henry was checkmated, and compelled to support his son's decision with a public display of enthusiasm. The Young King, Paul argues, was shrewdly exploiting his knowledge that 'the Limousin was a region where the memory of the crusades and commitment to the continued crusading enterprise had not waned since the time when so many of the region's knights and lords had headed for Jerusalem in 1096', and that while 'the kings of England, France, and Aragón had hesitated, the Viscount of Limoges, Adhémar V, and a number of other Limousin knights had traveled to the Holy Land in 1178'. Paul highlights the use of banners and other ceremonial cloths commemorating local crusading activities in this region, notably by the dynasty of the lords of Lastours, as a weapon in the contest between royal authority and local identity.[56] Interestingly it was from Lastours that emanated, according to Geoffrey of Vigeois, one of the earliest narrative accounts of the First Crusade. Geoffrey states that this was a long vernacular poem that took twelve years to write. It is now lost, though a fragment known as the *Canso d'Antioca* no doubt derives from it. Its author was the knight Gregory Bechada from the castle of Lastours, whose lord was the Gouffier of Lastours who distinguished himself in 1098 at the city of Ma'arrat-an-Nu'man.[57] The record of this reinforces the importance of crusade memorialisation in the region. At the same time the loss of this apparently massive work is a tantalising reminder of how far hitherto undiscovered, or permanently lost, material might affect our appraisal of the lyrics as evidence of public opinion of the time.[58]

Audiences, propaganda, impact

The case of Bertran de Born offers a telling instance of songs reflecting public opinion where this means the opinion of the knightly classes. In interpreting the value of other texts as evidence of wider opinion it is important, but not always easy or indeed possible, to identify the primary target audience, to consider the extent to which they can be regarded as propaganda on behalf of a particular person or group or to discover any evidence of their impact on the audience's opinions or actions.

Sometimes the primary target audience is clear: the song has a specific short-term goal and seeks to influence particular people in particular cirumstances. Richard the

---

[56] N. L. Paul, *To Follow in Their Footsteps* (Ithaca, 2012), pp. 131–33.
[57] C. Sweetenham and L. M. Paterson, *The* Canso d'Antioca. *An Occitan Epic Chronicle of the First Crusade* (Aldershot, 2003), pp. 5–6.
[58] Peter the Deacon reports the existence of an important eleventh-century medical treatise, a translation into Romance of the works of Constantine the African by a pupil of his who was chaplain to Empress Agnes (†1077), which has not survived: see Paterson, *The World of the Troubadours* (Cambridge, 1993), p. 193.

Lionheart's *Ja nus homs pris* (RS 1891), written while he was in prison in Germany and sent to France and England, puts pressure on his vassals and suzerain to pay his ransom. It is addressed principally to them, while also aiming to create a climate of opinion that will increase such pressure. Raimbaut de Vaqueiras targets the emperor of Constantinople and his council to press them to fulfil the emperor's promise to make Marquis Boniface of Monferrat ruler of Thessalonica (BdT 392.9a) – which he did. And when Louis IX, after his release from captivity in Egypt, is deliberating whether to return to France or stay behind to try to secure the release of prisoners, an anonymous trouvère composes a song to combat the efforts of the 'cowards and flatterers' urging him to leave (RS 1887). He must have intended for this to reach the king's ears, or at least those of men who could influence the king's decision. The king decided to stay.

The primary audience of Old French *chansons de départie* is also little in doubt. These are the self-reflexive songs of an in-group, where aristocrats address each other expressing refined sentiments in artistically constructed compositions which reinforce their courtly and knightly values. Such songs were no doubt performed at court, but the court is essentially where the lord is, and hence movable; there are signs that some songs were composed and performed at staging-posts of departure on crusade.[59] Others may have heard and transmitted such songs, but they are above all the exclusive, self-promoting and self-confirming entertainment of the nobility – while no doubt also being designed to stiffen morale and commitment once crusading is under way.

Other songs were visibly designed for performance at particular courts or in particular places: for example, the Limousin court to which Gaucelm Faidit bids farewell as he leaves on crusade (BdT 167.9), or the Malaspina court where Maria-Luisa Meneghetti very precisely identifies the audience as that of *homines de masnada*, i.e. members of Alberic's feudal family, a compact group of unfree knights (the *Dienstritter* of Germanic tradition).[60] When Raimbaut de Vaqueiras is holed up in Thessalonica while Boniface of Monferrat is off fighting the Wallacho-Bulgarians, never to return, the troubadour sings to others in the fortress to keep up their spirits and his own (BdT 392.24). The anonymous *Chevalier, mult estes guariz* (RS 1548a) is explicitly addressed to a knightly audience, while the use of proverbs with a mercantile flavour in RS 1967 suggests a bourgeois public. Many of the Occitan *sirventes* address rulers and other members of the nobility by name, though there is a wider circle involved, its nature varying according to the particular circumstances of composition and performance.

---

[59] For example, GcFaid BdT 167.50 and Anon BdT 461.122. Neither of these is a *chanson de départie* that is strictly analogous to those of the trouvères, though both express the pain of separation from the loved lady.

[60] M.-L. Meneghetti, 'Uc de Saint Circ tra filologia e divulgazione', in *Il medioevo nella Marca: trovatori, giullari, letterati a Treviso. Atti del Convegno, Treviso 28–29 settembre 1990*, ed. M.-L. Meneghetti and F. Zambon (Dosson, 1991), pp. 115–28 (p. 127).

Whatever the primary audience, songs may well have reached other listeners. A short section of the account of the First Crusade on p. 187 of MS Hatton 77 of the Bodelian Library depicts the performance of rotrouenges and other songs as entertainment on crusade, describing how, after a great loss of life, the Christian camp fell silent at night, when throughout the night there was no *rotrouenge ne neis un vers de son* to be heard. A rotrouenge is a type of lyric; a *vers de son* could be a line or stanza or section of a song, perphaps lyric, perhaps epic.[61]

As we have seen, Dijkstra and Barbieri describe songs of exhortation as propaganda texts which often relaunch themes expressed in preaching, papal bulls and official documents of kings and lords. This raises the thorny issue of what constitutes propaganda, but these horatory texts can reasonably be so regarded in the sense that they seek to 'propagate' a particular doctrine or practice and persuade people to commit to specific action.[62] They may have been assimilated with preaching activity in contemporary consciousness: Stefano Asperti has observed that there is at least one explicit piece of evidence for this, in the prose *razo* to Folquet de Marselha's song BdT 155.15 which supports Alfonso VIII of Castile in his fight against the king of Morocco, and presents the song as *una prezicansa*.[63]

But the term *prezicx* in fact has a wider extension than the sense which we normally attribute to preaching. An interesting occurrence of the word occurs in a song by the troubadour Guillem Fabre of Narbonne, which probably dates from 1284 during preparations in the Narbonne region for the so-called Aragonese crusade. This was launched by Pope Martin IV against King Peter III of Aragon, and led by King Philip III of France and his nephew Charles of Anjou, then king of Sicily, with the support of Peter's brother King James II of Mallorca (BdT 216.2). Guillem is deeply hostile to the looming conflict, which threatens not only internecine cruelty but also neglect of the holy places and God's cause: the great princes, he declares, should be directing their mustering and *prezicx* at the heathens rather than each other. While it could in theory be imagined that the leaders on each side of the Pyrenees are ordering preachers to pronounce sermons on the religious justification of their cause, there is no evidence for this. What does exist is a series of short songs authored by troubadours including the king of Aragon which constitute a kind of flyting match or ritual exchange of insults, to be heard by the public at large in

---

[61] 'unques icele nuit d'entor ne d'environ / n'ot chante rotrouenge ne neis un vers de son / car le mielz de lur gent ont laissie el sablon', privately signalled by Simon Parsons.

[62] SOED s.v. 2. 'Any association, systematic scheme, or concerted movement for the propagation of a particular doctrine or practice'.

[63] S. Asperti, 'Testi poetici volgari di propaganda politica (secoli XII e XIII)', in *Propaganda politica del basso medioevo, Atti del XXXVIII Convegno storico internazionale, Todi, 14–17 ottobre 2001* (Spoleto, Centro Italiana di Studi sull'Alto Medioevo, 2002), pp. 533–59 (p. 536); *Biographies des troubadours*, ed. Boutière, Schutz and Cluzel,, no. LXXI, E, pp. 482–83. Trotter, *Medieval French Literature*, p. 176, referring to Hölzle, *Die Kreuzzüge*, pp. 40–41, argues that the idea of crusade songs as sermons is attested by the poets' vocabulary: '*sermo, prec, conseil, prezicansa* in Provençal, *sermon* or *preecheman* in French'.

Narbonne on the one hand and Aragon on the other, and designed to stiffen the resolve of those who have already taken sides. Our edition translates *prezicx* here as 'public addresses': if there is preaching, it is preaching to the converted and intimidation of the enemy.

Many of the references to crusading and the Holy Land in our corpus are to be found in political *sirventes*, particularly those of a Ghibelline persuasion.[64] Martin Aurell assumes these to constitute political propaganda, and describes their function as raising the prestige of a patron or transmitting messages favourable to him by creating a climate of opinion and putting pressure on the group of listeners.[65] The listeners, he argues, intervene actively in the development of the song, as the creation and oral transmission of the *sirventes* allow for considerable improvisation and audience reaction, the listeners will recite the song and change it at will, and the repetition of a well-known tune and the *sirventes'* ability to make people laugh can make it very popular. There is evidence for this. At the end of the thirteenth century and the beginning of the fourteenth, some anticlerical *sirventes* by Peire Cardenal and Guillem Figueira were circulating in the Midi in bourgeois and popular milieux. Guillem Figueira's famous *sirventes* against Rome, composed in 1227 (BdT 217.2), was still being sung in Toulouse in 1274, when inquisitors asked a certain Bernart Raimon Baranhon, the son of a merchant of Toulouse and suspected of heresy, whether he owned, held or had seen a book beginning 'Roma Trichairitz'. He replied in the negative but said he had sometimes heard a song or some stanzas composed by a certain jongleur called Figuera recited in public in the presence of many people, which he thought began with the words 'du siruentes far en est so que magensa e sai ses doptar que naurai maluolensa dels fals de Mauples de Roma que ez caps de la chaensa que dechai tots bes'.[66] 'Roma trichairitz' is the first line of the third stanza of Guillem's invective, and the words cited by Bernart Raimon correspond in part to its opening stanza. Miriam Cabré has shown how the power of poetry to convey a political message effectively and exacerbate conflicts in northern Italy is exemplified by a poem by Peire de la Caravana, which encouraged Italian cities to fight together against Frederick II, and which provoked an edict by the *podestà* of San Gimignano banning any songs about Guelfs and Ghibellines

---

[64] Aurell (*La vielle et l'épée*, pp. 227–29) describes Ghibellinism as a movement aimed at countering the political action of the papacy and bishops in the Mediterranean, and the expansion of the house of France, by defending Frederick II and his descendants and helping to preserve their interests in the Midi.

[65] M. Aurell, 'Chanson et propagande politique: les troubadours gibelins (1255–1285)', in *Forme della propaganda politica nel Due e nel Trecento*, ed. P. Cammarosano (Rome, 1994), pp. 183–202 (pp. 184–86).

[66] See particularly S. Vatteroni, *Falsa clercia. La poesia anticlerical dei trovatori* (Alessandria, 1999), pp. 42–45, and also C. Léglu, 'Vernacular Poems and Inquisitors in Languedoc and Champagne', *Viator*, 33 (2002), 117–32 (pp. 118–21). For another example see Chapter 10, p. 186, n. 12.

in its castle or court.⁶⁷ The genre of the *sirventes*, Aurell maintains, is the medieval media par excellence: the fastest, most far-reaching and effective way of diffusing political propaganda and influencing public opinion.⁶⁸ The goal – or one of the goals – of these songs which combine crusading exhortations and political messages is not so much to persuade people to commit to the crusading cause as to harness crusading ideas in the denigration of, and resistance to, political opponents.

However, as Asperti has argued, the Occitan *sirventes* is a literary product, rooted in the expressive traditions of cultured lyric poetry, and celebrating from within the group the qualities and values of the knights and their leaders. In this respect it would be no different from the Old French *chansons de départie*. The Italian scholar observes that in many cases political *sirventes* containing references to the Holy Land are formally complex and sophisticated, and therefore there is more to them than simply their content. What is transmitted in the first instance is the culturally elevated form, the discourse perfected in line with the aesthetic rules of the time, sung to a fashionable tune (the *sirventes* normally adopts the pre-existing versification and melody of a *canso*, or love song). If it is legitimate to situate vernacular literary texts within the operation of some kind of political propaganda, he argues, the action that can be attributed to the majority of the texts analysed in his article is filtered through their formal aspects, hence through symbolic forms. So the action of propaganda will be predominantly indirect and will be explained on a level dictated by symbolic affirmation, not argumentation and persuasion. In other words, as Marco Grimaldi has put it, the expressive function is more important than the persuasive one.⁶⁹ This might be particularly true of songs in our corpus which combine crusading references with love songs or songs of general moral import, and where crusading themes may be included for the sake of reinforcing courtly and knightly values: 'everyone knows' that the courtly knight will want to serve God's cause.⁷⁰

As both Aurell and Asperti have remarked, one of the predominant features of the *sirventes* is its emphasis on the praise and blame of individuals and behaviours. Aurell sees this as part of the propaganda process, while Asperti distinguishes it from what he sees as the key feature of propaganda, namely its goal of persuading

---

⁶⁷ M. Cabré, 'Italian and Catalan Troubadours', in S. Gaunt and S. Kay, *The Troubadours: An Introduction* (Cambridge, 1999), pp. 127–40 (pp. 129–30). She emphasises that 'In addition to being a political weapon, poetry lent prestige to patrons and poets alike' (p. 130), and that the development of troubadour poetry in the Crown of Aragon confirms the importance of both social prestige and politics as factors in the adoption of this poetic tradition (p. 133). For interactions between vernacular songs and inquisitors in the light of the Avignonet massacre of 1242 see Léglu, 'Vernacular Poems'.
⁶⁸ Aurell, 'Chanson et propagande politique', p. 186.
⁶⁹ Asperti, 'Testi poetici volgari'; M. Grimaldi, 'Il sirventese di Peire de la Caravana (BdT 334,1)', *CN*, 73 (2013), 25–72 (p. 69).
⁷⁰ Cercam BdT 112.3a; ElBarj BdT 132.4; FqMars BdT 155.3; FqRom BdT 156.2; GcFaid BdT 167.58; GrBorn BdT 242.18; Cerv BdT 434a.20.

or convincing. The song's diffusion, he argues, is based above all on a pre-existing solidarity which may be established on common aversions rather than a coincidence of aims. The 'first' public, composed of those who are the nearest witnesses to particular events and situations, do not need to be informed or convinced: they are already in the know and have presumably already taken up a position in the face of the relevant dispute.[71] But this is not necessarily the whole picture. The song can be expected to be transmitted to others, even if we are not informed who they are; reputation mattered, and songs could damage reputations. When Olivier lo Templier (BdT 312.1) and Guillem de Mur (BdT 226.2) were urging James I of Aragon, who had just returned from his failed crusade of September 1269, to fulfil his crusading vow, Guillem concluded by reminding the king to *tener en pes son bon resso*, 'be mindful of his good name'. Luciano Formisano observes that the trouvères 'n'ignoraient pas le rôle politique que peut jouer la poésie, car au tout premier début du XII siècle Luc de la Barre avait payé de sa vie ses chansons contre Henri I Plantagenêt'.[72] Charles of Anjou feared the impact of hostile songs at a critical political juncture: after his execution of Conradin in 1268, in Perugia it was decreed that 'anyone composing, reciting or singing a song against Charles of Anjou, or saying anything injurious against him anywhere/in some way, should be fined a hundred *libras* of deniers for each instance. And if he could not pay the said fine his tongue should be cut out, as should be the case of those arguing in favour of Conradin, according to the manner of the statute.'[73] Marcabru's thirteenth-century *vida*, the basis for whose assertion is unknown, claims that the troubadour was put to death for having slandered the castellans of Guyenne.[74]

---

[71] Asperti, 'Testi poetici volgari', pp. 548–49.

[72] L. Formisano, *'Un nou sirventes ses tardar*: l'emploi du français entre pertinence linguistique et pertinence culturelle', in *O Cantar dos Trobadores: actas do congreso celebrado en Santiago de Compostela entre os días 26 e 29 de abril de 1993* (Santiago de Compostela, Xunta de Galicia, 1993), pp. 137–54 (p. 148).

[73] 'Item quicumque fecerit cantionem contra regem Karolum, vel dixerit vel cantaverit, solvat pro qualibet vice centum libras denariorum, vel aliqua, iniuriam contra eum dixerit. Et si non posset solvere dictam penam amputetur ei lingua secundum quod amputari debet intenzantibus pro Churradino ex forma statuti', cited from P. Larson, 'Primordi della ballata politica italiana', in *Comunicazione e propaganda nei secoli XII e XIII. Atti del convegno internazionale (Messina, 24–26 maggio 2007)*, ed. R. Castano, F. Latella and T. Sorrenti (Rome, 2007), pp. 413–29 (p. 425), in turn citing the Archivio di Stato di Perugia, Archivio storico del Comune di Perugia, *Consigli e riformanze*, n. 6, c. 310r–v.

[74] *Biographies des troubadours*, ed. Boutière, Schutz and Cluzel, p. 13. For the relation between certain *sirventes* and slander laws see C. Léglu, 'Defamation in the Troubadour *sirventes*', *MAe*, 66 (1997), 28–41. See also C. Sweetenham, 'Reflecting and Refracting Reality: The Use of Poetic Sources in Latin Accounts of the First Crusade', in *Literature of the Crusades*, ed. S. Parsons and L. Paterson (Cambridge, 2018), p. 37, who cites *inter alia* Orderic Vitalis describing how Henry I ordered a certain Luca to be blinded 'pro derisoriis cantionibus ... indecentes de me cantilenas facetus coraula composuit, ad iniuriam mei palam cantavit, malivolosque michi hostes ad cachinnos ita sepe provocavit'.

In the end, the implied audience of a particular song and the question of whether or not its crusading references constitute propaganda may or may not be inferable on an individual basis, and the symbolic and persuasive aspects of crusade songs are not mutually exclusive. Of the songs in our corpus, most if not all reflect Asperti's view that, on one level at least, they are the self-reflexive, symbolic production of an in-group, and in many – but not all – cases the affirmation of its values takes precedence over, or even excludes, any instrumental, propagandistic purpose. But often we can but surmise. When Richard the Lionheart asked Folquet de Marselha to sing for him on his arrival in Marseille on 31 July 1190, where his fleet was to join him for final departure on the Third Crusade, was this for reasons of personal propaganda? The song the troubadour produced (BdT 155.3) is mainly about love, which sets the aristocratic tone; but it also sets the record straight over Richard's determination to go on the crusade, after criticisms of his long delays.

Modes of performance

The troubadours' most highly regarded lyric genre was the *canso*, or love song, where not only the words but also, normally, the tune and versification were newly invented. Other genres such as the *sirventes* and the *tenso* (a dialogue song) would usually be modelled on the melody and versification of a *canso*. The Old French manuscripts have preserved a much higher proportion of tunes than the Occitan ones, and this is true for the texts of our corpus: over half of the Old French lyrics (29/51, all *cansos*), a ninth of the Occitan (17/151).[75] The available information suggests that all the Occitan ones bar a *tenso* (BdT 189.5) have original versification (in some if not all respects) and music.[76] Two were composed for special occasions: one celebrates the election of Boniface de Montferrat as leader of the crusaders in 1201 (BdT 392.3); the other is a *planh* (funeral lament) for Richard the Lionheart (BdT 167.22), one of only two Occitan songs whose melody has been preserved in as many as four manuscripts, three of which (WXη) are French. The others include Marcabru's magisterial *Pax in nomine Domini* (BdT 293.25), the highly unusual

---

[75] See Appendix C.

[76] The troubadours invented highly complex and varied verse forms, involving upwards of 900 different metrical structures: see I. Frank, *Répertoire métrique de la poésie des troubadours*, 2 vols (Paris, 1953–1957), and D. Billy, *L'Architecture lyrique médiévale: analyse métrique et modélisation des structures interstrophiques dans la poésie lyrique des troubadours et des trouvères* (Montpellier, 1989). Among the troubadours in our corpus whose music has been preserved, eleven have versification that is original in all respects (rhyme scheme, line lengths, rhyme sounds): unica GrRiq BdT 248.48, 248.87; Mbru BdT 293.35; RbVaq BdT 392.24; Anon BdT 461.122; and imitated by others, GcFaid BdT 167.15, 167.22; JfrRud BdT 262.6; Peir BdT 366.29; RbVaq BdT 392.3; RmMir BdT 406.12. Five others have some original aspect, whether rhyme sounds alone (FqMars BdT 155.3 [with a rotation of rhymes], PVid BdT 364.36, 364.4) or rhyme sounds and line lengths (BdT Gr Riq BdT 248.79; PVid BdT 364.11).

song *Finament / et jauent* (BdT 461.122) in a hybrid language preserved in French manuscripts (*Wd*, known as French MT), a *canso* by Gaucelm Faidit (BdT 167.15) and three songs by Guiraut Riquier which he designates as *vers*, a term he adopts as part of a strategy of reclassifying poetic genres and claiming prestige for his own productions.[77] In short, all have a claim to a high level of artistry.

It is very hard to know how any of these songs were first performed and how they were received as performances, whether from the dramatic or the vocal point of view.[78] Some crusade songs have more than one tune preserved in the manuscripts, so it is difficult to know what was the original tune, let alone be absolutely sure that the author of the poem is the composer of any of those surviving.[79] Nevertheless, from the interweaving of verbal and musical effects scholars have been able to make some plausible suggestions about the performance style of particular pieces, whatever the actual occasion of the performance that corresponded most closely to the surviving tune. Vincent Pollina highlights the Gregorian flavour of the melody to *Pax in nomine Domini*, which he qualifies as a cantor's piece, and the balanced rhythm of its incipit, which reinforces the solemnity of the Latin. The piece exemplifies what a later *trobairitz* described as Marcabru singing *a lei de prezicaire* (in the manner of a preacher).[80] Pollina's analysis of Gaucelm's dirge-like *planh* for Richard the Lionheart (BdT 167.22) shows how the melody is designed to highlight key textual elements such as the break after the fourth syllable in the opening line (*Fortz causa es | que tot lo maior dan*), the name *Richartz* (v. 6), the emotive phrase *es mortz* emphasised by its position after an enjambement and before a powerful caesura following the second syllable of the line (v. 7).[81] Anna Radaelli demonstrates

---

[77] See S. Asperti, 'Generic poetici di Cerveri de Girona', in *Trobadors a la península ibèrica. Homenatge al Dr. Martí de Riquer*, ed. V. Beltran, M. Simó and E. Roig (Barcelona, 2006), pp. 29–71 (p. 62).

[78] Robert Lug has shown that riders sang songs, incuding *cansos*, on horseback (R. Lug, 'Chevaliers chantant à cheval. Nouvelles observations sur la rythmique des troubadours', in *Toulouse à la croisée des cultures. Actes du Ve Congrès International de l'Association Internationale d'Etudes Occitanes, Toulouse, 19–24 août 1996*, ed. J. Gourc and F. Pic, 2 vols (Pau 1998), I, pp. 337–47).

[79] See G. Le Vot, 'Les chants courtois relatifs aux croisades dans le chansonnier de Saint-Germain-des-Prés (Paris, BnFr. 20050)', in *Lettres, musique et société en Lorraine médiévale. Autour du 'Tournoi de Chauvency'*, ed. M. Chazan and N. F. Regalado (Geneva, 2012), pp. 487–519, who concludes (p. 511) that the vocal–oral dimension of the courtly lyric is a very foreign *terra londhana*.

[80] V. Pollina, 'Les mélodies du troubadour Marcabru: questions de style et de genre', in *Atti del Secondo Congresso Internazionale della 'Association Internationale d'Etudes Occitanes'*, ed. G. Gasca Queirazza (Turin, 1993), pp. 289–306 (p. 290) and *'Si cum Marcabrus declina': Studies in the Poetics of the Troubadour Marcabru* (Modena, 1991), p. 40; see also M. Switten, in *Songs of the Troubadours and Trouvères: An Anthology of Poems and Melodies* (New York and London, 1998), pp. 21–24 and p. 51.

[81] V. Pollina, 'Word/Music Relations in the Work of the Troubadour Gaucelm Faidit: Some Preliminary Observations on the Planh', *CN*, 47 (1987), 263–78, on p. 272; see Giorgio

how the musical notation of the Old French crusade song RS 401 serves to clothe the text in solemnity while reproducing the prosody of the words being declaimed, indicating vocal inflections and providing stylistic information about where to lose emphasis, lower the voice or impose stress.[82] Margaret Switten explores Peire Vidal's blending of unique versification and refined melody, 'a bravura piece of remarkable energy', to produce 'a tone both serious and mocking' (BdT 364.11).[83]

Polemical *sirventes* often call for trenchant vehemence rather than poised solemnity or beguiling elegance. Martín de Riquer gives an idea of how one of our heavily ironic songs (BdT 245.1) might have been performed, citing the fourteenth-century grammatical and rhetorical treatise the *Leys d'Amors* on irony: 'e fa se ab elevatio de votz, enayssi que a la maniera del pronunciar enten hom que·l contrari vol dir' (it is done with the voice raised, so that from the manner in which it is pronounced people understand that the opposite is intended).[84] Troubadours speak of a difference between high, clear singing and a poor voice that is thin and squeaky or hoarse and rasping.[85] A grating voice, risible in a courtly love song, is actively desirable in the *trobar brau*, the rough style characteristic of many of Marcabru's *vers* and of later satirical *sirventes*.[86] Duran Sartor de Paernas's caustic attack on those who are failing to fight for the southern cause during the Albigensian wars (BdT 126.1) chooses clipped and harsh rhyme-sounds in *-oc, -ics, -ort, -ap*, reinforced by their hammering repetition in *coblas singulars* (where all lines of each stanza end in the same sound), suggesting a biting, aggressive performance style.

* * *

The book traces a broadly chronological path. It is envisaged, and indeed hoped, that this book will be read by a variety of readers, academic and non-academic, so each chapter begins with basic background historical information before presenting and commenting on the songs themselves. Discussion of particular poets, events or concurrent crusades may induce deviation from strict chronological order;

Barachini's discussion in his online edition.

[82] A. Radaelli, '*voil ma chançun a la gent fere oïr*: un appello anglonormanno alla crociata (London, BL Harley 1717, c. 251v)', *CN*, 73 (2013), 361–99 (p. 388); for a shorter version in English see Parsons and Paterson, eds, *The Crusades*, pp. 129–30.

[83] M. Switten, 'Music and versification', in Gaunt and Kay, *The Troubadours*, pp. 141–63 (pp. 153–55).

[84] M. de Riquer, 'El trovador Giraut del Luc y sus poesías contra Alfonso II de Aragón', *Boletín de la Real Academia de Buenas Letras de Barcelona*, 23 (1950), 209–48 (p. 228); M. Gatien-Arnoult, *Monuments de la littérature romane depuis le quatorzième siècle* (Toulouse, 1843), p. 258.

[85] In a famous satire on other troubadours Peire d'Alvernhe mocks Giraut de Borneil's 'thin, mournful singing' (*son chantar magre dolen*, BdT 323.11, v. 15) and complains that Guillem de Ribas 'performs all his pieces hoarsely' (*di totz sos vers raucamen*, v. 33).

[86] Paterson, *Troubadours and Eloquence*, pp. 52–54.

Appendix B provides a chronological overview. While the numbering of crusades (First Crusade and so on) can now be regarded as arbitrary and misleading, if not simply absurd, given the numerous expeditions that do not slot into such tidy pigeonholes, such terminology has been included simply because many readers will be familiar with it and because it serves as a shorthand for particular expeditions. The main focus of discussion in the main chapters is historical. Appendix A offers an analysis of the poets' crusading rhetoric, while Appendix C provides information about the survival of their melodies, and the project website contains some musical (and spoken) performances and commentary.

I have quoted extensively from the online editions, so as to let the poets speak in their many varied voices. Of course, these voices come to us through the medium of manuscripts that were nearly all transcribed many years after the songs were originally composed and performed, and after going through various stages of written and oral transmission. It has been the aim of the editors involved in this project to present texts that approach their authors' creations as faithfully as possible. The process of editing, translating and historically and culturally contextualising the online texts has often led to eureka moments, even from such details as realising that a small scribal slip obscured an otherwise perfectly clear and significant statement or, conversely, that a word in the manuscript was, contrary to received scholarly opinion, actually the right one.[87] Readers interested in the arguments which have led to the establishment of a text, its dating and its historical background can 'drill down' into these online editions.

---

[87] See BdT 312.1 and L. Paterson, 'James the Conqueror, the Holy Land and the Troubadours', *CN*, 71 (2011), 211–86, on pp. 233–38; and BdT 437.8 (translation and notes).

I

Early Expeditions

The 'Via de Hispania' and the 'via Jerusalem'

The triumphant First Crusade spawned many narratives, Latin and vernacular. But romance lyric responses to the crusading movement emerge only in the 1130s, in the context not of the Holy Land but Iberia.[1] The first troubadour, Duke William IX of Aquitaine, fought in both places. Despite the enormous contingent of southerners following Raymond of Saint-Gilles to Jerusalem, William did not take part in the main expedition to the Holy Land. In 1101 he led his own. It was a disaster. His army was ambushed and wiped out in Anatolia, though he himself managed to escape and make his way to Jerusalem, where he fulfilled his vows. The chronicler Orderic Vitalis relates that on his return with some of his companions he often recited the miseries of his captivity in the presence of kings and magnates and groups of Christians, using rhythmical verses with elegant modulations.[2] The hypothesis that his song *Pos de chantar m'es pres talenz* might be one of them, and refer to his departure on crusade, has not met with acceptance; rather, the duke was anticipating his departure from the world through death.[3]

---

[1] Much has no doubt been lost. Geoffrey of Vigeois tells us that Gregory Bechada, a knight of the castle of Lastours, wrote a massive account of the crusade in vernacular verse, an account which was probably the root of a later surviving Occitan fragment (Sweetenham and Paterson, *The 'Canso d'Antioca'*, p. 6). Compare Introduction, n. 59.

[2] See J. Riley-Smith, *The Crusades. A Short History* (New Haven and London, 1987), pp. 35–36; *The Ecclesiastical History of Orderic Vitalis*, ed. M. Chibnall, 6 vols (Oxford, 1969–1975), V, p. 342 and the note on p. 343; J. Martindale, 'Cavalaria et orgueill', in *The Ideals and Practice of Medieval Knighthood II: Papers from the Third Strawberry Hill Conference*, ed. C. Harper-Bill and R. Harvey (Woodbridge, 1988), pp. 87–116 (p. 112). No satisfactory explanation has ever been proposed for the reference to William's 'captivity': see L. Paterson, 'Occitan literature and the Holy Land', in *The World of Eleanor of Aquitaine: Literature and Society in Southern France between the Eleventh and Thirteenth Centuries*, ed. M. Bull and C. Léglu (Woodbridge, 2005), pp. 83–99 (p. 88).

[3] See S. Melani, 'Il cammino della croce e gli artigli della lussuria: ipotesi sulle "perdute" *cantilenae* composte da Guglielmo IX in occasione della sua crociata', in *Le letterature romanze del Medioevo: testi, storia, intersezioni*. Atti del V Convegno Nazionale della SIFR,

William also fought against the Muslims in Spain, at the battle of Cutanda in June 1120. Jane Martindale observes that the *Chronique de St-Maixent* gives the impression that the *Via de Hispania* and the *via Jerusalem* were regarded in Poitou as being of similar or even or equal importance, so that Christian victories in Spain match those 'in Jerusalem', and the disaster of the *Ager Sanguinis* (Field of Blood) in 1119 is counterbalanced not only by King Baldwin's great victory of the following year but also by the Christian success at Cutanda. In the St-Maixent annals this appears as a great victory: 'Count William, duke of the Aquitanians, and the king of Aragon fought with Abraham (Ibrahim) and four other Spanish kings on the field of Cutanda; and they conquered and killed 15,000 Moabites and made innumerable prisoners. They captured 2000 camels and other beasts without number, and they subjugated many castles.'[4]

This double perspective of the Holy Land and Spain prevails in the earliest response to the crusading movement on the part of lyrics in Occitan and Old French. During the winter of 1137–1138 the troubadour Marcabru, who spent his early years at the court of Poitou and moved to Spain on the death of his patron Duke William X of Aquitaine in April 1137, praises King Alfonso VII of Castile-León for his heroic efforts against the Saracens, and contrasts them with the feebleness of the French the other side of the Pyrenees (BdT 293.22). Marcabru's interest in the crusades here is bound up with the food and gift-giving (*conduich* and *do*) on which he and his associates in a patron's household depend, and crusading would seem to offer a good employment opportunity.[5]

---

ed. P. Antonio (Soveria Mannelli, 2000), pp. 281–93, and the refutation by W. Meliga, '*Pos de chantar m'es pres talenz*: l'adieu au monde du comte-duc', in *Guilhem de Peitieus, duc d'Aquitaine, prince du trobar* (Ventadour, 2015), pp. 193–203.

4   Martindale, '*Cavalaria et orgueill*', p. 103. See her n. 59 for numerous extended entries in the chronicle to the conflicts both in the East and in Spain from the 1090s onwards. Paul observes that in 1089 Urban II appealed to all the nobles and potentates and their followers from the regions of Barcelona and Tarragona 'to aid in the reconquest of Tarragona, promising that assistance in the campaign would be rewarded with a remission of sins similar to that gained by a visit to a shrine "in Jerusalem or in other places"' (Paul, *To Follow in Their Footsteps*, p. 265). Jonathan Phillips claims that 'Since 1113–14 the wars against the Spanish Muslims had been accorded the same status, and given the same spiritual rewards, as campaigns in the Holy Land' (J. Phillips, *The Fourth Crusade and the Sack of Constantinople* (London, 2005), p. xx), and see his *The Second Crusade: Extending the Frontiers of Christendom* (New Haven and London, 2007), pp. 246–48). He argues that it is probably safer to view the period between 1095 and c.1113–1114 as an evolutionary period; 'From the latter dates onwards, however, there are clearer signs of closer parallels between crusading to the East and Iberia and the existence of ties between the two theatres of war' (p. 247), and compare N. Housley, *Contesting the Crusades* (Oxford, 2006), pp. 102–4.

5   Much ink has been spilled on the definition of *joven* in the troubadours in general and Marcabru in particular, and on the *soudadiers* (those depending on payment) with whom he identifies himself. See in particular the index to R. Harvey, *The Troubadour Marcabru and Love* (London, 1989).

Pois lo fills de Dieu vos somo
qe·l vengetz del ling Farao,
ben vos en devetz esbaudir;
c'outra·ls Portz faillen li baro,
lo plus, de conduich e de do,
e ja Dieus no·ls en lais gauzir!

Mas en cels de lai es romas,
ad ops d'Espaigna e del Vas
en devetz ben l'afan sofrir,
e·ls Sarrazis tornar atras,
del aut orguoill f*a*r venir [bas],
e Dieus er ab vos al fenir.   (vv. 7–18)

Since the son of God summons you to avenge Him against Pharaoh's descendants, you should indeed rejoice; for beyond the Pyrenees most of the barons are lacking in hospitality and generosity, and may God never allow them to derive benefit from it!

Since those men over there are neglecting it, you should indeed carry the burden for the good of Spain and the holy sepulchre, drive the Saracens back, lay low their lofty pride and then God will be with you at the end.

The song is one of the earliest manifestations of an approach to the Christian–Muslim conflicts in Spain that sees them in crusading terms, an approach which, according to Richard Fletcher, properly begins in the second quarter of the twelfth century. The Saracens here are the Almoravids, Berber devotees of an Islamic fundamentalist sect who overran Muslim Spain between about 1090 and 1120. For the Christian authorities in Spain, Fletcher argues, their successes were one of the factors contributing to 'the replacement of a policy of expoitation of their Muslim neighbours by a programme of reconquest which was given a sharper edge by the notion of crusade'.[6] Their ascendancy Marcabru blames on the sybaritic apathy of the 'lords beyond the Pyrenees':

Als Amoravis saill conortz
per las poestatz d'outra·ls Portz
q'an pres una tela ad ordir
de drap d'enveia e de tort,
e ditz cadaüs q'a sa mort
·s fara de sa part devestir.

---

[6] R. A. Fletcher, 'Reconquest and Crusade in Spain, c. 1050–1150', *Transactions of the Royal Historical Society*, 37 (1987), 31–47 (especially pp. 38 and 47), Ruth Harvey's notes on dating in S. Gaunt, R. Harvey and L. Paterson, *Marcabru: A Critical Edition* (Cambridge, 2000), p. 309, and R. Harvey, 'A propos de la date de la première "chanson de croisade": *Emperaire, per mi mezeis* de Marcabru (PC 292.22), *CCM*, 42 (1999), 55–60 (p. 59).

Mas de lai n'ant blasme li ric,
c'amon lo sojorn e l'abric,
mol jazer e soau dormir,
e nos sai, segon lo prezic,
conquerrem, de Dieu, per afic
l'onor e l'aver e·l merir.   (vv. 19–30)

The Almoravids take heart because of the powerful lords beyond the Pyrenees, for they [the lords] have begun to weave a web of cloth from envy and wrong, and yet each one says that he will give up his share at his death.

But the rich men over there have the blame for this, for they love comfort and their cosy, sheltered spots, soft beds and sweet sleep, while we over here, according to the preaching, will conquer through our effort the honour and the wealth and the reward which are God's.

Rousing the Christian rulers of Spain to join together in a massed drive against the Muslims, he sharply reminds the recently crowned King Louis VII of France that, while he may have subjected Poitou and Berry to his rule, he himself is subject to a higher power to which he owes obligations:

Mas Franssa Peitau e Beiriu
aclin'a un sol seignoriu,
veign'a Dieu sai son fieu servir!

Q'ieu non sai per que princes viu,
s'a Dieu no vai son fieu servir!   (vv. 55–59)

Since France subjects Poitou and Berry to a single jurisdiction, let him come here to God to earn his fief!

For I do not know why a prince lives if he does not go to God to earn his fief!

Marcabru had personal as well as political reasons to dislike French control of Poitou. William's death in April 1137 was followed in July by the wedding of the future French king to William's heiress Eleanor of Aquitaine. A few days later Louis' effective rule of France began, and through his marriage he temporarily extended the Capetian lands to the Pyrenees. Marcabru was bereft of a patron, and headed for Spain.[7] His strictures to Louis echo lines in the troubadour Cercamon's *planh* for William (BdT 112.2a) in which he declares that Louis will be much to blame if he does not fight the Muslims:

---

[7] See Gaunt, Harvey and Paterson, *Marcabru*, p. 3 and poem IVb, 55–60 on p. 84. Cercamon also bemoans the loss of his patron William X in a *tenso* with Guillelmi, composed at the end of April or beginning of May 1137, despite the latter's optimistic assurances that 'Great fortune will come to you from France if you will only wait for it' (BdT 112.1 in Harvey and Paterson, *The Troubadour Tensos*, I, p. 246).

Plagnen lo Norman e Franceis
e deu lo be plagner lo reis,
cui laisset la terra e·l creis;
pos aitan grant honor li creis,
mal estara si non pareis
chivauche sobre Serrazis.   (vv. 37–42)

Normans and French mourn for him, and the king to whom he bequeathed the land and his offspring should certainly mourn for him: since his territory expands so much, it will be unseemly if he is not seen to be riding against the Saracens.

Although Marcabru mentions 'the good of Spain and the holy sepulchre', no one has questioned where Cercamon has it in mind that Louis should be fighting, and presumably he is thinking of the *via de Hispania*: there was no call at this time for a French king to involve himself in the frontier skirmishes and internal squabbles of the crusader states.[8] Ruth Harvey has pertinently suggested that the two troubadours may be reflecting contemporary reactions to the transfer of the ancestral lands of the house of Poitou to Capetian control. Louis VI arranged for 500 knights to escort his son and then the young married couple as they toured round Eleanor's domains, domains which had never been under the possession of Louis' forebears. Martindale has observed that 'This company of over five hundred of "the best knights of the kingdom" sounds more like an army prepared to deal with trouble and put down resistance than a peaceful wedding-escort.' Marcabru, who is elsewhere sensitive to the territorial and legal interests of the dukes of Aquitaine, appears to jib at French suzerainty, and Cercamon's words also seem to carry a negative tone. Harvey concludes that Marcabru's words to Louis at the end of BdT 293.22 seem not merely to concern holy war in Spain, but also to allow a glimpse of mistrust or anxiety felt by some of the late duke of Aquitaine's subjects in the face of what the French might represent for the customs of the former independent duchy. These lines would therefore be marking the end of an era at the same time as announcing a new chapter of the Reconquista.[9]

---

8 For 'driblets' of armed pilgrim companies and knights who joined the military orders arriving in the Holy Land during 1101–1147 see S. Runciman, *A History of the Crusades*, 3 vols (Harmondsworth, 1971, first published Cambridge 1951–1954), II, p. 249.
9 J. Martindale, 'Succession and Politics in the Romance-Speaking World, c. 1000–1140', in *England and Her Neighbours, 1066–1453. Essays in Honour of Pierre Chaplais*, ed. M. Jones and M. Vale (London, 1989), pp. 19–41 (p. 39), and Harvey, 'À propos de la date', pp. 59–60. A further reference to crusading in Spain occurs in BdT 293.12a, where Marcabru says that 'If the lord of Gerona rises, he will rise still further, / provided that he turns his mind to defeating the pagans, for Jesus commands him to do this'. Its date cannot be pinned down beyond the period 1122–1162. The 'lord of Gerona' may be either Guerau III de Cabrera, or his father, Pons II.

The Second Crusade

At Christmas 1144 Edessa fell to Zengi. The West's reaction seems to have been lukewarm.[10] Pope Eugenius III turned to Louis VII for help, and the following Christmas Day at Bourges the French king spoke of his intention to take the cross, only to be met with an underwhelming response from the lay nobility. The king then wrote to the charismatic Bernard of Clairvaux to enlist him in preaching the crusade. Once it was known that he would speak on 31 March at Vézelay, people flocked from all over France to hear his 'incomparable rhetoric'. 'Men began to cry for Crosses – "Crosses, give us Crosses!" – It was not long before all the stuff that had been prepared to sew into crosses was exhausted; and Saint Bernard flung off his own outer garments to be cut up. At sunset he and his helpers were still stitching as more and more of the faithful pledged themselves to go on the Crusade.'[11]

An anonymous Old French song echoes his appeal (RS 1548a). Addressed specifically to knights, it deploys the language of feudal law to illuminate the justice of God's cause.

> Chevalier, mult estes guariz
> quant Deu a vus fait sa clamur
> des Turs e des Amoraviz
> ki li unt fait tels deshenors,
> cher a tort unt cez fieuz saisiz!
> Bien en devums aveir dolur,
> cher la fud Deu primes servi
> e reconuu pur segnnur. (vv. 1–8)

Knights, you are under strong safeguard, since it is to you that God has lodged his lawsuit against the Turks and the Almoravids, who have done him such dishonour, for they have seized his fiefs. It is right that we grieve at this, for there God was first served and acknowledged as Our Lord.

A refrain at the end of each of the seven stanzas promises listeners,

> Ki ore irat od Loovis
> ja mar d'Enfern n'avarat povur,
> char s'alme en iert en Pareïs
> od les angles nostre Segnor.

Whoever will now go with Louis will never have fear of Hell, for his soul will be in Paradise with the angels of Our Lord.

---

[10] P. J. Cole, *The Preaching of the Crusades to the Holy Land, 1095–1270* (Cambridge, Mass., 1991), p. 40, questioning Runciman's claim (*History*, II, p. 248) that the news 'horrified the West'.

[11] Runciman, *History*, II, pp. 252–53.

The poet reminds his listeners of the capture of Edessa, whose churches are burned and ruined; Holy Communion is no longer offered there. He imagines the crusade as a tournament between Hell and Heaven, to which God summons all his followers to support him, and stirs the audience's desire for salvation through God's service and the implementation of his vengeance.[12]

Among the troubadours, there is no lyric that is unquestionably and wholly devoted to preaching this crusade. However, in a song primarily about the nature and value of love (BdT 112.3a), a matter of much contemporary debate, Cercamon promotes this expedition as a way of achieving salvation:

> Ara·s pot hom lavar et esclarzir
> de gran blasme, silh q'en son encombros;
> e s'i es pros, yssira ves Roays,
> e gurpira lo segle perilhos,
> et ab aitan pot si liurar del fays,
> qu'assatz en fai trabucar e perir.   (vv. 43–48)

Now a man can cleanse and purify himself of great guilt, if he is burdened with it; and if he is brave, he will set out for Edessa and abandon the perilous world, and he can thereby free himself of the burden which causes many to stumble and perish.

These lines follow a plea to God that he may enjoy his lady,[13] and are in turn followed by a statement that 'anger at love means fear and trepidation and a man cannot long live or die by this', for 'good Love never deceived or became flawed, but brings joy to bold lovers'. Lucia Lazzerini asks why, after singing of the *joy* that renews him and of the beauty of his love, Cercamon should suddenly change the subject by starting on the entirely different theme of the crusade. It does seem strange that this troubadour should see no incompatibility between crusading – even 'abandoning the perilous world' – and love of a woman, and she may be right to see the love presented here as crusading: 'Crusading as an Act of Love'.[14] On

---

[12] According to H. Gelzer, 'Zum altfranzösischen Kreuzugslied, *Chevalier, mult estes guariz*', ZRP, 48 (1928), 438–48, and U. Mölk, *Das älteste französische Kreuzlied und der Erfurter Codex Amplonianus 8°* (Göttingen, 2001), pp. 19–20, §5 ('Zur Sprache des Autors'), the text is probably of Poitevin origin. L. Lazzerini, *Les Troubadours et la sagesse* (Ventadour, 2013), pp. 101–02 sees a 'polyphonic discourse' taking place between this piece and Cercamon's *Puois nostre temps comens'a brunezir* (BdT 112.3a), see below.

[13] 'q'us joys d'amor me reverdis e·m pays, / e·m puesc jurar qu'anc ta bella no fos: petit la vey, mas per ella suy gays / e jauzions, e Dieus m'en do jauzir!' (for a special joy of love renews and nourishes me, and I can swear that there was never such a lovely lady: I see her but little, yet I am merry and joyful on her account, and God grant I may enjoy her!).

[14] Lazzerini, *Troubadours*, pp. 100–01. The argument is complicated but interesting, even if not all of her allegorical interpretations of Cercamon, Marcabru and Jaufre are convincing.

the other hand several other troubadour songs contain a switch from the topic of courtly love to a short crusading exhortation.[15]

We know that Jaufre Rudel went on the Second Crusade, for Marcabru sends one of his songs to him *outra mar*. A love song of Jaufre's (BdT 262.6) contains a final stanza, preserved in five of its thirteen manuscripts, which urges the need to follow Jesus to Bethlehem. Unless it is apocryphal, it is likely to be a call to go on crusade rather than a vaguer one to lead a spiritual life. The southern crusaders arrived Acre in April 1148, and stanza VI could have been composed before or during Jaufre's stay in the East. In this version of the song the poet moves from evocations of the joy of the simple, natural possession of love, to the longing for love not yet possessed, to anxiety and frustration at its non-fulfilment, to a decision to abandon this in favour of a different kind of love:

Amors, alegre·m part de vos
per so quar vau mo mielhs queren;
e sui en tant aventuros
qu'enqueras n'ai mon cor jauzen:
mas pero per mon Bon Guiren,
que·m vol e m'apell'e·m denha
m'es ops a parcer mon voler.

E qui sai rema deleitos
e Dieu non siec en Belleen,
no sai cum ja mais sia pros
ni cum ja venh'a guerimen;
qu'ieu sai e crei, mon escien,
que selh cui Jhesus ensenha
segur'escola pot tener.   (vv. 29–42)

Love, happily I part from you, because I go to seek what is best for me; and I am fortunate inasmuch as my heart already rejoices at it; but on account of my Good Protector, who wants me and calls me and judges me worthy, I need to restrain my yearning.

And if a man remains here in a life of pleasure and does not follow God to Bethlehem, I know not how he will ever be excellent, nor how he can ever attain salvation; for I know and firmly believe that anyone taught by Jesus can rely on a sure school.

Much discussion has taken place over the concept of love, particularly *amor de lonh* (distant love), in Jaufre's poetry as a whole, and its possible relationship to the crusades.[16] Whatever the truth of this, Marcabru appears to have had little truck

---

[15] For example, BdT 155.3, 364.11, 364.4, 323.5.
[16] For recent contributions to this debate see Lazzerini, *Troubadours*, especially Chapters 4 and 6, and compare F. Zufferey, 'Nouvelle approche de l'amour de loin', *CN*, 69 (2009), 7–58.

with either Jaufre's idea of love or his moral worth as a crusader. In a hard-hitting satire he attacks those who take the cross who allow themselves to be duped by 'lurve' (BdT 293.7). The poem is part of a dialogue between Marcabru and Jaufre and appears to have been composed either during the winter of 1148–1149 or, if Jaufre returned from the Holy Land, after his return.

> Ans que·l terminis verdei
> chantarai et ai ben drei.
> Qui que d'amor s'esbaudei,
> ieu no·n ai ni so ni quei.
> A nuill home que dompnei
> no quier peior malavei:
> Be mor de fam e de frei
> qui d'amor es en destrei!   (vv. 1–8)

Before the season grows green, I shall sing and rightly so. Whoever else may be cheered by love, I get nothing out of it. On any man who goes courting I wish no worse sickness. Anyone under love's tyranny is certainly starving and freezing to death!

With its uncourtly tone and its dinning repetition of rhyme sounds in *coblas singulars*, where each stanza uses a single rhyme for its eight lines, it hammers home a misogynistic attack on female venality and male, lust-driven gullibility. It concludes by saying that 'the man whom love will deceive should never sign himself with the cross [become a crusader]!' – probably an allusion to Jaufre himself.[17]

Around the same time he sends a 'refined' song on love (BdT 293.15) to Jaufre in Outremer, criticising women who love more than one man. This is generally taken to echo allegations of Eleanor of Aquitaine's misconduct in Syria with her uncle Raymond of Antioch.[18]

> Mesura es en gent parlar
> e cortesia es d'amar;
> et qui no vol esser mespres

---

[17] See L. Paterson, 'Marcabru's Rhetoric and the Dialectics of *trobar*: *Ans que·l terminis verdei* (PC 293.7) and Jaufre Rudel', in *Conjunctures: Medieval Studies in Honor of Douglas Kelly*, ed. K. Busby and N. Lacy (Amsterdam and Atlanta, 1994), pp. 407–23.
[18] N. Vincent, 'A Letter to King Henry I from Toulouse', *JEH*, 63 (2012), 331–45 (p. 340, and n. 30). Vincent suggests that the mutual understanding between Eleanor and Raymond, and Louis' deep resentment of it, may have been 'more political than sexual in nature, being based upon Eleanor and Raymond's shared desire to vindicate their inherited rights to Aquitaine and to loosen the Capetian influence established there as a result of Eleanor's marriage to Louis'. Compare Phillips, *The Second Crusade*, pp. 207–12, on this and the reasons behind Louis' decision to head south for Damascus instead of supporting the strategic needs of the Antiochenes.

> de tota vilania·is gar,
> d'escarnir e de foleiar,
> puois sera savis, ab que·ill pes.
>
> C'aissi pot savis hom regnar
> e bona dompna meillurar;
> mas cella q'en pren dos o tres
> e per un no si vol fiar,
> be·n deu sos prez asordeiar
> e sa valors a chascu mes.   (vv. 19–30)

Moderation lies in noble speech, and courtliness comes from loving; and a man who does not want to be misjudged should guard against all base, deceitful and excessive/wild behaviour, then, although it might not make him any happier, he will be wise.

For in this way, a wise man can live well and a good lady can improve, but she who takes two or three lovers and does not want to pledge herself to one alone, well, her reputation and worth decrease as a result with every month that passes.

Marcabru concludes ironically by saying he wants the song to cheer up the 'French' (the French crusaders of the royal domain of the Île-de-France):

> Lo vers e·l son voill enviar
> a·n Jaufre Rudel oltramar,
> e voill que l'aion li Frances
> per lor coratges alegrar,
> que Dieus lor o pot perdonar,
> o sia peccaz o merces.   (vv. 37–42)

I want to send the *vers* and the melody to Sir Jaufre Rudel, in Outremer, and I want the French to have it, to cheer their hearts, for God can allow them this, whether it is a sin or a good deed.

This reference to the French crusaders is likely to highlight the sly allusion in stanza V to their queen's behaviour.[19] The implications of the final remark are ambiguous: on the one hand it may insinuate that these crusaders like listening to sinful secular songs, though as this one is a condemnation of sin they may not enjoy it. On the other it might imply criticism of the French for not fostering courtly activities.

All of Marcabru's songs about Louis' crusade are negative in one way or another. His earliest, likely to date from the summer of 1147, contains a complaint against the call to arms and preaching ordered by the French king (BdT 293.1). However, the interplay of voices in this composition is equivocal. Although the troubadour

---

[19] See Harvey, *Marcabru*, pp. 136–39, for a detailed analysis of Marcabru's response to Cercamon's piece and the rumours of Eleanor's conduct in Syria.

very frequently adopts a preaching persona, here he does not. Instead his first-person speaker is a philanderer who stays behind in the West and tries to seduce a young girl weeping because her lover is departing overseas.

> 'Jhesus', dis elha, 'reys del mon,
> per vos mi creys ma gran dolors,
> quar vostra anta mi cofon,
> quar li mellor de tot est mon
> vos van servir, mas a vos platz.
>
> Ab vos s'en vai lo mieus amicx,
> lo belhs e·l gens e·l pros e·l ricx;
> sai m'en reman lo grans destrix,
> lo deziriers soven e·ls plors.
> Ay! mala fos reys Lozoïcx,
> que fai los mans e los prezicx
> per que·l dols m'es el cor intratz!'
>
> Quant ieu l'auzi desconortar,
> ves lieys vengui josta·l riu clar:
> 'Belha', fi·m ieu, 'per trop plorar
> afolha cara e colors;
> e no vos qual dezesperar,
> que selh qui fai lo bosc fulhar
> vos pot donar de joy assatz.'
>
> 'Senher', dis elha, 'ben o crey
> que Dieus aya de mi mercey
> en l'autre segle per jassey,
> quon assatz d'autres peccadors;
> mas say mi tolh aquelha rey
> don joy mi crec; mas pauc mi tey,
> que trop s'es de mi alonhatz.' (vv. 17–42)

'Jesus', she said, 'King of the world, because of you my great sorrow is increasing, for your shame is my undoing: the best of all this world are going to serve you, since it is your will.

My love, the handsome, courtly, brave and noble, departs with you; great distress, frequent longing and tears stay here with me. Oh! Cursed be King Louis, who orders the call to arms and the preaching which are the cause of this grief entering my heart!'

When I heard her lamenting, I went up to her by the clear stream. 'Pretty lady,' I said, 'too much crying spoils the looks and complexion, and you don't need to despair, for He who makes the woods come into leaf can give you much joy.'

'Sir', she said, 'I do believe that God will have mercy on me forever in the next world, as He will on many other sinners; but here He is taking away from me the one person who gave me joy (through whom my joy increased), but he thinks little of me, for he has gone so far away from me.'

While the listener's sympathies lie with the woman rather than the man, it is probably too simple merely to adopt her point of view, for she could be identified with one of those whose attractions risk diverting their men from their spiritual duty.[20] What is remarkable is that Marcabru passes up an obvious opportunity to preach, and that he allows a sympathetic character to curse the French king.[21] This delicate and original piece is unique among the texts attributed to Marcabru, and anticipates by some seventy years the lyric use of a feminine voice lamenting separation from a crusader lover.[22]

A further Marcabrunian song (BdT 293.21) attacks 'false Christians':

Sist falsa gen crestiana
qu'en crim pec fremilla
a la fi ves Corrosana
vira l'escobilla,
que·l baptismes de Jordan a
lur notz e·ls perilla.   (vv. 43–48)

---

[20] See Baldric of Bourgueil's account of Urban II's preaching of the First Crusade written in c. 1108 (*The Historia Jerosolimitana of Baldric of Bourgueil*, ed. S. Biddlecome (Woodbridge, 2014), p. 9): 'Non uos demulceant illecebrosa blandimenta mulierum necque rerum uestrarum, quin eatis' (Do not let the seductive lures of your possessions persuade you not to go', translation L. and J. Riley-Smith, *The Crusades: Idea and Reality* (London, 1981), p. 52), and compare Guibert de Nogent ('Historia quae dicitur Gesta Dei per Francos', *RHC (Historiens occidentaux)*, 5 vols (Paris, 1844–1895), IV, p. 124, translation L. and J. Riley-Smith, *The Crusades: Idea and Reality*, p. 56), writing before 1108, who praises those for whom 'Uxores pulcherrimae quasi quiddam tabidum vilescebant' (the most beautiful wives became as loathsome as something putrid).

[21] For subtle readings of this song see M. Bruckner, 'Marcabru et la chanson de croisade: d'un centre à l'autre', *CCM*, 53 (2010), 219–36, and S. G. Nichols, 'Urgent Voices: The Vengeance of Images in Medieval Poetry', in *France and the Holy Land. Frankish Culture at the End of the Crusades*, ed. D. H. Weiss and L. Mahoney (Baltimore and London, 2004), pp. 22–42 (pp. 22–27).

[22] See Chapter 5 for RS 21 by Guiot de Dijon (first third of the thirteenth century?) and the anonymous RS 191 (second half of the thirteenth century?). For a different interpretation of Marcabru's poem see Lazzerini, *Troubadours*, pp. 86–88, who sees Marcabru as launching a 'violente invective' against Louis, and the young lady as the *civitas* of the prophet Jeremiah's Lamentations: 1–2: 'quomodo sedit sola civitas plena populo / facta est quasi visua domina gentium / [...] plorans ploravit in nocte et lacrimae eius in maxillis eius / non est qui consoletur eam ex omnibus aris eius' (p. 87).

These false Christians, who persist in foolish crime, in the end turn their filth towards Khorassan, for the baptism of the Jordan harms and endangers them.

The references suggest the song was composed at the time of the Second Crusade; the 'false Christians' may be those crusaders who, abandoned at Attalia and left to make their own way to the Holy Land when Louis VII and others sailed to Antioch, threw in their lot with the Turks.

After the abortive siege of Damascus in July 1148, the abandonment of the Second Crusade under French leadership and the conquest of Tortosa on 31 December of the same year by Count Ramón Berenguer IV of Barcelona with the assistance of the Templars, Marcabru returns to his support of the Reconquista in his famous *vers del lavador* (BdT 293.35).[23] Taking his cue from Cercamon but opposing his declaration that a man can cleanse himself from great guilt by crusading in the Holy Land, he now explicitly extols Spain over the East as a place of spiritual cleansing:

Pax in nomine Domini!
Fez Marcabruns los moz e·l so.
Auiaz qe di:
cum nos a fait per sa dousor
lo seignorius celestiaus,
probet de nos, un lavador
c'anc for outramar no·n fon taus
en de lai enves Josaphat;
e d'aquest de sai vos conort.   (vv. 1–9)

Peace in the name of the Lord! Marcabru made the *vers* and the tune. Hear what he says: how the heavenly Lord in His loving-kindness has created for us, in our vicinity, a washing-place such as never existed before, apart from over there near the valley of Josaphat in Outremer; but it is about the one over here that I exhort you.

Paul has demonstrated that by this time the papacy and Ramón himself understood his campaigns in Iberia to be completely equivalent to crusades in the East.[24] Marcabru goes so far as to present the Spanish *lavador* as the more worthy of support. Although he calls on all to avenge God the wrongs being done to Him 'both here and over there towards Damascus', the contrast he draws between the Spanish and the French could hardly be more conspicuous. On the one hand he lauds Ramón Berenguer (now also marquis of Tortosa) and the Templars; on the

---

[23] As well as being one of the most anthologised troubadour songs in modern times, citations attest to its impact and lasting popularity in the Middle Ages: see Harvey, *Marcabru*, pp. 3–4.
[24] Paul, *To Follow in Their Footsteps*, p. 268.

other he derides the miserable, craven performance of the French leaders, planning to make their way home after their unsuccessful siege of Damascus:

> En Espaign'e sai lo Marques
> et cill del temple Salamo
> sofron lo pes
> e·l fais del orgoill paianor,
> per que jovens cuoill avol laus;
> e·l criz per aqel lavador
> versa sobre·ls plus rics captaus,
> fraich-faillit de proessa las,
> que non amo joi ni deport.
>
> Desnaturat son li Frances,
> si del afar Dieu dizo no,
> qu'eu sai cum es!   (vv. 55–66)

Here [in Guyenne and Poitou] and in Spain the marquis and all of Solomon's Temple bear the weight and the burden of pagan pride, which is why youth gathers a base reputation; and the public outcry relating to that other washing-place pours down on the highest-ranking leaders: broken failures, weary of valour, who love neither joy nor delight,

The French are perverted if they say no to God's cause, for I know how things stand!

Of the surviving songs connected to the Second Crusade, only one is French. It uncritically supports Louis' expedition, and may be part of its preaching programme. The seven troubadour songs securely connected to that expedition demonstrate the persistence of the commitment to the Reconquista shown in the two pieces composed before the Second Crusade, and a more critical stance towards the French-led crusade to the Holy Land. If Jaufre Rudel joins it and Cercamon flags it briefly as a source of salvation, Marcabru denigrates its crusaders' lack of moral integrity, the value of their efforts and, finally, their defeatism in the face of failure. He was not alone in such criticisms. From a variety of sources these reached the point that some disparaged the idea of crusading in general, and it took four decades and the cataclysmic fall of Jerusalem to Saladin in 1187 for an expedition on a comparable scale to set out from the West.[25]

---

[25] M. Hoch, 'The Price of Failure', in *The Second Crusade. Scope and Consequences*, ed. J. Phillips and M. Hoch (Manchester, 2001), pp. 183–85, and Cole, *The Preaching of the Crusades*, p. 52.

2

After Damascus: Reconquest, Settlement and Pilgrimage

After the failure of the Second Crusade, armed and unarmed pilgrims and small groups of crusaders continued to flow to the Holy Land, 'demonstrating that although Christians had been demoralized by the failure of the Second Crusade and were not inspired to mount a major expedition, their faith and commitment to the Holy Land were not shaken'.[1] To judge by the surviving records, this was not enough to inspire our lyric poets. For the next quarter of a century they had little to say about Palestine. However, the troubadours continued to be interested in the Reconquista; then by the 1170s and 1180s we catch a glimpse of activity in the crusader states and see two troubadours travel to Outremer on pilgrimage.

In the immediate aftermath of the crusade Marcabru's famous *Vers del lavador* turned attention back towards the *via de Hispania*. A decade later, in 1157–1158, Peire d'Alvernhe, defending the reputation of his oft-maligned predecessor, also writes in support of the Reconquista (BdT 323.7):

> Reis, per Cristians faillis,
> quar Masmutz nos faun sobransa:
> coms ni dux non senh sentura
> mieils de vos feira de lansa;
> per l'emperador me dol
> c'a moutas gens fai fraitura:
> tals en plora que n'a iais.
>
> Vostre coratges s'esclarzis
> quar n'avetz bon'esperansa:
> sobre paguans, gen tafura,
> cavalguatz cenes duptansa;
> premiers penres Labadol,
> e si anatz ab dreitura,
> tro a Marroc faran lais.   (vv. 8–21)

---

[1] Riley-Smith, *The Crusades. A Short History*, p. 108.

King, you are missed by the Christians [?], since Muslims are overpowering us: there is no count or duke girding his sword who could strike better than you with a lance. I grieve for the emperor, who is missed by a great many people: there is one who weeps over it who is delighted.

Your heart brightens because you have good hope: against the host of pagan ruffians, ride without hesitation; first you will capture Labadol [Badajoz?], and if you go with rectitude [on your side], they will lament as far as Morocco.

Probably addressed to King Sancho III of Castile, the song refers to the death of Sancho's father, Alfonso VII, and, probably, King Sancho VII 'the Wise' (1150–1194) of Navarre, who took advantage of Alfonso's death to enlarge the boundaries of his kingdom. The troubadour highlights the threat of Muslim ascendancy, the impediment to Christian success of internecine war and the common crusading theme of the need to fight with the right intention.

The Reconquista continued to be in the thoughts of troubadours in the 1180s. In a love song which turns to political matters, Peire Vidal comments on certain events taking place in Poitou-Charente and attacks the kings of Spain for their internal struggles that impede their religious war against the Muslims (BdT 364.36):

> Als quatre reis d'Espanh'esta mout mal,
> quar no volon aver patz entre lor;
> quar autramen son ilh de gran valor,
> adreit e franc e cortes e leyal,
> sol que d'aitan gensesson lur escuelh,
> que viresson lor guerr'en autre fuelh,
> contra la gen que nostra lei no cre,
> tro qu'Espanha fos tota d'una fe.   (vv. 49–56)

The four kings of Spain are in a bad way, for they do not wish for peace among themselves; otherwise they are of great worth, just and noble, courtly and loyal, if only they improve their conduct and redirect their war against the people who do not believe in our religion, so that all of Spain are of one faith.

Finally in a *planh* (funeral lament) composed in 1184–1185 the Catalan troubadour Guillem de Berguedà celebrates the deeds of Pons de Mataplana, who died fighting against the Moors in Spain (BdT 210.9).

Two songs by the troubadour Peire Bremon lo Tort composed in the 1170s afford a small glimpse of life in the crusader states. Peire is working closely in the administration of an unidentified Philip of Montreal in Syria and is having to return to the West with him, leaving a lady behind. The earlier song (BdT 331.2) shows him setting off:[2]

---

[2] While the piece itself contains no datable allusions, it is reasonable to assume it was composed just before BdT 331.1: see the notes on Rialto.

> Qu'era roman en Suria
> mos jois et eu tenc ma via
> en las terras on nasquei.
> Jamais midonz non veirei.
> Gran mal mi fan li sospir
> que per lei m'aven a far,
> que la nuoch non posc dormir
> e·l jorn m'aven a veillar.   (vv. 9–16)

For now my joy stays in Syria and I'm taking the road to the lands where I was born; I'll never see my lady again. The sighs I must sigh for her give me great pain, so that I can't sleep at night and yet must stay awake during the day.

In the second he is back in the West, asking William Longsword of Montferrat to go to comfort his lady after their painful separation (BdT 331.1):

> Ben gent me saup lo cor emblar,
> quan pris comjat de chai venir,
> que non es jorns qu'eu non sospir
> per un bel semblan que·ill vi far;
> qu'ella·m dis tuta maria:
> 'Que fara la vostr'amia,
> bels amics? Per qe·m vols laissar?'
>
> [...]
>
> Chanzos, tu·t n'iras oltra mar
> e per Deu vai a midonz dir
> q'e gran dolor et en conssir
> me fai la nuoich e·l jorn estar.
> Di·m a'N Guillem Longaespia,
> bona chanzos, qu'el li dia
> e que·i an per lei confortar,
>
> qe Filippe de Monreal
> me ten pres en sa bailia,
> et am tan sa compagnia
> qe sens lui no m'en puesc tornar.   (vv. 29–35, 43–53)

When I took my leave to come here, she stole my heart away very softly, for not a day passes without me sighing for a beautiful glance I saw her give; for she said to me, so saddened: 'What shall your beloved do, sweet friend? Why do you want to leave me?' [...] Song, you will go away over the sea and for God's sake tell my lady that day and night I am in great pain and anguish. Good song, tell Lord William Longsword for me that he should go to her to comfort her and tell her that Philip of Montreal keeps me close in his administration, and I so love his company that I cannot return without him.

This song can be dated to some time between the summer of 1175, when the nobility of the Kingdom of Jerusalem offered William the crown, and the late summer of 1177, when news of his death in Sidon in June probably first reached western Europe. In an interesting contrast to later French *chansons de departie*,[3] where crusading poets sing sorrowfully of leaving their beloved lady at home in France, these songs lament the separation from a lady left overseas in Syria while the poet returns to the West. According to his *vida*, this troubadour was from the Dauphiné, and may be the same man as the Petrus Bermundi who witnessed donations to the Templars of Roaix between 1163 and 1168, and in two acts in 1176. His address to William Longsword suggests that he may have had a fairly senior position in Philip's retinue.

Before Gillingham and Harvey set the record straight in 2003, on the basis of historical and literary evidence, scholars unanimously believed that the troubadour Giraut de Borneil had accompanied Viscount Aimar V of Limoges on the Third Crusade. This is wrong. Aimar did not go on crusade; at this time 'Aimar se trouvait tranquillement chez lui'. However, ten years earlier, in 1179–1180, he made a pilgrimage to the Holy Land, and Giraut travelled with him.[4] It is not known for certain whether two songs Giraut composed in Syria (BdT 242.24 and BdT 242.30) belong to this pilgrimage or to his later journey on the Third Crusade. For reasons I shall give in the next chapter, I believe they are more likely to post-date the fall of Jerusalem (1187). In BdT 242.28, mainly a love song, Giraut praises Alfonso II of Aragon's victories over the Saracens and refers to himself as the king's obedient servant overseas.

> Ara·m trai
> vas Mon Segon
> ad esple
> tot mantenen,
> e port prezen
> al rei n'Anfos
> de mos sos;
> c'autra manentia
> non ai mais de dir
> que l'aus perufrir.
> Car a valen
> e mante
> pretz, mi cove
> qu'ieu l'istei'aclis
> sers outramaris.

---

[3] See pp. 50–53.
[4] J. Gillingham and R. Harvey, 'Le troubadour Giraut de Borneil et la troisième croisade', *RST*, 5 (2003), 51–72 (p. 57).

> Razos es ben
> s'el mante
> vas San Sere,
> car trop mais conquis
> sobre Sarrazis.   (vv. 76–95)

Now I hasten straight away towards My Rival and bear the gift of my melodies to the honoured king, Lord Anfos; for no other riches can I offer him but my poetry. Since he has and maintains true reputation, it is right I should remain his obedient 'overseas' servant.

He is right to hold fast near Saint–Céré, for he has won far greater victories over the Saracens.

Contrary to previous opinion, this song is likely to have been connected not to the Third Crusade but to Alfonso's involvement in conflicts in the Limousin near Saint–Céré in c.1183 or 1186. Alfonso had known Giraut from at least the 1170s,[5] and probably knew that Giraut had been on pilgrimage.

Just before Saladin's cataclysmic victory over the Christian forces at the Horns of Hattin, Peire Vidal turned his attention from the Reconquista to the East, announcing his intention to go to Holy Land (BdT 364.9).

> Et irai m'en lai on fo mortz e vius
> Nostre Seigner per nos totz pechadors;
> E socora·m la soa grans doussors,
> si cum es fis, cars e verais e pius;
> e·m lais faire del tot lo sieu plazer.
> Et al bon rei don Dieus forsa e lezer
> c'aissi puosca son bon pretz mantener.   (vv. 43–49)

I shall go to that place where Our Lord died and rose again for all us sinners; may His great sweetness aid me, since he is noble, dear, true and gentle; and may he let me do His will in all things. And to the good king may God give the strength and opportunity to maintain his good name.

In his only song known to have been composed in Outremer (BdT 364.2) he is to be found at the court of Count Raymond II of Tripoli.[6] Although he claims to be a on a pilgrimage, his song hardly treats the idea of crusading seriously. The poet

---

5   Harvey and Paterson, *The Troubadour Tensos*, II, p. 704.
6   The piece dates from before the count's death on 17 October 1187 and after BdT 364.9 (February 1187?), when Peire was still in Occitania, and almost certainly before the fall of Jerusalem to Saladin on 3 October 1187, since he does not mention this catastrophe or the Third Crusade, which he does elsewhere (BdT 364.4, 364.8, 364.11).

maintains that he is overseas because his cruel lady has sent him into exile, and that what he really wants is to slip back home secretly.

> Assatz par que lonhar
> me volc de sa reio,
> quan passar mi fes mar,
> per qu'ieu la n'ochaizo.
> Mas no·i ai sospeisso,
> qu'ieu·l servi ab cor fi,
> tan quan puec a bando,
> e no·n aic guizardo,
> mas sol d'un pauc cordo.
> Si agui, qu'un mati
> intrei dins sa maizo
> e·lh baiziei a lairo
> la boca e·l mento.
> So n'ai agut e no mais re
> e sui totz mortz, si·l plus rete.
>
> Sospirar e plorar
> mi fai manta sazo,
> qu'alegrar e chantar
> volgra mais, si·l fos bo;
> mas cor a de drago,
> qu'a me di mal e ri
> als autres deviro,
> e·m fai huelhs de leo:
> per aital faillizo
> fes de mi pelegri,
> qu'anc romieus d'orazo
> mais ta forsatz no fo.
> E qui·l ver en despo,
> totz hom deu percassar son be,
> ans que mals seinhers lo malme.   (vv. 16–45)
>
> Pus pauzar ni finar
> no puesc nulha sazo,
> retornar et anar
> m'en vuelh ad espero
> entr'Arle e Tolo
> a tapi, quar aqui
> am mais un pauc cambo,
> qu'aver sai Lo Daro,
> ni aver Lo Toro
> N'Ibeli: mas frairi

fals lauzengier gloto
m'an moguda tenso
e lunhat del Peiro,
e·N Drogomans no m'au ni·m ve,
quar mon car Amic part de se.   (vv. 76–90)

It is most apparent that she wished to banish me from her land when she made me go overseas, which is why I reproach her. Yet I am not afraid of doing so, for I have served her with a faithful heart, to the utmost of my ability, and I had no reward for it other than a small piece of cord. Yet I did – for one morning I entered her house and stole a kiss on her mouth and chin. This I had and no more, and I die utterly if she withholds the rest.

Many a day she makes she makes me sigh and weep, when if it pleased her I would rather be happy and sing; but she has a dragon's heart, for she speaks harshly to me and she laughs with others near by, and glares at me like a lion: because of this fault she made me into a pilgrim, and never was a traveller so forced into a pious journey. If truth be told, every man ought to pursue what is good for him before an unkind lord mistreats him.

Since I can never find rest or pause, I want to return and spur back in secret to [the land] between Arles and Toulon, for I would rather have a small field there than Daron here, or Toron or Ibelin; but the base, false, wretched slanderers have stirred up hostility towards me and driven me from the Steps [in Toulouse], and Sir Interpreter does not hear from me or see me, since he is sending my dear Friend away.

Whatever lies behind the playful troubadour's reasons for travelling overseas,[7] his claim to be making a 'pious journey' appears equivocal at best. The song shortly preceded the events which were to shock the West into a new crusade; meanwhile the court of Tripoli was evidently happy to welcome a poet singing of his love adventures. This seems to reflect a settled feeling in this part of Syria, where there is leisure to cultivate courtly values and be entertained by a zany character who makes no claims to religious seriousness, claims he has been forced to come on pilgrimage to the Holy Land because of an unfortunate episode in which his lady banished him from her presence and declares that he would much rather be back home in Provence, where a small field (no doubt a metonymic expression for the lady) would be more attractive than the lordship of one of the Syrian territories.

If there is any trouvère song referring to the crusades to have survived from this period, it is Conon de Bethune's *Bele douce dame chiere* (RS 1325). It post-dates 1182 but could also have been composed after the start of the Third Crusade. The first of its two antithetical stanzas praises a lady to the skies; in the second, the first-person speaker attacks her fickle, grasping, promiscuous nature and declares she has sent

---

7   See the notes to this piece on Rialto.

him off to Syria. There is little sign of any autobiographical element here. The song forms part of a network of poetic homage between Conon and two troubadours, Conon imitating the versification of a song of Bertran de Born, and Raimbaut de Vaqueiras in turn echoing Conon's piece in his multi-lingual *descort*.[8] The idea of a poet's exile induced by a lady's coldness goes back at least to Bernart de Ventadorn's *Can vei la lauzeta mover*,[9] though Peire Vidal claims more specifically in BdT 364.2 (see above) that he was in the Holy Land for this reason. The song tells us little about contemporary attitudes to crusading, but provides an example of the increasing interaction of trouvères and troubadours during the crusading period from this time on.[10]

The few songs dating from the years leading up to the Third Crusade give no inkling of the disaster to come. As Runciman observes, 'In spite of all the appeals that had come from the kingdom of Jerusalem in recent years, no one in the West, except perhaps at the Papal Court, had realized the urgency of the danger. The knights and pilgrims that had journeyed eastward had found in the Frankish states a life more luxurious and gay than any that they had known at home. They heard tales of military prowess; they saw commerce flourishing. [...] Now, suddenly, they heard that it was all ended.'[11]

---

[8] Barbieri, 'A mon Ynsombart part Troia', pp. 272–76.

[9] BdT 70.43, 'e vau m'en pus ilh no.m rete, / chaitius, en issilh, no sai on', ed. S. G. Nichols, J. A. Galm et al., *Bernart de Ventadorn: The Songs of Bernart de Ventadorn* (Chapel Hill, 1962), 43, 55–56.

[10] Barbieri, 'A mon Ynsombart part Troia', p. 265. Barbieri observes that nearly the whole of Conon's poetic corpus is involved in the play of intertextual relations between Bertran de Born and Raimbaut de Vaqueiras (p. 269).

[11] Runciman, *History*, III, p. 3.

3

The Third Crusade (1187–1192)

On 3 July 1187 at the Horns of Hattin, near Tiberias and the Sea of Galilee, Saladin routed the Christians and captured the unbelievably precious relic of the True Cross. The king of Jerusalem, Guy of Lusignan, was taken prisoner and on 2 October the Holy City surrendered. Pope Urban III is said to have died of shock and grief. Within ten days his successor, Gregory VIII, issued an impassioned appeal for a new crusade, explaining the catastrophe in terms of punishment for the sins not only of the Latin settlers but also of all Christians, whom he summoned to acts of penance.[1] Meanwhile Conrad of Montferrat and the surviving remnants of the nobility and military forces of the Kingdom of Jerusalem took refuge behind the walls of Tyre, courageously defending it against Saladin's onslaughts and sending desperate messages to the West.[2]

Richard the Lionheart took the cross as soon as he heard the news. Other leaders showed less sense of urgency. Richard's father, Henry II, and King Philip Augustus of France continued to wage war on each other, to outraged public reaction. Eventually they called a truce at Gisors in mid-January 1188, took the cross and agreed to levy the so-called Saladin tithe (10 per cent on all movable property and income). However, it took a long time for the crusade to get off the ground. Richard, Philip and Henry continued fighting. Henry died shortly after taking the cross, and Richard was crowned on 3 September 1189. The delays caused a storm of protest, 'not only from ecclesiastics but also from troubadours and trouvères: there can be no doubt that public opinion was scandalized'.[3] By contrast, Frederick Barbarossa of Germany had responded quickly and decided on a land route to the Holy Land, but after he had successfully marched an army through hostile territory and Asia Minor, he died suddenly as he was attempting to cross a river. After this the German contribution more or less collapsed.[4] This was to have disastrous consequences: Runciman comments that 'Saladin was right to see his salvation in

---

[1] Riley-Smith, *The Crusades. Idea and Reality*, pp. 63–67.
[2] Runciman, *History*, II, pp. 471–72.
[3] Riley-Smith, *The Crusades. A Short History*, p. 110.
[4] Riley-Smith, *The Crusades. A Short History*, pp. 111–13.

the Emperor's death', and 'the grim fiasco of the Emperor's Crusade made it more than ever urgent that the kings of France and England should arrive in the East'.⁵

Philip and Richard evenually met at Vézelay in July 1190 and began their march to the coast from where they would set sail. Mediterranean sea conditions led to them overwintering in Sicily from September to March/April. Philip finally reached Acre in April, and Richard in June after landing at various Mediterranean islands and conquering Cyprus. They retook Acre from Saladin on 12 July 1191, and divided the city between them. Philip left for home on 31 July. When there were difficulties over his payment of the agreed ransom of the survivors of the garrison, Richard ordered the massacre of some 2,700 men, women and children in the sight of the Turkish army. He carried off a number of successes during the crusade, campaigning impressively against Saladin but failing to recapture Jerusalem. On his way home a shipwreck forced him to travel through Austria in disguise, where he was taken prisoner by Leopold of Austria. He was eventually released in 1194 after the payment of a gigantic ransom.

The Third Crusade provoked the most numerous lyric responses among both troubadours and trouvères. The dating of some of their pieces is complicated by the fact that some were updated by the poets themselves in the light of moving events. This period produced a variety of songs of exhortation, songs of departure and complaints about the leaders' delays in setting out, as well as evidence of a cultural change to which certain individual troubadours sought ways to adapt themselves.

Exhortation and departure

One of the most influential, as well as one of the earliest, songs of this period is Conon de Bethune's justly famed *Ahi! Amors, com dure departie* (RS 1125). Composed soon after the fall of Jerusalem, around the end of 1187 and the beginning of 1188, it enjoyed a huge success.⁶

> Ahï! Amors, com dure departie
> me convenra faire de la millor
> ki onques fust amee ne servie!
> Diex me ramaint a li par sa douçour,
> si voirement ke m'en part a dolor.
> Las! k'ai je dit? Ja ne m'en part je mie!
> Se li cors va servir Nostre Signor,
> li cuers remaint del tot en sa baillie.
>
> Por li m'en vois sospirant en Surie,
> car je ne doi faillir mon Creator;
> ki li faura a cest besoig d'aïe,

---

⁵ Runciman, *History*, III, pp. 16–17.
⁶ L. Barbieri, 'Le canzoni di crociata, pp. 2–4.

saiciés ke il li faura a grignor;
et saicent bien li grant et li menor
ke la doit on faire chevallerie
ou on conquiert Paradis et honor
et pris et los et l'amor de s'amie.

Diex est assis en son saint iretaige:
ore i parra se cil le secorront
cui il jeta de la prison ombraje,
quant il fu mors ens la crois ke Turc ont.
Saichiés chil sont trop honi ki n'iront,
s'il n'ont poverte ou viellece ou malaige;
et cil ki sain et jone et riche sont
ne poevent pas demorer sans hontaige.

Tous li clergiés et li home d'eaige
qui ens ausmogne et ens biens fais manront
partiront tot a cest pelerinaige,
et les dames ki chastement vivront
se loiauté font a ceus qui i vont;
et s'eles font par mal consel folaige,
as lasques gens et mauvais le feront,
car tot li boin iront en cest voiaige.

Ki chi ne velt avoir vie anuieuse
si voist por Dieu morir liés et joieus,
ke cele mors est douce et savereuse
dont on conquiert le resne presïeus;
ne ja de mort nen i morra .i. sels,
ains naisteront en vie glorïeuse;
ki revenra moult sera eüreus,
a tos jors mais en iert honors s'espeuse.

Diex! tant avons esté prex par huiseuse,
or i parra ki a certes iert prex;
s'irons vengier la honte dolereuse
dont chascuns doit estre iriés et hontex;
car a no tans est perdus li sains lieus
ou Diex soffri por nos mort angoisseuse;
s'or i laissons nos anemis mortex,
a tos jors mais iert no vie honteuse.   (vv. 1–48)

Ah, Love, how hard it will be for me to part from the best lady who was ever loved and served! May God in his sweetness bring me back to her, as truly as I leave her in sorrow. Alas! What have I said? I am not leaving her at all! If my body goes off to serve our Lord, my heart remains entirely in her service.

Sighing for her, I set out for Syria, since I must not fail my Creator. If anyone should fail him in this hour of need, be aware that he will fail him in a greater; and may great and small know well that a man ought to perform knightly feats in the place where one wins paradise and honour, reputation, and praise, and the love of one's beloved.

God is besieged in his holy heritage; now it will be manifest how those whom he released from the shade of prison, when he died upon the cross held by the Turks, will assist him. Shame on all those who stay behind, unless they are poor or old or ill! But those who are healthy and young and rich cannot remain behind without disgrace.

All the clergy and the old men who stay behind performing deeds of charity and good works will have their share in this pilgrimage, as well as the ladies who live chastely and remain faithful to those who go there; but if they ill-advisedly commit folly, they will be doing so with cowardly wicked people, for all the good ones will go on this voyage.

Let anyone who does not wish to lead a discreditable life go and die gladly and joyfully for God, for that death through which one wins the precious realm is sweet and delectable; and not a single one of them will die there from death, but rather all will be born into glorious life; anyone who returns will be most happy; glory will for ever more be his spouse.

Oh God! we have been so long valiant in idleness; now it will be clear who really *is* valiant, if we go off to avenge the painful humiliation at which each one of us should feel sorrow and shame; for in our times the holy place where God suffered agonising death on our account has been lost; if we now leave our mortal enemies there, our life will be evermore stained with infamy.

Barbieri (see the online edition) has observed that this is the first crusade song of exhortation to absorb the themes and style typical of the courtly love lyric. This development marks a turning-point in the history of crusade songs, namely the creation of the *chanson de départie* or 'song of departure': a typically French variation of the crusade song, progressively emphasising the theme of love at the expense of its political and religious side and its tone of exhortation or invective. He also identifies numerous specific echoes in the second part of the text of themes and motifs typical of papal documents and contemporary preaching: ideas of the double reward, spiritual and worldly (vv. 15–16), the lost heritage (v. 17), Christ's passion understood as the highest manifestation of his love, requiring reciprocation, and hence the duty to assist the one who died for our salvation (vv. 19–20 and 45–48), exemption from crusade service accorded to the poor, the old and the sick (vv. 21–24), the promise of an indulgence to those who contribute financially to the expedition (vv. 25–26), dying in order to be reborn (vv. 37–40) and the need to avenge God (v. 43).

In a second song of departure, composed in March or perhaps October 1188 (RS 1314), Conon responds angrily to the imposition of the Saladin tithe, which he sees as the consequence of greed by those who have taken the cross in order to profit from it: a theme common in Third Crusade preaching and particularly emphasised by the French theologian and poet Peter of Blois.

> Ne ja por nul desirier
> ne remanrai chi avoc ces tirans,
> ki sont croisiet a loier
> por dismer clers et borgois et serjans;
> plus en croisa covoitiés ke creance,
> et quant la crois n'en puet estre garans,
> a teus croisiés sera Dieus mout soffrans
> se ne s'en venge a peu de demorance.   (vv. 25–32)

I have absolutely no desire to remain here with these tyrants who have taken the cross out of self-interest, to tax clerics, burghers and men-at-arms/sergeants; greed more than faith has made them take the cross, and since the cross cannot (suffice to) protect them, God will certainly prove very patient with such crusaders if he does not swiftly take vengeance on them.

The text shows many points of contact with Giraut de Borneil's song BdT 242.41, probably composed in 1188–1190, and there is also a dense network of reciprocal cross-referencing between Conon de Béthune and Bertran de Born.

Conon took the cross at the time of the Third Crusade, but although his movements are unknown, by the time of the trouvère Huon d'Oisy's death on 20 August 1189 he had not left for the Holy Land. Huon was distantly related to Conon, who indicates him as his master in the art of poetry (RS 1314, vv. 51–52). Whatever their affinity, Huon composed a sarcastic song deriding Conon for failing to fulfil his crusading vow (RS 1030):

> Maugré tous sains et maugré Diu ausi
> revient Quenes, et mal soit il vegnans!
> Honis soit il et ses preechemans,
> et honis soit ki de lui ne dist: 'fi'!
> Quant Diex verra que ses besoins ert grans,
> il li faura, quant il li a failli.
>
> Ne chantés mais, Quenes, je vos em pri,
> car vos chançons ne sont mais avenans;
> or menrés vos honteuse vie ci:
> ne volsistes pour Dieu morir joians,
> or vos conte on avoec les recreans,
> si remarrés avoec vo roi failli;
> ja Damedius, ki sor tous est poissans,
> del roi avant et de vos n'ait merci!

Molt fu Quenes preus, quant il s'en ala,
de sermoner et de gent preechier,
et quant uns seus en remanoit decha,
il li disoit et honte et reprovier;
or est venus son liu recunchiier,
et s'est plus ors que quant il s'en ala;
bien poet sa crois garder et estoier,
k'encor l'a il tele k'il l'emporta.   (vv. 1–22)

Despite all the saints and despite God himself Conon is returning, and a curse on his return! Shame on him and his preaching, and shame on anyone who does not say to him 'fie upon you'! When God sees him in great need he will not help him, just as *he* has not helped *him*.

Sing no more, Conon, I pray you, for your songs are no more pleasing. Now you will live a shameful life here; you did not choose to die joyfully for God, and now you are counted among the cowards, so you will stay here with your failed king. May Our Lord, who has power over all people, have no pity, first on the king and [then] on you!

When he set off, Conon was very brave in giving sermons and preaching to people, and if a single man stayed behind, he covered him in shame and reproach. Now he has returned to soil his home [his nest?], and he is filthier than when he left. For sure, he can keep his cross and stow it away, as it is in the same state as it was when he carried it away.

Barbieri (see the online edition) comments that Huon's text testifies to the rapid reception and popularity of Conon's crusade songs, since it is almost entirely made up of more or less literal responses to RS 1125 and RS 1314. But he cautions that Huon's harsh sarcasm should not necessarily be interpreted literally, as it might simply constitute a literary game.

Two *chansons de départie* by the Châtelain de Coucy (RS 679 and 985) belong either to this period or else to the time of the Fourth Crusade. As Barbieri has shown (see the online edition), they are essentially love songs, exacerbating the tension of separation and presenting the crusade as an unavoidable and painful duty, in which the idealising and religious spirit typical of the songs of exhortation, still present in Conon de Béthune's texts, finds no place. The focus is on the exaltation of the beloved lady, along with the psychological analysis of the lover's suffering as he is forced into departure.

Ne me vaut pas Diex por noient doner
tos les deduis k'ai eüs ens ma vie,
ains les me fait c(h)ierement comperer,
s'ai grant paour chis loiers ne m'ochie;
merchi Amors, s'ainc Diex fist vilonie,
ke vilains fait boine amor desevrer:

ne je ne puis l'amor de moi oster
et si m'estuet ke jou ma dame lais.

Or seront lié li faus losengeor
cui tant pesoit des biens k'avoir soloie,
mais ja de çou n'ere pelerins jor
ke ja vers aus boine volenté aie;
por tant porrai perdre tote ma voie,
car tant m'ont fait de mal li traïtor,
se Diex voloit k'il eüssent m'amor,
ne me porroit cargier plus pesant fais.   (RS 679, vv. 25–40)

Not for nothing has God wished to grant me all the delights I have had in my life; instead he makes me pay dearly for them, to the point where I fear that this price will be my death. Have pity, Love, if God ever acted basely, it is a cruel thing to sunder good love: but I cannot free myself of love, and yet I am obliged to leave my lady.

Now the false slanderers who so resented the good things I used to have will be glad, but I shall never be so penitent as ever to be well disposed towards them; for this reason I could lose all the benefits of my pilgrimage, because the traitors have done me so much harm that if God desired me to love them, he could not burden me with a heavier load.

The success of his songs is demonstrated both by the romance of which he is the protagonist (the *Roman du Châtelain de Coucy*) and by their insertion into the main romances containing lyric quotations: Jean Renart's *Guillaume de Dole*, Gerbert de Montreuil's *Roman de la Violette* and the *Châtelaine de Vergi*. To whichever crusade the song RS 679 belongs, it is one of the oldest songs of departure with a male first-person speaker.[7]

---

[7] Two undatable songs possibly belonging to this period are by Gautier de Dargies, who lived between c. 1170/75 and 1236: see A. M. Raugei, *Gautier de Dargies, Poesie* (Florence, 1981), pp. 30–33. This trouvère was a contemporary and apparently a close friend of Gace Brulé, whom he regarded as his poetic master and model. In RS 1575 he refers to having been abroad for a long time, facing many hardships and dangers and living constantly in sadness and fear (vv. 1–9). Although this piece contains no direct allusions to a crusade, it forms part of a fairly uniform group of texts on separation from the lady, some of which refer to crusading explicitly. RS 795 refers to him being on his way to 'the port', which may be a real port of embarkation or perhaps mean metaphorically his end or death; a stanza which is probably apocryphal relates that he is heading for Syria 'most downcast because of her' (vv. 73–76). If not by Gautier himself, the stanza shows how the song was interpreted by the time of its transmission in the manuscripts.
 Also plausibly relating to the Third Crusade is an attack on adulterous husbands in the style of Marcabru (BdT 323.5) which includes a brief prayer for crusade leaders to 'Sancta Maria d'Orien' (St Mary of the East). The reading of the majority of the manuscripts, giving

One of the most fascinating Old French crusade songs of the Third Crusade (RS 401) has survived in part of what was previously a loose parchment leaf inserted at the end of the British Library manuscript Harley 1717 devoted to the *Chronique des Ducs de Normandie* of Benoît de Sainte-Maure. Anna Radaelli has argued that the anonymous author was probably a scribe of the Plantagenet royal chancery, and wrote his composition in an Angevin environment between January and November 1188, during a rare moment of truce between the English and French kings and of peace in the domestic struggles between Henry II and his sons. It calls on people to go to God's aid in the consciousness that 'neither counts nor dukes nor crowned kings can escape death'. Out of the generic themes of the second and third stanzas, she has teased specific allusions to the Plantagenet princes.

> Cunte, ne duc, ne li roi coruné
> ne se pöent de la mort destolir,
> kar quant il unt grant tresor amassé
> plus lur covient a grant dolur guerpir.
> Mielz lur venist en bon jus departir,
> kar quant il sunt en la terre buté
> ne lur valt puis ne chastel ne cité.
>
> Allas, chettif! Tant nus sumes pené
> pur les deliz de nos cors acumplir,
> ki mult sunt tost failli e trespassé
> kar adés voi le plus joefne enviellir!
> Pur ço fet bon paraïs deservir
> kar la sunt tuit li gueredon dublé.
> Mult en fet mal estre desherité! (vv. 8–21)

Neither counts nor dukes nor crowned kings can escape death, and the greater the treasure they have amassed, the greater will be their grief on leaving it. It

---

'kings' in the plural, supports a date of 1187–1190 and points to the kings Philip Augustus, Henry II or Richard, and Frederick Barbarossa. On the other hand the reading of some manuscripts gives 'king' in the singular. This would indicate the Second Crusade, when Louis VII and Conrad III took the cross at Vézelay in 1146, in which case the song would have been composed between the launching of the crusade in 1145–1146 and the departure of the two sovereigns in May and June 1147. But as Beggiato has argued (F. Beggiato, '"Belha m'es la flors d'aguilen"', *CN*, 48 (1988), 85–112, and see the online edition), troubadour references to crusading at this earlier time are rare, Marcabru's being focussed on Spain, and the single Old French crusade song *Chevalier, mult estes guariz* referring to Louis VII but not to the emperor; what is more, Conrad III died in 1152 without ever having been crowned emperor. Beggiato links 'Sancta Maria d'Orien' to a church dedicated to the Virgin in Saint-Sernin (now Saint-Sernin-sur-Rance) in the diocese of Rodez, built by the Hospitallers in the twelfth century. He also suggests a number of plausible though inconclusive arguments to support the authorship of Bernart de Venzac.

would be better for them to divide it up by good agreement, since once they are thrown into the earth neither castle nor city will be of any help to them.

Alas, wretches that we are! We have taken so many pains to satisfy the pleasures of our bodies, so that many [of us] have prematurely faded and passed away, and I see the youngest continually growing older! For this reason it is good to gain paradise, for there all rewards are doubled. How terrible to lack an inheritance!

She argues that the futile obsession with material pleasures and many premature deaths point towards Henry's two elder sons, the Young King Henry and Count Geoffrey of Brittany, who both died young and not in battle, while the last remaining heir and the youngest, John 'Lackland', is still landless and has the prospect of growing old without an inheritance.[8] The song ends on a movingly personal note. After further exhortations, the poet's thoughts return to his 'good lords':

> [E] il otroit a sa merci venir
> mes bons seignurs, que jo tant ai amé
> k'a bien petit n'en oi Deu oblié!   (vv. 43–45)

And may He receive into His grace my good lords whom I have loved so much that I was almost forgetting God!

This piece from the peripheral tradition of Old French manuscript transmission provides a riveting example of a personal take on contemporary events expressed, as is typical of medieval lyrics, in universalising terms.

Exhortation and delay

As soon as Richard the Lionheart took the cross, Bertran de Born was quick to exult and rouse people to arms (BdT 80.30).

> Nostre Seigner somonis el meteis
> totz los arditz e·ls valenz e·ls prezatz,
> q'anc mais guerra ni cocha no·l destreis,
> mas d'aqesta si ten fort per grevatz;
> qar presa es la vera crotz e·l reis,
> e·l sepolcres ha de socors fraichura,
> don tuit crezem ab lial fe segura
> qe lo saintz focs i deissen, q'om o ve,
> per qe no fai nul esfortz qui so cre.

---

[8] Although John was known as 'Lackland', he had been betrothed to the heiress to the Gloucester earldom since 1176 and designated king of Ireland in 1177, so if this is an allusion, it is not a straightforward one.

Cel qui es coms e ducs e sera reis
s'es mes enan, per q'es ses prez doblatz,
q'el vol mais prez q'om de las doas leis:
dels cristians ni dels non-bateiatz.
E s'el vol prez, a las obras pareis;
q'el vol tan prez e tan bon'aventura,
– per que sos prez creis ades et meillura –,
q'el vol lo prez del mal e·l prez del be;
tant ama prez q'ambedos los rete.   (vv. 1–18)

Our Lord himself summons all bold, valiant and worthy men, for war nor mêlée never grieved him, yet he holds himself deeply injured on account of this one: for the true cross and the king are captive, and no one comes to the aid of the sepulchre on which, as we all believe with firm loyal faith, the holy fire descends: people see it, so there is no difficulty in believing it.

The one who is count and duke and will be king has stepped forward, which doubles his merit, for he loves merit more than anyone of the two religions, the Christians and the unbaptised. And his love of merit can be seen in his deeds, for he so loves merit and happiness – so his merit constantly grows greater and more perfect – that he wishes the merit of evil and the merit of good, and he loves merit so much that he retains both.

He probably composed these two stanzas at the beginning of November 1187, and added a third when the king of France took the cross in January 1188:

Aras sai eu qu'adreitz vol esser reis
lo reis Felips, que dizen qu'es crozatz;
et anc Carles en tal pretz no s'empeis
cum el fara, d'aiso s'es ben vanatz.   (vv. 19–22)

Now I know that King Philip wants to be a legitimate king, for they say he has taken the cross; and Charlemagne never attained such merit as he will: he has publicly committed himself to this.

Despite his connections with Conon de Béthune, the tone and approach to the crusade are very different. Bertran, this 'poet of arms' as Dante dubbed him,[9] waxes lyrical at the prospect of action: no elegiac thoughts of separation from his beloved (he is not tempted to go himself), no sorrowful dwelling on the suffering and death of Christ upon the cross, but vigorous anger, justified vengeful violence and a faith inspired by the miracle of the holy fire.[10]

---

[9] Dante, *De vulgari eloquentia*, ed. S. Botterill (Cambridge, 1996, reprint 2006), II, 10 (pp. 52–53).
[10] According to a legend much reported in medieval chronicles, candles placed on the holy

THE THIRD CRUSADE

In spite of the rulers' commitments to leave on crusade, the kings of England and France continued to fight against each other and delay their departure, and hence the arrival of crucial help to Conrad of Montferrat in Tyre. At the end of spring 1188 Bertran refers to Conrad's defence of the city against Saladin (BdT 80.17) and blames Philip and Richard, who was not yet king, for their tardiness.

> Ara parra de prez qals l'a plus gran
> de totz aqells qi·s leveron mati:
> mesier Conratz l'a plus fin, ses enjan,
> qe·s defen lai a Sur d'En Saladi
> e de sa mainada croia.
> Dieus l'acorra, qe·l secors vai tardan.
> Sols aura·l prez, pos sols suefre l'afan.
>
> Mesier Conrat, a Jesu vos coman,
> q'ieu fors lai, ab vos, so vos afi,
> mas laissei m'en qan vi qe li plus gran
> si croiçavan, li rei e li primsi.
> Pueis vi midons, bella e bloia,
> per qe mos cors mi vai afreollan,
> lai for'ab vos, s'ieu en saupes aitan.
>
> D'En Oc-e-No mi vauc ara duptan,
> qar peza li si nuilha re·l casti,
> e·l reis frances vai si trop apriman
> ez ai paor qe veinha sobre mi.
> Mas anc al seje de Troia
> non ac tan duc, primce ni amiran
> con ieu ai mes, per chantar, a mon dan.   (vv. 15–35)

Now it will be clear who has the greatest merit of all the early risers [pilgrims]: Lord Conrad's is the purest and truest, for he is defending himself overseas at Tyre against Lord Saladin and his vile troops. God will help him, for help is slow in coming! He alone will have the prize, since he alone suffers the hardship.

Lord Conrad, I commend you to Jesus, for I would be there with you, I assure you, but I held back when I saw the greatest men were taking the cross, the kings and the princes. Then I saw my lovely blonde lady, who makes my heart grow weak, but I would be with you if I knew as much about it as they do.

Now I'm afraid of Lord Yes-and-No (Richard), as he doesn't like me to rebuke him in the least, and the French king is being far too sensitive and I'm afraid he

---

sepulchre would light spontaneously on Holy Saturday (G. Gouiran, *L'Amour et la guerre: l'œuvre de Bertran de Born*, 2 vols, Aix-en-Provence, 1985, p. 669).

will come down on me like a ton of bricks. But I've braved more dukes, princes and emirs in song than were ever at the siege of Troy.

Bertran sends the song to Conon de Béthune, the Isombart of the *tornada* (v. 36), and the first line, 'Ara parra de prez qals l'a plus gran', is thought to respond to lines in Conon's crusade song *Ahi! Amors, com dure departie* (see above).[11] Bellicose in goading others to hurry up and leave for the Holy Land, Bertran offers lame excuses for himself: first, there was no point in rushing off to help Conrad once he saw the great leaders taking the cross, and second, his lady held him back. The latter move was perhaps suggested by Conon's new emphasis on the *dure departie*, the difficult parting of lady and crusader.

The manuscript tradition of this song is complicated, and the text appears to have been reworked on at least two occasions.[12] The first reworking must have occurred after Richard succeeded his father in July 1189, if not after his coronation on 3 September (BdT 80.4). Bertran again blames Philip and Richard, now referred to as king, for delaying their journey:

> Seingner Conrat, eu sai dos reis q'estan
> d'aiudar vos. Ara entendatz qui:
> lo reis Felips es l'us, qar vai doptan
> lo rei Richart; et el lui dopt'aissi.
> Ar fos usqecs d'els em boia
> d'En Saladi, pos van Deu galian,
> qar son crosat e d'anar mot non fan.
>
> Seingner Conrat, tot per vostr'amor chan,
> ni ges no·i gart amic ni enemi;
> mas per so·l fatz qe·ls crosatz vauc reptan
> del passage q'an si mes en obli.
> Non cuidon q'a Deu enoia
> q'ill se paisson e se van sojornan?
> E·us enduratz fam e set, e·ill estan!   (vv. 15–28)

Lord Conrad, I know of two kings who hold back from assisting you. Now hear who they are: King Philip is one, because he fears King Richard who in turn fears him. Would they were now both in Sir Saladin's chains, for they are cheating God: they have taken the cross and do nothing about leaving.

Lord Conrad, I sing for love of you alone, and pay no heed to friend or enemy. I do so because I'm upbraiding the crusaders for having forgotten the crossing. Do they imagine they won't annoy God by banqueting and having a good time? You endure hunger and thirst, but they are at a standstill!

---

[11] 'Dieus est assis en son saint iretaige; / ore i parra con cil le secorront / cui il jeta de la prison ombraje', and 'or i parra ki a certes iert preus' (vv. 17–19 and 42).
[12] For details see the Gouiran edition of BdT 80.17 on Rialto.

His excuse that there was no point in rushing off to help Conrad once he saw the great leaders taking the cross is no longer relevant, since the leaders are not in fact leaving. He now asserts that he held back because the leaders were dawdling so much.[13]

> Seigner Conrat, a Jesu vos coman,
> q'eu fora lai a Sur, so vos afi,
> mas laissei m'en qar s'anavan tardan
> li comt'e·ill duc, li rei e li princi.
> Pois vi midonz bell'e bloia,
> per qe s'anet mos cors afebleian,
> qu'eu fora lai, ben ha passat un an. (vv. 8–14)

> Lord Conrad, I commend you to Jesus, for I would be there at Tyre, I assure you, but I held back because the counts and dukes, kings and princes were delaying. Then I saw my lovely blonde lady, and my heart went weak, otherwise I would have been there over a year ago.

The second reworking, shown from stanza VI of the version in MSS DcFIKd and apparently added at the time of the general assembly of Vézelay on 4 July 1190, qualifies his criticism of Richard and Philip and announces their imminent departure.

> Seingner Conrat, lo reis Richartz val tan
> (si tot, qan voill, de lui gran mal m'en di)
> q'el passara ab tal esfortz ogan
> qon far poira, so aug dir tot de fi;
> e·l reis Felips en mar poia
> ab autres reis, q'ab tal esfortz venran
> qe part l'Arbre-Sec irem conquistan.
>
> Bels Papiols, vas Savoia,
> ten ton camin e vas Branditz brocan,
> e passa·l mar, q'al rei Conrat ti man.
>
> Can seras lai, no te noia,
> tu li diras qe, s'ar no·ill vaill ab bran,
> e·il valrai tost, si·ll rei no·m van bauzan.
>
> Mas ben es ver q'a tal dompna·m coman,
> si·ll passatges no·ill platz, non crei qe i an. (vv. 36–50)

Lord Conrad, King Richard has so much worth (even if, when I want to, I speak very badly of him) that he will make the crossing this year with the greatest force

---

[13] Paul (*To Follow in Their Footsteps*, pp. 131–32) takes this as evidence that the rulers' inaction 'had deeply damaged enthusiasm for the expedition'.

he can muster – I hear this for sure; and King Philip is setting sail with other kings, who will come with such a vast army that we'll go conquering beyond the Dry Tree.

Fair Papiol, make your way to Savoy, spur towards Brindisi and cross the sea, for I send you to King Conrad.

When you arrive, may you come to no harm: you will tell him that if I am not now helping him with my sword, I will soon do so, if the kings are not deceiving me.

But it is certainly true that I depend on such a lady that if the crossing displeases her, I don't believe I shall go.

Gouiran observes that the content of stanza VI is obscure: Richard will make the crossing, while Philip 'is setting sail with other kings', and moreover this news is recent and uncertain, since the *tornada* indicates a restriction, 'if the kings are not deceiving me'. Despite this, he argues, events must have unfolded as Bertran describes them, and the troubadour composed stanza VI in the light of the kings' planned itinerary after they separated at Lyon, Philip to Genoa and Richard to Marseille, even if there is no trace of the 'other kings' who were supposed to accompany Philip (perhaps an element of propaganda), though once the crusaders moved off, the troubadour probably lost all contact with them and had to rely more and more on rumour.

During the period following Richard's coronation on 3 September 1189 and the early months of 1190, when the latter is passing through Aquitaine before leaving on crusade, Bertran goads Philip for not being as bellicose as he was in the wars of 1188–1189: he has not yet set out for the Holy Land, where he could cover himself with glory (BdT 80.3).[14]

> Le seinher de cui es Manta
> e Murols / s'es de prim tersols
> tornatz. Ab qe sai non rest!
> Sieus seria, si·s n'anava
> lai, Roais, / Trevaganz,
> Alaps e Aranz.
> E fera filhol / dels Persanz.   (vv. 21–30)

The lord who rules Mantes and Murol has become a tercel instead of a female hawk.[15] Let's hope he doesn't stay here! If he went overseas, Edessa, the god Tervagan, Aleppo and Syria would be his, and he would make a godchild of the Persians [i.e., convert them].

---

[14] Gouiran, *L'amour et la guerre*, pp. 631 and 645.
[15] The female hawk is a third larger than the male tercel and was considered more vigorous and better for hunting.

But this prompts the question: is Bertran actually more interested in local fights than in crusading? He goes on tell his jongleur to urge Richard, now that he is solidly established in his northern domains of Normandy and England, to make more war in Aquitaine.

> Vas Mon Oc-e-No t'avanta,
> Papiols, / qar sieus es Bristols
> E Nortzecrentz e Suest
> e Londres e Titagrava
> e Carais / e Roanz,
> e Toars e Canz.
> Pos tot ha qan vol, / sai s'eslanz!
>
> Entre Dordoinha e Charanta
> es trop mols
> so·m dis N'Auriols,
> q'enqier no·i a ren conqest.
> Et er l'anta si·s suava
> ni qe lais
> benenanz
> e gorts e tiranz
> cels q'amar non sol
> e poissanz.
>
> Enaps e copas mazanta
> e orçols
> d'argen e pairols
> e sec ribiera e forest,
> e sai tolli'e donava!
> No·s biais
> dels afanz:
> preisas e mazans,
> Gerras ab tribol
> l'er ennanz. (vv. 41–60)

Go to my Yes-and-No (Richard), Papiol: he reigns over Bristol, Northampton, Sussex, London, Titgrave, Carhaix, Rouen, Thouars and Caen. Since he has all that he desires, let him hurry here!

Between the Dordogne and Charente he shows himself too soft, according to what Sir Auriol tells me, for he hasn't yet conquered anything. And he'll be put to shame if he relaxes and leaves his customary enemies prosperous, fat and rebellious and powerful.

He clinks goblets, cups, silver jugs and kettles, and goes hunting along the river-banks and in the forests, and here he used to seize and give! He shouldn't steer clear of hardship: mêlées and tumult, wars and discord will be to his advantage.

Speeding Philip on his way to the Holy Land may be ironic: a means of leaving the field clear for the Plantagenet.

Richard arrived in Marseille on 31 July 1190, and his fleet joined him there on 22 August. On his arrival he apparently asked the troubadour Folquet de Marselha to sing for him, perhaps because he wanted him to counter negative publicity about the delays to his departure. Folquet's piece (BdT 155.3) begins as a rhetorically polished love song. After four stanzas he turns to praise of the king:

> E qui·l bon rey Richart qui vol qu'ieu chan
> blasmet per so quar non passet dese,
> ar l'en desmen si que chascus o ve;
> qu'areire·s trais per miels salhir enan:
> qu'el era coms, ar es rix reys ses fi,
> quar bon secors fai Dieus al bon voler;
> e s'en dis ben al crozar, ieu dis ver,
> et ar vei m'o, per qu'adonc no menti.   (vv. 33–40)

But if anyone has blamed the good King Richard, who wants me to sing, for not immediately making the passage [to the Holy Land], he now gives the lie to him so that all can see it; for he takes a step back in order the better to leap forward: for he was count and is now a powerful king without limits, for God grants good assistance to good will; and if I spoke well when he took the cross, I spoke the truth, and now I see it for myself, for he did not then lie.[16]

Changing times: courtly culture and crusading

Giraut de Borneil

While Bertran at regular intervals follows the progress of the crusade leaders, or the lack of it, bent principally on goading them to action abroad or at home, two other troubadours engage with the crusade in contrasting ways, both seeking to uphold a courtly way of life apparently out of joint with the times. Giraut de Borneil and Peire Vidal had already voyaged to the Holy Land, Giraut on a pilgrimage with Viscount Aimar V of Limoges, Peire to the court of Count Raymond II of Tripoli (see Chapter 2). After his pilgrimage to the Holy Land in 1179–1180 and before setting out again on the Third Crusade, Giraut clearly remained in the West long enough to chide the tardy rulers, but it is unknown exactly when he left. He may

---

[16] No song attributed to Folquet contains lines in which he 'spoke well when he took the cross'. Stroński suggests that this might in fact be BdT 9.10, attributed to Aimeric de Belenoi by its two manuscripts (S. Stroński, *Le Troubadour Folquet de Marseille* (Kraków, 1910), p. 19*). As Stroński remarks, there is no proof; moreover BdT 9.10 is unlikely to date from this period (see Chapter 8, p. 169).

have gone with local lords, perhaps Raimon II of Turenne in the spring of 1190 before Richard the Lionheart's departure. His earliest surviving song composed after the loss of Jerusalem (BdT 242.41) signals a major shift in public attitude towards the way of life devoted to courtly joy, and his concern both to defend it and to adapt to the change.

> Jois sia comensamens
> e fis ab bon'aventura
> d'un nou chan qu'eras comens;
> qar sobravinens
> es e bona ma razos.
> De faire chansos
> sol hom dir qu'es faillimens,
> et es bes e chauzimens
> c'uns qecx chan
> e digu'e mostr'en chantan
> can ric guizardo n'aten
> cel q'a Dieu ser bonamen.
>
> Per qu'ieu, que n'er'alqes lens,
> no·m tenc per man d'Escriptura
> c'al chantar non torn iauszens,
> tant mi sembla gens
> e fis lo mestiers! C'ap sos
> hi vueill far sermos
> e precx contrals no-calens,
> cui cors faill enans c'argens,
> per qu'estan
> c'al servizi Dieu no van
> de paians e d'avol gen
> desliurar lo monimen.   (vv. 1–24)

May joy and good fortune begin and end a new song which I am now beginning; for it is very pleasing and my theme is good. People tend to say it is wrong to compose songs, and yet it is a good and wise thing for each and everyone to sing and tell and show in song how richly God rewards the man who truly serves him.

So although I have been somewhat slow in returning joyfully to song, no command of the Scriptures prevents me from doing so, since it seems to me such a fair and noble pursuit. For here I wish to compose musical sermons and prayers against the indifferent, who lack heart rather than silver, because they hold back from leaving, in God's service, to deliver the sepulchre from pagans and vile people.

Evidently some people were critical of courtly entertainment at a time when the West was awash with calls for penitent soul-searching. The immediate answer for this troubadour, whom Dante dubbed the model poet of rectitude, and who according to his *vida* used to spend the winters teaching 'letters',[17] is to appeal to scriptural authority – nothing there rules against the pleasure of song, he declares – and to adopt a preaching mode. The *sirventes* goes on to exhort men to prove their worth in a way that is compatible with, and indeed essential to, the aristocratic way of life, once knightly prowess and even costly display are directed to God's service.[18]

> E qui dels fals mescrezens
> non pensa ni·s dona cura
> com caia lur ardimens
> viu con recrezens;
> c'anc meiller luecx non cre fos
> d'esproar los pros.
> C'armat de bels guarnimens
> sobre lur destriers correns
> conquerran
> benanans'e valor gran,
> don seran pueis viu manen
> e si morran eissamen.   (vv. 25–36)

A man who gives no thought or care to how the insolence of the false infidels may be crushed lives the life of a coward. I do not believe there was ever a more rewarding opportunity for men to prove their excellence, since, clothed in fine armour on their swift chargers, they will conquer fortune and great renown, which will make them rich if they live and equally rich if they die.

Acknowledging the very real fear that people had of the dangers and hardships facing the crusader,[19] he appeals both to their aversion to the stigma of cowardice

---

[17] *Biographies*, ed. Boutière, Schutz and Cluzel, p. 39.
[18] See also BdT 242.24, 25–36: 'Per que·s degra·l plus richs plus fort / esforsar con mais li plagues, / pos gens garnirs ni bels conres / ni cortezia ni deportz / no·il notz des que Sains Esperitz / hi met razitz, / ni ia per sos bels garnimens, / des que sa vid'es avinens, / non deu doptar / que nostre Senher dezenpar / los genseis tenens ni·ls plus pros, / si no·ls en tol autra razos' (The richer and more powerful a man is, the harder he should strive to please him, since fine clothes and splendid banquets, courtly ways and pastimes do him no harm once the Holy Spirit has taken root in him; nor on account of his fine clothing should he fear, as long as his life is seemly, that Our Lord will disinherit those who are more elegantly dressed or the most refined, unless they are dispossessed for some other reason), and compare BdT 242.33, particularly vv. 5–11 and 67–72. For the full range of Giraut's crusading songs see <http://www.rialto.unina.it/autori/Crusades.htm>.
[19] This is brought out graphically by Phillips, *The Fourth Crusade*, pp. 14–19.

and to their jusitified hope in God's protection, also warning them of what awaits them in the afterlife (vv. 73–84).

Several of his crusade-related songs show him treading a fine line between courtly and religious matters, either distancing himself from courtly life with its customary joys of spring in the face of the leaders' delays and quarrels and 'such great peril' – the Muslim threat – 'being borne as lightly as this' (BdT 242.6), or else exploring ways of making crusading and courtly values mutually compatible. One approach is to draw attention to the art of playful folly which is an essential component of Occitan courtly sociability, while artfully reminding his audience of his serious credentials as a promoter of the crusades (BdT 242.18).

Ben deu en bona cort dir
bon sonet qi·l fai,
per q'ieu retrairai
un levet, et qi l'apren,
parra d'ome non-chalen;
c'aissi con si no·m chalia,
faz lieugiers sonetz,
per qe·l plus greus sembla sia
leus e bos a faire.

Mas un petit vueil gequir
– e si faillirai –
so don chantarai,
pos qe·il rei entre lor gen
an pres tal acordamen.
Bo·m sab qe d'esta paria
sorg' als Mors esfretz,
e cil n'aion manentia
cui n'er mal a traire.

E Dieus los en lais iauzir,
q'ieu m'entrametrai
d'aisso qe m'eschai;
q'eu no m'azaut de trop sen
n'en trop foudat no m'enten.
Pero senz, pretz e follia
chascunz a sas vetz,
qi be·ls assembla ni·ls tria,
segon mon veiaire.

If someone composes a fine song, he ought to perform it in a fine court, so I will sing a light one, and anyone learning it will think it the song of a light-hearted man; for I make light and easy songs that seem effortless, so that the hardest gives the appearance of having been simple and easy to compose.

But for the moment I wish to leave aside the subject of my song – even if I commit a fault – because the kings have graciously come to such an agreement among themselves. I am pleased that from this alliance the Moors may be struck with fear, and those who will bear the suffering may receive a rich reward.

And God grant them joy in this, while I [now] turn to personal matters; for I neither delight in excessive seriousness nor aim for too much playful folly. However, seriousness, worth and folly all have their time and place if one combines and chooses them well, to my way of thinking.

Rather than travelling to the Holy Land with Richard, who arrived in Acre on 8 June 1191, Giraut probably set out in the spring of 1190, and was staying in either Antioch or Tripoli, which were then under the authority of Bohemond III of Antioch. In a song composed in Syria[20] in May–June 1191 (BdT 242.15) he refers to Richard having put ashore at Cyprus on 11 May 1191.

> Era, que Dieus en sia guitz,
> repayre fes e venha patz,
> e ferm se valors e vertatz,
> de que ia·s crolav'uns grans pans,
> e gens bobans;
> qu'ieu crei, si sai non fos ganditz,
> que fos faillitz.
> Mas era cobrara son drei,
> en cant eu vei,
> pos lo reis Richartz es passatz,
> e pueis el es lai aribatz,
> n'i a tans valens companhos,
> derga son cap Crestiandatz,
> c'un petit l'a trop baissat ios!   (vv. 43–56)

Now with God's help let faith return and peace arrive, and let virtue and truth strengthen their fortifications, which have largely been falling in ruins, and let courtly splendour do the same; for I believe that if it had not taken refuge here it would have perished. But now it will recover its rights, as far as I can see, since King Richard has made the crossing; and now that he has put to shore over there and has so many valiant companions with him, let Christendom lift up its head, for it has been lowering it a little too much!

---

[20] The Middle Ages commonly referred to the Holy Land as Syria or the kingdom of Syria, a designation including present-day Syria, Palestine and much of the western Middle East up to the boundary with Egypt.

Richard brings hope of the revival of both Christendom and 'courtly splendour', and Giraut reiterates his intention to continue to 'play the fool in a wise way' (vv. 79–80).[21]

It is not known for certain whether two other songs he composed in Syria (BdT 242.24 and 242.30) belong to the period of Giraut's crusade or to his earlier pilgrimage. However, their preoccupation with a defence of the courtly way of life in the face of the prevailing spiritual ethos seems to fit particularly well with the aftershock of Saladin's triumph.[22] In BdT 242.30 Giraut is in the Holy Land, having made the crossing on the encouragement of his lord, and defends cultural activities against indifference and the accusation that courtly songs are frivolous nonsense.

De chantar / ab deport
mi for'eu totz laissatz;
mas quant soi ben iratz
estenc l'ir'ab lo chan
e vau mi conortan.
Qu'estiers non fora patz
entre l'ir'e·l coratge;
qu'ieu vei d'un mal usatge
que puei'ades e creis,
car es faillitz domneis,
don sol hom esser gais,
e pretz non pot ni iais
revenir entretans;
qu'er es de cels damans
per cui degra valer.
E ges pretz sens poder
loniamen sans non dura

---

[21] In stanza VII, when Giraut says he would have returned earlier had the king of Aragon not detained him, he is referring to his previous journey to the Holy Land, when he accompanied Viscount Aimar V of Limoges there on a pilgrimage in 1179–1180: see Chapter 2 and Gillingham and Harvey, 'Le Troubadour Giraut de Borneil'. BdT 242.6 also anticipates Richard's arrival in the Holy Land. Two other songs by Giraut, not in our corpus, probably refer to the Third Crusade: a love song (BdT 242.57) where the troubadour refers to having made the passage towards Ascalon (R. V. Sharman, ed., *The Cansos and Sirventes of the Troubadour Giraut de Borneil* (Cambridge, 1989), poem 39, v. 63; Sharman notes on p. 231 that this was where Richard the Lionheart went after the siege of Acre), and BdT 242.32 (Sharman, ed., poem 66, vv. 56–65), which probably refers to Frederick Barbarossa and Germans making their way to the Holy Land and Castilians being involved in the Reconquista (Gillingham and Harvey, 'Le Troubadour Giraut de Borneil', pp. 68–69).

[22] In BdT 242.24 Giraut gives thanks to God for the travellers' safe arrival, reminds his listeners of their duty to serve him gratefully and in the right spirit in the sure hope of heavenly reward (vv. 1–12), and once more defends the threatened compatibility of courtly ways with the crusading ethos (vv. 25–48).

sens clam o sens rancura.

Alegrar / mi voill fort
e son aisi passatz,
e si non sembles fatz,
no camiera·l talan;
mas tenon s'a masan
mains bos sonetz qu'eu fatz
vilan d'avol linatge,
qu'anc pros hom de paratge,
s'en ben auzir ateis,
de l'escoutar no·s feis
ni·l plaszer no n'estrais.   (vv. 1–31)

I would give up singing and pleasant pastimes altogether, but when I feel sad I comfort myself by drowning my sorrows in song. Otherwise my heart would have no peace from sadness; for I see that an evil way of life is constantly on the rise and increase. The courting of ladies, which used to make men glad, has fallen into disuse, and in the meantime worth cannot return, or joy either; for worth is now complaining about those through whom it should be strong, and without strength it cannot stay healthy for long without grievance or complaint.

I wish to live most joyfully and have crossed to the Holy Land in this spirit. If I did not look a fool I should not change my inclination; but churlish, base-born people think many of the fine melodies I compose are a form of rowdiness, even though any excellent man of noble birth who takes care to hear them properly has never excused himself from listening to them or abstained from the pleasure they afford. Is not a man who takes no pleasure in joy or song a miserable wretch? Anyone who cannot remember such delight, and prohibits the pleasure of it, and begrudges other people's enduring joy, is an utter fool.

It seems that Giraut had a particularly difficult time during the voyage on account of the attitude of some noblemen, and that his lord intervened to calm his ruffled feelings and dissuade him from making more vociferous and pointed complaints.

D'un affar / mi conort
don degr'esser iratz;
que be·m fora clamatz
d'aisso que l'ausor fan
e del mal e del dan
qe·ls en a desviatz,
mas en gran volpilatge
m'an mes vilan passatge,
qu'ie·n parlera forseis,
e·l seyner qui·m n'espeis,
quan m'abatera·l fais,

a·m comandat que mais
no sia coreillans
plus qu'il son de lur dans,

I am comforted about one matter which ought to make me sad, as I would certainly have complained about what the nobles are doing, and the evil and damage that has sent them off course; but [I will still say that] in a very base way they have caused me [to have] a wretched crossing. I would speak about it more strongly, but the lord who encouraged me [to make the crossing] has commanded me, however hurt and oppressed I feel, not to complain any further about their wrong-doing, any more than they do themselves, and not to be much concerned about others' failings.

It is true that complaints of the 'decline of the world' are commonplace in medieval literature, not least among the troubadours. But there is clearly a particular event behind Giraut's grumbling. Moreover it can hardly be denied that the trauma of Saladin's triumph brought about a major shift of sensibility among the nobles, at least for a time. The contrasting great courts of Mainz in 1184 and 1188 present a striking example of this, the courtly extravagance of the first dissolving into the religious humility of the second.[23]

Peire Vidal

By the fall of Jerusalem in October 1187 Peire Vidal had already gone to stay at the court of Raymond II of Tripoli. To judge by the only song he composed there to have been preserved (BdT 364.11), he does not give the impression of taking his pilgrimage – if pilgrimage it was – particularly seriously. The main part of it is a love song, composed before 1180, to which he added one stanza (VIII) in 1184 and another after the fall of Jerusalem. The update seems little more than a nod in the direction of topicality and none of his surviving fifty songs focuses primarily on crusading.

En Fransa et in Beriu
et a Peitieus et a Tors
quer nostre Senher secors
pels Turcs que·l tenon faidiu,
que tolt l'an e·l vas e·l riu
on mondava·ls pechadors;
e qui ara no·s revella
contr'aquesta gen fradella
ben mal sembla Daniel
que·l dragon destruis e Bel.   (vv. 51–60)

---

[23] Paterson, *The World of the Troubadours*, pp. 115–16.

In France and Berry, Poitiers and Tours Our Lord seeks help on account of the Turks who keep him in exile, for they have stolen from him the sepulchre and the river where he purified sinners; and whoever does not now rise up against this race of villains can never be compared to Daniel, who destroyed the dragon and Bel.

Peire was probably back in Languedoc or Provence in the period after the end of October 1187, when Richard vowed to go on crusade, and before Richard's coronation on 3 September 1189. Here the troubadour composed another love song, to which he appended one complete stanza and two *tornadas* referring to the capture of the True Cross and the loss of the holy sepulchre (BdT 364.4).

> Lai vir mon chan, al rei celestial,
> cui devem tug onrar et obezir,
> et es mestier que l'anem lai servir,
> on conquerrem la vid'esperital;
> que·lh Sarrazi, deslial Caninieu,
> l'an tout son rengn'e destruita sa plieu,
> que sazit an la crotz e·l monimen:
> don devem tug aver gran espaven. (vv. 49–56)

I direct my song over there [in the Holy Land] to the heavenly king whom we must all honour and obey, and it is needful that we should go and serve him there where we shall win spiritual life; for the Saracens, faithless Canaanites, have stolen his kingdom and destroyed his people, and have seized the cross and the sepulchre: we should all feel great terror at this.

The first *tornada* reproaches the king for not yet having set out, and for not having given him money he apparently claims the king had promised him.

> Coms de Peitieus, de vos mi clam a Dieu
> e Dieus a mi per aquel eis coven,
> qu'amdos avetz trazitz mout malamen,
> lui de sa crotz e me de mon argen,
> per qu'en devetz aver gran marrimen. (vv. 57–61)

Count of Poitiers, I complain of you to God and God likewise complains to me, for you have betrayed both of us very badly, Him over his cross and me over my money; so you ought to be very sorry for it.

It would be impossible to imagine Giraut de Borneil making light of God's cause in this way.

The second *tornada*, found only in MS B, suggests that Richard has now satisfied both God and the impecunious troubadour, and was doubtless added later. It is unknown to what this money refers; there is certainly no evidence to suggest it was supposed to finance another oriental journey.

> Coms de Peitieus, bels seigner, vos et ieu
> avem lo pretz de tota l'autra gen,
> vos de ben far et eu de dir lo gen.   (vv. 62–64)

Count of Poitiers, fair Sir, you and I are prized by everyone else, you for doing good and I for saying so gracefully.

The troubadour's priorities are his verbal art and the system of gift-giving that supports it.

If these two pieces suggest that crusading is little more than an adjunct to his usual cultivation of courtly songs, a third piece (BdT 364.43), like several of Giraut de Borneil's, aims for a fusion of courtly love and crusading. But his strategy is very different from that of the *poeta rectitudinis*. Where Giraut is troubled and defensive, Peire goes on the attack through his uniquely extravagant, zany persona. The Occitan tradition of entertainment and sociability may blend seriousness with folly, as Giraut argues rather solemnly, but Peire Vidal takes the *foudat* to comical extremes. He begins with a defiant maintenance of courtly values in the face of 'trouble and anxiety':

> Si·m laissava de chantar
> per trebalh ni per afar,
> ben leu diria las gens,
> que non es aitals mos sens
> ni ma gallardia,
> cum esser solia.
> Mas be·us puesc en ver jurar,
> que mais tan no·m plac jovens
> ni pretz ni cavallairia
> ni domneis ni drudaria.   (vv. 1–10)

If I abandoned singing because of trouble and anxiety, people would very easily say that my wits and gaiety are not what they used to be. But I can truly swear to you that youth and merit and chivalry, courting and gallantry never pleased me more.

While 'trouble and anxiety' are open to interpretation as some personal situation on the troubadour's part, what follows suggests that he is thinking alternatively – or at the same time – of the situation in the Holy Land (and the word *afar* may even suggest the *afar Deu*, 'God's business'), for he postures outrageously as a swaggering warrior who, single-handed, can recapture the sepulchre:

> E s'ieu podi'acabar
> so que m'a fait comensar
> mos sobresforcius talens,
> Alexandres fon niens
> contra qu'ieu seria:

> e s'a Dieu plazia,
> que m'en denhes aiudar,
> ja·l sieus verais monumens
> lonjamen non estaria
> sotz mal serva senhoria. (vv. 11–20)

If I could accomplish what my overpowering desire made me begin, Alexander would be nothing in comparison with what I would be: and if it pleased God to deign to assist me, his true sepulchre would not long remain under an evil, shameful lordship.

We are not told what his 'overpowering desire' is, but there can be little doubt that it refers to his courting of his lady's favours. These would soon make him a superhero!

On a more serious level, while crusade songs often remind listeners of death in order to impress upon them the need for penitence and God's service, Peire does so to stress the value of 'speaking and acting well' and behaving 'in a courtly way'.

> Hom no·s deuria tarzar
> de ben dir e de ben far,
> tan cum vida l'es prezens:
> que·l segles non es mas vens,
> e qui plus s'i fia
> fai maior follia.
> Qu'a la mort pot hom proar
> com pauc vaal aurs als manens:
> per qu'es fols qui no·is chastia
> e non renh'ab cortesia. (vv. 21–30)

A man should not delay in speaking and acting well as long as life is still with him: for the world is but wind, and the one who relies on it most commits the greatest folly. At death a man can discover how little gold is worth to the wealthy, so anyone who does not correct his behaviour and conduct himself in a courtly way is a fool.

There are different kinds of folly, and he makes it clear that his is the positive kind: comical braggadocio is better than the hypocrisy of a ruler who puts on a long face because of the losses in the Levant but is too avaricious to do anything about them.

> Mas tant ai de que pensar,
> qu'ieu non puesc ben desliurar
> totz mos honratz pensamens.
> Pero bos comensamens
> mostra bona via,
> qui no s'en cambia.
> Mas ieu per sobresforsar

cug dels fellos mescrezens
en breu recobrar Suria
e Domas e Tabaria.

Qu'ieu no m'aus desesperar
a lei d'un rei flac avar,
cui sobra aurs et argens,
e cuida, quar es manens,
qu'autre Dieus non sia
mas sa manentia,
qu'avers lo fai renegar;
mas quan venra·l jutgamens
car comprara sa feunia
e l'engan e la bauzia.   (vv. 31–50)

But I have so much to think about that I cannot carry out all my magnificent ideas. However, a good begining shows a good path to one who does not stray from it. But I, through tremendous effort, believe I can quickly recover Syria and Damascus and Tiberias from the evil miscreants!

For I dare not despair in the manner of a flabby, miserly king who has gold and silver in abundance and imagines because he is wealthy that there is no other God but his wealth, so that possessions make him into a renegade; but at the Last Judgement he will pay dearly for his betrayal, his deceit and hypocrisy.

Peire Vidal's style is inimitable, but he is not the only troubadour to treat the subject of the crusade light-heartedly. In a fictive *tenso* (debate) between the troubadour Peirol and Love (BdT 366.29), probably composed before Henry II's death in July 1189, Peirol deflects Love's criticism of his failure to pay attention to his lady by focussing on the crusade. The choice of genre and the light-hearted tone makes this a novel way of combining criticism of the tardy crusade leaders with the theme of lovers' parting.

'Peirol, metes en oblit
la bona donna valen
qe tan gen vos acuilhit
e tan amorosamen,
tot per mon comandamen?
Trop aves leugier talan,
e no·n era ges semblan,
tan gais e tan amoros
eras en vostras chansos.'

'Amors, anc mais no·n failhit
mas ar failh forsadamen,
e prec Dieu Jesus qe·m git

> e qe trameta brieumen
> entre·ls reis acordamen,
> qe·l socors vai trop tarzan
> ez auria mestier gran
> qe·l marqes onratz e pros
> n'ages mais de compainhos.'
>
> 'Peirol, Turc ni Arabit
> ges per vostr'envazimen
> no laisseran Tor Davit!
> Bon conseilh vos don e gen:
> amas e chantas soven.
> Ires vos e·l rei no·i van?
> Veias las gerras qe fan,
> ez esgardas dels baros,
> cossi trobon ochaizos.'   (vv. 19–45)

'Peirol, are you forgetting all about the good and noble lady who welcomed you so sweetly and so lovingly, all at my command? You are too fickle and yet there was never any sign of this because you were so happy and loving in your songs.'

'Love, I never failed in this before, but I fail now against my will, and I pray to God that Jesus should be my guide and make peace quickly between the kings, for help [for the Holy Land] is too long in coming and the brave and worthy marquis [Conrad] has great need of more companions.'

'Peirol, the Turks and Arabs will never leave the Tower of David on account of your attacks! I'm giving you good and sound advice: love and sing often. Will you go there when the kings [themselves] won't? Look at the wars they wage and see how the barons find pretexts [for not going].'

A humorous dialogue between Aimeric de Peguilhan and Elias d'Ussel (BdT 10.37) may also date from this period. Aimeric asks for advice about whether to keep a promise to his lady, who has agreed to go to bed with him for one night on condition he goes no further than kissing and embracing. Elias announces that if he were in his friend's position he would make love to her with a laugh and a jest, and then weep for it until she forgives him, then go as a pilgrim beyond Tyre seeking God's forgiveness for breaking his oath.[24]

* * *

---

[24] W. P. Shepard and F. M. Chambers, *The Poems of Aimeric de Peguilhan* (Evanston, Ill., 1950), p. 8, suggest a possible date of c.1208, but Harvey and Paterson, *Tensos*, I, p. 60, are more inclined to place it in the early 1190s.

Saladin's victories and the events of the Third Crusade sparked a wide variety of lyric responses. Aside from the variety of the composers' backgrounds and personal agendas, some trends emerge: contact and interaction between northern and southern composers; the development of songs of separation; an increased production of songs of exhortation, as often as not political and polemical songs aimed at tardy leaders; and a growing awareness of a new sober climate at odds with the traditional values of a secular courtly society, to which poets respond in diverse ways, sometimes humorously, sometimes through explicit arguments. Even the Old French songs of departure could be seen as a subtle form of resistance to ecclesiastical propaganda: a way of preserving the aristocratic value system of the courtly nobility.

The Third Crusade ends with the five-year peace treaty signed by Richard and Saladin on 2 September 1192. For the next ten years the northern French trouvères will ignore God's business. Ironically, the only Old French song in our corpus[25] is Richard's plea for ransom. But in the South, troubadours will show considerable interest in his captivity, legacy and even potential as a future crusader – not to mention as a patron. Also, unlike their northern counterparts, they will turn their attention back to the Reconquista.

---

[25] See Appendix B, Chronology: the songs of Gautier de Dargies and Gontier de Soignies can only be roughly dated to within a forty-five-year period.

4

The Aftermath of the Third Crusade

Richard the Lionheart's captivity

On his way home from the Third Crusade in December 1192 Richard was captured and imprisoned by Duke Leopold of Austria. This was despite the fact that Richard was a crusader-pilgrim, and such an action was strictly forbidden by the Church and punishable by excommunication. In February 1193 Leopold handed him on to his brother-in-law, the Holy Roman Emperor Henry VI, and the king spent nearly a year and a half being moved from one prison to another. William of Newburgh reported that Richard himself later said that he had at first been treated well, but that after the French king's cousin Philip of Beauvais came to the imperial court he was loaded down with chains so heavy that a horse or a donkey would have struggled to move, and Peter of Blois wrote in a letter to Archbishop Conrad of Mainz that 'Richard was held in chains and made to go hungry, his face pale and his body weak.' Gillingham suggests that 'if anything like this did happen it is likely to have been in the weeks immediately after Easter 1193 when he was imprisoned in the castle of Trifels'.[1] From here he was rescued by the diplomacy of William of Longchamp, who persuaded Henry to allow him to return to the imperial court and negotiated a date for his release. Gillingham relates that 'Longchamp was then sent back to England with letters from both Richard and Henry VI exhorting the prisoner's subjects to find the money as quickly as possible, with similar letters being sent to other parts of Richard's dominions.'[2] This is likely to have been when he composed his famous song in Old French (RS 1891) to help raise his ransom.[3]

---

[1] See J. Gillingham, 'The Kidnapped King: Richard I in Germany, 1192–1194', *German Historical Institute London Bulletin*, 30 (2008), 5–34 (p. 22).
[2] J. Gillingham, *Richard I* (New Haven and London, 1999), p. 239.
[3] Comments on this text draw almost entirely on Charmaine Lee's interpretation and analysis in her Rialto edition and 'Richard the Lionheart: the Background to *Ja nus homs pris*', in Parsons and Paterson, *Literature of the Crusades*, pp. 134–49.

Ja nus homs pris ne dira sa raison
Adroitement si con hon dolanz non;
Mes par confort puet il fere chanzon.
Pro ai d'amis mes povre sont li don;
Honte i auront se por ma raençon
     Sui ça deus ivers pris.

Ce sevent bien mi home e mi baron,
Englais, Normant, Poitevin et Gascon,
Qe je n'avoie si povre conpaignon
Qe je laissasse por avoir en prison.
Je nel di pas por nulle retraçon,
     Mes encor sui je pris.

Or sai je bien de voir certainement
Qe morz ne pris n'a ami ne parent,
Qant hom me lait por or ne por argent.
Molt m'est de moi, mes plus m'est de ma gent,
Q'apres ma mort auront reprocement,
     Se longement sui pris.

N'est pas merveille se j'ai le cor dolent
Qant mi sires met ma terre en torment.
Se li menbrast de nostre serement
Qe nos feïmes amdui comunaument,
Bien sai de voir qe ja plus longement
     Ne seroie ça pris.

Ce sevent bien Angevin et Torain,
Cil bachaler qi sont delivre e sain,
Q'engonbrez sui loing d'eus en autrui main;
Forment m'aidassent mes il ne voient grain.
De belles armes sont ore vuit li plain
     Por ce qe je sui pris.   (vv. 1–30)

No prisoner will speak his mind fittingly unless he does so as a man in sorrow; but he can, for consolation, make a song. I have friends enough but the gifts are few; they will be shamed if for want of my ransom I am for two winters here a prisoner.

This my men and my barons – English, Norman, Poitevin and Gascon – know full well: I never had a companion so poor I would leave him in prison for the sake of wealth. I do not say this as a reproach, but I am still a prisoner.

Now I well and truly know for certain that a dead man or a prisoner has no friend or family, since I am left here for the sake of gold or silver. I fear for myself, but even more so for my people, for after my death they will be dishonoured, if I am long held prisoner.

It is no wonder I have a grieving heart when my lord causes havoc in my land. If he were to remember our oath which we both made together, I know for sure that I would no longer be here a prisoner.

The men of Anjou and Touraine, those youths who are free and healthy, know full well that I am held far from them in another's hands; they would help me greatly but see no money coming. The plains are now empty of fine arms because I am a prisoner.

Composing in Old French, Richard opens with an emotive appeal to his 'friends', playing on their sympathies and their sense of shame. He moves on to address the whole of the Angevin Empire – much of which, as Lee observes (see the online edition), had rebelled in his absence – deliberately effacing hierarchical differences by naming his vassals his 'companions', reminding them of his own open-handedness, calling on their sense of honour and insistently stressing his captivity with the refrain word *pris*. He then targets King Philip Augustus of France, Richard's own lord for his French lands. Despite their non-aggression pact made before the crusade, Philip was in league with Richard's brother John to undermine support for him in Normandy, Toulouse and Angoulême, and was exploiting his absence to take large areas of his territory. Richard further appeals to the centre of the Angevin Empire and the marcher lords William of Cayeux and Geoffrey of Perche, important lords who had been Richard's companions during the crusade, but whose allegiance was now in doubt.

> Mi conpagnon qe je amoie e qe j'ain,
> Cil de Chaieu e cil de Percerain,
> Chanzon, di lor q'il ne sont pas certain:
> Q'onques vers els ne oi faus cuer ne vain.
> S'or me gerroient trop feront qe vilain
> Tant con je soie pris. (vv. 31–36)

My companions whom I loved and love still – the lords of Cayeux and of Perche – tell them, Song, that they are not men to rely on: the heart I had for them was never false nor faltering. If they now wage war on me, they will act most basely, as long as I were to remain a prisoner.

The king was finally released on 4 February 1194, after the payment of a ransom of 100,000 marks and the promise of a further 50,000.

Apart from his own song, no French lyrics alluding to his imprisonment and return have survived, but several Occitan songs evoke these events. His captivity features in a *sirventes* by Peire Vidal composed during Richard's captivity (14 February 1193–4 February 1194) on the traditional theme of the decline of the world (BdT 364.35). Complaining of the death of courtly values and the ubiquitous triumph of evil, Peire first blames the folly and sinfulness of the pope and the 'false doctors', the corrupt clergy, for the rise of heresy, which has driven people to unorthodoxy by setting them a bad moral example.

> Qu'a Rom'an vout en tal pantais
> l'Apostolis e·lh fals doctor
> Sancta Gleiza, don Dieus s'irais;
> que tan son fol e peccador,
> per que l'eretge son levat.
> E quar ilh commenso·l peccat,
> greu es qui als far en pogues;
> mas ieu no·n vuelh esser plaies.   (vv. 9–16)

In Rome the pope and the false doctors have thrown the Holy Church into such disarray that God is angry; for they are so foolish and sinful that the heretics are on the rise. And since it is they (the clergy) who are the first to sin, it is difficult for anyone else to behave otherwise, though I do not wish to defend such people.

The Cathar heresy had been firmly established in Occitania since 1167, when Occitan, French and Lombard Cathars assembled at Saint-Félix-de-Caraman with Nicetas, Cathar bishop of Constantinople, and established dioceses in France, Toulouse, Carcassonne (which included Catalonia), Albi, Agen and Lombardy.[4] Pope Celestine III (1191–1198) was about eighty-five years old on his election, and not in a position to pursue heretics with the vigour of his successor, Innocent III. Nevertheless in 1191 in a bull confirming the appointment of the new archbishop of Narbonne he drew attention to various heresies and sects overrunning the region, and in a letter of the same year he gave the archbishop of Arles the authority to punish and excommunicate heretics and those who received and showed favour to them.[5] Peire probably began his poetic career at the court of Count Raymond V of Toulouse, who died in December 1194, ten months after Richard's release, and would have been well aware of the pressures on the count to stop supporting the heretics, many of whom were in fact to be found among his relatives and close associates.[6] This is one of the earliest cases of anticlerical satire in the vernacular, at a time when the Church tolerated it in Latin but not in a language accessible to the populace.[7] Peire is therefore

---

[4] M. Lambert, *The Cathars* (Oxford, 1998), pp. 45–49; E. Griffe, *Le Languedoc cathare de 1190 à 1210* (Paris, 1971), p. 52.
[5] Griffe, *Le Languedoc cathare de 1190 à 1210* (Paris, 1971), pp. 198 and 200–01.
[6] Griffe, *Le Languedoc cathare*, pp. 23–33.
[7] Vatteroni, *Falsa clercia*, pp. 12–13 and 51–53. Prior to 1137 the troubadour Marcabru had attacked the venality of Rome (BdT 293.33, vv. 13–18); as Vatteroni points out (following A. Roncaglia, 'Marcabruno: *Lo vers comens quan vei del fau* (BdT 239.33)', *CN*, 9 (1951), 25–48), although the terms of the attack give an impression of generality, it probably refers to the specific situation of events following the papal schism between Innocent II and the antipope Anacletus II, the latter being supported by Marcabru's patron William X of Aquitaine.

being daringly outspoken, and is certainly not repeating a literary commonplace. He takes the wise precaution of declaring that he is not trying to defend heretics.

He goes on to attack Philip Augustus, who left the Third Crusade after the capture of Acre on 3 August 1191, for abandoning the sepulchre to busy himself with trade, and the Holy Roman Emperor for violating Richard's safe-passage.

> E mou de Fransa totz l'esglais,
> d'els qui solon esser melhor,
> que·l reis non es fis ni verais
> vas pretz ni vas Nostre Senhor.
> Que·l sepulcr'a dezamparat
> e compr'e vent e fai mercat
> atressi cum sers o borzes:
> per que son aunit siei Frances.
>
> [...]
>
> Et anc pus lo guit de Dieu frais,
> non auzim pueis l'Emperador
> creisser de pretz ni de bontat.
> Mas pero s'ueimais laiss'en fat
> Richart, pus en sa preizon es,
> lor esquern en faran Engles. (vv. 17–24, 27–32)

The whole horror stems from France, from those who used to be better, for the king is not faithful or true towards merit or towards Our Lord. He has abandoned the sepulchre and buys and sells and deals just like a servant or burgher, which is why his French subjects are put to shame.

Never since he infringed God's safe-passage have we seen the emperor grow in merit or goodness. However, if from now on he foolishly lets Richard go, now he is in his prison, the English will vent their scorn on him.

Why should Peire think that Henry might be considering letting Richard go? Gillingham (personal communication) has suggested that soon after Easter 1193, just after Henry had put Richard on trial at Speyer, reports had circulated about Richard's successful defence of his reputation and in consequence Henry giving Richard a kiss of peace. According to Roger of Howden, immediately after this Richard agreed to pay Henry 100,000 marks as a fee for Henry reconciling him with Philip Augustus, with – very curiously – Henry promising he would let Richard return home without taking any money from him if he (Henry) failed to reconcile them. This very soon came to nothing, but it may be that for a few weeks after the public ritual of the kiss of peace rumours circulated that Richard might

---

There is then a gap of at least fifty years until in 1188 Giraut de Borneil criticises the laxity of monastic rule (BdT 242.32, 84–91, see Sharman, *Giraut de Borneil*, p. 431).

soon be simply set free. This would make good sense of Peire's remark. Henry is caught in a double bind: his imprisonment of the king brings him into disrepute, but he will look a fool if he backtracks.

Finally the troubadour turns to the Reconquista, accusing the kings of Spain of acting cravenly in the face of the Moors and pursuing their internecine conflicts.

> Dels reis d'Espanha·m tenh a fais,
> quar tant volon guerra mest lor,
> e quar destriers ferrans ni bais
> trameton als Mors per paor:
> que lor erguelh lor an doblat,
> don ilh son vencut e sobrat;
> e fora miels, s'a lor plagues,
> qu'entr'els fos patz e leis e fes.   (vv. 33–40)

I am heavy-hearted on account of the kings of Spain, because they are so keen for war among themselves, and because they send grey and bay chargers to the Moors out of fear; they have redoubled the latters' pride through which they themselves are subdued and defeated; and it would be better, if it pleased them, for there to be peace and lawfulness and faith among themselves.

This piece reflects disquiet in the aftermath of the Third Crusade. The Church's corruption is provoking rather than curbing the rise of heresy; the French king has abandoned God's cause; the emperor has imprisoned the real hero of the crusade; and the Spanish rulers are fighting each other and appeasing the Moors.

Richard's return

Richard landed back in England on 13 March 1194 and had himself crowned in Winchester for a second time. By 12 May he was setting sail for Normandy to confront the massive problems facing him everywhere in his continental domains. His reception in Barfleur was ecstatic. After some notable successes in Normandy he marched south in June to the Touraine, where he rapidly reasserted his authority, and thence to Aquitaine to clamp down on rebels. His capture of the town of Angoulême in July marked 'the culmination of two months of remarkable military success'.[8] A year-long truce between Richard and Philip arranged at Tillières on 23 July 1194 'was probably also a war of attrition' taking place in the marches of Normandy, while Richard may also have been supervising the early stages of a campaign in Berry. But on 19 July 1195 the Castilian army under the command of Alfonso VIII suffered a massive defeat by the Almohad caliph of Morocco Abû-Jûsûf beneath the walls of Alarcos. When news of this reached the English and French

---

[8] Gillingham, *Richard I*, pp. 251, 273, 283, 287–89; see also Gouiran, *L'Amour et la guerre*, vol. II, pp. 695–96.

kings at the end of July they tried to patch things up, arranging a short extension of their truce till November.⁹

Among the troubadours news of the English king's return set off a whirl of excitement. Characteristically, Bertran de Born focuses on the stirring prospect of local war, but others evoke the crusades.¹⁰ In a jocular fictive dialogue (BdT 305.12) the Monk of Montaudan, in dispute with God over the rights and wrongs of his life as a worldly troubadour, has God reprove him for not immediately hurrying to see the English monarch.

> 'Morgues, ben mal o fezis
> que tost non anies coitos
> al rei cui es Olairos
> que tant era tos amis:
> per que lau que t'o afraigna.
> Ah, cans bos marcs d'esterlis
> aura perdutz els tieus dos,
> qu'el te levet de la faigna!'   (vv. 33–40)

'Monk, it was very wrong of you not to rush off immediately to the king who rules Oléron, for he used to be such a friend to you; so I recommend him to break off his friendship with you. Ha! What a lot of fine sterling marks he will have lost by making you gifts, for he raised you from the mud!'

Here, as elsewhere in the *tenso*, the poet mischievously assigns to God the rôle of persuading him that he ought not to return to the cloister. The Monk's bantering riposte blames God for allowing Richard to be captured in the first place, which has meant among other things that while Richard was out of action, Acre was, and still is, left defenceless if there is another wave of Saracen attacks. While his tone is humorous, he slyly undermines the crusading enterprise: if God can't arrange things better, why should men risk their lives?¹¹

> 'Seigner, ieu l'agra ben vis,
> si per mal de vos non fos,
> car anc sufris sas preizos!
> Mas la naus dels Sarrazis,
> no·us membra ges consi·s baigna:

---

⁹ Gillingham, *Richard I*, pp. 290–94.

¹⁰ BdT 80.5 and 80.8, for example: see Gouiran, *L'Amour et la guerre*, poems 36 and 35.

¹¹ See G. Gouiran, 'Os meum replebo increpationibus (Job, XXIII, 4). Comment parler à Dieu sans prier, ou la contestation contre Dieu dans les lyriques occitane et galaïco-portuguaise', in *O cantar dos trobadores. Actas do Congreso celebrado en Santiago de Compostela entre os días 26 e 29 de abril de 1993* (Santiago de Compostela, 1993), pp. 77–98, for this and other troubadour songs questioning God's ways, and compare Daspol's fictive *tenso* with God in Chapter 12.

car, si dins Acre·s cuillis,
pro i agra enquer Turcs felos:
fols es qui·us sec en mesclaigna!'   (vv. 41–48)

'Lord, I would certainly have seen him had it not been Your fault for ever tolerating his imprisonment! But have You completely forgotten what the Saracen ship is like when it takes a bath? If it finds its way into Acre, there will be plenty of wicked Turks there: anyone who follows You into battle is a fool!'

Dario Mantovani has argued that the Monk's *tenso* belongs to a cycle of three songs responding to Richard's return.[12] The others are a *canso* uncertainly attributed to Folquet de Marselha (BdT 155.12), and one of the *sirventes* of Bertran de Born already mentioned (BdT 80.8). The *canso* makes no reference to crusading, but simply wishes that Richard were further south than the Limousin so that the poet could see him more often. However, after renewed pressure by the Turks led Henry VI to vow to leave on a new expedition to the Holy Land (2 April 1195), Folquet composed a *sirventes* urging Richard to follow his example.

Doncs, nostre baron que fan
ni·l reis engles, cui Dieus sal?
Cuida aver fait son jornal?
Mout i aura lait engan
s'il a fait la messio
et autre fai la preiso:
que l'emperaire·s percassa
cum Dieus cobres sa reio!
Que primiers cre que·i socor
si Dieus li rent sa honor:
be·s taing, tant es rics lo dos,
c'aitals sia·l guizerdos.   (vv. 49–60)

So what are our barons doing, or the English king, God save him? Does he think he has finished his day's work? It would be a really ugly trick if he goes to the expense and another wins the spoils: for the emperor is trying to see how God might recover his kingdom! I think above all that he will help there if God gives him back his lands: it is fitting, the gift is so rich, that this should be the reward.

---

[12] D. Mantovani, 'Prove di dialogo fra i trovatori: Bertrand de Born, Monge de Montaudon, Folquet de Marselha, Palais', in *La Lirica romanza dei Medioevo. Storia, tradizione, interpretazioni. Atti del VI Convegno triennale della Società Italiana di Filologia Romanza (Padova-Stra, 27 Settembre–1 Ottobre 2006)*, ed. F. Brugnolo and F. Gambino (Padua, 2009), pp. 197–216.

A further stanza, which may have been added by someone other than Folquet, adds that Philip should also join such a new expedition, in order to make amends for his early departure from the Third Crusade in 1191 (BdT 155.7):

> Al rei frances lau refassa
> ·l tornar, c'om no·l teng'a bo;
> per qu'eu dic, s'era·i socor
> qu'es ops, que no·s don paor,
> e s'ar no·i vai qu'es saisos
> dic c'aunit[z] es per un dos.[13]   (vv. 61–66)

I advise the French king to make amends for his return, for I do not consider it a good thing; so I say, if he goes to help there now because it is needful, he should not be afraid, and if he does not go now that it is time, I say that he is doubly shamed.

Richard returned at a time of widespread demoralisation. Not only were Jerusalem and the true cross in Muslim hands, but a new threat was also emerging in Spain: the North African Almohad dynasty, 'whose defeat of Alfonso VIII of Castile at Alarcos in 1195 [...] was in some ways comparable to the Christian defeat at Hattin in 1187'.[14] Between 1190 and 1194 the Catalan troubadour Guiraut del Luc, a bitter political enemy of Alfonso II of Aragon, launched two virulent poetic attacks on the king. In 1190 the Templars had conquered the frontier castle of Polpís del Mastrazgo and received it in donation from him. The troubadour accuses Alfonso of robbing it from the Templars (BdT 245.1) and, in what is probably the earlier of the two pieces (BdT 245.2), selling it back to the delighted Muslims:

> Gauch n'ant las gens d'outra·l Nil
> car lor fai tant gen socors,
> c'us feus de lor ancessors
> c'avion conquist li fraire
> vendet, mas ges non pres gaire
> vas q'era grans la ricors.
> Dieus! Cal gaug n'ant part Valenssa,
> car Polpitz torn'en tenenssa
> del rei marrochin, qui fai
> son esqern delai!
> Et anc tant gran descrezenssa
> non vim pois la leis ebraia,
> e Barbaria·is n'apaia.

---

[13] See P. Squillacioti, *Le poesie di Folchetto di Marsiglia* (Pisa, 1999), pp. 322–23.
[14] Paul, *To Follow in Their Footsteps*, p. 281.

Qui qe·l vis franc ni humil
era·l pot trobar aillors
fin de malvazas lauzors,
qe·l fetz son oncl'e son fraire
justiziar e desfaire,
don fo pechatz e dolors.
E no·m par c'aia crezenssa
ni vergoigna ni temenssa
reis que son fraire deffai
e son oncle trai;
e car pres per covinenssa
don del rei engles part Blaia
det presset vermeill per saia.   (vv. 14–39)

Anc pois asset Berbesil
no·l destreis pretz ni amors
ni poc far tan avol qors.   (vv. 53–55)

The people beyond the Nile are overjoyed that he is giving them such kind assistance, for he has sold [them] some of their ancestors' fiefs which the Brothers [Templars] had conquered, though he did not gain much in relation to their high value. My God, how they are celebrating the other side of Valencia! Polpís is back in the hands of the Moroccan king, who is laughing at us over there! Never have we witnessed such great impiety since the Hebrew religion, and Barbary is delighted at it.

Whoever found him noble and gracious will now find him changed, refined through obloquy, for he had his uncle and his brother put on trial and destroyed, which was a sin and a tragedy. It does not seem to me that a king who destroys his brother and betrays his uncle can have faith or a sense of shame or qualms; and by taking a gift in exchange for an agreement with the English king the other side of Blaye he gave scarlet perse for wool.

Never since he passed through Berbezilh did he have any care for merit or love, nor could he make a baser journey.

The other piece continues to blame him for this and other 'perfidies', as well as for fraternising with Arabs, consorting with Jewish women and 'going native' in his dress.

Li Sarrazin de Fraga e d'Aytona
l'an enseignat cum entr'els si razona:
salem alec, volon que lor respona,
per ualica zalem, cui Deus confona;
mas bels arnes li presta Na Maimona
qan viest la çupa ab l'obra salamona.   (vv. 19–24)

The Saracens of Fraga and Aytona, God confound them, have taught him how they speak to each other: they want people to answer their 'salem alec' with 'ualica zalem'; but Lady Maimona lends him fine clothes when he wears her skirt with the Solomonic design.[15]

Paul argues that behind many of Guiraut's barbs lay Alfonso's failure to lead a crusade as his father had done.

The terms and images employed in Giraut's political songs are important in that they openly contrast the kind of crusading conquest conducted by Alfonso's predecessors, his father Ramón Berenguer IV and his great-uncle Alfonso the Battler, who worked in concert with the Templars, with the war for parias and profit waged in the absence of crusading rhetoric in Iberia. Living in harmony with Muslims, and entering into agreements with them, were seen to be in fundamental opposition to crusading ideology, and by sparing the Muslims in Spain, he was providing succor to their counterparts in the East whom the armies of the Third Crusade (1189–92) were at that moment engaging in desperate conflict.[16]

By selling back the castle of Polpis to its Muslim overlords, Alfonso was undermining the work of reconquest itself.

Guiraut ends this song by addressing a jongleur named Arnaut with denigratory remarks, intended humorously and typical of many such troubadour addresses.

> Arnaut joglar, mal huillat, cara trona,
> ab ben fer temps passaras la Botona,
> que la nuoich gela e·l dia plou e trona,
> e tu non as enqer souta ta gona.
> Rendetz la·l oste, anz que trop vo·n somona,
> q'ie·us pagarai al laus de Na Peirona.   (vv. 25–30)

Arnaut, you wall-eyed, snub-nosed jongleur, you will cross the Boutonne in dreadful weather, for it is freezing at night and raining and thundering in the day and you have not yet redeemed your over-tunic. Give it back to the innkeeper before he demands it from you too insistently, for I will pay you with Madam Peirona's consent.

The links to France in these pieces are the references to a deal between Alfonso and an English king beyond Blaye and to Alfonso passing through Barbezieux (245.2); and to the jongleur Arnaut heading north to cross the River Boutonne, a tributary

---

[15] *salem alec* = *al-salām 'alayka* 'peace be upon you', and *ualica zalem* = *u-alayka al-sālam* 'and upon you peace': see M. de Riquer, *Los trovadores: historia literaria y textos*, 3 vols (Barcelona, 1975), vol. I, p. 552. Riquer sees the name *Maimona* as Moorish, but it is also a Jewish name. The *obra salamona* is likely to refer to decoration formed from a star of David pattern.
[16] Paul, *To Follow in Their Footsteps*, p. 284.

of the Charente (245.1). As we have seen, Richard was campaigning in the region in July 1194, which culminated in his capture of Angoulême, 67 km from Chef-Boutonne and 35 km from Barbézieux. It would make sense to see the jongleur heading north in the hope of Richard's patronage.[17]

Alarcos

The defeat of the Castilian forces at Alarcos on 19 July 1195 incited several troubadours to urge renewed efforts against the Saracens in Spain. In his exhortations Folquet de Marselha produces the unusual argument that there is no excuse for men not to support the Reconquista since there is no sea crossing to fear (BdT 155.15).

> Oimais no·i conosc razo
> ab que nos poscam cobrir,
> si ja Dieu volem servir,
> pois tant enquier nostre pro
> que son dan en volc sofrir:
> que·l sepulcre perdet primieiramen
> et er sofre qu'Espaigna·s vai perden,
> per so car lai trobavam ochaiso
> mas sai sivals non temem mar ni ven;
> las! cum nos pot plus fort aver somos,
> si doncs no fos tornatz morir per nos.   (vv. 1–11)

Henceforth I know no pretext behind which we can hide if we ever wish to serve God, since He seeks so much what is good for us that he has been willing to suffer harm to himself. First of all he lost the sepulchre, and now he lets Spain suffer losses, because there [in the Holy Land] we had an excuse, but here at least we fear neither sea nor wind. Alas, how can he summon us more forcefully other than by coming back to die for us again!

Unlike the jocular Monk of Montaudon, this future bishop and persecutor of heretics explains Christian losses, both in the Holy Land and now in Spain, as the self-sacrifice which God's generosity in his own self-sacrifice on the cross has made it possible for true Christians now to make.

> De si mezeis nos fetz do
> quan venc nostres tortz delir,
> e fetz so sai agrazir

---

[17] Arnaut's identity is unknown, but it is tempting to speculate about the troubadour Arnaut de Mareuil from Mareuil in the Périgord, some 100 km south of the source of the river in Chef-Boutonne. Arnaut dedicated a song to Alfonso II, and the king features in the *razo* to one of his songs, BdT 30.19: see the notes on Rialto to the edition of BdT 245.1.

quan si det per rezensso;
doncs qui vol viven morir
er don per Dieu sa vida e la presen,
qu'el la donet e la rendet moren,
c'atressi deu hom morir non sap co;
ay! cum mal viu qui no·n a espaven!
que·l nostre viures don em cobeitos
sabem qu'es mals et aquel morir bos.   (vv. 12–22)

He made us a gift of himself when he came to erase our crimes, and he made us thankful here for this when he gave himself for our redemption. Therefore whoever wishes to die into eternal life should now give and offer his life for God, for he gave it and renounced it through his death, and a man also must die one way or another. He leads such a bad life if he has no fear of this! For we should realise that our life, which we covet so much, is bad and dying in that way is good.

Saverio Guida has suggested in addition that his words to Alfonso VIII of Castile may reflect an idea current on both sides of the Pyrenees that the disaster of Alarcos was divine punishment for his sins.

E ja non pretz fol resso
lo reis castellans ni·s vir
per perdre, qu'anz deu grazir
a Dieu que·l mostra el somo
qu'en lui si vol enantir;
et autre esfortz ses Dieu torna e nien:
c'aissi valra sos bos pretz per un cen
si acoill Dieu oimais a compaigno;
qu'el non vol ren mas reconoissemen:
sol que vas Dieu non sia orgoillos,
mout es sos pretz honratz et envejos.   (vv. 45–55)

And may the king of Castile disregard foolish gossip and not turn aside because of losing; instead he should thank God who, by calling him to his service, shows him that he wishes to exalt himself through him. But any exploit other than with God is futile: his good name will be worth a hundred times more if he welcomes God as his companion from now on; for all he desires is acknowledgment of his suzerainty. His [the king's] reputation is highly honourable and enviable as long as he is not arrogant towards God.

According to the chronicles of the time, after his marriage to Eleanor of England he had entered a seven-year relationship with a beautiful Jewish woman from Toledo, forgetting his duties as a spouse and sovereign.[18]

---

[18] Guida, *Canzoni di crociata*, pp. 382–83.

At this same time the troubadour Gavaudan grimly evokes the growing threat of the Iberian Muslims (BdT 174.10). The Almohad caliph Abû Jûsûf Ya'qub al-Mansur was pressing towards areas of northern Spain which had hitherto long been beyond the reach of the Arabs, traditionally considered to be an impregnable bastion of the western world, and from where he was threatening to move across the Pyrenees and into the south of France.

> Senhors, per los nostres peccatz
> creys la forsa dels Sarrazis:
> Jherusalem pres Saladis
> et encaras non es cobratz;
> per que manda·l reys de Marroc
> qu'ab totz los reys de Crestias
> se combatra ab sos trefas
> Andolozitz et Arabitz
> contra la fe de Crist garnitz.
>
> Totz los alcavis a mandatz:
> Masmutz, Maurs, Goitz e Barbaris,
> e no·y reman gras ni mesquis
> que totz no·ls aya·n ajostatz:
> anc pus menut ayga non ploc
> cum elhs passon e prendo·ls plas;
> la caraunhada dels milas
> geta·ls paysser, coma berbitz,
> e no·y reman brotz ni razitz.
>
> Tant an d'erguelh selh qu'a triatz
> qu'els cujo·l mons lur si'aclis;
> Marroquenas, Marabetis
> pauzon a mons per mieg los pratz;
> mest lor gabon: 'Franc, faiz nos loc!
> Nostr'es Proensa e Tolzas,
> entro al Puey totz lo mejas!'
> Anc tan fers gaps no fon auzitz
> dels falses cas, ses ley, marritz.   (vv. 1–27)

Lords, because of our sins the Saracens' strength increases: Saladin captured Jerusalem and it is still not reconquered. As a consequence the king of Morocco makes known that he will fight all the kings of Christendom, with his perfidious Andalusians and Arabs armed against the faith of Christ.

He has summoned all his lieutenants, Masmudes, Moors, Goths and Berbers, and there remains not one, fat or thin, whom he will fail to line up in his army. Never was rainfall so dense as they are when they pass through and take the plains; he throws them carcasses to graze on that have been left for the vultures, as if they were sheep, and [when they have passed by] not a shoot or root remains.

Those he has hand-picked are so arrogant that they think the world is subject to them; masses of Moroccans and Marabouts take rest in the fields and boast among themselves: 'Franks, make way for us! Provence and the Toulousain are ours, and all the land to Le Puy!' You never heard a more terrifying threat than that of these false cursed pagan dogs.

In this time of doom he rouses all peoples of the West to crusade not only against the Spanish Saracens but also against the renegade Christians who have joined forces with them. This probably refers to Christians under Alfonso IX of León or Sancho VIII of Navarre who, after Alfonso VIII's defeat at Alarcos, had formed alliances with the Muslims against Castile.[19]

> Emperaire, vos o aujatz,
> e·l reys de Frans'e sos cozis,
> e·l reys engles, coms peitavis:
> qu'al rey d'Espanha secorratz!
> Que anc mais negus mielhs no poc
> a servir Dieu esser propdas:
> ab Luy venseretz totz los cas
> cuy Bafometz a escarnitz
> e·ls renegatz outrasalhitz.   (vv. 28–36)

> Non laissem nostras heretatz,
> pus qu'a la gran fe em assis,
> a cas negres outramaris;
> q'usquecx ne sia perpessatz
> enans que·l dampnatge nos toc!
> Portogals, Gallicx, Castellas,
> Navars, Aragones, Serdas
> lur avem en barra gequitz
> qu'els an rahuzatz et aunitz.

> Quan veyran los baros crozatz,
> Alamans, Frances, Cambrezis,
> Engles, Bretos et Angevis,
> Biarns, Gascos, ab nos mesclatz,
> e·ls Provensals, totz en un floc,
> saber podetz qu'ab los Espas
> romprem la preyss'e·l cap e·ls mas,
> tro·ls ajam mortz totz e delitz;
> pueys er mest nos totz l'aurs partitz.

---

[19] See the notes on dating and historical circumstances to BdT 370.5 on Rialto.

Profeta sera·n Gavaudas
que·l digz er faitz. E mortz als cas!
E Dieus er honratz e servitz
on Bafometz era grazitz.   (vv. 46–67)

Emperor, hear this, and you, the king of France, and you, his cousin, and the English king, the count of Poitou: come and assist the king of Spain! For never could anyone be more close at hand to serve God: with his assistance you will vanquish all the curs that Mohammed has deceived, and the renegades who have gone over to his side.

Let us not abandon our patrimony, since we are established in the great faith, to black dogs from overseas: let each man think on this before the damage touches us! Men of Portugal, Galicia, Castile, Navarre, Aragon and Cerdagne we have thrown against them as a barrier, but they have routed and humiliated them.

When they see the barons who have taken the cross, the Germans, French, Cambresians, English, Bretons and Angevins, men of Bearn and Gascony, united with us, and the Provençals, in a great multitude, then you can be certain that with the Spaniards we shall smash the rabble, and the head and hands [of the enemy], until we have killed and destroyed them all; then all the gold will be divided up among us.

Gavaudan will be a prophet in this: what he has said will be done. Death to the dogs! And God will be honoured and served where Mohammed used to be worshipped.

Giraut de Borneil refers to a campaign in Spain in which he apparently intends to participate (BdT 242.74, 69–90), perhaps in c.1195–1196, and shortly after the end of April 1196 Perdigon hopes to see Peter II of Aragon and Alfonso VIII of Castile united against the 'renegades' (BdT 370.5, 51–60). This latter song is sent to a certain Arias, most probably a Galician, and the details of the text suggest that it was composed shortly after the accession of Peter of Aragon at the end of April 1196, whether in renewed efforts against the Muslims, for whom the designation *renegatz* might be accepted, or, more plausibly, as in Gavaudan's case, against renegade Christians of León or Navarre.

Death and reputation: Richard the Lionheart and Aimar V of Limoges

Two years later Innocent III became pope, and quickly announced his desire for a new crusade. In August 1198 he issued his first crusade encyclical, addressed to all prelates, counts, barons and Christian people. Richard and Philip Augustus were fighting again, and Innocent called on them to establish a five-year truce. But within a year Richard was dead. His death inspired one of the best-known *planhs* of the troubadour tradition (BdT 167.22), Gaucelm Faidit's *Fortz cauza es*.

Fortz cauza es que tot lo maior dan
e·l maior dol – las! –, qu'ieu anc mais agues,
e so don dei totztemps plaigner ploran
m'aven a dir en chantan e retraire:
car selh qu'era de valor caps e paire,
lo rics valens Richartz, reys dels engles,
es mortz. Ai Dieus! quals perd'e quals dans es,
quan estrang mot, quan salvatge a auzir!
Ben a dur cor totz hom c'o pot suffrir.   (vv. 1–8)

Grave is the cause for which it befalls me to declare and relate in song the greatest tragedy and the greatest grief – alas! – which I have ever experienced, and for which I must forever lament in weeping: the one who was the pinnacle and origin of all worth, the noble and valiant Richard, king of the English, is dead. Ah God! what a loss and how damaging this is, what a terrible, cruel word to hear! Hard indeed is the heart of any man who can bear it.

Never in the last thousand years, he laments, was there a man to equal him: so valiant, so open-handed, so noble, so bold, so free-spending! Now that he is no longer here, what will happen to deeds of arms and packed tournaments, rich courts and munificence? And what will become of those in his service waiting for release from ill-treatment and for their due reward? They will live out their lives in sorrow, wretchedness and perpetual grief; and the Saracens, Turks, Pagans and Persians, who used to fear him more than any man of woman born, will advance their cause with such arrogance that the sepulchre will take a very great deal longer time to win back – but God wills it, for if he did not, and Richard were still alive, they would infallibly be driven from Syria.

A! Senher reys valens, e que faran
hueimais armas ni fort tornei espes
ni ricas cortz ni belh don aut ni gran,
pus vos no·i etz qui n'eratz capdelaire?
Ni que faran li liurat a mal traire,
silh qui s'eran en vostre servir mes,
qu'atendion que·l guazardos vengues?
Ni que faran cilh que·s degran aucir,
qu'aviatz faitz en gran ricor venir?

Longua ira e avol vida auran,
e tostemps dol, qu'enaissi lor es pres!
E Sarrazi, Turc, Payan e Persan,
que·us duptavon mais qu'ome nat de maire,
creisseran tan d'erguelh e[n] lur afaire
que plus tart n'er lo sepulcres conques.
Mas Dieus o vol, que s'El non o volgues

e vos, senher, visquessetz, ses falhir
de Suria los avengr'a fugir. (vv. 28–45)

Ah Lord, valiant king, what will henceforth become of deeds of arms and tough tightly packed tourneys and sumptuous courts and fine gifts, splendid and abundant, now that you who were their leader are not here with them? And what will become of those abandoned to ill-treatment, those who had placed themselves in your service and who were waiting for the reward to come? And what will become of those who ought to kill themselves, whom you had brought to great power?

Abiding sorrow and a wretched life will be theirs, and perpetual grief, because such is their fate. But Saracens, Turks, pagans and Persians, who used to fear you more than any man of woman born, will so grow in arrogance in all their actions that it will be even later before the sepulchre is reconquered. But God wishes it, for had he not wished it and you, Lord, were alive, they would infallibly have been made to flee from the Holy Land.

The troubadour, who was in fact to leave for the Holy Land in two years' time, has little hope here of a king or a prince being able to take on Richard's mantle, and indeed this was to prove one of the difficulties faced by Innocent's enterprise.

Not everyone spoke well of Richard. In a *planh* which was almost certainly dedicated to his memory (BdT 242.73), Giraut de Borneil mourns a king who inspired fear among the pagans beyond Edessa. Sharman notes that, despite the king's popularity with some troubadours, many opposed him.[20] Here Giraut complains of those who would seek to denigrate his achievements:

Er aug del rei q'era plus pros
e plus valens e mains assais
de totz cels que vianda pais,
que sobret meians e maiors
e crec sos pretz e sas honors,
e non temi'afan ni fais,
que, si lo plaignon dui,
lo tertz lor o destrui,
qe·m par mal enseignatz.
Q'ieu non cre q'anc fos natz,
se Carlemagn'en sai,
reis per tant bel assai
mentaugutz ni prezatz;
mas ia leu non crezatz
c'afars tant mal estei
q'ensems lo plaignant trei!

---

[20] Sharman, *Giraut de Borneil*, p. 479, note to vv. 65 ff.

E que val doncs bella faissos
ni grans poders, q'aissi s'abais?
E ia passava part Roais
lo noms e·l pretz e la paors
entrels paians galiadors,
q'anc us sols plus areir no·ls trais!
Per que faill qui·s desdui,
pois aissi leu s'esdui
so c'om plus vol ni·l platz,
de q'ieu teing per grevatz
cels que mais podon sai,
si non adoban lai,
qan camiara·ill rictatz,
qu'aiant cal que solatz
de lor gran carlabei
denant la maior rei.   (vv. 65–96)

Nowadays I hear things said of the king who in many trials was the most excellent and the most valiant of all mortals [*literally*: of those fed on meat], who defeated both lesser and greater men, and extended his reputation and lands, fearing neither pain nor burden: I hear it said that if two mourn him, the third blackens his name. This seems churlish ignorance to me, for I do not believe there was ever a king born since Charlemagne's day who was so famed or admired for such a fine enterprise. Despite this, why imagine that things have come to such a pass that as many as three should mourn for him!

But what is the good of handsome features or great power when they fall into decline like this? And yet his name and reputation and the fear he inspired would pass beyond Edessa among the treacherous pagans, and no one man ever drove them further back than he did. Consequently a man is wrong to indulge in pleasure, since what he most desires and enjoys is so ephemeral. I therefore believe that those who have the greatest power here on earth are carrying a great burden unless they set up some store in heaven, when their rank will be overturned, so that they may have some joy of their great tournament in the presence of the highest king.

Giraut uses the *planh* genre to explore the processes by which a man's life can and will be judged. Here he condemns the ignorant who are quick to write off the king's unparalleled crusading achievements. Does he also obliquely imply that Richard was a pleasure-seeker and will need to answer for this at the Last Judgement? Or does he simply mean that in view of the ephemeral nature of not only earthly pleasure but also earthly reputation, men need to concentrate on their spiritual capital? The ambiguity may well be intentional.

The nature and control of reputation also feature in his second *planh* (BdT 242.56), this time for his own lord, Aimar V of Limoges, who like Richard died in 1199. Giraut had accompanied him, almost certainly not on the Third Crusade but on a pilgrimage to the Holy Land in 1179–1180.[21] There is genuine affection in Giraut's evocation of Aimar's kind, cultured nature, his love of 'fine folly' and 'gracious jesting', his learning and nobility, his charming conversation, his warmth to strangers and light-hearted way of dealing with boors or fools. After such sympathetic testimony Giraut moves on to a more difficult matter: an unspecified fault for which men and God may judge him unfavourably.

> Ren non desir
> saber aitan,
> ni no·n seria tan pagatz,
> si d'els non era·l plus prezatz
> que lor meneron leialmen,
> plus francs contra lor faillimen.
> Qu'en gran afar
> notz pauc petit'erranza
> qui ben s'acusa ni's repren,
> per qu'ieu cre que sos torz l'er pars;
> e·n Dieu n'ai esperanza!
>
> Qu'el deing auzir
> cels que·l querran
> qu'a l'arma don repaus e patz,
> e·l Sanz Vas en qu'el fon pausatz
> – qu'ie·l vi baisar mot humilmen
> li si'en luec de bon guaren;
> c'anc plus pros bar
> de lui no·n portet lanza
> ni non ac totz comunalmen
> los aibs ab que·s fassa lauzars
> ni per que prez s'enanza.   (vv. 67–88)

I desire nothing so much, and nothing would please me more, as to know he were esteemed the most highly by those who conducted themselves loyally, [being] more generous towards their failings; for a slight error does no real harm to a great undertaking [*gran afar*] if a man truly owns up to it and chides himself [takes appropriate responsibility]. For this reason I believe his sin will be forgiven him, and I place my hope in God for this.

May he deign to hear those who beseech him to grant rest and peace to his soul, and may the holy sepulchre in which he was laid – which I saw Aimar kiss most humbly – serve as his protector; for a more noble baron never bore lance or

---

[21] Gillingham and Harvey, 'Le troubadour Giraut de Borneil', pp. 56–58.

possessed all the qualities combined through which praise may be won, or which enhance reputation.

Sharman may be right in seeing the *gran afar* as an allusion to the Third Crusade: since Giraut appears to have a particular sin (the singular *tortz*) in mind, perhaps this is Aimar's failure to go on that crusade, though this can only be a matter of speculation.

From his captivity in 1192 until his death in 1199 Richard continued to occupy the minds of troubadours and their public as they thought about the business of fighting God's enemies. Excited by Richard's return, some troubadours thought of heading towards him, and one at least hoped he would go back to the Holy Land to pick up where he left off. In Spain the Catalan Giraut del Luc, while accusing the king of Aragon of undermining the work of the Reconquista, also showed awareness of the charismatic leader's renewed presence in France. The Christian defeat at Alarcos focused minds on the need for action in Spain, while 1199 seems to mark a pause, when Richard's death induced reflections on the past. But another crusade was brewing, which would lead men in a very new direction.

5

The Fourth Crusade and its Aftermath

In preparation for a new crusade, in 1198 and 1199 Innocent III introduced a number of reforms. One of them was to promise crusaders that their military service would give them full remission of their sins and would absolve them of any punishment due, in this world or the next, provided they showed 'penitence in voice and heart' for their transgressions.[1] This indulgence made a great impression on his contemporaries. Geoffrey of Villehardouin reports that 'The hearts of the people were greatly moved by the generous terms of this indulgence, and many, on that account, were moved to take the cross.'[2] But from the outset the crusade was bedevilled by financial problems. Warfare was becoming more and more expensive. Despite the general enthusiasm for a new venture, without royal involvement knights were reluctant to commit themselves. But the kings of France and England were quarrelling again, and Richard's death put paid to a truce arranged in 1199. Innocent's response to the issue of finance was to impose the first direct taxation of the universal Church, a fortieth of all revenues for one year. This encountered some resistance and took a long time to collect. Nevertheless the nobles showed some interest, and at a tournament in Ecry-sur-Aisne on 28 November 1199 the young counts Thibaut III of Champagne and Louis of Blois took the cross, along with many of their men. Others followed suit.

Two months later, a meeting at Compiègne gave six men, including the chronicler Villehardouin and the sixty-year-old trouvère and diplomat Conon de Béthune, powers to negotiate transport arrangements with the maritime cities. The Venetians promised to provide ships which would have to be paid for, adding to these fifty galleys (armed ships) and committing themselves to the crusade as equal partners with equal share in the spoils. The fleet, which represented 'a level of commitment unprecedented in medieval commerce [requiring] the suspension of practically all other commercial activity with the outside world',[3] would be ready by the end

---

[1] T. Asbridge, *The Crusades. The War for the Holy Land* (London, 2010), p. 524.
[2] Villehardouin, *La Conquête de Constantinople*, ed. E. Faral, 2 vols (Paris, 1938), vol. I, §2, p. 4 (henceforth GV), translated into English by M. R. B. Shaw in *Joinville and Villehardouin, Chronicles of the Crusades* (Harmondsworth, 1963), p. 29.
[3] Phillips, *The Fourth Crusade*, p. 61. He observes that the cost of transport, 85,000 marks, was equivalent to around twice the annual income of King John of England or King Philip

of June 1202. But the French delegates had vastly over-estimated the size of the crusading forces, and by late 1200 the actual body of crusaders amounted to no more than a third of the predicted number. A further complication was the leaders' readiness to deceive their followers about their plans. They secretly agreed between themselves to sail not to the Holy Land but to Egypt, as there was a growing, probably realistic, conviction that the Holy Land could only be secured by taking war to the centres of Muslim power in the region. But the mass of crusaders dreamed of Jerusalem and would be likely to jib at deviation – as many of them indeed did, when the crusade veered off route, not to Africa but to Christian lands.

Thibaut of Champagne had been designated leader of the crusade, but before the fleet was ready to set sail he fell terminally ill, and an Italian, Boniface of Montferrat, patron to the troubadour Raimbaut de Vaqueiras, was chosen in his stead. Boniface had links with Greece and was also a personal friend of Philip of Swabia, who was married to Irene Angelus, a Greek whose father had been deposed, blinded and imprisoned, together with her brother Alexius, by her uncle Alexius III. At Christmas 1201 Boniface was in attendance at the court of Philip of Swabia when young Alexius arrived having escaped from prison and fled to the West to appeal for help on his father's behalf. This was to have repercussions before long.

By the summer of 1202 the great shortfall in the number of crusaders meant that they had accumulated a massive debt of 34,000 marks for ships already built. The Venetians threatened to cut off the crusaders' supplies if they were not paid, but made a deal: they would postpone the debt if the crusaders would help recapture the port of Zara (Zadar) on the Dalmatian coast. Its ruler was the king of Hungary, a Christian who had himself taken the cross. Many crusaders were understandably disturbed, and abandoned the expedition. Villehardouin, who along with the leaders was trying to hold it together, saw their concerns in terms of factions being determined to break up the army. The leaders saw no option but to fall in with the Venetians' demands, and in 1202 a fleet of over 200 ships left Venice and landed at Zara. The pope was horrified, and wrote a letter forbidding an attack on any Christian city, naming Zara in particular. Nevertheless the crusaders conquered and sacked it on 24 November, splitting the booty between the Venetians and themselves.

Shortly afterwards, envoys from Philip of Swabia arrived to propose on behalf of Alexius that the crusaders should conquer Constantinople on their way to the Holy Land and restore him and his father to the throne of Greece. 'In return Alexius, with the easy generosity of a pretender, promised the earth: reunion of the Orthodox Church with Rome, huge sums of money for the Venetians and the crusaders and support for the crusade in the shape of 10,000 Byzantine soldiers as soon as he was restored to power.'[4] In addition he pledged to maintain 500 knights in Palestine at his own expense for the rest of his lifetime. Again seeing no other

---

of France (p. 66).

[4] H. E. Mayer, *The Crusades*, translated by J. Gillingham (Oxford, 1988, first published in German, Stuttgart, 1965), p. 200.

solution to the problem of debt, the leaders agreed, tempted also by the prospect of Greek participation in the crusade and the reunification of the Church, which had been divided since the schism of 1054.[5] A long-standing dislike of the Greeks also played a part, and there was the added lure of the incredible mass of holy relics which were to be found in Constantinople: it was easy to assert that 'the schismatic Byzantines were no longer worthy to be the custodians of the richest treasure of relics in the world'.[6] But more crusaders were troubled in their consciences, and left the army. The remaining crusaders were flagrantly disobeying the pope, and were automatically excommunicated, but the army bishops gave them provisional absolution while a delegation went to Rome to explain their action and to ask for forgiveness. The pope was in a quandary: if he did not relent, his crusade might simply collapse. So he was prepared to absolve the crusaders as long as they restored what they had taken illegally and did not invade other Christian lands.

In April 1203 the crusaders sailed from Zara, and on 5 July they landed at Galata, the chief port of Constantinople. An attack on the city failed, but despite this Alexius III fled in panic and blind Isaac Angelus was released from prison. Reluctantly he confirmed the deal done with his son, and on 1 August the young Alexius was crowned co-emperor. The crusaders thought they would soon be off to the Holy Land, but the situation in Constantinople rapidly went downhill. Alexius had paid the first instalment of the promised cash, but fights broke out between Greeks and Catholics, the payments dried up; a coup d'état removed Alexius and his father from power, and amidst a wave of anti-Catholic xenophobia another ruler was crowned with the title of Alexius V, otherwise known as Murzuphlus ('the bushy-eyebrowed'). The crusaders could afford to go neither to the Holy Land nor back home. Short of provisions, in a hostile environment, they decided to capture Constantinople and take over the Byzantine empire. Again, spiritual concerns led many to leave for France or head directly to the Holy Land. The leaders concocted elaborate justifications to defend the plan, based on the Greeks' alleged sin in abetting the murder of their emperor and their schismatic status, and agreed with the Venetians to divide up the spoils. The attack on the city was successful: the emperor fled, and for three days it was given over to killing and looting.

Unlike the French chroniclers Villehardouin and Robert de Clari, the lyric poets refer but fleetingly to the marvellous treasures, the priceless relics and the ruthless sack of Constantinople.[7] While the marshal Villehardouin strives to create an impression of impartiality, the poets are more like Clari in that they speak of

---

[5] For the East–West schism that precipitated the formal separation between the Eastern Christian churches and the Western Church, see <http://www.britannica.com/event/Schism-of-1054>.

[6] Mayer, *The Crusades*, p. 200; N. G. Chrissis, *Crusading in Frankish Greece: A Study of Byzantine–Western Relations and Attitudes, 1204–1282* (Turnhout, 2012), p. 54.

[7] GV, II, pp. 52–55, §§ 250–51; Shaw, *Joinville and Villehardouin*, pp. 92–93, and especially Robert de Clari, *La Conquête de Constantinople, edition bilingue*, ed. and trans. J. Dufournet (Paris, 2004), pp. 168–85 (ch. LXXX–XCII).

their personal involvement. Besides exhorting others to take part in the expedition, they evoke their vows, their support for Boniface, the time of preparation and parting from loved ones, their journey and homecoming. And while Villehardouin upbraids deserters for wilfully undermining the crusade, lyric poets betray anxiety about its deviation from its original goal.

Exhortation

After Boniface of Montferrat was elected leader of the crusade at Soissons in early August 1201, the troubadour Raimbaut de Vaqueiras excitedly celebrated the honour shown to his patron and urged others to follow him in his noble cause (BdT 392.3).

> Ara pod hom conoisser e proar
> qe de bons fatz ren Dieus bon guisardon
> c'al pro marques n'a fait esmend'e don,
> qu'el fai son pretz sobr·els meillors puiar
> tan que il crozat de Franc'e de Chanpaingna
> l'an quist a Dieu per lo meillor de totz
> e per cobrar lo sepulcr'e la crotz
> on Jhesus fon; qu'el vol en sa compaingna
> l'onrat marques et a·l Dieus dat poder,
> de bons vassals e de terr'e d'aver
> e de rric cor per far miels so que·l taingna. (vv. 1–11)

Now people can know and be certain that God gives a good reward for good deeds because He has made a recompense and gift to the noble marquess, making him surpass the best in worth so that the crusaders of France and Champagne have asked God for him, as the best of all men, to recover the holy sepulchre and the cross where Jesus was crucified; for he wants the honoured marquis in his company, and God has given him might, good fighters, and land and riches and a strong heart, the better to fulfil what he must do.

Knighted by Boniface some seven years previously,[8] Raimbaut adopts the language of chivalric epic to rouse crusaders in East and West to deeds of glory:

> Nostr'estol guit sans Nicolaus de Bar,
> e·il Campanes dresson lo gonfanon,
> e·l marques crit 'Monferat e·l leon!',
> e.l coms flamencs 'Flandres!' als grans colps dar;
> e fiera·i quecs d'espaz'e lansa fraingna,

---

[8] Probably in 1194. See *The Poems of the Troubadour Raimbaut de Vaqueiras*, ed. J. Linskill (The Hague, 1964), p. 15.

que leu aurem los Turcs totz morz e rrotz,
e cobrarem en camp la Vera Croz
c'avem perdut; e·il valen rei d'Espaingna
fassan granz ostz sobre Mors conquerer,
que·l marques vai ost e setje tener
sobre·l soudan e pass'en breu Romaingna.   (vv. 56–66)

May St Nicholas of Bari guide our fleet, and let the men of Champagne raise their standard, and the marquis cry 'Montferrat and the lion!', and the Flemish count 'Flanders!' as they strike great blows; and let every man there strike with his sword and break his lance and we shall easily have smashed and killed all the Turks and on the battlefield we'll recover the True Cross, which we have lost. And may the valiant kings of Spain conquer the Moors with a great army, for the marquis is going to summon his army and lay siege to the sultan and will shortly pass through the Eastern Empire.

Peire Vidal also urges men to support the crusade, referring to the incentive of the pope's indulgence, issuing the customary dire threats to those who refuse to serve God in the East (BdT 364.8) and reviling Philip Augustus in particularly aggressive terms for failing to live up to the example of his father Louis VII, leader of the Second Crusade:

Reis auniutz val meins que pages,
quan viu a lei de recrezen
e plora·ls bes qu'autre despen
e pert so que·l paire conques.
Aitals reis fari'ad aucir
et en lach luec a sebelhir,
qui·s defen a lei de contrag
e no pren ni dona gamag.   (vv. 41–48)

A dishonoured king is worth less than a peasant when he lives like a coward and deplores the wealth that another spends and loses what his father won. Such a king deserves to be killed and buried in a loathsome place, when he defends himself like a cripple without taking or giving a blow.

The song was still being sung after Boniface set sail on August 1202, for one manuscript refers to him being *oltra mar*.[9] Gaucelm Faidit also castigates Philip Augustus' indifference to God's cause: 'the king who owns Paris prefers to gain silver coins in Saint Denis or over there in Normandy rather than all that Safadin has or holds in his power' (BdT 167.9, 57–62). These 'silver coins' represent the money provided for

---

9   MS O, v. 13, *Qes oltra mar*: see Peire Vidal, *Poesie*, ed. A. S. Avalle, 2 vols (Milan and Naples, 1960), pp. 112–13.

in the treaty of Goulet which Philip agreed with King John of England on 22 May 1200, which was followed by John's visit to Saint Denis and Paris on 31 May 1201.[10]

Departure, deviation and desertion

Of the troubadours and trouvères setting out on this crusade, not all were entirely enthusiastic, particularly in view of the attack on Zara and the deviation to Greece. Some followed the leaders all the way; others were troubled about the purity of the crusaders' intentions. The Vidame de Chartres was one of those who, according to Villehardouin, accompanied Renaud de Montmirail from Zara on a mission to the Holy Land and broke his oath to come back.[11] On his return home, probably in 1203, he composed two love songs referring briefly to his stay away from his homeland and expressing his happiness at being back in Blois (RS 421 and 502).

Other French trouvères who went on the Fourth Crusade include Hughes de Berzé, Conon de Béthune and the Châtelain de Coucy. The French crusaders set out after Pentecost (8 June) 1202, crossed the Alps near the pass of Mont-Cénis and passed through northern Italy, probably arriving in Venice at the end of June or beginning of July and eventually sailing in October or November.[12] The Châtelain died at sea during May–June 1203 on the way to Constantinople and was buried at sea; it is uncertain whether his crusade songs belong to this or the Third Crusade (see Chapter 3).[13]

Of Hughes de Berzé, Villehardouin simply records that he took the cross.[14] A few allusions in the trouvère's *Bible* indicate that he took part in the siege of Zara and the conquest of Constantinople. He remained in the East until at least 1205, and probably also completed a pilgrimage to the Holy Land. After he had taken the cross on 14 September 1201 he composed a song of farewell to his lady (RS 1126), where he says that to avoid the pain of separation it is preferable to send

---

[10] The details securely place the song at the time of the Fourth Crusade. 'Normandy' may refer to the region where Goulet was situated, but more probably alludes to the invasion unleashed by Philip in May 1202 following the judgement depriving the Plantagenets of their continental possessions. See Meliga's edition of this piece on Rialto, under 'Datazione e circostanze storiche'. There is no evidence, *pace* Mouzat, that Gaucelm went on the Third Crusade. See the important articles on the dating and historical circumstances of his crusade songs by R. Harvey, 'On the Date of Gaucelm Faidit's Dialogue with Albertet (BdT 16,16), with a Note on *Ara nos sia guitz*', *CN*, 71 (2011), 9–21, and W. Meliga, 'Gaucelm Faidit et la (les) croisade(s)', in *Gaucelm Faidit: amours, voyages et débats. Trobada tenue à Uzerche les 25 et 26 juin 2010* (Ventadour, 2011), pp. 25–36, which present essential reconsiderations of J. Mouzat, *Les poèmes de Gaucelm Faidit* (Paris, 1965).
[11] GV, I, §102, Shaw, *Joinville and Villehardouin*, p. 52.
[12] See Barbieri's edition of RS 1126, 'About the text'.
[13] GV refers to him in §§7 (when he took the cross), 114 (in Corfu) and 124 (when he died); see Shaw, *Joinville and Villehardouin*, pp. 30, 55, 58.
[14] GV, §45; Shaw, *Joinville and Villehardouin*, p. 39.

greetings to his lady from 'Lombardy' (Italy). This suggests that it may have been written during the journey in Italy, probably during the second half of June 1202.[15] The song includes an accusation against God for separating lovers, a theme which had already been explored by the Châtelain de Coucy (RS 679) and later by Guiot de Dijon (RS 21), and an anonymous song of separation, which like Guiot's was written from a female point of view (RS 191).[16]

> Mult a croissiés amorous a contendre
> d'aler a Dieu ou de remanoir ci,
> car nesuns hom, puis k'Amors l'a saisi,
> ne devroit ja si grief fais entreprendre:
> on ne puet pas servir a tant seignor;
> proec qe fins cuers qi bet a haute honor
> ne se poroit de tel chose deffendre,
> por ce, dame, ne m'en devés reprendre. (vv. 25–32)

A crusader in love must well ponder whether to go towards God or to remain here, for no one, once Love has taken hold of him, ought ever to assume such a heavy burden: one cannot serve more than one lord; but since a noble heart that aspires to high honour cannot avoid doing this, you ought not, my lady, to blame me for it.

Barbieri observes that the songs of separation composed by Conon de Béthune, the Châtelain de Coucy and Hughes de Berzé demonstrate the change in crusade songs which occurred at the time of the Third and Fourth Crusades and that it may be significant that the three are likely to have known each other through the expedition to Constantinople.[17]

Despite his enthusiastic promotion of Boniface's leadership, Raimbaut de Vaqueiras did not accompany the marquis to Soissons, and Linskill believed the troubadour was actually reluctant to take the cross himself, referring to lines 74–75 in BdT 392.3, where he tells his beloved *Bel Cavalier*,

> non sai si·m lais per vos o·m leu la croz,
> ni sai com m'an ni sai com m'en romaingna. (vv. 74–75)

I do not know whether for your sake I should refrain or should take the cross, nor do I know how I am to go or how I am to remain.

As Linskill observes, this strikingly contradicts the troubadour's previous statement,

---

[15] See Barbieri's edition of RS 1126. He observes that the song may have been written on two occasions, first in Burgundy before departure and then during the journey in Italy.
[16] Barbieri, 'Le canzoni di crociata', p. 54. This theme, also presented from a female point of view, is found as early as 1146–1147 in BdT 293.1: see Chapter 1, p. 35.
[17] See Chapter 3, p. 50, and Barbieri, 'Le canzoni di crociata', p. 54.

Mas Dieus es gautz per c'om si seingn'en crotz,
per que non pot perdre qui lui gasaigna;
per qu'eu am mais, s'a lui ven a plazer,
de llai morir que sai vius romaner
en aventura, fos mia Halamaingna.   (vv. 51–55)

> But God, for whom men make the sign of the cross, is joy, which is why anyone who wins him cannot lose; which is why, if it please him, I prefer to die over there than stay here alive but in peril, even if all Germany were mine.

He concedes that 'such hesitation may be no more than a traditional concession to the conventions of courtly love' – and indeed it was highly topical – but nevertheless observes that 'Raimbaut's reluctance to take the cross at this time is confirmed by a passage in the *Epic Letter* (II, 26–31) which affords clear evidence that he did not finally decide to join his patron overseas until the spring of 1203'.[18] He suggests that Raimbaut spent the winter of 1202 in Marseille at the court of Uc des Baux after Boniface's departure for Venice in the autumn of 1202, and that upon the decision to move against Constantinople taken at Zara,

> even though the diversion against Constantinople was a deviation from the purpose of the Crusade, it is clear that the faithful servant of Boniface could no longer refrain from participating in an expedition destined to bring such great glory to his patron. The whole passage attests therefore once again Raimbaut's devotion to the marquis, since he could truthfully claim to have sacrificed the hospitality he was enjoying among friends in his native Provence in order to brave a hazardous sea journey and fight against the Greeks, with whom he had no quarrel.

He suggests that the troubadour probably composed his song in Italy in 1201, and sailed east from Marseille in the spring of 1203.[19]

Gaucelm Faidit

The troubadour Gaucelm Faidit composed several songs about his involvement in the Fourth Crusade, but it is not easy to trace his movements or even his eventual destination. We know that he made his vows to the accompaniment of some ceremony and, not being privy to the leaders' secret plans to head for Africa, he believed he would be departing for the Holy Land (BdT 167.36).

E quar estauc que ades no·m empenh
ves Suria? Dieus sap per que m'ave:
que ma domna e·l reys engles mi te,

---

[18] Linskill, *Raimbaut de Vaqueiras*, p. 224, note 74.
[19] Linskill, *Raimbaut de Vaqueiras*, p. 222, *Epic Letter*, II, vv. 26–29, and pp. 328–29.

l'us per amor e l'autre per pauc faire
del gran secors que m'avia en coven.
Ges non remanh, mas ben iray plus len;
quar d'anar ai bon cor, don ges no·m vaire,
qu'e nom de Dieu ai levat entresenh.   (vv. 33–40)

But why do I still delay spurring to Syria? God knows why this befalls me: because my lady and the English king hold me back, the one through love and the other for doing little about the great assistance he had promised me. I am not in fact staying behind, but I shall certainly go more slowly; I have the firm intention of going and am not being irresolute about it, for I have raised the sign in God's name.[20]

Apparently at the moment of departure, he invokes God's support and protection for the crusaders' persons and goods which they have 'raised up' in God's service (BdT 167.33):

Oimais es sazos
d'anar am Dieu lo paire.
Qi pres mort per nos,
[nos] sia chapdelaire
ez als compaignos,
qi son nostre cofraire
per obedïenza
(aid'er me lor crezenza!);
e·us cors e·us avers,
c'an el sieu servir ders,
teinha en sa prezenza
e·il sia douz vezers
l'afanz e·l mals parsers.   (vv. 66a–78a)[21]

Now it is time to go with God the Father. May he who suffered death for our sake be a guide to us and to the companions who are our fellows in the duty of obedience[22] (may their faith now assist me!); and may he receive for himself

---

[20] The *entresenh* is likely to have been one of the distinctive signs assumed by pilgrims when they made a public commitment to undertake the journey. Phillips (*The Fourth Crusade*, p. 87) mentions the rite according to the first liturgical text to describe the event: after a blessing the cross was presented to the crusader, accompanied by the words 'Lord, bless this ensign of the holy cross that it may help forward the salvation of Thy servant'. The crusader then attached the cross to his shoulder, and was given the traditional insignia of staff and scrip.
[21] This stanza is in MS a¹; MS T has a different one.
[22] Perhaps knights, armed to provide personal security for other pilgrims. Villehardouin refers to pilgrims, knights and sergeants among those who sailed from Marseille (GV I,

the persons and goods which these have dedicated to his service, and may the torment and harsh suffering be sweet in his sight.

A song of farewell to his beloved Limousin (167.9) shows that he expected to receive inducements to settle in the Holy Land,[23] but that he intended, God willing, to come back after the start of the following May:

> Mas cals que sia·l critz
> del remaner auzitz,
> ia negus bes qu'eu aia
> ni rics locs aizitz
> no·m tenra ni conquistz,
> s'avia·ls votz complitz,
> c'apres calenda maia
> non sia garnitz
> del torn, si Dieus l'aizis.   (vv. 17–25)

But whatever appeal to stay behind is heard, no riches I might have, nor any noble pleasant place, nor gain, will ever stop me, if I have fulfilled my vows, from being ready to return after the start of May, if God allows it.

He also refers to these inducements on his return (167.19):

> Ben dei Dieu merceiar
> pos vol qe sanz e fortz
> puesc'el pais tornar,
> un val mais uns paucs d'ortz
> qe d'autra terr'estar
> rics ab gran benananza.   (vv. 13–18)

I surely ought to thank God, since he wishes me to return healthy and strong to the country where a certain corner of a garden is worth more than having riches and prosperity from another land.

His intention to return after the start of the following May corresponds to the agreement of 1201 between the Venetians and the French barons concerning the sea crossing. Villehardouin records that the Venetians had committed themselves for one year after the fleet's departure, which took place on 8 November 1202, after a delay from the set date of 24 June because of various problems, including finance, and Gaucelm was evidently aware of this agreement.[24]

The manuscripts transmit two versions of the *tornada* (stanza VI), both probably addressed to Hugh IX of Lusignan. The one in MS R, unlike the other in

---

p. 124, § 121; Shaw, *Joinville and Villehardouin*, p. 57).
[23] Meliga, 'Gaucelm Faidit', p. 27.
[24] Meliga, 'Gaucelm Faidit', p. 28.

CIKe, refers to the crusade.²⁵ The poet asks God to allow 'us pilgrims' to arrive in Syria with Count Baldwin of Flanders and the valiant marquis, namely Boniface. Following Crescini, Meliga argues that there was originally a single *tornada* referring to Maria de Ventadorn but also Baldwin and Boniface, and that R rewrote it, setting aside the more 'worldly' version, in the interests of reinforcing the 'serious' nature of the song and giving an ending more suitable for a crusade song which had just ended on references to the Virgin and God. Whatever the authenticity of the R version, it can at any rate be said that the scribe or his source thought Gaucelm was on crusade with Baldwin and Boniface.

In BdT 167.15 Gaucelm states that he has not yet left for the East because he needs his lady's pardon for some fault (vv. 51–54).

> E s'aquest tortz, dona, ·m fos perdonatz,
> passad'agra la mar part Lombardia;
> mas non cuich far leialmen romavia,
> si no m'era vas vos adreichuratz.   (167.15, 51–54)

And if this wrong, lady, were forgiven me, I should have passed over the sea beyond Italy; but I do not think to make the pilgrimage legitimately, without having set things right with you.

This courtly declaration probably blends with the religious idea of the need to resolve disputes before setting out on crusade.²⁶ Although Mouzat (who wrongly thought the song referrred to the Third Crusade) suggested that Gaucelm was writing while he was in northern Italy, the line *passat agra la mar part Lombardia* only shows that he wanted to sail from Italy, not that he was in Italy at the time. He probably did travel there in Boniface's company, since in BdT 167.14, probably composed in 1201 or 1202 as preparations for the Fourth Crusade were getting under way, he prays for the salvation of 'My Treasure' – almost certainly a *senhal* for Boniface – whom he is leaving there (vv. 50–52).²⁷

---

²⁵ See Meliga's first set of variants in his Rialto edition, and the notes to the English translation.
²⁶ See Barachini's note to vv. 53–54 and Matthew 5. 22–24, in which Jesus said no one should offer a sacrifice to God without having become reconciled with those with whom he has quarrelled. This last *cobla* is not in all MSS, so could be a later addition, as in the case of stanza VI of 167.33.
²⁷ Boniface did not leave with the bulk of the expedition but rejoined it at the end of 1202, as GV relates (p. 47); see Meliga, 'Gaucelm Faidit', p. 31, and his edition of BdT 167.14 on Rialto, n. 52 and GV I, p. 80, §79 (Shaw, *Joinville and Villehardouin*, p. 47). Lewent, 'Das altprovenzalische Kreuzlied', p. 344, and V. De Bartholomaeis, *Poesie provenzali storiche relative all'Italia*, 2 vols (Rome, 1931), I, p. 100, date the song from after the marquis' election in Soissons as leader of the crusade, a diplomatic journey he made in France and Germany, and his return to Italy in March 1202, and before August of the same year, when he travelled to Venice for the army's departure; Robert Meyer, *Das Leben des Trobadors Gaucelm Faidit*

At some point on his journey Gaucelm refers to the marquis waiting for the crusaders in the springtime.[28]

Can vei reverdir li jardis
et hoi los hoizelos chanter
e nos aten don[c] li marchis
me renoveilon mei penser;
ladonc me soven d'un cler vis,
que ge ne puis pas emblier.
*Qu'e tal daima ai pausé mon cuer,
don muir e·n viu, e·n viu e·n muer.*   (167.50, 1–8)

When I see the garden grow green again and hear the little birds sing, and so the marquis awaits us, my thoughts revive me; then I remember a bright face that I cannot forget. *For I have placed my heart in such a lady in whom I die and live, and live and die.*

The song is very unusual, if not unique, among troubadour lyrics in that Gaucelm seems to have intended to write it in French, or at least intended it to sound French. The second stanza shows that he was writing in a crusading context, as he claims that his lady has made him 'make the crossing from the other side of the sea' (v. 10). He evidently found himself in the company of French crusaders and composed the song for a largely French audience, or for some important Frenchmen. Under what circumstances might he have done this? If the marquis is waiting for the crusaders it would seem that they are at some stopping point between Italy and the East. One possibility is that they were at Zara, in April 1203, when the crusaders were about to set sail for Corfu, 'where the first to arrive would wait for the late-comers, until they had all collected'.[29]

Gaucelm's much-anthologised and vividly personal song of thankfulness for his joyful, healthy homecoming expresses his relief at escaping the troubles of the ports and the perils of the sea: the lighthouse by the straits of Messina, the contrary winds, the fear of pirate or enemy ships (BdT 167.19), the rolling of his own.

Del gran golfe de mar
e dels enoios portz
e del perillos far

(Heidelberg, 1876), pp. 41–42 placed it more generally between the end of the summer of 1201 and spring 1202, while Mouzat suggested the slightly later date of c. 8 October 1202, when the bulk of the expedition set sail from Venice. For further details and discussion see Meliga's edition of BdT 167.14.

[28] The rhyme word *marchis* in v. 3 of MS V has been the subject of much discussion. For my arguments in favour of the manuscript reading see the notes to the Rialto edition.

[29] GV, I, pp. 112–14, §§110–11, and Faral's note 3 on p. 115; Shaw, *Joinville and Villehardouin*, p. 54.

soi, merce Dieu, estortz;
don posc dir e comdar
qe mainta malananza
i hai suffert e maint turmen.
E pos a Dieu platz q'eu torn m'en
en Limozi ab cor iauzen,
don parti ab pesanza,
lo tornar e l'onranza
li grazisc, pos El m'o cossen.

Ben dei Dieu merceiar,
pos vol qe sanz efortz
puesc'el pais tornar,
un val mais uns paucs d'ortz
qe d'autra terr'estar
rics ab gran benananza.
Qar sol li belacuillimen
e·il onrat fag e·ll dig plazen
de nostra domna [e]·il prezen
d'amoros'acoindanza
e la douza semblanza
val tot qan autra terra ren.

Ar hai dreg de chantar,
pos vei ioi e deportz,
solatz e domneiar,
qar zo es vostr'acortz.
E la[s] font[z] e·l ri*u* clar
fan m'al cor alegranza,
prat e vergier, qar tot m'es gen,
q'era non dopti mar ni ven
garbi, maïstre ni ponen,
ni manaus no·m balanza
ni no·m fai mais doptansa
galea ni corsier corren.   (vv. 1–36)

From the great gulf of the sea, and from the troubles of the ports and from the perilous lighthouse, thanks to God, I have escaped. So I can say and relate that I have endured many hardships there, and many torments. And since it pleases God that I should return with a joyful heart to the Limousin which I left sorrowfully, I thank him for the return and the honour, since he grants me this.

I surely ought to thank God, since he wishes me to return healthy and strong to the country where a certain corner of a garden is worth more than having riches and prosperity from another land. For the fair welcoming words and honourable actions and pleasing conversations of our lady alone, and her gifts of amorous intimacy, and her sweet expression, are worth all that any other land can offer.

Now I am right to sing, since I witness joy and merriment, sociability and the courting of ladies, since this is your good pleasure; and the bright springs and streams, the meadows and orchards bring happiness to my heart, for everything is a delight to me now that I fear neither sea nor Garbin (south-west), Maïstre (south) nor Ponen (west) wind, and my ship doesn't roll, and I'm no longer terrified by galleys or swift warships.

Phillips describes the ships transporting crusaders as rounded tubs, a little shorter than a modern aeroplane such as an Airbus A320 but twice as wide. 'As they huddled below decks, rolling from side to side in the dark, dank underbelly of the ship, many a passenger must have regretted ever leaving dry land.'[30] Gaucelm's conclusion cleverly mirrors in the ship's rolling and tossing the spiritual turmoil of the man who goes on pilgrimage with the wrong intentions:

> Qi per Dieu gazaignar
> pren d'aitals desconortz,
> ni per s'arma salvar,
> ben es dregs, non ges tortz.
> Mas cel qi per raubar
> e per mal'acordanza
> vai per mar, un hom tan mal pren,
> em pauc d'ora s'aven soven
> qe, qan cuj'om pujar, deissen,
> si c'ab desesperanza
> il laissa tot e 'slanza
> l'arm'e·l cor e l'aur e l'argen.   (vv. 37–48)

It is right and certainly not wrong for a man to take on such adversities in order to win God and save his soul. But if anyone with evil intent goes to sea, where one suffers so many torments, in order to rob, it often happens in a short space of time that, when he thinks he's going up, he's going down, so that in despair he abandons everything and throws away life and soul and gold and silver.

The need to go on crusade with the right intentions is a commonplace of crusading preaching and poetry. But is there more to it than this? Time and again, generalising commonplaces in troubadour poetry can be shown to have relevance to particular circumstances known to its audience. Why should Gaucelm choose to end his song by speaking of the man who sets sail *per mal'acordanza* (with evil intent) with the intention of robbery (*raubar*)? Was he pointing the finger of blame

---

[30] Phillips, *The Fourth Crusade*, p. 74; see his further graphic details.

at those who were corrupting the crusade? After all, the sack of the Christian port of Zara was robbery pure and simple.

In his account of the Fourth Crusade Villehardouin presents the point of view of the leaders attempting under very difficult circumstances to maintain the unity of the army, and energetically condemns those whom he blames for trying to break it up. At each stage he can see crusaders, who had committed themselves to serving God in the Holy Land, abandoning the expedition, profoundly disturbed by the deviation to Constantinople and the conquest of the Christian city of Zara, whose ruler, the king of Hungary, had himself taken the cross. The chronicler relates that during the whole winter of 1202–1203 many men of the lower ranks escaped in merchant ships, followed by barons and knights send on a mission to Syria who broke their oath to return to the army. These desertions continued until Easter, when the fleet left for Corfu, where the new arrivals would wait for the rest of the crusaders.[31]

Gaucelm's song proves that he did indeed voyage overseas. But where did he go? The song says nothing of this. Once back in the comfort of his home environment Gaucelm no doubt indulged in many traveller's tales, and the troubadour Elias d'Ussel pokes fun at him for it (BdT 136.3a):

Manenz fora·l francs pelegris,
mas son aver mes al Santor;
mout lai estet a grant onor
per cho si ac dan Sa*f*adis.
E si no fos lo granz ventres qu·ill pen,
car conpreron li Turc son hardimen!
Ancaras dis el qe lai vol tornar,
mas laissa s'en pe·l bel fill eretar.

The sincere [noble?] pilgrim would be rich, but he spent his wealth on [visiting] the sepulchre; there he stayed for a long time in great honour, which caused harm to Safadin.[32] And if it were not for the great belly that hangs down in front of him, the Muslims would have paid dearly for his boldness! He has also said that he wants to go back there, but abandons the idea in order to provide an inheritance for his handsome son.

This *cobla* might mean that Gaucelm completed his pilgrimage to Jerusalem (and therefore did not follow the crusaders to Constantinople). On the other hand Elias may well be questioning, through his sarcastically hyperbolic tone, whether Gaucelm ever went there at all.

---

[31] GV I, pp. 100–02, §§100–02 and pp. 110–12, §§108–10; Shaw, *Joinville and Villehardouin*, pp. 52 and 54.
[32] Despite Mouzat and Riquer, it is generally accepted that Saladin (v. 4) in the MSS is a scribal error for Safadin: see Barachini's edition on Rialto.

In short, we know that Gaucelm took a crusading vow in the belief that he would be travelling to the Holy Land, intending to return home after the start of May 1203; that he probably travelled to north Italy with Boniface, where they separated; that in the spring of 1203 he appears to have been in the company of French crusaders about to set sail to join the marquis who was waiting for them at a stopping-point on the way eastwards; and that he returned home, remarking on the importance of crusading to gain salvation rather than plunder. It is uncertain whether he reached Constantinople, or joined defectors to go straight to the Holy Land, or returned home with others without fulfilling his vow. A reasonable hypothesis is that he composed *Can vei reverdir li jardis* at Zara, when Boniface was in, or on his way to, Corfu waiting for the remaining crusaders to follow; and that shortly afterwards our troubadour abandoned the army in disillusionment.[33]

Life, politics and war in Greece

After the conquest of Constantinople there were two contenders for the imperial throne: Baldwin of Flanders and Boniface of Montferrat. An election was held, and Runciman maintains that the Venetians made sure the position went to the 'weaker and more tractable' Baldwin, who was ceremoniously crowned on 16 May 1204.[34] Any thought of the crusade to the East was forgotten: the crusaders set about establishing themselves as rulers of Frankish Greece, otherwise known as Romania. The pope was at first delighted at the fall of Constantinople; then, when he heard about the atrocities of the sack, he was deeply shocked. But he managed to reconcile himself to the *fait accompli*, hoping that Frankish Greece in the longer term would help the cause of Christendom and that the Greek Orthodox Church would soon be reunited with Rome.

It had been agreed in advance that the losing contender would receive all of Asia Minor and the Morea (the Peleponnese), but what Boniface wanted was the crown of Thessalonica, which had been promised to his brother Renier by Manuel I Comnenus.[35] A rift developed between Boniface and Baldwin, and it was agreed to put Boniface's wish before a council of barons. Thomas Madden observes that the

---

[33] Immediately after the sack of Zara, while the troops were encamped close to the harbour, Simon de Montfort, 'one of the great barons in command of the forces, having made an agreement with the King of Hungary, went over to his side', along with many others (Shaw, *Joinville and Villehardouin*, p. 54; see GV I, pp. 110–12, §109). Gaucelm had already visited Hungary (BdT 167.6, ed. Mouzat, 63, 25) and may have had particular sympathies for the king whose territory had been so illegitimately attacked.

[34] Runciman, *History*, III, p. 124.

[35] T. F. Madden, 'The Latin Empire of Constantinople's Fractured Foundation: The Rift between Boniface of Montferrat and Baldwin of Flanders', in *The Fourth Crusade: Event, Aftermath, and Perceptions, Papers from the Sixth Conference of the Society for the Study of the Crusades and the Latin East, Istanbul, Turkey, 25–29 August 2004*, ed. T. F. Madden (Aldershot, 2008), pp. 45–52 (p. 45).

council in general and Conon in particular were not well liked by Boniface or his court,[36] and the troubadour Raimbaut de Vaqueiras voiced strong opinions about it, as we shall see. Madden suggests that the emperor probably told the marquis that it was beyond his power to grant his request at that time, and matters were delayed while the commission was slowly deciding on the division of territorial spoils. The quarrel erupted into outright rebellion during the summer of 1204, when Boniface professed to the Greek citizens of Demotica and Adrianople that he had abandoned his Latin allies and was now fighting to restore the Angelan dynasty through Manuel, the eldest son of Margaret (Maria) of Hungary and Isaac II Comnenus. The quarrel was put for arbitration before a council of barons in Constantinople consisting of Count Louis of Blois, the diplomat and trouvère Conon de Béthune, the doge of Venice Enrico Dandolo and the marshal and chronicler Geoffrey of Villehardouin.[37]

Raimbaut was deeply disappointed that Baldwin had been elected emperor instead of his patron Boniface, and resented Baldwin's delay in honouring his promise to the marquis concerning Thessalonica. The negotiations were difficult, and the emperor's councillors were urging him to break his promise. Through a hard-hitting *sirventes* (BdT 392.9a) the troubadour lobbies the emperor directly, intervening forcefully in the dispute and attempting to bypass the influence of his privy council.[38] He begins by sarcastically labouring the idea of council, councillors and counsel, disparaging Baldwin's lack of authority over his barons, and targeting in particular Conon de Béthune and the seneschal Thierry of Loos.

> Conseil don a l'emperador
> pois per conseil fai totz sos plais,
> e non faria meins ni mais
> mas tant con sei conseillador
> li volun far dir'e faire:
> e·il conseil, s'el vol esser pros,
> qe don, sens conseil, derenan;
> e, ses conseil ab sos baros,
> creza·l conseil del plus prezan,
> q'aissi·s conseils d'emperaire.
>
> Pueis eu li conseil sa honor,
> creza m'en, si·n vol, o s'en lais;
> e se·l senescal no·s n'irais
> ni Coine del cosseil major,
> eu serai bos cosseillaire,

---

[36] Madden, 'The Latin Empire', p. 49.
[37] Madden, 'The Latin Empire', p. 47.
[38] Linskill, *Raimbaut de Vaqueiras*, p. 230, n. 14, suggests that the *cosseil major* was probably the small privy council consisting of the emperor's officials and intimate friends, as distinct from the general council of the barons.

e darai conseil a els dos,
qant lur segnor consseillaran,
qe·il cosseillen de far rics dos;
mas no sai s'amdos m'en creiran,
ni eu no·ls en forzi gaire. (vv. 1–20)

I offer counsel to the emperor, since he conducts all his affairs by council, and would not do anything other than his councillors would have him say and do: and if he aspires to excellence I counsel him to make gifts from now on without counsel; and without consulting his barons' council let him accept the counsel of the worthiest man; for this is counsel fit for an emperor.

Since I counsel him what will bring him honour, let him believe me or not as he pleases; and if the seneschal and Conon of the Privy Council are not vexed, I shall be a good counsellor, and I shall counsel both of them, when they counsel their lord, to counsel him to give rich gifts; but I do not know whether the two of them will heed me, and I am hardly forcing them to do so.

Raimbaut deftly makes light of his own rôle in offering counsel: Baldwin can choose whether or not to accept it – but since it is to his honour, how can he refuse? Thierry and Conon may be irritated by his intervention, but are they not free to ignore it? But the emperor, despite his natural advantages of birth, will do so to his cost, for he risks alienating his allies, and he will need both valour and unity in the face of the enormous of the task ahead of him, with hostile forces on all sides.

E si no·s meillur'en la flor,
lo frugz poiri'esser malvais;
e gart se q'al seu tort non bais,
qe pujatz es en grant honor,
et es bels e de bon aire;
e se vol creire mos sermos,
ja no·i aura anta ni dan,
anz sera granz honors e pros,
car se pert cels c'ab lui estan,
tart venran de son repaire.

E non tema freg ni calor,
ni·s baign ni sojorn em palais,
qe al col a cargat tal fais
qe, s'el non es de gran valor,
greu lo poira a cap traire;
qe li Blac e·il Coman e·il Ros
e·il Turc e·il Paian e·il Persan
seran contra lui ab Grifos;
e si per pretz non trai afan,
tot qant a faig pot desfaire. (vv. 21–40)

But if the fruit does not develop well in the flower it may prove rotten; and let him take heed not to decline to his own detriment, for he has risen to great honour, and is handsome and of good lineage; and if he is willing to heed my words there will never be shame or harm in them; instead there will be great honour and profit, for if he abandons those who stand by him they will be reluctant to belong to his house.

Let him fear neither cold nor heat, or take baths and rest in his palace, as he has taken such a weight upon his shoulders that without great valour it will be hard for him to bring matters to a conclusion. The Vlachs and the Cumans and the Russians, the Turks and Pagans and Persians will be against him, with the Greeks; and if he does not suffer the burden for glory, he may undo everything he has done.

Raimbaut also plays on the spiritual anxieties of Baldwin and other crusaders who feel guilty at having sacked Christian cities and religious foundations. This can only be justified, he implies, in the context of the ultimate goal of taking the crusade further to Africa and the Holy Land, and he warns that the Venetians are not to be trusted not to divert it yet again from this purpose.

> Qu'el e nos em tuig pecchador
> dels mostiers ars e dels palais,
> on vei pecar los clercs e·ls lais;
> e se·l sepulchre non secor,
> serem vas Dieu plus pechaire,
> q'en pechat tornara·l perdos,
> e se·l conqis no 'stai enan;
> mas s'el es larcs ni coratjos,
> ben leu pot anar osteian
> a Babiloni'e al Caire.
>
> Tota sa forz'e sa vigor
> taign qe mostr'als Turcs part Roais,
> qe tuit li soudan e·il alcais
> e·il amirail e·il almassor
> n'esperan lansar e traire;
> et er n'encolpatz Nevelos,
> e·ls doz'electors blasmaran,
> se·l sepulchr'es mais en preizos;
> e·l dux m'er apellatz d'enjan
> si·l vol del socors estraire.   (vv. 41–60)

For he and we are all guilty of burning monasteries and palaces, and I see both clergy and laymen sin in this; and if he does not assist the sepulchre, and if our conquest does not make progress, our sin against God will be all the greater, for the pardon will turn to sin; but if he is liberal and courageous, he can very easily take his armies to Babylon and Cairo.

He needs to display all his might and strength to the Turks beyond Edessa, for all the sultans and cadis and emirs and caliphs are waiting for him to hurl lances and fire missiles; and Névelon will be accused, and they will blame the twelve electors, if the sepulchre remains in captivity; and the doge will be accused of deceit if he tries to divert him from bringing this assistance.

He concludes with an appeal to Geoffrey of Villehardouin, of whom he seems to approve, in contrast to Conon and Thierry. He also seems to think that Villehardouin and Milon of Brabant are more likely than the other two leading members of the court to support his cause (vv. 61–66).[39] Boniface was successful in his bid for Thessalonica. 'The settlement of the dispute in Boniface's favour was apparently effected in precisely the way advocated by the poet.'[40] But the task ahead was indeed enormous. Chaotic events erupted in February 1205, when the Greeks rebelled against Latin rule in Demotica and Adrianople, and on 14 April Baldwin suffered a disastrous defeat at this latter city, never to be seen again. The doge died soon afterwards. Johannitz, tsar of the Wallacho-Bulgarians, invaded the Latin empire and at the end of May Boniface rushed north from the Peleponnese to meet the serious threat to Thessalonica.

A song Raimbaut composed in June–July (BdT 392.24) shows that he was not with Boniface on his last campaign.[41] It begins on a despondent note, looking back to a lost time of love and courtly pleasures.

> No m'agrad'iverns ni pascors
> ni clars temps ni fuoills de garrics,
> car mos enans mi par destrics
> e totz mos majer gaugz dolors,
> e son maltrag tuit miei lezer
> e desesperat miei esper;
> e si·m sol amors e dompneis
> tener gai plus que l'aiga·l peis!
> E pois d'amor me sui partitz
> cum hom issillatz e faiditz,
> tot'autra vida·m sembla mortz
> e totz autre jois desconortz.   (vv. 1–12)

---

[39] Linskill, *Raimbaut de Vaqueiras*, p. 230, points out that Villehardouin frequently mentions Thierry, Conon and Milon together, 'i.e. precisely those leading members of the court who are also mentioned in our poem'.
[40] Linskill, *Raimbaut de Vaqueiras*, p. 229 and p. 230, n. 7–10.
[41] See v. 96.

Neither winter nor spring delights me, nor cloudless days nor leaf of oak, for to me my advancement seems loss, and all my greatest joy but sorrow, and sufferings are all my pleasures, and my hopes transformed to despair; yet love and courting used to keep me merrier than a fish in water! And since I have parted from love, like one ruined and sent to exile, every other life seems death to me, and every other joy desolation.

Warfare for the sake of gain is little consolation:

> Bels armatz e bos feridors,
> setges e calabres e pics,
> e traucar murs nous et antics,
> e vensser bataillas e tors
> vei et aug; e non puosc aver
> ren qe·m puosc'ad amor valer!
> E vauc cercan ab rics arneis
> gerras e coitas e torneis,
> don sui conqueren enriquitz;
> e pos jois d'amor m'es faillitz,
> totz lo mons no·m parri'us ortz,
> ni mos chans no m'es mais confortz. (vv. 25–36)

Fine armed warriors and stout fighters, sieges, catapults and pickaxes, and holes being smashed through walls old and new, and fortifications and towers being won, I can see and hear; but I can have nothing to avail me in love! And, clad in rich armour, I seek out wars and frays and mêlées where I am enriched by conquest; yet since the joy of love is denied me, the whole world [if I had it] would seem to me [less than] one garden, and my song no more consoles me.

The last part of the text reads like a self-conscious effort to make the best of a grim situation. Raimbaut stoically puts on a cheerful face and thinks positively of the proven martial competence of the marquis and his allies – but does not forget to pray for reinforcements.

> Pero no·m comanda valors,
> se be·m sui iratz ni enics,
> q'ieu don gaug a mos enemics
> tan q'en perda pretz ni lauzors,
> q'ancar puosc dan e pro tener,
> e sai d'irat joios parer
> sai entre·ls Latins e·ls Grezeis;
> e·l marques, que l'espaza·m seis,
> gerreia Blacs e Drogoïz,
> et anc pos lo mons fon bastitz
> nuilla gens non fetz tant d'esfortz
> cum nos, cui Dieus a gent estortz.

Lo marques n'es honratz e sors
e·l Campanes e·l coms Enricx,
Sicar, Montos e Salanicx
e Constantinople socors,
quar gent sabon camp retener,
e pot hom ben proar en ver:
qu'anc mais nulha gent non ateis
aitan gran honor, apareys.
Per bos vassals, valens, arditz,
es nostr'emperis conqueritz,
e Dieus trameta nos esfortz
coissi·s tray'a cap nostra sortz!   (vv. 49–72)

Yet, even if I am troubled and sad, valour does not command me so to gladden my enemies as to lose my reputation and honour, for I can still do harm and good, and I know how to seem merry even in sadness, here among the Latins and the Greeks; and the marquis, who girded me with the sword, is warring against the Vlachs and Drogobites, and never since the world was made has any people accomplished such exploits as we, whom God has graciously delivered.

The marquis is thereby honoured and exalted, so too the man of Champagne[42] and Count Henry, and Sicar, Modon, Salonika and Constantinople relieved, for [these men] well know how to be masters of the field, and this indeed can easily be shown: it is manifest that no people ever attained such great glory. By fine warriors, valiant and intrepid, has our empire been won, and may God send us reinforcements so that our destiny may be fulfilled!

Raimbaut is unusual in his attempt to imbue the Fourth Crusade with epic qualities. Peter Noble, focusing on the narrative sources, remarked that none of the writers who wrote about this crusade was in the least interested in presenting it through epic or in glorifying its participants as epic heroes.[43] In contrast, the troubadour wistfully evokes legendary heroes whose achievements are surpassed in the new Latin empire, and which he foresees leading on to the final liberation of the Holy Land:

---

[42] The 'man of Champagne' is probably William of Champlitte, a councillor of Boniface, who conquered the Peleponnese in the winter of 1205 along with the marshal's nephew. Count Henry is the emperor Baldwin's brother Henry of Flanders, who had saved the army and the capital after the disaster of Adrianople (Linskill, *Raimbaut de Vaqueiras*, p. 250, n. 62).

[43] P. Noble, '1204, The Crusade without Epic Heroes', in *Epic and Crusade. Proceedings of the Colloquium of the Société Rencesvals British Branch Held at Lucy Cavendish College, Cambridge, 27–28 March 2004*, ed. P. E. Bennett, A. E. Cobby and J. E. Everson (Cambridge and Edinburgh, 2006), pp. 89–104 (p. 104).

Anc Alixandres non fetz cors
ni Carles ni·l reis Lodoics
tan honrat, ni·l pros n'Aimerics
ni Rotlans ab sos poignadors
non saubron tan gen conquerer
tan ric emperi per poder
cum nos, don poja nostra leis;
q'emperadors e ducs e reis
avem faitz, e chastels garnitz
prop dels Turcs e dels Arabitz,
et ubertz los camins e·ls portz
de Brandiz tro al Bratz Sain Jorz.

Per nos er Domas envazitz
e Jerusalem conqueritz
e·l regnes de Suri'estortz,
que·ls Turcx o trobon en lur sortz.   (vv. 73–88)

Never did Alexander or Charlemagne or King Louis make such a glorious invasion, nor were the valiant lord Aimeri or Roland with his warriors able to conquer by force, in such noble fashion, such a powerful empire as we have won, whereby our Faith is in the ascendant; for we have created emperors and dukes and kings, and have garrisoned fortresses near the Turks and Arabs, and opened up the roads and ports from Brindisi to St George's Straits [the Bosphorus].

By us Damascus will be attacked, and Jerusalem conquered, and the realm of Syria liberated, for the Turks find this in their prophecies.

But the end is bitter, and sad.

Los pellegris perjurs, fraiditz,
qi nos an sai en camp geqitz,
qi los manten e cortz es tortz,
que chascuns val mens vius que mortz.

Belhs dous Engles, francx et arditz,
cortes, essenhatz, essernitz,
vos etz de totz mos gaugz conortz,
e quar viu ses vos, fatz esfortz.   (vv. 89–96)

Whoever maintains in courts those perjured, treacherous pilgrims who have deserted us here on the battlefield is a crook, for each one of them is worth less alive than dead.

Fair, gentle *Engles* [Boniface], noble and bold, courteous, well bred and distinguished, you are the inspiration of all my joys, and in living without you I perform a miracle.

The 'perjured, treacherous pilgrims' were armed crusaders (7,000 according to Villehardouin) present in the harbour of Constantinople who fled panic-stricken by the news of the disaster at Adrianople. They abandoned the almost defenceless capital, 'and despite the entreaties of the military and religious leaders sailed for home on April 17th'.[44] Boniface was to die shortly afterwards on this campaign, and of our troubadour we hear no more.

After the marquis' death on 4 September 1207 the political future of the kingdom of Thessalonica and its relationship with the Latin empire under Baldwin's successor, his brother Henry of Flanders, was in doubt. One party supported Boniface's son Demetrius's claim to the throne. Demetrius's mother was Margaret of Hungary, former wife of the Greek emperor Isaac II, who had formed a part of Boniface's policy of legitimising and strengthening his rule in Thessalonica. Stirred up by the Greeks who identified themselves with Demetrius and Margaret, this party proposed to submit to Henry's authority in order to retain some internal autonomy within the kingdom. Various Lombard lords in Thessalonica, including Rolandino and Albertino of Canossa, Guido Pelavicino Marchesopulo of Parma and Ravano dalle Carceri of Verona, formed a conspiracy against her, fearing that Henry and the French would enter Thessalonica to take up the reins of power and redistribute fiefs. Openly rebelling against Henry's authority, they hoped for the intervention of the new marquis of Monferrat, William VI, Boniface's son by his first marriage. In the winter of 1208 Henry was advised to travel to Thessalonica in order to obtain the fealty of the Lombards on behalf of Demetrius, while the Lombards were plotting to place William VI of Montferrat on the throne and make it independent of Constantinople. After holding his Christmas court at Vigneri and travelling around western Greece, Henry found his path to Thessalonica blocked. This was in the middle of winter, when he and his men were at serious risk of death from hypothermia. While he took refuge in a monastery in Choriatis, 15 km east of Thessalonica, he sent for Conon de Béthune to go to Thessalonica and talk to the Lombards. Conon succeeded in negotiating Henry's entry into the city before 6 January 1209, when Demetrius was crowned king, and was in and out of Thessalonica during the next two months. The Lombards continued to plot, with Conon being involved in peace-making at Ravennika at the beginning of May, though Ravano dalle Carceri and others did not turn up to the arranged meeting. Ravano

---

[44] Linskill, *Raimbaut de Vaqueiras*, p. 252, n. 89–92 and GV, II, §§376–79, pp. 184–88 and p. 189, n.1; Shaw, *Joinville and Villehardouin*, pp. 125–26.

During the time when Boniface was king of Thessalonica (1204–1207), Peire Vidal composed BdT 364.38, *Pus ubert ai mon ric thesaur*, in which he urges Peter of Aragon to put his whole efforts into destroying pagans 'over there', and boasts that he will destroy all those 'over here'. Avalle (Peire Vidal, *Poesie*, p. 301) thinks the first are probably the Muslims in Spain, the second those in Malta and Sicily, the poet having probably composed the song in Malta; for further details see p. 286.

eventually sent word for a truce on about 20 May and the Lombards then yielded all their fiefs and lands to the emperor.⁴⁵

Ravano was the lover of a married woman named Isabella, and wed her in 1212 after the death of her unidentified husband and a papal dispensation. She was a woman of no small fortune: after Ravano's death in 1216 she and her daughter Berta inherited a third of the island of Euboea, and Berta married Geoffrey of Villehardouin, nephew of the historian of that name and prince of Achaea. Isabella was celebrated by the troubadour Elias Cairel, with whom she exchanged a playful *tenso* while in Greece,⁴⁶ and who was a spokesman for the rebel leaders. In a song probably composed in the autumn of 1208 (BdT 133.9) Elias composed a stinging *sirventes* attacking William of Montferrat for his lack of interest in his Greek inheritance and failing to follow the example of his father Boniface.

> Marques, li monge de Clonic
> vuoill que fasson de vos capdel
> o siatz abas de Cistel,
> pois lo cor avez tan mendic
> que mais amatz dos bous et un araire
> a Monferrat, qu'aillors estr'emperaire:
> be·n pot hom dir qu'anc mais fills de lioupart
> no·s mes en cros a guisa de rainart.   (vv. 9–16)

> Lo regesme de Salonic
> ses peirier'e ses manganel
> pogratz aver, e maint chastel
> – d'autres qu'ieu no mentau ni dic –
> per Dieu, Marques, Rotlandis e sos fraire
> e Guis Marques e Ravas lor confraire,
> Flamenc Frances Borgoignon e Lombart
> van tuit dizen que vos semblatz bastart!   (vv. 33–40)

Marquis, what I want is for the monks of Cluny to make you their superior or for you to be abbot of Cîteaux, since you have such a niggardly heart that you prefer two oxen and a plough in Monferrat to being emperor elsewhere. People can surely say of this that a leopard's son never hid in his lair like a fox.

You could have the kingdom of Salonika without [recourse to] petrary or mangonel, as well as many other castles I do not name or mention. For God's sake, Marquis! Roland and his brother, and their associates Marquis Guy and

---

⁴⁵ See L. Paterson, 'Greeks and Latins at the Time of the Fourth Crusade: Patriarch John X Kamateros and a Troubadour *tenso*', in *Languages of Love and Hate. Conflict, Communication, and Identity in the Medieval Mediterranean*, ed. S. Lambert and H. Nicholson (Turnhout, 2012), pp. 119–39 (pp. 124 and 132).
⁴⁶ Harvey and Paterson, *The Troubadour Tensos*, II, p. 841.

Ravano, the Flemish, French, Burgundians and Lombards are all saying you look like a bastard!

Once the Lombards had made peace with Henry, Elias tried to mend fences with Conon de Béthune in a song addressed to him (BdT 133.3). I have suggested elsewhere that Conon replied in a cleverly veiled political attack on Elias' patroness Isabella delle Carceri, who had had no small rôle in fomenting the civil war.[47]

The marriage of Isabella's daughter to Geoffrey of Villehardouin, nephew of the chronicler, proved a shrewd move. His independent principality of Achaea in the Peleponnese survived until 1277, when it passed to the control of Charles of Anjou, and lasted in some form until 1432. Under Henry's successors 'the Latin Empire went inexorably downhill'. The kingdom of Thessalonica fell in 1224. Pope Gregory IX (1227–1241) was prepared to accept participation in the struggle in Greece as satisfactory fulfilment of crusading vows, but Emperor Baldwin II of Constantinople (1228–1261) lived in abject poverty, travelling all over the world from England to the Nile to raise cash by the sale of his European estates and of precious relics from Constantinople: 'Even the Crown of Thorns was pawned to the Venetians to be redeemed in 1238 by Saint Louis of France and taken to the Sainte Chapelle in Paris.'[48] The end of Frankish rule in Constantinople came suddenly one day in 1261, when a passing Greek commander noticed the Latins were relying on a truce and leaving the city undefended. He simply marched in and took it.

---

[47] Paterson, 'Greeks and Latins', pp. 128–37, but see L. Formisano, 'Prospettive di ricerca sui canzonieri d'autore nella lira d'oïl', in *La filologia romanza e i codici. Atti del convegno, Messina, Università degli studi, Facoltà di lettere e filosofia, 19–22 decembre 1991*, ed. S. Guida and F. Latella (Messina, 1994), vol. I, pp. 131–52 (p. 145).

[48] Mayer, *The Crusades*, pp. 207–08.

6

The Fifth Crusade, of Damietta, and the Albigensian Crusade

The early thirteenth century saw the intersection of several crusading ventures and European wars. In Greece, a crusade against Christians had produced a new but shaky empire facing external and internal threats, which continued to call, in vain, for support from the West. In 1208 Innocent III launched another crusade against Christians, this time nearer home. The story of the Albigensian Crusade is well known, and still resonates today. A French army under Simon de Montfort headed south, sacking Béziers, massacring its population, occupying Carcassonne and burning heretics.[1] Occitan resistance to Simon de Montfort's army fell apart at the battle of Muret, on 12 September 1213, with the death of Peter II of Aragon. Then three years after proclaiming the Albigensian Crusade, in 1211, Innocent ordered the preaching of a new crusade in Spain, which resulted in the stunning Christian victory over the Moors in July the following year at Las Navas de Tolosa. Meanwhile at the end of 1211 or the beginning of 1212 Frederick II laid claim to the Holy Roman Empire and joined Philip Augustus of France in his war against John of England and the then Holy Roman Emperor, Otto IV of Brunswick. The war culminated in the battle of Bouvines on 27 July 1214, marking the permanent English loss of Brittany and Normandy and Frederick's acquisition of the imperial crown. And five months before the battle of Muret, to launch a new crusade to the Holy Land, the pope issued his great crusade encyclical *Quia major*, which was to be the main focus of the Lateran council held in 1215. During the second half of April and early May 1213 copies of this supreme example of papal crusade propaganda were issued to almost all the provinces of Latin Christendom.[2] Then at the

---

[1] The story of the Albigensian Crusade has been told many times: see Introduction, n. 26, p. 8. For a complete list of texts relating to the Albigensian Crusade, not indicated here, see Alvira Cabrer, 'Del *Sepulcro* y los *sarracenos meridionales*', pp. 216–17, and for a detailed account of Occitan literary views of the crusade see Ghil, *L'Age de Parage*. For papal thinking and its justification of crusading against Christians see Housley, *The Later Crusades*, pp. 234–35.
[2] See Riley-Smith, *The Crusades. Idea and Reality*, p. 118.

1215 council sentence was pronounced on Raymond VI of Toulouse, depriving him definitively of his lands and provisionally sequestering those of the count of Foix.

When Innocent died on 16 July 1216, Honorius III enthusiastically took over his predecessor's programme. From late 1217 crusaders began to arrive in Acre in dribs and drabs, and the army eventually made its way to Damietta, which surrendered to the crusaders in August 1218. However, by the early winter it was struck down by a serious epidemic, an icy winter was followed by a burning summer, some crusaders sailed for home, and poor decisions were made in negotiations with Sultan al-Kāmil. A crusade which came near to success ended in failure. By 8 September 1221 it was over and the sultan entered Damietta.[3]

The Fifth Crusade

The crusade to Damietta provoked a mixed response in both North and South. Initial enthusiasm gave way to doubts and eventually, in the light of the Albigensian Crusade, to cynicism.

Even before Innocent issued his bull *Quia major*, troubadour song was apparently being recruited in appeals for a new oriental expedition. After accepting a five-year truce with Sultan al-Adil which would come into force in July 1212, the recently crowned king of Acre, John of Brienne, sent repeated messages to the pope, urging him to proclaim a new crusade to coincide with the truce's end. It is at this time, after the coronation of Otto IV as Holy Roman Emperor in 1209 and before Frederick II laid claim to the Empire at the end of 1211 or the beginning of 1212, that Carlo Pulsoni situates an anonymous Occitan crusade song which exhorts Philip, Otto and John to put an end to their fratricidal wars and direct all their energies towards the reconquest of the Holy Land (BdT 323.22).

> Al rei Felip et an Oto
> et al rei Ioan eisamen,
> laus que fasson acordamen
> entr'els e segon lo perdo,
> e servon a Sancta Maria,
> don sos fils pert la senhoria
> de Suria, del comte de
> Sur tro al regne d'Egipte.   (vv. 33–40)

I urge King Philip and Lord Otto, and King John as well, to make peace among themselves and pursue the pardon, and serve Holy Mary whose son has lost the lordship of Syria, from the county of Tyre to the kingdom of Egypt.

The troubadour sends the song to an unspecified lord in Germany: some minor nobleman, Pulsoni suggests, conceivably Otto von Bolentauben, count of Hennen-

---

[3] Runciman, *History*, III, pp. 144–70; see also Asbridge, *The Crusades*, pp. 551–62.

berg and Anhalt, who lived for many years in Syria, where in 1206 he married Beatrice, daughter of Joscelin III (or IV), seneschal of Jerusalem.

Quia maior sparked off several troubadour crusade songs, some supporting the pope's plans, some critical. Writing in northern Italy at the court of William Malaspina, Aimeric de Peguilhan urged men to go to the rescue of the holy sepulchre under the guidance of 'the constant, wise and good Pope Innocent' (BdT 10.11):

> Ara parra qual seran enveyos
> d'aver lo pretz del mon e·l pretz de Dieu,
> que bel poiran guazanhar ambedos
> selh que seran adreitamen romieu
> al sepulcre cobrar. Las! Cal dolor
> que Turc aian forsat Nostre Senhor!
> Pensem el cor la dezonor mortal
> e de la crotz prendam lo sanh senhal
> e passem lai, que·l ferms e·l conoissens
> nos guizara, lo bos pap'Innocens.   (vv. 1–10)

Now is the time when it will be apparent who wishes to have the world's esteem and God's esteem, for the ones who will rightfully be pilgrims to recover the holy sepulchre will be well able to gain both. Alas! How painful it is that the Turks have violently assaulted Our Lord! Let us reflect in our hearts on this deadly dishonour, let us take up the holy sign of the cross and make the voyage overseas, for the constant, wise and good pope Innocent will guide us.

Praising his patron for being swift to take the cross, he exhorts Marquis William VI of Montferrat to do likewise, and blames the kings and the emperor for not making peace. His incipit, *Ara parra ...*, echoes Bertran de Born's call for the support of Conrad of Monferrat in Tyre, and Bertran's model, Conon de Béthune's famous *Ahi! Amors, con dure departie* (RS 1125).

The troubadour Pons de Capdoill, a nobleman from the Auvergne, does not actually name Innocent as Aimeric does, but he responds no less explicitly, and at first positively, to the pope's preaching drive (BdT 375.8):

> Seignor, pois sai nos a trames
> per cardenals e per legatz
> absout cel q'es en loc pausatz
> de saint Peire, cui Dieus promes
> q'en cel et en terra pogues
> solver chascun de sos pechatz,
> qui so non cre, al mieu veiaire,
> fals es e fellos e trichaire
> e de nostra lei mescrezens.[4]   (vv. 13–21)

---

4   I have added a comma in v. 16 to Mulholland's text; the translation is hers.

Lords, since St Peter's representative, to whom God promised that in heaven and on earth he might absolve each one of his sins, has sent us an indulgence here through cardinals and legates, it seems to me that whoever does not believe this is false and treacherous and deceitful and one who misbelieves our religion.

His address to *Seignor* mirrors the term used by ecclesiastical preachers in vernacular sermons aimed at a lay audience,[5] and the terms in which he introduces the indulgence echo *Quia major* in summary: 'For we [...] by that power of binding and loosing that God has conferred on us [...] grant to all those submitting to this labour personally or at their own expense full forgiveness of their sins.'[6] Like Aimeric, Pons wishes Philip and Frederick, Otto and John would make peace, and seeks to persuade his listeners that going on crusade will make even the lowest of men noble and courtly (*pros e cortes*), and so cleansed of their sins that they will not need to be tonsured or suffer hardship in a strict monastic order. Francesco Saverio Annunziata suggests that the troubadour may be alluding negatively to the choice of some of his contemporaries to enter the monastic life as a means of expiating their sins after a dissolute life, and observes that from the earliest days popes were in fact inclined to present the duty to go on crusade as the main form of penance for *milites*.[7]

As Annunziata has observed, a second song by this troubadour (BdT 375.22), probably composed shortly afterwards, is very different in tone. While he still blames the lay rulers for staying in the West 'making war for silver and for land', he turns against the clergy, specifically attacking them for losing all interest in the oriental expedition: they are more concerned to disinherit Christians at home, and to censor criticism by accusing people of sinfulness – perhaps even heresy.

> Cui que sabon las leise a las leissos
> e·ls bes e·ls mals no·i volon jes anar;
> q'ie·n sai de tals c'amon deseretar
> mais crestians que sarrazis fellos;
> e si·n parlatz diran vos q'etz pechaire;
> e cill qe·is fant dels autres predicaire
> deurion si predicar eissamen,
> mas cobeitatz tol a clercia·l sen.   (vv. 33–40)

---

[5] For details of specific echoes of *Quia major* in this text see Annunziata's commentary on <http://www.rialto.unina.it/PoChapt/375.8/375.8(Mulholland-idt).htm>, accessed 6 December 2016. For this particular point see his n. 13, referring to M. Zink, *La Prédication en langue romane avant 1300* (Paris, 1976), p. 140.
[6] Riley-Smith, *The Crusades: Idea and Reality*, p. 121.
[7] See Annunziata, n. 31–32 on <http://www.rialto.unina.it/PoChapt/375.8/375.8(Mulholland-idt).htm>, accessed 6 December 2016.

> Those who are experts in the Scriptures and lessons do not want to go there (to the Holy Land) at all; for I know some that prefer to disinherit Christians rather than the evil Saracens; and if you speak of it they will say you are sinful; but those who act like preachers to others should preach to themselves in the same way, but greed makes the clergy lose their senses.[8]

Annunziata explains this shift of viewpoint in relation to events of the Albigensian Crusade and the circumstances of the troubadour's own life. The composition ends with a dedication to the king of Aragon, whom Pons praises for his ability to serve God, and who is likely to have been Peter II, one of the victors at the battle of Las Navas de Tolosa (17 July 1212). At the beginning of June 1213 Innocent III, pressed by the papal legates in the Midi, gave new impetus to the crusade against the Albigensians, and Peter became the focal point of southern barons anticipating the decisive encounter with the crusaders. On the more personal front Pons had also for many years found himself in conflict with episcopal power supported by the French Crown in his territorial holdings in the Velay. Fighting against Robert bishop of Clermont in support of Guy and Dalfi of Auvergne, he ended up in 1211 losing the lordship of Vertaizon, and he was also at odds with the bishop of Le Puy, Robert of Mehun. There is no reason to doubt Pons' genuine commitment to the eastern crusade, for in this same song he announces his own intention to take part (v. 25). His *vida* says he did so, and that he died overseas, even if there is no historical corroboration of this. His personal conflicts with regional bishops may well have particularly rankled as he saw the pope's oriental project becoming obscured by the crusade against heresy in lands not far from his own, under the aegis of overbearing and self-serving prelates.

A third, more general and non-polemical song of exhortation by this troubadour (BdT 375.2) reminds those who seek conquest 'on this side of the sea' that they will have no benefit from this in the next world, and instructs those who are too old or ill to go to the Holy Land to give money to those who will. Annunziata observes that this last element is further evidence of Pons' familiarity with the bull *Quia major*, in which the pope introduced the new idea that those who contributed to financing soldiers to go on crusade without taking part themselves could share in the same spiritual benefits of the crusade.[9] No references to historical events or figures offer a clue to the dating, though the piece is generally thought to belong to the same period as his other two crusade songs. Lewent argues that its timelessness suggests it may be the earliest of the three; one might equally well speculate that the opening words, 'Ar nos sia capdels e garentia / cel qui guidet tres reis en Betleem' ('Now may He who guided the three kings to Bethlehem be our

---

[8] Mulholland: 'but covetousness makes learning meaningless', which is also possible.

[9] In 1187–1188 Conon de Béthune had already declared that 'All the clergy and the old men who stay behind performing deeds of charity and good works will have their share in this pilgrimage' (RS 1125, vv. 25–27), without explicitly stating that this involved financing soldiers (see Chapter 3, p. 50).

guide and protector'), would be particularly appropriate for a solemn moment of crusading commitment, perhaps when Pons took his vow, or even at the moment of departure.[10]

An Old French crusade song of exhortation by an unknown author may also be a consequence of *Quia major* (RS 1967). Its tone is very different from that of the troubadours, emphasising tender feelings rather than argument. It begins with an invocation to lovers at dawn:

> Vous ki ameis de vraie amor,
> anveilliez vos, ne dormeis pais!
> L'aluëte nos trait lou jor
> et si nos dist an ces refrais
> ke venus est li jors de paix
> ke Deus, per sa tres grant dousor,
> promet a ceaz ki por s'amor
> panront la creus et por lour fais
> sofferront poinne neut et jor.
> Dont vairait Il ces amans vrais!   (vv. 1–10)

You who love with true love, wake up, sleep no more! The lark brings us the dawn and tells us with its warbling that the day of peace has come which God, in his great sweetness, promises to those who for love of him will take the cross, and for their sins will suffer pain both night and day. Then he will see who truly loves him!

This is how Anna Radaelli (see the online edition) describes the mellifluously affective yet also hard-headedly mercantile appeal of this song:

> The opening is that of a *cantio vigilum*, which associates the song with the liturgical tradition of the *vigiliae* and morning hymns. The text takes the form of an announcement of good news, as if it were the expression of the biblical κήρυγμα (*kérugma*) in which the herald, God's official spokesman, publicly proclaims that the time is fulfilled and the faithful are invited to repent and amend their lives. The lark, messenger of the day, is the mystical reflection of the annunciation of Christ's coming and the opportunity to emerge from the darkness of sin and renew the pact of fidelity with God by taking the *votum crucis*. The use of traditional preaching motifs (the *dies irae*, the account of the Passion, the *memento mori*) together with the use of proverbs having a mercantile flavour, clothes the song in the garb of a public sermon, and reveals the type of lay, bourgeois audience to whom the song is addressed.

The dating is uncertain, but because of the song's relation to the work of Philip the Chancellor she proposes to situate it after the first decade of the thirteenth

---

[10] Lewent, 'Das altprovenzalische Kreuzlied', p. 352.

century, at a time when a new crusade was being preached: 'for example, the period beginning with the appeal launched by Innocent III in his bull *Quia maior nunc* of April 1213'.

But not all Old French songs unequivocally supported the Church's efforts. Huon de Saint-Quentin blames the plight of Jerusalem on the Church for allowing crusaders to commute their vows (RS 1576):

> Nostre pastour gardent mal leur berbis
> quant pour deniers cascuns al leu les vent,
> mais li pechiés les a si tous souspris
> k'il ont mis Dieu en oubli pour l'argent.
> Que devenront li riche garniment
> k'il aquierent assés vilainement
> des faus loiers k'il ont des croisiés pris?
> Saichiés de voir k'il en seront repris,
> se loiautés et Dius et fois ne ment;
> retolu ont et Achre et Belleent
> ce que cascuns avoit a Diu pramis.
>
> Ki osera jamais en nul sermon
> de Dieu parler em place n'em moustier,
> ne anoncier ne bien fait ne pardon,
> [*missing line*]
> chose qui puist Nostre Segneur aidier
> a la terre conquerre et gaaignier
> u de son sanc paia no räençon?
> Segneur prelat, ce n'est ne bel ne bon
> que son secors faites si detriier:
> vos avés fait, ce poet on tesmoignier,
> de Deu Rolant et de vos Guenelon.   (vv. 12–33)

Our shepherds take little care of their sheep when each of them sells them to the wolf for money, but sin has so taken hold of them that they have forgotten God for the sake of silver. What will become of the rich ornaments they acquire most shamefully with the fraudulent payment they have taken from the crusaders? Be well aware that they will be blamed for this, if loyalty and God and faith do not lie; they have stolen from Acre and Bethlehem what each had promised to God.

Who will dare to preach and speak of God any more in square or cloister, and announce benefits and indulgences, [when no one is disposed to perform] anything which can assist Our Lord to conquer and win back the land where He paid our ransom with His blood? Lord prelates, it is neither good nor just that you so delay his help: you, this can certainly be said, have made Roland of God and Ganelon of yourselves.

He is also particularly concerned about the plight of Christian prisoners in the Holy Land.

> En celui n'a mesure ne raison
> ki se conoist, s'il n'aïe a vengier
> ceuls ki pour Dieu sont dela em prison
> et pour oster lor ames de dangier.
> Puis c'on muert ci, on ne doit resoignier
> paine n'anui, honte ne destorbier:
> pour Dieu est tout quan c'on fait en son non,
> ki en rendra cascun tel guerredon
> que cuers d'ome nel poroit esprisier;
> car paradis en ara de loier,
> n'ainc pour si peu n'ot nus si riche don.   (vv. 34–44)

There is no wisdom nor intelligence in anyone who knows this without helping to avenge those who are over there in prison for God's sake, and to remove their souls from danger. Since one has to die here, one should not fear pain or torment, shame or harm: everything one does in his name is for God, who will give to each such a reward that the heart of man could not appreciate its worth; for he will receive paradise as a reward, and no one has ever had such a rich gift for so little.

This reference to prisoners has until recently led scholars to date the song to the months following the fall of Damietta, when in Europe the hostages' fate must have still been unknown (September–November 1221). Huon also composed a *Complainte de Jérusalem contre Rome* in which he explicitly alludes to the loss of Damietta. However, Barbieri has argued that its hortatory tone, the fact that his lyric makes no mention of Damietta and that it refers to key places in the Holy Land (v. 21) rather than Egypt suggests instead the initial phase of the crusade, at the time of the reverses suffered by the Christians in Palestine (November–December 1217), before the arrival of the new contingents and the beginning of the campaign in Egypt.

Preparations for the crusaders' departure for the East produced a further clutch of songs in both Occitan and Old French. After Frederick II was crowned King of the Romans in 1215 and took the cross for the first time, Guillem Figueira pressed him to fulfil the promise of this good beginning, exhorting all who were willing to 'die and live' for God to seek salvation in the Holy Land (BdT 217.7). He probably composed his song in Italy, perhaps at the emperor's own request or in the hope of his favour, addressing him in flattering terms:

> Reys Frederics, vos etz frugz de joven,
> e frug de pretz, e frug de conoyssensa,
> e si manjatz del frug de penedensa,
> feniretz be lo bon comensamen.   (vv. 49–52)

King Frederick, you are the fruit of youth [courtly qualities], and fruit of merit, and fruit of learning, and if you eat of the fruit of penitence you will end well the good beginning.

The Châtelain d'Arras composed a *chanson de départie* before setting out for Syria (RS 140) in which he sees his ship foundering, not literally as the result of the imminent voyage, but metaphorically because of the lady's siren allurements. Guiot de Dijon's well-known *Chanterai por mon corage* (RS 21), in the voice of a woman fearing for her lover's safety overseas, may also date from this period.

Troubadours and trouvères were in touch with each other at this time. The rubric to MS H of the Burgundian trouvère Hugues de Berzé's song RS 37a, composed between 1213 and 1221,[11] informs us that 'Sir Hughes de Berzé sent these *coblas* to Falqet de Romans by means of a jongleur who was called Bernart d'Argentau, to exhort him to come overseas with him.' The text begins by admonishing his friend that after spending a great part of their life in pleasure-seeking, 'par qe fareit ben esmender sa vie, / car a la fin es for de joglaria' ('it looks as if it would be good to amend one's life, for the time for diversion is coming to an end', vv. 7–8). He also invites Marquis William VI of Monferrat, at whose court Falquet was probably residing, to join him in a pilgrimage to Outremer, highlighting the kinship links between the Monferrat family and Frederick II, who was supposed to take part in the expedition and finance it from his own resources:

Ni ja d'aver porter ne seit pensis,
qe sos cosis l'emperere Freeris
n'avra assez, qui ne li faudra mie,
qu'il l'acuilli molt bel en Lombardie.   (vv. 25–28)

Do not worry about taking money, for his cousin, the emperor Frederick, will have plenty and he will not refuse it to him, since the marquis gave him a great welcome in Lombardy.

Although William of Monferrat took the cross and planned to lead an expedition to Egypt, he abandoned this idea once he became involved in the question of the succession in the kingdom of Thessalonica, and there is no evidence that Hugues de Berzé took the cross again on his return from the Fourth Crusade or left for the Holy Land a second time.

Other pieces whose dates are impossible to pin down beyond the likelihood of having been composed in the first half of the thirteenth century include an anonymous Old French song of courtly love from Outremer (RS 227b) and an extraordinary *lai* in hybrid Old French and Occitan (BdT 461.122). The latter was possibly composed by a member of the aristocratic family of Caumont La Force, and dram-

---

[11] The reference to Frederick as emperor does not necessarily mean the song pre-dates his coronation in November 1220: see Barbieri's discussion in his online edition under 'About the text'.

atises a lover's conflicting emotions as he heads for the ship that will take him away to the East. In some ways it typifies common themes of crusade songs: the lover's reluctance to abandon love of an earthly lady in favour of God's service in the Holy Land and the dangers and hardships of the sea crossing; but rather than treating these solemnly it does so with an engaging lightness of touch, self-deprecation and playful teasing. It is also, and above all, a virtuoso piece which interweaves complex versification, melodic themes and stanzaic forms, and a sophisticated handling of point of view, since while the first-person poet and lover seem the same, the lover appears to move spatially away from and then back to the lady, while the poet stands before an audience, in a beguiling blend of the real and the imaginary.[12]

The Albigensian Crusade

If Pons de Capdoill in the Auvergne decries the interference of the Albigensian crusade with the proper pursuit of God's business to which he is personally committed, in the Languedoc, troubadours' resentment at the French invasion deeply colours their view of any eastern expedition. Raimon de Miraval had a personal motive for hoping for King Peter of Aragon's support. The French had captured Carcassonne, seat of the viscounts of Béziers, in 1209, and the troubadour's castle of Miraval some time between then and 1211. The castle of Montagut fell to Simon in 1211, was taken back in the same year and then recaptured by him in 1213. By dedicating a song to the king, Raimon reminds him to recapture local territories, which include the troubadour's own castle (BdT 406.12).

> Chansos, vai me dir al rei
> cui jois guid'e vest e pais,
> q'en lui non a ren biais,
> c'aital cum ieu vuoill lo vei;
> ab que cobre Montagut
> e Carcasson'el repaire,
> pois er de pretz emperaire,
> e doptaran son escut
> sai Frances e lai Masmut.   (vv. 55–63)

Song, go on my behalf and tell the king, whom joy guides and clothes and nourishes, that there is nothing blameworthy in him, for I see him as I wish to see him; as long as he recovers Montagut and returns to Carcassonne, he will then be emperor of merit, and here the French, there the Muslims will fear his shield.

But soon Peter was dead on the battlefield, and worse was to come. At the Lateran council of 1215 Innocent pronounced sentence on Raymond VI of Toulouse,

---

[12] L. Paterson, 'Anonymous (Nompar de Caumont?). *Finament* (BdT 461.122)', *Lt*, 23 (December 2014), 1–35.

depriving him of his lands. Tomier and Palaizi, two urban knights from Toulouse, thundered their shock and outrage what they saw as this appalling treatment and urged him to defy the clergy and fight back (BdT 442.2).[13]

> Mas chascus pes e conssire
> et en Tolosa se mire:
> qu'i·l plus rics a pietz d'ausire;
> e qui sen avia,
> mais valria guerreges   que s'avol plag fazia.
>
> Mais val que hom si deffenda
> que hom l'ausia ni·l prenda,
> que mot n'a malvaiz'esmenda
> d'avesques, cui Dieus deissenda.
> Ar prec chascun que m'entenda
> cals fon la bausia
> que feiron a sel de Fois,   car en lor se plevia.   (vv. 10–21)

Let each man ponder and reflect, and contemplate Toulouse for himself: there the greatest nobleman has the worst mistreatment, and it is clear to anyone who has any sense that it would be better to wage war, for he made a base agreement. It is better for a man to defend himself than be killed or taken prisoner, for [if he surrenders] he has poor compensation from the bishops – God bring them low! I now ask everyone to realise what treachery they committed towards the count of Foix, because he trusted them.

Their focus is on the situation of Toulouse, its allies and defectors, particularly William of Baux, but at the same time the troubadours accuse the French and the clergy for indifference to the Holy Land and obstruction of the routes into to Syria:

> Pauc a en Deu d'esperanssa
> qui·l sepulcre desenansa,
> car clergue e sel de Franssa
> preson pauc la desonranza
> de Dieu, qu'en penra venjansa.
> C'ab lur raubaria
> an tout los camins e·ls portz   d'Acre e de Suria.   (vv. 43–49)

Anyone who abandons the sepulchre has little hope in God: the clergy and the Frenchman care little for the dishonour inflicted on God, but he will be avenged on them, for with their brigandage they have seized (rendered impassable) the paths and mountain passes to Acre and Syria.

---

[13] See F. S. Annunziata, 'Tomier e Palaizi, *Si co.l flacs molins torneia* (BdT 442.2), *Lt*, 6 (2013), 1–23 (http://www.lt.unina.it/Annunziata-2013).

Those of the Languedoc had particular reason to complain of the consequences for the Holy Land of the papacy's extension of crusading to the fight against Christian heretics. But they were not alone. Housley has shown that in 1207 Innocent III himself expressed concern about the risk of dissipating the Western resources which were essential for the survival of the Crusader States, 'and the representatives of Latin Syria proved quick to complain that "the most urgent need of the Holy Land" was not being helped by the offer to western knights of the same indulgence granted to those who went to Syria'.[14] The troubadours are tapping into wider concerns.

Burlesque

This period sees the notable troubadour development of the burlesque treatment of crusading themes. Shortly after 1212, Guillem Ademar (BdT 202.9) assures King Alfonso 'whom the Muslims fear', and 'the best count in Christendom' – likely to be Alfonso VIII of Castile and Raymond VI of Toulouse – of total forgiveness of sins if they take all the jealous husbands off to fight the Muslims. In a *descort* Guiraut de Calanson asserts that he would not need to make a pilgrimage to save his soul if his lady gave him what he most desires from her.[15] And in a debate poem composed some time between 1219 and 1245, Count Raymond Berenguer of Provence asks his debating partner Arnaut whether he is prepared to emit a great fart to help ladies on board a becalmed ship reach the Holy Land or return home (BdT 184.1).

> Amics N'Arnauz, cent domnas de parage
> van outramar e son a meça via,
> e non podon acomplir lor viage
> n'endrez tornar per nuilla ren qe sia
> se per vos non, qe es per tal coven
> c'un pez fassaz de qe·s movan tal ven
> que las domnas vadan a salvamen.
> Farez l'o non? Q'eu saber lo volria.   (vv. 1–8)

Friend Sir Arnaut, a hundred ladies of rank are going to the Holy Land and are half-way there, and they are unable to complete their voyage or to return directly home by any means but through you, namely on condition you let out a fart from which such wind will arise that the ladies will be saved. Will you do this or not? For I should like to know.

---

[14] Housley, 'Crusades against Christians', p. 29.
[15] BdT 243.1, ed. by W. Ernst, 'Die Lieder des provenzalischen Trobadors Guiraut von Calanso', *RF*, 44, 2 (1930), 255–406, poem 8, vv. 68–71 (pp. 325 and 342). Guiraut's datable songs were composed during the period from before 1202 to 1214.

It is unclear whether the count of Provence is participating in person or whether part of the joke lies in attributing scatalogical comments to him by means of a fictive speaker. The tone of both these pieces may represent a light-hearted rather than derisive treatment of crusading themes, though by the time Charles of Anjou is count of Provence and Sordel is harking back to the topic of maritime winds it has become noticeably more cynical.[16]

Amidst the distraction, resentment and disaffection brought about by the Albigensian Crusade, the failure of the crusade to Damietta and disenchantment at the commutation of crusading vows, the newly crowned emperor Frederick II of Hohenstaufen offered a beacon of hope. Troubadours sang in support of his crusading intentions. As he became embroiled in conflict with the papacy, this support would become more and more a matter of politics.

---

[16] See Chapter 9, p. 134. A song by Gontier de Soignies (RS 1404) may also belong to this period. The lovelorn speaker declares his desire to renounce the world, voyage overseas and live among the Templars, where he will no more hear love spoken of every day.

7

Frederick II and the Sixth Crusade

After Damietta: exhortations

When Frederick II took the cross in Aachen on 25 July 1215, during his second coronation as King of the Romans, he did so 'in the manner of a crusader, exhorted his followers to do likewise, and spent the following day, a Sunday, in the cathedral from dawn to dusk, listening to crusade sermons'. David Abulafia suggests that this act sprang not only from religious conviction and gratitude to God for His blessings, but also from subtle statesmanship. Frederick had acted without papal approval, implying that the leadership of the crusade lay at least as much with the secular arm as with the spiritual. As time would further show, he was not a 'great respecter of papal control over the crusading movement'.[1]

His solemn commitment was followed by years of delay, due to his political concerns in Germany and Sicily. Innocent III granted him leave to postpone his expedition until he had put the affairs in Germany in order. His successor, Honorius III, regarded Frederick's promises as genuine and sent messages to the crusaders in Egypt telling them to expect his army, and in November 1220 crowned him and his wife Constance Emperor and Empress. In return Frederick definitely promised to set out for the East next spring, but delayed again. On 30 August 1221 the defeated Christians agreed to abandon Damietta, which they did on 7 September, and to observe an eight-year truce.

Between this time and the summer of 1222 the troubadour Peirol made a pilgrimage to Jerusalem, possibly having been present at the final loss of Damietta on 7 September 1221 and visiting the Holy Land after the Christians vacated the city.[2] On his way home to Marseille he composed a song of thanks to God for

---

[1] D. Abulafia, *Frederick II: A Medieval Emperor* (London, 1988), pp. 121–22.
[2] Lewent, 'Das altprovenzalische Kreuzlied', p. 339. In this case, if we are to take seriously Peirol's reference to having been away for about a year, he would appear to have been part of a contingent that went to help those already involved in the Fifth Crusade. However, he could have set out on a pilgrimage directly to the Holy Land straight after the beginning of the truce.

letting him visit the holy places (BdT 366.28). Elation at his experiences blends with personal reminiscences, including some interaction with local Muslims. He singles out for particular mention the non-knightly brethren attached to the military orders, perhaps because he mixed with them.

> Pus flum Jordan ai vist e·l Monimen,
> a vos, vers Dieus, qu'es senher dels senhors,
> ne ren merces qar vos plac tan d'onors
> que·l sancte loc on nasques veramen
> m'avetz mostrat, don ai mon cor jauzen;
> quar s'ieu era em Proensa d'un an
> no·m clamarian Sarrazis Johan.
>
> Ara·ns don Dieus bona vi'e bon ven,
> e bona nau e bos governadors,
> qu'a Marcelha m'en vuelh tornar de cors,
> quar sieu[s] era de lay mar veramen.
> Acre e Sur e Tripol e.l sirven
> e l'Espital e·l Templ'e·l rey Johan
> coman a Dieu, e l'aigua de Rotlan.   (vv. 1–14)

Now that I have seen the River Jordan and the holy sepulchre, I give thanks to you, true God who are lord of lords, for having so graciously pleased to show me the holy place where you were truly born; this fills my heart with joy, for had I been in Provence for the last year, the Saracens would not be calling me 'John' [probably a generic term analogous to 'Tommy'].

Now may God give us a good passage and fair wind, and a good ship and good pilots, since I wish to speed back to Marseille, for truly [for a long time?] I was his [man] overseas: Acre and Tyre, Tripoli and the sergeant-brethren, and the Hospital and the Temple and King John I commend to God, and the waters of Roland.

He not only bids these places and people farewell but also signals his concern for what he leaves behind. There used to be great crusade leaders all over the Western world, he declares: but what will their successors be like? Following a general denigration of contemporary rulers he homes in on the emperor, who has taken 'many an oath from which he is now trying to extricate himself'. The imperial eagle risks dishonour from cowardice and indifference to the fate of Christendom:

> Emperador, Damiata·us aten,
> e nueg e jorn plora la blanca tors
> per vostr'aigla que·n gitet us voutors:
> volpilla es aigla qe voutor pren!
> Anta·y avetz, e·l soudan onramen,
> e part l'anta avetz hi tug tal dan
> que nostra ley s'en vai trop rezeguan.   (vv. 29–35)

Emperor, Damietta awaits you, and night and day the White Tower mourns for your eagle which a vulture has cast down from it: cowardly is the eagle taken by a vulture! In this you receive shame, and the sultan honour, and beyond the shame all of you suffer the damage of our religion heading for the rocks.

In the early years after the fall of Damietta, papal policy was to urge Frederick to take up arms against the Muslims in the East, and from 1223, in the face of widespread apathy, preachers had travelled to all parts of Europe to attempt to drum up enthusiasm for his crusade.³ Abulafia states that the papacy was helped in this by 'the propaganda poems of the troubadour Peirol'.⁴ There are in fact no other songs by Peirol which could be regarded in this light, but the Church could in theory have used this one for such purposes.⁵

Elias Cairel delivers two exhortations to Frederick in 1224–1225. He may have been supporting the Church's preaching drive, but he has other fish to fry, hoping that enthusiasm for crusading will have a knock-on effect on events in Greece. In 1224 he addresses the emperor with a mixture of flattery and criticism, reproaching him for overly delaying his departure for the Holy Land (BdT 133.13, vv. 33–40). However, in the second *tornada* he turns to William of Monferrat, goading him with accusations of cowardice and a warning that he will lose his supporters in Greece and a kingdom (vv. 45–48).

While in Thessalonica under the rule of Boniface of Monferrat, Elias had enjoyed the patronage of the Lombard lord Ravano delle Carceri and his mistress, then wife, Isabella, who had engaged in a bantering *tenso* with him and to whom he addressed several songs.⁶ After Boniface's death in 1207 various Lombard lords, including Ravano, refused to accept his two-year-old son Demetrius as his heir. Demetrius was Boniface's son by his wife Margaret (or Maria) of Hungary, former wife of the Greek emperor Isaac II Angelus, and had formed a part of Boniface's policy of legitimising and strengthening his rule in Thessalonica. Instead of Demetrius the Lombards sought to establish William of Monferrat,⁷ the son of Boniface by a

---

³ T. C. Van Cleve, *The Emperor Frederick II of Hohenstaufen, immutator mundi* (Oxford, 1972), p. 160.
⁴ Abulafia, *Frederick II*, p. 149, citing this piece only.
⁵ V. De Barthomolaeis ('Osservazioni sulle poesie provenzali relative a Federico II', *Memorie della Real Accademia delle scienze dell'Isituto di Bologna. Classe di scienze morali, sezione storico-filologica*, serie I, vol. 6, 1911–1912, pp. 97–124, on p. 103) argued that at the time of composition Peirol might have been at some Italian port from where the song could have reached him in Sicily, Calabria, Apulia or Campania.
⁶ See Chapter 5, p. 121.
⁷ Given as William IV in the *Dizionario Biografico degli Italiani*, ed. A. M. Ghisalberti and M. Pavan (Rome, 1960–), 60 (2003): see <http://www.marchesimonferrato.com/web2007/_pages/gen_summary.php?DR=all&URL=marchesidelmonferrato.com&LNG=IT&L=3&C=2&T=news&D=IT{96A4A08D-EDDA-C5FF-947D-9A982017484D}&A=0>, and as William VI in R. L. Wolff and H. W. Hazard, *The Later Crusades, 1189–1311*, vol. II of K. M. Setton, ed., *A History of the Crusades*, 6 vols (Madison and London, 1969–1989), p. 870 (Index).

previous marriage, as ruler. Elias had urged him to come and defend his hereditary rights, goading him with insults.[8] On his return from Greece Elias sought patronage in Spain and then at various courts in northern Italy, and for a while he was in the entourage of Frederick II, but in BdT 133.4, composed in the autumn of 1220 just before Frederick's coronation as Emperor,[9] he announces that he can no longer follow 'the gracious king who will now be emperor', and who 'keeps me so thin a file can't bite into me' (vv. 31–34).

Elias' complaint of the emperor's delayed departure is followed up during 1225, when he bemoans the continuing delay of Western rulers in setting out for the Holy Land and north Africa, and their failure to defend their interests in Greece (BdT 133.11).[10] He urges counts, kings, barons and marquises to stop killing each other in war: 'they will destroy Christendom like this, but they ought rather to kill Turks and pagans and recover our rightful home, Jerusalem, and conquer Cairo'. At the same time he presses William to avenge his father's death, and, now, in an about-turn, to prevent the disinheritance of his half-brother Demetrius, ousted by Michael Comnenus Ducas at the end of 1224 and fled to Italy. Instead of perceiving Demetrius as William's rival, as he had done in 1207, Elias realises that Thessalonica is lost to the whole house of Monferrat unless William acts with the utmost urgency in support of his half-brother's rights. He also sees Frederick's crusade as an opportunity to provide specific support for Greece and those whose interests he has long promoted, saying that the best way to the Holy Land is via Hungary and Greece, since they will find no opposition there and will be able to help Frederick's new wife, Yolanda (Isabella), the daughter of John of Brienne and queen of Jerusalem. Addressing the emperor in particular, Elias warns him that he will endanger his own soul if he fails to fulfil his crusading vow (vv. 41–48). But his admonitions to William are even less flattering:

> Marques Guillem, lo sojorn e·l dormir
> de Monferrat no voletz ges gurpir,
> tart venjaretz la mort del vostre paire
> ni·l deseret qu'om fai a vostre fraire.
>
> Be.n pot hom dir, 'Malvatz filhs de bon paire',
> e peza·m fort, mas no·n puesc alres faire. (vv. 49–54)

Marquis William, [if] you do not decide to abandon the comfort and repose of Monferrat, it will be difficult to avenge your father's death or the disinheriting of your brother.

---

[8] See Chapter 5, p. 121.
[9] For the dating see G. Lachin, *Il trovatore Elias Cairel* (Modena, 2004), pp. 333–34.
[10] For further details on the complex background to the piece see Lachin, *Elias Cairel*, pp. 392–401, especially pp. 398–401, and <http://www.rialto.unina.it/ElCair/133.11(Lachin).htm>.

People can well say of this, 'A bad son of a good father', and this grieves me much, but I can do no more about it.

It is hard to judge whether this piece was first performed in the presence of either, both or neither of these rulers.[11]

Some exhortations to Frederick may have been part of his own propaganda drive rather than that of the Church. On 25 July 1225 Frederick met with two papal legates at San Germano. Here he took an oath that he would start out for the East in August 1227, send 1,000 knights at once, and deposit 100,000 ounces of gold at Rome which would be forfeit to the Church should he break his vow. He summoned an imperial diet at Cremona over Easter 1226 to discuss his expedition, which Abulafia takes as an indication of how seriously he was in his crusading plans.[12] In a song likely to have been composed in Piedmont-Liguria at the court of Othon del Carret (BdT 156.2),[13] the troubadour Falquet de Romans urges him to make his move:

A l'emperador man,
pos valors renovella,
qe mov'ab esfortz gran
contra la gen fradella
ez haia en Dieus son cor,
qe Sarrazi e Mor
han tengut li destret
trop lonjamen
la terra on Dieus nasqet
e·l monumen,
e taing be qe per lui cobrat sia.   (vv. 45–55)

I send word to the Emperor, since valour is reviving, that he should move with a great army against the race of villains and have God in his heart, for Saracens and Moors have too long held sway over the sepulchre and the land where God was born, and it is right that they should be recovered for him.

Although there is no proof, Falquet could have produced it as a contribution to Frederick's relaunch of his crusading plans at Cremona.[14]

---

[11] On 25 July 1225 Frederick was in San Germano in Piedmont, and in Lombardy for the Diet of Cremona at Easter 1226. William was based in Monferrat all this time, prevented by illness from setting out on his expedition to Greece until the spring of 1226. In theory Elias could have produced his song straight after Frederick took his oath at San Germano, with it being known that Yolanda was or was soon to be Empress, and in theory William could have been there. On the other hand Elias may well have relied on the song being transmitted by others.
[12] Runciman, *History*, III, p. 177; Abulafia, *Frederick II*, p. 154.
[13] See the notes to this piece and to BdT 156.11 on Rialto.
[14] Abulafia, *Frederick II*, pp. 154–58.

Probably during the same period (end 1220–1227) Elias de Barjols composed a song which, like Falquet's, passes from the theme of love into a crusading exhortation (BdT 132.4). God, he declares, has chosen the emperor alone as crusade leader, and has now given him the means to act:

> Al valent emperador
> vuelh mostrar e dir
> que totz met Dieus en azir
> mas son servidor;
> e pus Dieus l'a donat de que,
> sierva·l a dreg l'emperaire,
> qu'om del mon no pot plus traire
> mas tant quant i fara de be.   (vv. 33–40)

To the noble emperor I wish to declare and announce that God disfavours all but his servant; and since God has given him the means, may the emperor rightly serve him [*or:* serve him justly], for a man can take no more from the world than the good that he will do in it.

The song was almost certainly composed in a Provençal environment. Frederick was never in Provence and there is no evidence that Elias ever travelled to Italy. Barachini tentatively suggests that he might have crossed the Alps and come into contact with the emperor's court between March and August 1226, the only time during the 1220s when Frederick was in north Italy.[15] An alternative is to see his exhortation as the expression either of his general standpoint concerning the next crusade, or else of his expectation that his message can be transmitted from Provence to the emperor's ears. Evidence from a Ghibelline *sirventes* by Falquet de Romans in 1228 (BdT 156.11, see below) shows that this was certainly possible.

During the two years 1225–1227 Frederick was trying to establish his rule in northern Italy against the 'determined enmity' of the Lombard League and so link up his German and south Italian lands. A song by Falquet de Romans (156.12), wholly devoted to crusading exhortation, bewails the spectacle of 'holy Christendom heading for disaster and destruction', 'the entire world lost and in turmoil', and 'counts and kings, dukes and emperors and many a baron and many a ruler [...] waging war out of sheer caprice'. Since it does not evoke the clergy or papacy, it is thought to date from the period following Frederick's coronation in 1220 but before the outbreak of papal–imperial hostilities after March 1227. Its allusions to war among secular rulers suggest the period of Lombard rebellion following Frederick's decision to hold the Diet of Cremona.

---

[15] As well as the Rialto edition see G. Barachini, *Il trovatore Elias de Barjols* (Rome, 2015), pp. 207–11.

Papal–imperial hostilities

In March 1227 Honorius died, and the new pope, Gregory IX, decided that it was imperative that Frederick now depart for the East. The emperor mustered a great army in Apulia throughout the summer of 1227, and although an epidemic of malaria struck the army, several thousand soldiers sailed from Brindisi in August under Duke Henry IV of Limburg. Frederick joined the army a few days later, and embarked on 8 September. Virtually immediately one of his companions fell desperately ill. The ship put in at Otranto, where his companion died and Frederick himself fell sick. He left the fleet, which he sent off to Acre under the patriarch of Jerusalem, Gerold of Lausanne, and went to recover his health at the spa of Pozzuoli. The Pope thought Frederick was yet again prevaricating. He excommunicated him at once, without even admitting into his presence the ambassadors who had arrived to explain the delay. Frederick issued a 'dignified manifesto to the princes of Europe denouncing Papal pretensions' and continued with his crusade preparations. Although the pope warned him he could not lawfully set out for Holy War while under interdict, he recovered from his illness and embarked from Brindisi with a small company on 28 June 1228. He arrived in Acre via Cyprus on 7 September; meanwhile news had arrived there that Gregory had excommunicated him again, this time for setting out on crusade before being absolved from his previous excommunication. This caused sharp divisions in the crusading army, because there was some doubt about whether oaths of fealty to him were valid. Despite lacking an army strong enough to strike a decisive blow against the Muslims, through this 'diplomatic crusade' Frederick succeeded in negotiating a ten-year peace treaty, signed on 18 February 1229, whereby Sultan al-Kāmil returned Jerusalem and other holy sites to the Crusader Kingdom and all prisoners on both sides were to be released.[16] He arrived home in June 1229, still under interdict. Now in open warfare against the papacy, his troops 'scored success after success against the papal forces. By the autumn of 1229 Frederick stood in full possession of his kingdom. It was now only necessary for him to make his peace with the defeated pope.' In May 1230 peace terms were drawn up, and on 28 August the excommunication was lifted.[17]

The troubadour Falquet de Romans evokes these turbulent events in a song of Ghibelline sympathies composed before Frederick's departure on 28 June 1228 (BdT 156.11). He declares that 'the world has been reduced to little worth, and definitely worst of all are the clergy, who ought to uphold the virtues but generally prefer war to peace, they are so in love with wickedness and sin', and begs 'the good emperor, who has taken the cross in order to serve God, to set out with force and vigour towards the land where God chose to die'. This apparently alludes to Frederick's illness the previous year and looks forward to his departure now that he has recovered his health. Disgusted by the present state of the world, Falquet expresses his wish to make the voyage himself on the first wave of crusaders. This was a song

---

[16] Runciman, *History*, III, p. 187.
[17] Wolff and Hazard, *The Later Crusades*, p. 461.

which clearly was expected to find its way from Provence to north Italy. There appear to be two main versions of it, both composed in Provence after Falquet's return there from Italy, one for a Provençal audience, the other for one in Liguria.[18] In both of them the troubadour appeals to the 'good emperor' (v. 41). Manuscripts from both versions (C and Tc) also address him in a tornada: 'Emperor, if you duly reflect on how God is doing your will you will show true love towards Him; for he wishes you to recover his inheritance, and you can be sure this is the truth' (vv. 61–65). The Tc version alone contains a second *tornada*, which sends the song across the Alps to Othon del Carret in Liguria, urging him to go to the Holy Land: 'Sirventes, pass Mont-Cénis and tell Othon del Carret that I am sending you as a messenger to tell him to go to where Jesus was born; then his good reputation will be crowned' (vv. 66–70).

Does the fact that he addresses the emperor mean that he expects the song eventually to be performed in his presence? Not necessarily. The direct appeals to Frederick may express a hope that it will come to his attention, or be simply a rhetorical device to signal his support for the emperor's crusade. He may have been encouraged to compose it by Frederick's supporters, such as his patron Othon del Carret. Abulafia (pp. 162–163) observes that the new situation under Gregory IX saw a generation of aggressive propagandists emerging from the University of Naples which Frederick had founded in 1224. It must be wondered to what extent Falquet's crusading exhortations belong to a propaganda drive ultimately directed by the emperor himself.

After Frederick's excommunication some of his German and Italian subjects changed sides to support the pope. They may be the particular target of Peire Cardenal's bitterly sarcastic *De sirventes sueilh servir* (BdT 335.18), probably composed in c.1228, just before Frederick's departure for the East. Unlike Alfonso VIII of Castile, who defeated the Saracen army at the battle of Las Navas de Tolosa in 1212, he declares, these men have criminally ignored God's cause in the Holy Land:

Dieus deu als barons grazir
qar ves lui son sort e mut,
qe·ll luec on fom rezemut
no volun tan possezir
qon l'autrui terra sazir,
e non crei qe·l reis n'Anfos
aitals fos,
anz volc envazir
turcs per crestianz aizir.   (vv. 28–36)

God should thank the barons for being deaf and dumb towards him, for they have less desire to possess the place where we were ransomed than to seize other people's land; but I do not believe that King Alfonso was like this; instead he wanted to attack Turks in order to ease the lot of Christians.

---

[18] For the arguments underpinning this statement and further details see the notes to the edition on Rialto, <http://www.rialto.unina.it/FqRom/156.11(Arveiller-Gouiran).htm>.

The war for the control of Cyprus

On 21 July 1228 Frederick landed in Cyprus. The king of that island, Hugh of Lusignan, had died in 1218 leaving his infant son Henry I as his heir, and the regency was taken over by Henry's mother, Alice of Champagne, who was linked by kinship to both the Lusignans and the Ibelins. She delegated it to Philip of Ibelin, John's younger brother, but after her remarriage to Bohemond of Antioch she tried to exclude Philip from the regency and to entrust it to another ambitious Cypriot nobleman, Aimery Barlais. This provoked a reaction on the part of the Cypriot court, which favoured the Ibelins, giving rise to the conflict which soon drew in Frederick II as well. After Philip's death in 1227 John of Ibelin, the 'Old Lord of Beirut', became regent of the island. Runciman describes him as at that time the greatest person in Outremer. 'He was rich; he owned the city of Beirut, and his wife was heiress of Arsuf. His personal qualities won him general respect. His birth, wealth and integrity had made him for some decades already the accepted leader of the baronage of Outremer. Half Levantine-French and half-Greek, he understood the East and its peoples and he was equally versed in the history and the laws of the Frankish kingdom.'[19]

When Frederick met with John at Limassol he presented him with rich gifts and invited him to a feast in his honour. His soldiers crept into the hall and stood behind each of the guests, with their swords drawn, whereupon Frederick demanded that John hand over his fief of Beirut together with all the revenues of Cyprus received since the death of King Hugh. John refused to be intimidated and declared that even if he were to be killed for it he would not break the laws of the land. Frederick broke out in threats and insults but finally agreed to submit his claims to the appropriate courts, demanding however that twenty nobles, including John's two sons, Balian and Baldwin, should be left with him as hostages and that John should come with him to Palestine. John withdrew to the castle known to the Franks as Dieu d'Amour (now Saint Hilarion), where he had already sent the ladies and the children of his household with ample stores of provisions. 'Feudal law laid down that, during a regency, the barons could not be ejected from castles entrusted to them by the late monarch. Frederick did not attempt now to flout the law.'[20] It was subsequently arranged that in exchange for the return of the hostages John would accompany Frederick to Acre and defend his right to Beirut before the High Court.

When Frederick returned to Acre in 1229 after his entry into Jerusalem, news from home forced him to compromise with the barons and the Templars, and to leave for Italy. On his return from Acre he made a fresh stop at Cyprus, where he sold the regency to five noblemen who had been instructed to exile all the friends of the Ibelins from the island.[21] These *baillis*, referred to by the trouvère Philippe

---

[19] Runciman, *History*, III, pp. 180–81.
[20] Runciman, *History*, III, p. 182.
[21] Runciman, *History*, III, p. 194.

de Novare, sought to procure the necessary sum at the expense of their political opponents, profiting from the absence of John of Ibelin, who had stayed in the Holy Land with his men, and in the meantime persuading Philippe de Novare to negotiate peace between them and the lord of Beirut. Once they had obtained money the five bailiffs decided to go back on the peace agreement and tried to have Philippe murdered. He found refuge with his men in the tower of the Hospitallers in Nicosia, from where he sent a plea for help to Balian of Ibelin. John, returning swiftly to Cyprus, confronted and defeated his enemies on the battlefield near Nicosia on 14 July 1229 (24 June according to the *Eracles*, followed by Mas Latrie 1852), subsequently besieging the castles where the bailiffs had taken refuge: Kyrenia, Dieudamour (Saint Hilarion) and La Candare (Kantara).[22]

In 1231, after making peace with the pope by the Treaty of San Germano on 23 July 1230, Frederick sent an army to the East under his marshal, the Neapolitan Richard Filangieri.[23] John left a small garrison in the castle of Beirut and sailed to Cyprus. Filangieri sent an ambassador to see King Henry of Cyprus with a message from Frederick telling him to banish the Ibelins and confiscate their lands. Henry replied that John was his uncle and that in any case he would not dispossess his own vassals. Filangieri then sailed straight for Beirut. The town which was ungarrisoned was handed over to him by its 'timorous bishop', and he set siege to the castle. Back in Acre, he called a meeting of the High Court and showed it letters from Frederick appointing him as *bailli*. The barons confirmed the appointment, then Filangieri proclaimed the forfeiture of Ibelin lands. This provoked protests from the barons: 'Estates could not be confiscated unless the High Court so decided, after the owner had had the chance of defending his case'. After a long struggle Filangieri eventually surrendered to Ibelins and others in April 1233, Cyprus was wholly restored to the rule of Henry and his Ibelin cousins, and the High Court accepted John's leadership, though this was still not the end of the story since Pope Gregory, trying to act correctly, declared that the Ibelins must stand trial before the High Court. The terms were unacceptable to the barons and the Commune, who ignored them, and at this point John died as the result of a riding accident.[24]

The struggle for control of Cyprus resonated in two very different groups of French and Occitan lyrics. The first consists of four compositions of a highly personal nature by the trouvère Philippe de Novare, who as we have seen was intimately caught up in its events. The second is a pair of Occitan *sirventes* composed a decade later expressing opinions on Frederick's conduct towards John of Ibelin. A 'Lombard' of unknown origin, but probably from family of the lesser Novarese nobility, Philippe was probably born towards the end of the twelfth century and built his fortune in the East under the protection of the Ibelins. As early as 1218–1219 he is known to have been present at the siege of Damietta and to be linked to the Cypriot nobility. Thanks to the Ibelins he became a figure of

---

[22] See 'About the text' in <http://warwick.ac.uk/crusadelyrics/texts/of/verseletter>.
[23] Runciman, *History*, III, p. 196.
[24] Runciman, *History*, III, pp. 202–04.

some influence, exploiting his diplomatic and legal talents during various high-level missions. In the last part of his life he became a trusted adviser of the king of Cyprus, Henry I. His chronicle of Frederick's crusade[25] is a lively history of the war for the control of Cyprus during 1223–1242. It provides essential, richly detailed information concerning little-known facts, but is written in a highly personal and partisan style, its author being a fervent supporter of the Ibelins as well as an intimate friend of the family. Inserted into it are five verse texts plus a few fragments, which are the texts under consideration here. Barbieri highlights the 'numerous ludic and comic elements in the verse texts which lend the whole work an ironic and satirical character approaching parody. Such elements reveal a taste for defiance and provocation on the author's part and enhance the superiority of the victors through the denigration of the enemy.'[26]

The first of these verse insertions (Verse Letter) refers to the events preceding the battle of Nicosia on 14 July 1229, probably at the end of May or the beginning of June. The introductory rubric to the text defines it as a letter in verse sent by Philippe de Novare to John's son, Balian of Ibelin, who was in Acre with his father. Philippe relates through comical literary allusions to the *Roman de Renart*, where protagonists are represented as fox, wolf and badger, how he refused to swear allegiance to the five bailiffs whom Frederick had installed as rulers of the island; he was arrested and thrown in the privy, escaped a plan to murder him during the night and fled to the Hospitallers' tower.[27] It urgently pleads with Balian of Ibelin to set aside his 'loves of Acre' (which may be an ironic allusion to the presence in Acre of a high number of prostitutes) to come and relieve the siege:

> Se vous aimés les femes, [qui] ont eü lor part,
> car les levés dou siege! Et Grimbers et Renart,
> qui devant l'Ospital ont mis lor estendars,
> toute nuit font gaiter o lances et o dars
> ceaus qui tienent la terre, et nous faillent d'esgart.
> Les dames sont dedens et .j. tout soul Lombart.
> Coment le soufrés vous, recreant et couart?
> De l'endemain de Pasque, se Damedeu me gart,
> me souvient quant jes voi, trestout le cuer m'en art,
> que chascun se fait rey, mais qu'il se truit soi quart.
>
> [...]

---

[25] Philippe de Novare, *Mémoires*, ed. C. Kohler (Paris, 1913); English translation J. L. LaMonte with M. J. Hubert, *The Wars of Frederick II against the Ibelines in Syria and Cyprus* (New York, 1936). See also the introduction to S. Melani, *Guerra di Federico II in Oriente (1223–1242)* (Naples, 1995).
[26] See Barbieri's notes in <http://warwick.ac.uk/crusadelyrics/texts/of/verseletter>.
[27] Runciman, *History*, III, p. 194, dubs this piece 'doggerel'. For an informed analysis of Philip's style in his verse texts see the notes in <http://warwick.ac.uk/crusadelyrics/texts/of/verseletter>.

Ne puis muër ne rie quant les voi au baillage:
Hue a la torte bouche, qui renee parage;
Guillaume de Rivet, qui tant cuide estre sage;
quy de son mal sarmon trestous les assouage;
et Renart, qui bien sait com l'on deste des gage;
Amaury et Gauvain ne sont pas d'un lignage;
bien les conoissés tous, n'i a nul si sauvage.   (vv. 61–70, 73–79)

If you love the women, who have had had their part [in the suffering], please save them from the siege! Both Grimbert and Renart, who have fixed their banners before the Hospital, make those who hold the village stand guard every night with lances and arrows, and deny us justice. The ladies are in there with just one single Lombard. How can you bear it, you cowardly recreant? When I see them (the bailiffs) I remember the day after Easter, God help me: my whole heart burns in fury, because each of them acts like a king as long as he has his share.

[...]

I cannot help laughing when I see them as regents: Hugh with his twisted mouth, who abjures nobility; William of Rivet, who thinks he is so wise, and lulls them with his evil speech; and Renart, who is an expert at breaking pledges; Amaury and Gauvain, who are not of the same lineage; you know them all well.

After their victory against the imperial army at Nicosia, the Ibelins' men besieged the castles in which the five bailiffs had taken refuge: Aimery Barlais, Amaury of Bethsan and Hugh of Gibelet in Dieudamour, Gauvain of Chenichy and his men in Kantara and William of Rivet in Buffavento. Philippe de Novare followed John of Ibelin and took part in the siege of Dieudamour, which lasted from the second half of July 1229 to May–June 1230. *A tout le mont vueil en chantant retraire* (RS 184a) was probably composed at the start of this siege and in any case before Easter (7 April 1230). It describes how the five bailiffs 'without the court's judgment and without appeal [. . .] deprived their peers and their lord of their legitimate fiefs' (vv. 5–7) and tried to prevent them landing back in Cyprus, and relates the Ibelins' landing at La Castrie, their conquest of the port, the battle of Nicosia, and the ignominious flight of the baliffs, some to Dieudamour, where they were imprisoning their king, Henry I. Philippe has no qualms about sanctioning the torture and mutilation of his enemies, branded as traitors, and as he sends the song off to the constable of Jerusalem, Odo of Montbéliard, he refers to the capture of someone dubbed 'Long-Tongue': 'I send you his tongue and nose to cut up.'

Philippe wrote *Nafré sui [je], mais encor ne puis taire* (RS 190a) after being wounded in the arm. He continues to revile Aimery Barlais as the Renardian fox, and sympathises with the poor fools who serve him:

Nafré sui [je], mais encor ne puis taire
de dan Renart et (de) s'autre compaignie,
qui pour luy est afamee et honie,

dedens Maucrois, ou il maint et repaire.
Mais se Renart a de son cors paour
que ont mesfait li autre vavassour
et ly sergent? Por quoi se laissent vendre?
Come bricons leur fait aucuns atendre.   (vv. 1–8)

I am wounded, but still I cannot be silent concerning Sir Renart and the rest of his company, which because of him is starving and dishonoured inside Maupertuis, where he is taking refuge. But if Renart is in fear for his life, what harm have the other vavassors and the sergeants done? Why are they allowing themselves to be sold? Someone is keeping them waiting [for reinforcements] like fools.

Written in the form of an *alba* or dawn song just after RS 190a, *L'autrier gaitay une nuit jusque(s) au jour* (RS 1990a) was also composed during the siege of Dieudamour. Philippe states that during the siege John of Ibelin went to Kantara to check the development of operations. Philippe appears to have followed him, because outside Kantara, when he was accompanying Ansel of Brie during a nocturnal watch, he claims to have heard the dialogue between the men besieged inside which gave rise to this piece: possibly a piece of propaganda designed to boost the morale of the Ibelins' side and deflate that of their opponents. Denigrating the five bailiffs and the dire consequences of Frederick's interference in the island, it graphically evokes the hardships inflicted on ordinary soldiers, who were allegedly lamenting, high up in a tower:

Lors respondy uns autres: 'Grant doulor
et grant peine souffrom, et grans tormens:
la nuit veiller, matin estre au labour,
poy a manger, et povres vestimens;
a la periere esteut que nous tirons;
tous les ennuis et tous les maus avons

[...]

Aprés dist .i.: 'En lermes et en plours
seront pour nous et amis et parens;
tous y morons, car leur trabucheour
nous fait nos fours (saens) trabucher si dedens,
murs et petreaus et creneaus et maisons.
S'on nous assaut, coment nous defendrons?
Car nostre gent est d'armes desgarnie.

[...]

'Abatu est le molin et le four;
d'atendre plus ne seroit pas grans sens.
Traï nous ont les baus de Deudamor,
et ont menti vers nous leur sairement.

Toly nous ont le roy en traïson,
et covenant fu que nous l'avriom.
Puis nous firent combatre a Nicossie,
pour eaus sauver et nous tolir la vie.

[...]

Mal veïmes onques l'empereor;
merci crier nous covendra par tens.'   (vv. 10–15, 19–25, 28–35, 39–40)

We are suffering great grief and great pain, and great torments: watching at night, toiling during the day, with little food and poor garments; we have to pull on the petrary; we have all the discomforts, and all the sufferings.

[...]

Friends and kin will be weeping and in tears for us: all of us will die here, for their trebuchet makes our ovens collapse right here inside, our walls and ramparts, crenellations and houses. If we are attacked, how shall we defend ourselves? Our people are unequipped with armour.

[...]

The mill and the oven are already ruined; it would not make much sense to wait any longer. The bailiffs of Dieudamour have betrayed us, and have broken their oath to us. They have treacherously robbed us of the king, and it was promised that we should have him. Then they made us fight at Nicosia to save them and to rob us of our life.

[...]

It was a disaster ever to set eyes on the emperor: soon we shall have to beg for mercy.

For the partisan Philippe de Novare, Frederick's intervention in Cyprus was uncompromisingly illegal and treacherous. For him the emperor's treatment of the Ibelins completely effaced any potential value of, or concern for, his crusade. The interest of the trouvère's verses lies in their personal, lived account of events, and the light directed at the sufferings of ordinary soldiers caught up in them, but also for their hostility to the emperor.

Frederick's conduct towards John of Ibelin in 1228 was still a live issue a decade later. In early 1239 the emperor was spending two months in Padua enjoying hunting and other courtly pastimes, with a great festival taking place there on 20 March, Palm Sunday. It was a famously extravagant and exotic affair, involving hunting with leopards and an elephant. On the very same day Pope Gregory IX bludgeoned him with yet another excommunication. A vitriolic attack on the emperor composed during 1–20 March, atttributed to the troubadour Guillem Figueira, expresses disgust at 'a lord who is base and peevish, greedy and tight-fisted, one who has hardly a shred of shame or fear of anything unseemly he might say or do'

(BdT 217.4a). He reminds his listeners of Frederick's actions in Cyprus and goes on to pour scorn on Frederick's plans for combatting the Lombards.

> Li franc baro d'outramar
> l'an ben cognogut,
> qe molt cuiet mal frut
> entre lor semenar,
> q'el volc deseritar
> lo segnor de Barut
> e·ls autres de repaire;
> mas no·l poc acabar,
> car Dieus per sa vertut
> l'en fon del tot contraire.
>
> Ara somon c'on l'aiut
> davas totaz partz,
> que, passat aquest martz,
> vol mostrar son escut
> a Melan, mas no·l cut
> ia sia tant auzartz
> qe s'en auz enanz traire,
> si tot l'a convengut,
> car es vils e coartz
> et avols guerreiaire.
>
> E cuia venzer Lombartz
> totz a son coman;
> pero qar vai chazan
> per bosc e per eissartz
> ab cas et ab leopartz,
> e qar men'aurifan?
> Ben es fols l'enperaire
> e nescis e musartz,
> si zo qe vai pezan
> cuia tot a cap traire.
>
> Non traira, per San Johan,
> ugan tot a cap
> son penzer ni sun gap;
> aisso·us pliu e vos man.
> Doncs de qe pessa tan?
> Q'unz penz'et autre sap,
> e totz nescis penzaire
> perchaza leu son dan
> tro que ven a mescap,
> si s'en pot leu estraire.   (vv. 31–70)

The noble barons of Outremer have recognised this well, for he thought he could do them some mischief: he wanted to disinherit the Lord of Beirut and the others of their homes, but he was unable to achieve this because God in his goodness was completely opposed to it.

Now they are summoning help for him on all sides, as after the end of March he wants to show his shield to Milan; but I do not think he will be so bold as to dare to move ahead, even if he has promised to do so, for he is base and cowardly and an abysmal fighter.

He thinks he can completely subject the Lombards to his command; so why does he go hunting through woods and clearings with dogs and leopards, and why is he dragging an elephant behind him? The emperor is quite mad and stupid and deluded if he thinks he can fulfil all that he has in mind.

By Saint John, he will not fulfil his ideas or his boast this year, I can tell you this for sure. So what is he thinking of all the time? For some people think and other people know, and any fool who spends all his time thinking is heedlessly heading for a fall until disaster strikes; and yet he can easily avoid this.[28]

These attacks make a conspicuous contrast with BdT 217.8, *Un nou sirventes*, which dates from around the same time. In its fourth stanza Guillem praises Frederick's virtuous conquests in Outremer. Instead of accusing him of baseness, cowardice and avarice, he praises him for being pure of baseness and full of largesse.

Mos fes otramar onrad'obra e neta
que Jheruzalem conques et Escalona,
que anc no·y pres colp de dart ni de saieta
can li fe·l soudan onrada patz e bona;
pueys tenc en Chipre sa carreyra
e la mostret tan bona fe
e [*missing*] lialtatz tan enteira
c'al don de Barut en sove,
cuy sols s'eretatz per gentil cortezia,
franc emperador que n'a tot lo cors ple,
e voyt e lavat de tota vilania,
ples de largetat; e qui·s vol, crea·n me.

E qui no m'en cre, demand en a Berreta
o al cavaier de Palma o de Cremona,
a qu'el det d'arnes cargat una carreta
e mil unsas d'aur. Ben aya c'aisi dona!

---

[28] The *sirventes* can be securely dated to before 20 March, before news of Frederick's excommunication had spread. This news made a deep impression in Padua, and previous scholars have pointed out that it would have been very surprising for the author not to have mentioned it, particularly in the case of the author of the famous *sirventes* against Rome.

> Tostems n'amaray may Figueira,
> que de luy lauzar no·s recre,
> ni non ditz paraula mesongieyra
> de l'emperador: que jasse
> lo sans Dieu li gart tota sa manentia
> si co ilh ama verai pretz e mante,
> et a mi don Dieus gaug d'amic e d'amia
> e don joy al comte Ramon c'onor soste.   (vv. 37–60)

He brought about an honourable, clean achievement in the Holy Land when he conquered Jerusalem and Ascalon, for before a bolt or arrow had been fired at him the sultan made him a good and honourable peace; then he continued on to Cyprus and there showed such good faith and [...] such impeccable lawfulness that it is remembered by the lord of Beirut, to whom the noble emperor handed back his lands with gracious courtesy, his heart being full of this, void and cleansed of all baseness, full of generosity: and anyone can trust me on this.

But if there is anyone who does not believe me, let him ask Berreta about it, or the knights of Palma or of Cremona, to whom he gave a cart loaded with armour and a thousand ounces of gold. A blessing on the man who gives like this! Henceforth Figueira will always love anyone who ceaselessly sings his praises and speaks no lying word of the emperor: may Holy God preserve his entire wealth for him since he loves and maintains true worth.

Ja de far un sirventes is factually correct when it states that Frederick wished to disinherit the Lord of Beirut and was unable to do so. The sycophantic *Un nou sirventes* glosses over his treacherous behaviour at the feast he gave in John's honour, putting a positive spin on these events by claiming that he acted with complete good faith, lawfulness and noble courtesy by handing John back his lands. The stress on lawfulness chimes with Abulafia's observation concerning the Ibelins' respect for legal requirements: 'it was precisely their attention to law, as they interpreted it, that brought them bitterly into conflict with Frederick.'[29] Also in contrast to *Ja de far un sirventes*, whose observations on Frederick's crusade of 1228–1229 are confined to his behaviour to the 'franc baro d'outramar', *Un nou sirventes* praises him for an honourable and bloodless conquest of Jerusalem and Ascalon, which concluded with the peace treaty with al-Kāmil. Such a positive spin seems to have been unusual: Runciman relates that the treaty met with 'immediate and universal disapproval', and 'the recovery of Jerusalem was of little profit to the kingdom', since Frederick's hurried departure left it an open city, impossible to police and open to recapture at any time.[30]

Most previous scholars have tried to explain the hostility of *Ja de far un sirventes* as a sarcastic spur to action against the Lombards on the part of Guillem Figueira,

---

[29] Abulafia, *Frederick II*, pp. 175–78 and 190–93.
[30] Runciman, *History*, III, pp. 187 and 193.

reflecting the disappointments of the more radical Ghibellines. One year later, it has been argued, Guillem composed a 'new *sirventes*' full of praise for the emperor, recognising that he had wronged him. The only dissenting voice was that of Giulio Bertoni, who suggested that manuscript a¹, whose attributions are often wrong, had mistakenly preserved the piece among Guillem Figueira's compositions.³¹ If Guillem Figueira was indeed the author of *Ja de far un sirventes*, the hope expressed in *Un nou sirventes* of entering his service (v. 3), and possibly fear (vv. 13–17), appears to have spurred him to recant from his previous criticisms in quite specific detail. What is much more likely is that Bertoni was right, and that Guillem is responding both to specific points of the negative propaganda of another misidentified troubadour, and to Frederick's excommunication. The peace treaty with al-Kāmil lay behind the earlier *sirventes*' accusation that Frederick was 'coartz / et avols guerreiaire' (vv. 49–50): a widely held view of a crusading leader who, instead of conquering through martial prowess, had talked his way into a deal.³² This was no doubt what prompted Figueira to lay special emphasis on the emperor's crusading successes, praising his 'honourable, clean achievement in the Holy Land'.

As Thomas Asbridge has remarked, 'Frederick II was one of the most controversial figures in medieval history. In the thirteenth century he was lauded by supporters as *stupor mundi* (the wonder of the world), but condemned by his enemies as the "beast of the apocalypse".'³³ At first the troubadours uncontentiously support his crusade, as they have so far supported any crusade to the Holy Land, whether in its favour in line with papal propaganda, or with the emperor's own after the Diet of San Germano. Once papal–imperial hostilities break out the troubadours tend to show their Ghibelline sympathies, in line with many anticlerical compositions of the period.³⁴ Passions run high, and by the time of renewed hostilities in 1239 an atypical, most probably misattributed Occitan piece directs a ferocious diatribe against the emperor's treatment of John of Ibelin in Cyprus. The troubadour Guillem Figueira counters it, no doubt self-servingly, by defending Frederick's conduct in Cyprus and praising his achievements in the Holy Land. In contrast to the majority of the troubadours, the only trouvère to comment on these events takes a personal stance against the emperor. Philippe de Novare took part in Frederick's crusade but was a close friend of the Ibelins, and his lyrics wickedly satirise the conduct of Frederick's five deputies in the Cyprus war.

---

³¹ G. Bertoni, 'Un serventese di Guilhem Figueira', *ZRP*, 35 (1911), 489–91 (p. 491), n. 2.
³² See also Abulafia, *Frederick II*, p. 183: 'Frederick's treaty with al-Kāmil was seen both in the Muslim and in the Christian world as a betrayal. For the Christians, it was an extraordinary spectacle to have a crusading emperor arrive amid such fanfares, and then, hardly even unsheathing his sword, to have him reach agreement for the return of Jerusalem by mere negotiation', and p. 189: 'The reaction of the Latins in the East deeply disappointed the emperor [. . .] The peace between al-Kāmil and the emperor was considered in no way praiseworthy.'
³³ Asbridge, *The Crusades*, p. 563.
³⁴ See Introduction, p. 17, and Chapter 8, p. 154.

8

The 'False Crusade': the Albigensian war of 1224–1233

The period of intense papal–imperial hostilities coincided with equally turbulent events taking place in the Midi, as Count Raymond VII of Toulouse struggled to recover his former lands. His supporters hoped that Frederick could be drawn to intervene against the French in the defence of his rights in the kingdom of Arles, and their hatred of the clergy there naturally merged with the anticlerical stance of Frederick's own supporters. Occitan troubadours voiced outrage at what they saw as a perversion of the true purpose of crusading, and contrasted the call of the Holy Land with the 'false crusade' of the French against Toulouse. They were not entirely unsupported by their northern colleagues.

By 1224 Raymond VII had retaken possession of many castles captured by the French, and restored them to their exiled holders. At the council of Bourges on 30 November 1225 he was excommunicated, and on 30 January 1226 Louis VIII took the cross and marched down the Rhône valley at the head of a powerful army, accompanied by the papal legate Romain de Saint-Ange. They reached Avignon after encountering no resistance on the way. As a result of an obscure misunderstanding, the city first yielded to the king, then defied him during a long hot summer of siege. Faced with growing discontent in his army as a result of the exorbitant cost of food and the spread of dysentery, Louis attempted an assault on the city, but failed. The defeat was generally ascribed to the treachery of some of his barons, particularly to the trouvère Thibaut de Champagne, who, according to Jonathan Sumption, had only joined Louis' crusade under duress. He had relatives inside Avignon and apparently remained in constant contact with them throughout the siege. Suffering from hunger and unaware of the gravity of Louis' situation, the Avignonese surrendered on 9 September, and more and more of Raymond's supporters submitted to the king, who marched triumphantly through the Languedoc.[1]

The response of Tomier and Palaizi to the imminent arrival of the king's army at Avignon's city walls highlights the bitterness in the region at the corruption of the very notion of crusade (BdT 442.1).

Tals cuia venir
ab falsa croisada,

---

[1] Sumption, *The Albigensian Crusade*, pp. 218–21.

qe·l n'er a fozir
sens fog d'albergada,
car ab ben ferir
venz hom leu maisnada.
Segur estem, seignors,
e ferm de ric socors. (vv. 17–24)

Some think they can come here on a false crusade, but they will have to flee before lighting a camp fire, for it is easy to defeat troops by striking well. *Let us stand firm, lords, sure of powerful aid.*

With its invigorating refrain, their song aims to stir the citizens to resistance in the hope that the emperor will come to their support. Aragon and Catalonia have proved ineffectual, they declare, but as ruler of the kingdom of Arles Frederick II has an interest in defending this part of his empire (vv. 25–40). This false crusade is waged at the expense of the Holy Land and the relief of Damietta, and the prelates, more interested in a life of ease and the acquisition of wealth, are leading men astray, since these 'crusaders' are destined to die without a valid absolution.

Al sepolcre an tout
socors e valenza
cil q'an la croz vout,
et es descredenza;
li fals nesci sout
veiran mal Argenza. (vv. 41–46)

Those who have turned the cross [against Christians] have withdrawn aid and support from the sepulchre, and this is contrary to faith; the false absolved fools will never see Argence.

Resistance was effective for a while, but only in the short term, and disappointingly the emperor was busy elsewhere and eventually distanced himself from the Toulousain cause.

When Thibaut de Champagne left the siege of Avignon after his short term of obligatory service, he did so without the king's permission. Louis died of dysentery a few months later, and some suspected Thibaut of having had him poisoned. He subsequently formed a group rebellious to the crown, which included among others Raymond VII of Toulouse, with whom he had ties of kinship and friendship.[2] He took part in the negotiations in Meaux and Paris, acting as mediator between the positions of the French crown and the count of Toulouse, but was frustrated in

---

[2] For the relations between Thibaut and the court of Paris, see L. Barbieri, 'Un sirventese religioso di Thibaut de Champagne: *Diex est ausis conme li pellicans* (RS 273)', *CN*, 73 (2013), 301–46, and the bibliography indicated in that article, and S. Melani, 'Aimeric de Belenoi, Thibaut de Champagne e le crociate', in *RST* 1 (1999), 137–57.

all his attempts to soften the harsh conditions imposed on Raymond by the treaty of Paris in 1229. Barbieri has noted some particularly interesting correspondences between Thibaut's song *Diex est ausis conme li pellicans* (RS 273) and two troubadour *sirventes*, one by Falquet de Romans (*Quan cug chantar eu planc e plor*, BdT 156.11)[3] and Peire Cardenal's *Li clerc si fan pastor* (BdT 335.31). Both of these form part of pro-imperial propaganda in Occitania.[4] They criticise the stance of the clergy who prefer war to peace, and they contain references to Frederick's activity in the East, which Peire Cardenal in particular highlights as hindered by clerical ambitions and hypocrisy. While Peire's anticlerical invective is often taken to concern the Inquisition, in fact it particularly targets the churchmen who, he declares, are attempting to bring down the emperor and take over supreme command of the Western world.

> Li clerc si fan pastor
> e son aussizedor
> e semblan de santor;
> can los vei revestir
> e prent m'a sovenir
> de n'Alengri, c'un dia
> volc ad un parc venir,
> mas pels canx que temia
> pel de mouton vestic,
> ab que los escarnic,
> pois manget e trazic
> la cal que l'abelic.
>
> Rei et emperador,
> duc, comte e comtor
> e cavallier ab lor
> solon lo mon regir;
> eras vei possezir
> ha clercs la seingnoria,
> ab tolre et ab trair
> et ab ypocrizia,
> ab forssa et ab prezic,
> e tenon s'a fastic
> qui tot non lor ho gic,
> et er fait, cant que tric.
>
> [...]
>
> Ia non aion paor
> alcaicx ni almassor
> qe abat ni prior

---

[3] See Chapter 7, p. 142.
[4] Barbieri, 'Un sirventese religioso', pp. 314–17.

los anon envazir
ni lors terras sazir,
que afans lor seria,
mas sai son en consir
del mon comsi lor sia,
ni com en Frederic
gitesson de l'abric;
pero tals l'aramic
c'anc fort no s'en iauzic.   (vv. 1–24, 49–60)

The clergy make themselves out to be shepherds and are killers; and they seem holy when I see them putting on their habit; but I remember Sir Ysengrin (the wolf in the *Roman de Renart*), who wanted to enter a sheep pen one day, but for fear of the dogs he dressed in a sheepskin through which he tricked them, then ate and swallowed whatever he pleased.

Kings and emperors, dukes, counts, *comtors* and knights along with them used to rule the world; now I see the clergy holding power through robbery and betrayal, through hypocrisy, through violence and through preaching; they are disgruntled if people refuse to yield them everything, and this will be done, however they delay [the inevitable].

Let *alcaydes* and *almansors* [Arab commanders and princes] have no fear that abbots or priors will go and attack them or seize their lands, for this would be too much trouble for them, while here they are giving thought to how the world might be theirs, and how they might dislodge lord Frederick from his refuge; yet one man did challenge him and was none too happy about it afterwards.

While a date for this song of 1245–1246, a later period of acute papal–imperial conflict, cannot be ruled out, Peire's recent editor Sergio Vatteroni argues persuasively in favour of the earlier period of 1229–1230. When Frederick was away in the Holy Land the French clergy and Blanche of Castile had profited by his absence to impose on Raymond VII the humiliating treaty of Paris, which had also damaged Frederick's imperial rights in the kingdom of Arles. If the one who defied the emperor was Pope Gregory IX, it would make sense to say that he would not have been happy about it afterwards because Frederick, soon after his return, invaded the papal state and routed the pontifical army. Before Gregory and Frederick made peace at San Germano, the pope found himself expelled from Rome, bankrupt and without arms, abandoned by the Lombards and unsupported by the Western kings.[5] The idea of dislodging Frederick from his refuge would refer to the invasion of the kingdom of Naples during his absence by pontifical troops led by his father-

---

[5] S. Vatteroni, *Il trovatore Peire Cardenal* (Modena, 2013), 2 vols, I, pp. 465–66, discusses the possibility that *tals* (v. 59) might refer to John of Brienne himself, though seems inclined to prefer the first identification.

in-law John of Brienne, whom Frederick had dispossessed of his title of King of Jerusalem. On Frederick's return in 1229 John was forced to raise the siege of Gaeta and took refuge at Gregory's court.[6] Vatteroni suggests the earlier dating could also explain why the clergy are not supporting a crusade. When on the eve of his departure for the Holy Land in August 1227 the emperor was detained in Brindisi by an unexpected epidemic, this gave Gregory a pretext to initiate hostilities: Frederick was accused of failing to meet the deadline set for his departure and was excommunicated on 29 September. It was soon clear to contemporaries that this was indeed a pretext: the pope had no intention of resolving their conflict. Because he could not refuse absolution to a repentant Frederick who was ready to leave on crusade, he made a series of new accusations, creating all sorts of difficulties in the West to try to obstruct his voyage to Palestine, in order to acquire in the eyes of public opinion the right to expropriate Sicily and depose Frederick as emperor. It even seemed that the pope had stirred up the Lombards and the inhabitants of the papal domains to obstruct and rob the crusaders on their way to southern Italy. Gregory's attempts to boycott the crusade had wide resonance, especially in Germany. In turn, Frederick published encyclicals responding point by point to the pope's accusations. Shortly after Frederick's departure from Brindisi (28 June 1228) Gregory released the Germans and Sicilians from their oath of fidelity to the emperor, sent Franciscan envoys to the Holy Land to sow discord among the ranks of the crusaders, entered Sicily with the pontifical army and with the help of Lombard rebels soon succeeded in taking over many continental provinces of the Regno. These events could explain the allusions to the clergy's lack of desire to take part in the crusade and attempts to chase the emperor from his *abric*, the kingdom of Sicily.

---

[6] Alternatively, the details of the piece might correspond to events of 1245–1246, when the clergy, instead of supporting Louis IX's crusade which had been in preparation since 1244, were thinking about how to expel Frederick from his empire. The Council of Lyon deposed him on 17 July 1245, and vv. 61–63 ('Clergy, anyone who chose you without a treacherous wicked heart miscalculated') might refer to the choice of cardinals for the Council of Lyon, which spoke out in favour of this. Those opposing this position have argued that vv. 59–60 cannot be explained by a date of 1245 since, if the one who is defying Frederick is Innocent IV, it is unclear how he can be said to have been unhappy about it afterwards (*no s'en iauzic*): Innocent continued his struggle against the emperor after the Council of Lyon, and Frederick never succeeded in achieving his aim of capturing that city. However, Vatteroni concedes that these arguments are not decisive. The poet uses the preterite tense, and could be making a poorly veiled threat against Innocent IV by reminding him of the unhappy end of whoever, before him, had dared to defy the emperor. And the lines referring to the Holy Land could be explained by the situation following the Council of Lyon, when Innocent IV concentrated all his efforts on the struggle against Frederick: in 1246 he ordered preaching against the pagans in Germany to be broken off and a crusade against the emperor to be launched, and on 9 November 1247 he declared that the crusade against the heretic Frederick was more important than the crusade to the Holy Land.

Thibaut's song *Diex est ausis conme li pellicans* (RS 273) lacks specific references to contemporary events, but it seems clear that it concerns crusading because of the trouvère's evocation of the 'deficient and slow' repayment of God's suffering for mankind's sake. This is graphically depicted in the image of the pelican whose chicks are killed by the Devil: the father kills itself with its own beak, 'and from the painful flow of blood brings its chicks immediately back to life'.

> Diex est ausis conme li pellicans
> qui fait son nif el plus haut arbre sus,
> et li mauvais oisiax, qui est dejus,
> ses oiseillons ocist, tant est puans;
> li peres vient destroiz et angoisseus,
> dou bec s'ocist, de son sanc doulereus
> fait revivre tantost ses oiseillons.
> Diex fist autel quant fu sa passïons:
> de son dous sanc racheta ses anfanz
> dou dëable, qui tant par est puissanz.
>
> Li guerredons en est mauvais et lens,
> que bien ne droit ne pitié nen n'a nus,
> ainz est orguiex et baraz au desus,
> felonie, traïson et bobans.
> Moult par est ore vostre estaz perilleus,
> et se ne fust li exemples de ceus
> qui tant ainment et noises et tençons –
> ce est des clers qui ont laissié sermons
> por guerroier et por tuer les gens –
> jamais en Dieu ne fust nus hons creanz.   (vv. 1–20)

God is similar to the pelican which makes its nest up in the highest tree; and the evil bird underneath kills its chicks, it is so foul. The father returns full of distress and anguish, kills itself with its beak and from the painful flow of blood brings its chicks immediately back to life. God did the same in the hour of his passion: with his sweet blood he ransomed his children from the Devil, who is so enormously powerful.

Repayment is deficient and slow, for no one harbours goodness or justice or pity; so pride, fraud, disloyalty, treachery and arrogance prevail. Now your situation is extremely dangerous, and were it not for the example of those who so love both uproar and disputes – that is, the clergy who have abandoned sermons to wage war and kill people – no one would have faith in God any more.

The trouvère inveighs against both clerics and barons: the clergy, loving uproar and disputes, 'have abandoned sermons to wage war and kill people'; 'the heavy guilt lies largely with the barons, who grieve when anyone wants to give proof of valour'; while religious hypocrites 'are truly repulsive and stinking and evil: they kill all the good people, who are God's children, through their false words'. As with Peire Cardenal's song, there are two dating possibilities, in this case 1229–1230 or 1236–1239. Like Vatteroni, Barbieri favours the earlier period, namely the final period of the Albigensian Crusade, which presents a series of events that could have provided the starting-point for his song: the siege of Avignon (March–June 1226), which constitutes the beginning of Thibaut's rebellion against the French crown; the excommunication of Frederick II (29 September 1227); the emperor's departure on crusade without the support of the French crown or, obviously, of the pope (May–September 1228); the treaty of Paris (12 April 1229), where the intransigence of the clergy and the hypocrisy of the court sanctioned the humiliation of the count of Toulouse; and the failure of Thibaut's diplomacy at the council. Barbieri importantly demonstrates that Thibaut's song is in dialogue with the troubadours' polemical literary tradition, highlighting numerous textual correspondences with the two songs by Falquet de Romans and Peire Cardenal, and observing that the source of the rare version of the pelican legend found in this text seems to be an Occitan homily. He suggests that his analysis of the song reveals a less well-known aspect of Thibaut's character, which is more Ghibelline and pro-emperor than previously realised, and highlights his closeness to the count of Toulouse.[7]

A further song by Peire Cardenal (BdT 335.51) may also belong to this period. It laments the advance of the Saracens in the Holy Land and the sinfulness and apathy towards this on the part of the princes and clergy:

Aissi·ns layssa Dieus dechazer
per los falhimens qu'en nos son,
que·ls sarrazis fa tan valer
que sobre nos son aurion;
qu'enveiar l'autruy sai cofon
clercx e primses e l'autra gen:
quascus quan pot de l'autre pren
e fa·n temen ben   e grieumen,
e·l sepulcre[s] es del tot oblidatz
e la terra on Iesu Crist fon natz.   (vv. 41–50)

God lets us so decline for the faults that are in us that he makes the Saracens prosper to the point that they are eagles above us; coveting other people's goods in this world confounds clergy and princes and others: each takes what he can from the other and does good timidly and reluctantly, and the sepulchre is completely forgotten, and the land where Jesus Christ was born.

Vatteroni (see the online edition) suggests the poem could date either from 1229, Frederick II's entry into Jerusalem, or from 1244–1254, when the city was occupied by Kwarismanian troops and re-entered the orbit of the sultan of Egypt, and the abandonment of the first crusade of Louis IX of France.

7   Barbieri, 'Un sirventese religioso'.

THE 'FALSE CRUSADE': THE ALBIGENSIAN WAR

The most violently outspoken of the Occitan Ghibelline poets was Guillem Figueira. His long, hammering invective against Rome (BdT 217.2) is justly famed. Composed during the time of Raymond VII's resistance to French aggression and occupation in the South, Guillem's invective flays a power-hungry Rome both for its crusade against Christians and for its attempts to sabotage the emperor's rightful crusade to the Holy Land. It is no surprise if people stray into error, he declares, for Rome has pitched the world into war and turmoil, betrayed its supporters and fleeced its flock; it is Rome's fault that Damietta was lost through its devious deals and stupidity; Rome has misled the barons of France through a false indulgence, promising them paradise for crusading against Christians and thereby steering the soldiers towards the torments of hell; it has caused the death of King Louis VIII, done little to damage the Saracens yet plunged Greeks and Latins into carnage; and it has been responsible for the deaths of many, closing to them the gates of salvation. In what scripture, he demands, do you find any justification for killing Christians? But if Count Raymond lives another two years, France will be sorry for your deceitfulness! Vengefully he anticipates the emperor's triumph:

> Roma, be·m conort
> quez en abans de gaire
> venrez a mal port,
> si l'adreitz emperaire
> mena adreich sa sort
> ni fai so que deu faire.
> Roma, eu dic ver,
> que·l vostre poder
> veirem dechazer.
> Roma, lo vers salvaire
> m'o lais tost vezer.   (vv. 133–43)

Rome, I comfort myself well that in no time at all you will arrive at a bad port, if the righteous emperor properly fulfils his destiny and does what he has to do. Rome, I tell you truly that we shall see your power collapse. Rome, may the true Saviour let me see this soon!

Rome perpetrates many base acts and crimes; it so longs to rule the world that it has no fear of God or his prohibitions. If its power is not curtailed, the world will collapse into death and defeat, all worth destroyed: a miracle brought about by its pope! The cardinals think of nothing but selling God and his friends, its priests are false deceivers, and the pope does evil work when he disputes with the emperor over the right to the crown (of Jerusalem?[8]), pronounces him excommu-

---

[8] See vv. 199–202. At the time of composition (1227–1229) Frederick had sought the crown of Jerusalem through marriage to Yolanda of Brienne, crowned queen of Jerusalem in 1225. By 1228 she was dead and Frederick no longer king and the queen's husband but guardian of the infant king Conrad, his son. Nevertheless in 1229, on entering Jerusalem, Fred-

nicate and officially pardons his soldiers for renouncing their allegiance to him. Rome, the troubadour contends, you deserve to have your brains extracted: you and the Cistercians brought about an appalling massacre at Béziers, and you are a rabid wolf in lamb's clothing, a crowned serpent sired by a viper, and the Devil takes care of you like one of his own!

This same troubadour's *sirventes Del preveire maior* (BdT 217.1) seems to have been composed at around the same time, in 1228, when Frederick had recovered from his illness and was actively preparing to embark for Cyprus and Acre in May and finally departing on 28 June. Here the troubadour rails against the futility of the conflict between pope and emperor, when what counts is the afterlife and the need to set out on God's business in the Holy Land. 'I wish the pope and the emperor would make peace among themselves to give the Turks and Arabs cause to grieve', he laments, 'but each of them is conducting his quarrel with great bitterness, and they are wasting their efforts; for all that is visible is nothing in comparison with what is to come.' He claims he would dearly love to make the sea crossing but has not the wealth to make the passage honourably, and is despondent to think that this will diminish his hope of eternal joy, since 'those who will be God's servants in the place where He lived in humility will be thanked more than all other people'.

Unlike Falquet de Romans, who wished to set out on the first wave of crusaders, Guillem stresses the need for all determined fighters to make the passage in a single body.

> Qe·l bon envazidor
> e·l bon combatedor
> e l'ardit feridor
> devon tut az un crit
> pasar, gerer complit
> ab gran afortimen
> de cobrar lo sant monimen;   (vv. 41–47)

For the good assailants and good fighters and bold strikers, perfect warriors highly determined to recover the holy sepulchre, ought to make the passage all together.

Gregory's insistence on maintaining Frederick's excommunication caused sharp division in the crusading army and this led to different groups leaving at different times, which could explain the stress Guillem lays on the need for all the key fighters to depart together.

In the second *tornada* Guillem sends word to 'the noble, valiant count of Toulouse' that God has singled him out as one he particularly wishes to 'serve him in his birthplace'.

---

erick crowned himself in the Church of the Holy Sepulchre (see Runciman, *History*, III, pp. 174–89). Frederick was under interdict at the time, at loggerheads with Gregory IX.

> Al pro comte valen
> de Toloza·m digaz breumen,
> estiers, qe·l sapcha veiramen,
> qe per so·l volc Dieus part totz enantir
> qe lai on ell nascet l'anes servir. (vv. 56–60)

In addition, immediately tell the noble, valiant count of Toulouse on my behalf, so that he may be truly aware of this, that this is why God wished that he, more than anyone else, should go to serve him in his birthplace.

This *tornada* appears to have been added on after the treaty of Paris of 12 April 1229, whereby Raymond VII undertook *inter alia* to do penance for five years fighting the infidel. In this light the emphasis with which the troubadour singles out the count *part totz* (v. 59, 'above all') as one who should follow his injunctions to expiate his sins in the Holy Land, is interesting. Given Guillem's invective against Rome and his loyalty to his natural lord during the Albigensian wars, the troubadour may not be implying Raymond's particular sinfulness; rather, once Raymond had taken the cross he could be seen as a leader who could reinforce Frederick's as yet unfinished campaign overseas.

The defence of Rome was taken up by the *trobairitz* Gormonda from Montpellier, a town that remained staunchly orthodox during the Albigensian Crusade (BdT 177.1). Her viewpoint is unlikely to be an individual one: she is likely to be the Church's mouthpiece, and to have had her song vetted and informed by the ecclesiastical authorities. Her rhetoric is the demonstrative kind, consisting of praise and blame, as well as some violent threats. Rome is the source of all perfection and salvation, she proclaims; Guillem is a 'rabid madman who broadcasts so many false words', and her peroration invokes God's assistance in making him 'die under the same law and with the same punishment by which a heretic dies'. Her response to crusading is that heretics are worse than Saracens, 'and more false-hearted'. Far from supporting Frederick's efforts in the East, she declares that those seeking salvation 'should at once take the cross in order to crush and wreck the false heretics'. She predicts that within two years Rome and France will succeed in destroying the 'false silent heretics who fear no prohibitions and believe in secret teachings', when the 'arrogant' Raymond VII of Toulouse 'will have to give up his tricks and his dubious faith and set all the damage to rights', disavowing 'the false people of Toulouse', all of whom covertly and outrageously flout God's commands and destabilise the world. Bracketing the count of Toulouse and the emperor together, she claims to take great comfort in the fact that they are achieving little despite their military efforts, now that they have turned aside from Rome; however, she sends a somewhat conciliatory if unappealing message to Frederick: 'of the emperor I say that if he does not reconcile himself with you [Rome] his crown will come to great dishonour, and rightly so; but anyone who confesses his wrongs with a good grace and is tormented by them easily finds pardon from you.' Her tirade precedes the treaty of Paris in April 1229, when Frederick was in the East and might be thought to be achieving some success by negotiating the ten-year truce in February 1229 with al- Kāmil, who returned Jerusalem and other holy sites to the Crusader Kingdom – even if this proved to be of no lasting benefit and was unappreciated by nearly all concerned at the time.[9] Furthermore, ironically, on his return home in June 1229 Frederick's troops were highly successful against the papal forces.

While the city of Avignon, jealous of its independent rights, temporarily opposed the advance of the French, the count of Provence, Raymond Berenguer, had little reason to sympathise with Raymond VII of Toulouse. In 1230 the latter launched a major attack on him. Before the treaty of Paris of 1229 the counts of Toulouse owned rights over the imperial lands to the left of the Rhône. The treaty forced Raymond VII temporarily to renounce them, but he immediately set about attempting to regain them. At the time of the attack the nobles and cities, particularly Marseille, were revolting against Raymond Berenguer's authority. The count of Toulouse crossed the Rhône, made allies of the citizens of Tarascon and drove forward to Marseille. By the end of 1230 he had formed a league consisting of Tarascon and Marseille, along with Uc and Raimon of Baux and other Provençal nobles, and on 7 November the people of Marseille offered him sovereignty over their city. Raimon Berenguer in turn sought the support of the king and the emperor, and by 1232 Frederick had distanced himself from the count of Toulouse. The emperor's intervention on the side of the count of Provence proved decisive, imposing peace on the region. During this war the troubadour Bertran d'Alamanon, a loyal servant of Raymond Berenguer, was captured by Raymond VII or one of his allies, and Asperti argues that it was while Bertran was in prison, most probably in the winter of 1232–1233 or the beginning of spring, when he composed a complex and allusive political *sirventes* (BdT 76.16) attacking Raymond VII and the Provençal rebels. The particular point of interest as far as crusading is concerned is that Bertran mocks Raymond's claim to have committed himself to go on crusade. The count

> se cuid'esser a Deu offertz,
> – qar l'an en cort entrepausat –,
> ez a·s al dos la crox leuat
> per anar segurs pels desertz.   (vv. 15–18)

> thinks he has offered himself to God – since they have coerced him in court – and is carrying the cross on his back so that he can wander safely through the deserts.

This picture of Raymond as crusader refers to one of the conditions of the treaty of Paris, whereby he had to promise to go on crusade to the East (which he never did). The comment that by wearing the cross on his back the count will be safe in the deserts is no doubt comical on a literal level, but also metaphorical in the context of his imminent defeat in Provence.

---

[9] See Chapter 7, p. 142.

A further anticlerical invective by Peire Cardenal (BdT 335.54), perhaps composed in the later 1230s, attacks the religious orders for their sale of pardons and other abuses, and their avoidance of any personal commitment to the Holy Land:

Per deniers trobaretz perdos
ab elhs, s'avetz fag malestan,
e renoviers sebelliran
per aver, tant son cobeitos;
mas ges lo paupre sofrachos
per nuil temps non er sebelir
ni vizitar ni acuillir
si non era pozestados.

E d'aquo baston lur maizos
e belhs vergiers ont elhs estan,
mas ges li turc ni li perssan
non creiran Dieu per lurs sermos
qu'elhs lur fasson, car paoros
son del passar e del morir,
e volo mais de sai bastir
que lay conquerre los fellos.   (vv. 17–32)

For money you will get pardons from them, if you have committed an unseemly act, and they will bury usurers for lucre, they are so greedy; but the needy pauper must never be buried or visited or welcomed unless he is powerful.

And with this they build their houses and fine orchards where they reside, but the Turks and Persians will never believe in God through any sermons they might preach to them, as they are afraid of travelling overseas and of dying, and they would rather build over here than conquer the wicked over there.

Vatteroni suggests the reference to orchards may allude to the 'Garrigue gardens' to which the Dominicans of Toulouse moved in 1230, around Christmastime, after having abandoned the convent of Saint-Romain for lack of space. He adds that a date during the second half of the 1230s might be indirectly supported by the situation of profound aversion for the *ordo Praedicatorum* recorded in Toulouse at this time, whether on the level of a citizens' revolt against the brothers or with regard to the politics of Raymond VII and his contacts with the emperor, which were particularly strong during the period 1236–1240.[10]

It was not only the numerous Occitan texts which bore witness to the diffusion of powerfully anticlerical polemics at this time. Some Old French authors also show solidarity with the southern troubadours and attack the behaviour of the Church.[11]

---

[10] Vatteroni, *Il trovatore Peire Cardenal*, p. 681.
[11] Vatteroni, *Falsa clercia*, and Barbieri, 'Un sirventese religioso', pp. 311–17.

A song wrongly attributed to Moniot d'Arras, which begins by lamenting the death of kin in the Albigeois at the hands of the all-conquering French, blames the clergy for crusading failure overseas at Damietta (RS 640):

> Trop vit clergiez desloiaument;
> par tot lo mont voi Deu traïr;
> sa grant besogne fist perir
> outre mer, n'a pas longement,
> que nostre haut conquierement
> fist tot en perte revertir.   (vv. 9–14)

The clergy lives most dissolutely; all over the world I see God betrayed; not long ago they made His great business perish overseas, for they turned our high conquest into failure.

During the same period anticlerical invectives are also diffused outside the lyric: for example, in Huon de Saint-Quentin's *Complainte de Jérusalem contre Rome*, which refers explicitly to the loss of Damietta, the Albigensian Crusade, John of Brienne and the pontifical legate Pelagius; in Gautier de Coinci's *Vie de sainte Léocade*, also referring to Damietta; and in the *Besant de Dieu*, written in 1226–1227 by Guillaume le Clerc from Normandy, who castigates Frenchmen who hound the Albigensians but are no better than they:[12]

> Que dirra il a ces Franceis,
> Qui si preisiez chevalers sont,
> Qui par devant croizer se font
> Sovent contre ces Aubigeis?
> Il i a plusors de ces Franceis
> Qui autretant a blamer font
> Come font cil sor qui il vont.

What will he say to these Frenchmen who are such esteemed knights, who in preference often take the cross against those Albigensians? There are several of those Frenchmen who are as much to blame as those they are attacking.

Sympathy for the southern cause and criticism of the 'false crusade' was a matter of political and family allegiances, and lay hostility to the power of the Church. It was not sympathy for heretics. This is strikingly exemplified by Thibaut de Champagne, as he prepared for the next crusade to the Holy Land.

---

[12] *Huon de Saint-Quentin, poète satirique et lyrique, étude historique et édition de textes* (Madrid, 1983), ed. A. Serper, p. 87; *De Sainte Leocade : au tans que Sainz Hyldefons estbit arcevesques de Tholete cui Nostre Dame donna l'aube de prelaz : miracle versifié*, ed. E. Vilamo-Pentti (Helsinki, 1950), vv. 910–16, p. 157; *Le Besant de Dieu de Guillaume le Clerc de Normandie*, ed. P. Ruelle (Brussels, 1973), vv. 2484–90 (p. 133).

9

The Barons' Crusade, or the crusade of Thibaut de Champagne

Exhortation, separation and departure

In 1239 the treaty made between Frederick II and al-Kāmil in 1229 came to an end. Thibaut de Champagne, who in 1230 had first publicly declared his intention to go on crusade in anticipation of the end of the truce, became king of Navarre in 1234, and the crusade was preached at the end of that year. Preparations were complicated, and five years later, in the summer of 1239, Pope Gregory IX sent out agents to preach the crusade again, in both France and England. The emperor Frederick had been hoping to lead it but was prevented by events in Italy, and Thibaut was left in charge. By early summer he was ready to set sail, and he arrived at Acre on 1 September, where an army of around 1,000 knights assembled during the next few days. This period saw the production of a number of preaching songs, and also of songs of separation, in whose development Thibaut himself was particularly innovative.

Thibaut preceded his departure by presiding over the burning of more than 180 heretics at Mont-Aimé in Champagne. According to Michael Lower, this powerfully bolstered both his finances and his public image as a penitential crusader.[1] He himself contributed to the preaching of the crusade (RS 6):

> Seignor, sachiez, qui or ne s'an ira
> en cele terre ou Diex fu mors et vis
> et qui la croiz d'outremer ne penra
> a painnes mais ira en paradis.
> Qui a en soi pitié ne remembrance,

---

[1] M. Lower, *The Barons' Crusade: A Call to Arms and Its Consequences* (Philadelphia, 2005), pp. 94–111. Lower comments that Thibaut had a number of reasons for punishing heretics at that time and in that way: he had financial incentive, namely a claim on their property; and it helped him meet the penitential demands of crusading, since it was regarded as a pious act likely to win divine favour (pp. 109–11).

au Haut Seignor doit querre sa vanjance
et delivrer sa terre et son païs. (vv. 1–7)

> Lords, know this: whoever will not now go to that land where God died and rose again, and whoever will not take the cross to Outremer will find it hard ever to go to heaven. Whoever has pity and good remembrance in his heart must seek to avenge the Highest Lord and liberate his land and his country.

His composition draws on many of the motifs and arguments typical of crusade songs of exhortation: the hope of salvation and fear of hell, compassion for Our Lord's suffering, the need to avenge it and liberate the holy places that rightfully belong to God, the concern for personal reputation, the cowardice and lechery of those who stay behind. Barbieri suggests that, despite this exploitation of traditional material, he is perhaps the only poet to express so vividly and dramatically the possible objections of the man who hesitates to leave his loved ones:

Tuit li mauvais demorront par deça
qui n'ainment Dieu, bien ne honor ne pris;
et chascuns dit: 'ma fame que fera?'
'je ne lairoie a nul fuer mes amis'.
Cil sont cheoit en trop fole atendance,
qu'il n'est amis fors que Cil, sanz doutance,
qui por nos fu en la vraie croiz mis. (vv. 8–14)

> All the base men who do not love God, goodness or honour or reputation, will remain here; and each says: 'What will my wife do?', 'There is no way I would leave my friends.' These are embroiled in vain preoccupations, since there is certainly no true friend apart from the one who was placed upon the true cross for us.

As he remarks, 'the thought here is not with the *trouvère*'s courtly lady, but, more realistically, with his wife', and he sympathetically highlights 'the understandable concern over losing what is most dear [which] makes men cautious about armed expeditions to the Holy Land'.[2]

A single Occitan preaching song (BdT 9.10) may date from this period of preparation. With mixed emotions the troubadour Aimeric de Belenoi expresses compassion for the count, his lord, 'who has taken the cross to serve God', while celebrating the fact that 'God in His great kindness grants us such a leader'. His exhortations target the nobility:

---

[2] See the notes to Barbieri's edition. The song has traditionally been assigned to this period of preparation. It might go back as far as 1230, when Thibaut first pledged to go to the Holy Land, or to 1235, when he first took the cross and the enthusiasm aroused by the preachers was such that the pope strove to dissuade the crusaders from leaving prematurely.

> Caisi com son princes ausor,
> e Dieus lur ha dat mais valor
> es qui·n rema plus encolpatz;
> e qui, per creiser sa ricor,
> quant auzira·ls autres passatz,
> resta e los dezenansa
> contra Dieu s'es aconseillatz,
> e Dieus penra en venjansa
> tal qu'el corn del taulier n'er matz.　　　　(vv. 27–35)

For just as princes are more important and God has given them more prestige, one who stays behind is more guilty; and if someone stays to increase his riches when he hears the others have gone overseas, and does them damage, he has decided against God, and God will take such revenge that he will be checkmated in the corner of the chessboard.

Drawing on standard hortatory topoi, he thanks God for choosing such an excellent leader, 'who is count and will be called king' (*qu'es coms et er reis apelatz*, v. 57). Although this line has been thought in the past to refer to Richard the Lionheart, Aimeric's datable songs span 1216–1241, and his recent editor Caterina Menichetti (see the online edition) argues that he is most probably alluding to Thibaut de Champagne.

A sombre trouvère song (RS 1020a), uncertainly attributed to Richard de Fournival, a canon of Amiens, evokes the dreadful day of wrath when God will punish all who fail to answer His call:

> Au pesme jour coureçous et plain d'ire
> que li fieus Dieu venra fiers et iriés,
> et mousterra ses plaies a delivre
> en ses costés, en ses mains, en ses piés
> qu'il ot pour nous et fendus et perciés,
> n'i avra saint qui ost un seul mot dire.
> Li plus hardis vauroit estre croisiés
> tant douteront son mautalent et s'ire!　　　　(vv. 17–24)

On the dread dark day of wrath, when the Son of God will come, terrible and wrathful, and will openly reveal the wounds in his side, in his hands, in his feet, pierced and nailed for us, then there will be no saint who dares to utter a single word. The bravest will wish he had taken the cross, so much will they fear his fury and his ire!

The piece appears to refer to a truce, or lack of it, in the Holy Land:

> Outre la mer, en cele sainte terre
> ou Dieus fu nés et ou fu mors et vis,
> devons aler nostre iretaje qerre,

car a grant tort en fu pour nous hors mis.
Ki n'i venra, il n'ert pas ses amis
car il n'i a pais ne trieves ne terme
Dieus nous i laist si aler et venir
k'en paradis puissons aler sans guerre!   (vv. 25–32)

Overseas, in that holy land where God was born and where he died and lived again, we should go to claim our inheritance, for he was most wrongly expelled from there on our account. Anyone who does not go will not be his friend, for there is no peace, nor truce, nor respite there.

The truce in question may be the one concluded by Frederick II in 1229 for a period of 10 years, 5 months and 40 days, and its expiry would place the text in or around 1239, though this is uncertain.

A further song of exhortation (RS 1152) by Thibaut himself refers to a period of poisonous conflict in 1236–1239 between Gregory IX and Frederick II:

Au temps plain de felonnie,
d'envie et de traïson,
de tort et de mesproison,
sanz bien et sanz courtoisie,
et que entre maint baron
veons le siecle empirier,
et voi esconmunnïer
ceus qui plus offrent raison,
lors vuel faire une chançon.   (vv. 1–9)

In this time full of treachery, envy and betrayal, of injustice and error, void of goodness and courtliness, when amongst many barons we see the decline of the world, and I see excommunicated those who would make the best contribution, then I wish to compose a song.

The reference to excommunication probably concerns Gregory's anathema against Frederick on 20 March 1239, whose sentence was announced to the whole of Christendom after 7 April. The emperor was refusing to take on the leadership of a crusade before the end of his ten-year truce with al-Kāmil. While Thibaut suggests that Frederick would be the best person to lead the crusade, he is doubtful about the participation of many of the barons, since it is essential for crusaders to go with the right intention and purity of heart:

Li royaumez de Surie
nous dist et crie a haut ton,
se nouz ne nouz amendon,
pour Dieu que n'i alons mie:
n'i feriemes se mal non.   (vv. 10–14)

> The kingdom of Syria tells us and cries aloud that if we do not amend our lives, it is better for God if we not go there: we shall do nothing but harm.

The second part of the song moves to a debate over whether to depart from the beloved lady, which suggests that it was composed before the first days of August 1239, when the crusaders left the port of Marseille, or perhaps, as Wallensköld suggests, 24 June of the same year, when Thibaut probably left Champagne for Lyon, where the crusaders were assembling to await departure and were still hoping for Frederick's involvement. Barbieri observes that, despite the claims of the continuator of the chronicle of William of Tyre that the French barons considered the emperor to be a collaborator of the Moslem enemy, and therefore would have set out without him, the official documents speak of a much more diplomatic relationship between the emperor and the crusaders. Frederick, caught up in his political interests and the conflict with the pope, which made him reluctant to waste time on a new crusade, seems to have offered the crusaders all the help he could, leaving them to believe until the last minute that he really did wish to head the expedition; for their part the crusaders postponed departure several times, and Frederick's letter of 9 March 1239 seems to support the idea of his participation; but only a few days later the papal interdict precipitated matters by making this impossible, and further delay pointless. Barbieri also remarks that the impression gained from reading the text is that of an appeal from a man who already feels invested with a certain authority over the other crusaders – in other words, he is now the leader – and that in exhorting his companions to action he is also intending to seek precise guarantees from them, being aware that conflicts, divisions, acts of insubordination and individual interests can only damage the outcome of the expedition and personal prestige.[3]

Before crusaders finally set sail on their expeditions there must have been a good deal of time when they were simply waiting around for everyone to join forces. This is likely to have been the case on the Barons' Crusade, when they were hoping for Frederick to come and take charge. As Thibaut and his companions assembled at Lyon before setting off for Marseille, were they accompanied by members of their family and escort? The days and weeks of waiting would have offered an ideal opportunity for poet–musicians to provide entertainment, and it seems no coincidence that this period gives rise to courtly songs of separation and departure, modelled on Conon de Béthune's celebrated *Ahi! Amors, com dure departie* (RS 1125). Such songs include *Li departirs de la douce contree* (RS 449) by Chardon de Croisilles, formally elegant but entirely based on quotations from other examples of the genre, in which he is probably celebrating Thibaut de Champagne's wife. The song is clearly addressed to a courtly audience and makes no attempt at crusading exhortation.

These songs also include Thibaut de Champagne's song *Dame, ensint est qu'il m'en covient aler* (RS 757). If autobiographical, it indicates that the author is about to leave his lady, whether in Champagne, Lyon or Marseille. Barbieri comments that in the first more traditional part of this *chanson de départie* Thibaut exploits

---

[3] See Barbieri's edition of RS 1152.

the Châtelain de Coucy's pessimistic approach (RS 679), according to which the crusade is an unavoidable duty to be faced with scant enthusiasm since it takes the lover away from love:

> Dame, ensint est qu'il m'en covient aler
> et departir de la douce contree
> ou tant ai malx apris a endurer:
> quant je vos lais, droiz est que je m'en hee.
> Dex! pour quoi fu la terre d'outremer,
> qui tant amant avra fait dessevrer
> dont puis ne fu l'amours reconfortee,
> ne ne porent la joie remenbrer?
>
> [...]
>
> Je ne voi pas, quant de li sui partiz,
> que puisse avoir bien ne solaz ne joie,
> car onques riens ne fis si a enviz
> con vos lessier, se je jamés vos voie!
> Trop par en sui dolanz et esbahiz;
> par maintes foiz m'en serai repantiz
> quant j'onques vos aler en ceste voie,
> et je recort voz debonaires diz.   (vv. 1–8, 17–24)

Lady, it is destined that I should leave and depart from the sweet land where I have so much learned to endure sufferings: since I am leaving you, it is right I should hate myself for it. God, why did the Holy Land ever exist? It will have separated so many lovers whose love has never since been able to recover its strength, and who were never able to revive their joy.

[...]

Since I am separated from it/her, I cannot see how I can have any comfort, happiness or joy, for I have never done anything so reluctantly as to leave you – and if only I may be allowed to see you again one day! This makes me utterly grief-stricken and broken-hearted. I shall repent time and time again of ever wishing to undertake this journey, and [when] I call to mind your gracious words.

Noting that in the second part of the song the text changes register, Barbieri argues that it develops in an innovative way the attempt to reconcile love for the lady with crusading values, and concludes that Thibaut arrives at a mystical interpretation rarely found in this type of song, according to which earthly love is surpassed or absorbed into divine love:

> Bien doit mes cuers estre liez et dolanz:
> dolanz de ce que je part de ma dame
> et liez de ce que je sui desirranz

de servir Deu, qui est mes cuers et m'ame.
Iceste amors est trop fine et poissanz:
par là covient venir les plus saichanz;
c'est li rubiz, l'esmeraude et la jame
qui touz garit des viez pechiez puanz.

Dame des ciels, granz roïne poissanz,
au grant besoing me soiez secorranz!
De vos amer puisse avoir droite flame!
Quant dame per, dame me soit aidanz.   (vv. 33–44)

My heart must surely be happy and sad: sad because I leave my lady, and happy because I am full of the desire to serve God, to whom belong my heart and soul. This [divine] love is most pure and powerful; the wisest must perforce arrive at this; it is the ruby, the emerald and the gemstone which cures all from vile and stinking sins.

Lady of the heavens, great and powerful Queen, be my support in my great hour of need! May I feel the proper fervour to love you! When I lose a lady, may a lady be my aid.

Once overseas – whether in the Holy Land or on the way – Thibaut composed another *chanson de départie* (RS 1469), whose themes, Barbieri suggests (see the online edition), take on a new and more 'historical' tone.

> Quant me covient, dame, de vos loignier
> onques certes plus dolanz hons ne fu,
> et Dex feroit, ce croi, por moi vertu
> se je jamés vos pooie aprochier,
> que touz les biens et toz les max
> que j'aieai je par vos, douce dame veraie,
> ne ja sanz vos nuns ne me puet aidier:
> non fera il, qu'il n'i avroit mestier.
>
> Ses granz beautez, dont nuns hons n'a pooir
> qu'il en deïst la cinquantisme part,
> li dit plaisant, li amoreus regart
> me font sovent resjoïr et doloir:
> joie en atent, que mes cuers a ce bee,
> et la paors rest dedanz moi entree;
> ensi m'estuet morir par estovoir
> en grant esmai, en joie et en voloir.
>
> Dame, de cui est ma granz desirree,
> saluz vos mant d'outre la mer salee
> com a celi ou je pans main et soir,
> n'autres pansers ne me fait joie avoir.   (vv. 25–44)

When I had to part from you, my lady, there was certainly not a more sorrowful man than I, and God would, I think, perform a miracle for me if I were ever able to approach you, for all the good and bad things I have, I have from you, sweet true lady, and no one but you can assist me: they would not do so, since it would be useless.

Her great beauty, a fiftieth of which no one has the power to describe, her delightful words, her loving glances make me often rejoice and suffer: I expect joy from her, for my heart aspires to this, but fear takes hold of me once more, so I am perforce compelled to die in great distress [*or:* from privation], in joy and in longing.

Lady, for whom is my great desire, I send you greetings from over the salt sea, as to the one of whom I think day and night, and no other thought gives me joy.

In this way, Barbieri suggests, Thibaut 'deliberately moves between *topoi* typical of the courtly love song, in particular those focussing on the lover's timidity, and themes characteristic of songs of separation, more grounded in reality'. These songs express feelings which crusaders may well have felt in anticipation of their journey overseas; at the same time they reinforce their aristocratic authors' self-perception as the embodiment of refined courtly values.

The Gaza ambush

After arriving in the Holy Land at the beginning of September 1239 crusaders assembled in Acre, but the fluid situation of the enemy and tensions between the sultanates of Syria and Egypt suggested it would be better to delay action and await favourable developments. Enforced idleness was frustrating both to a number of the barons and to the lesser knights who had mortgaged their lands and whose resources were running out.

Some barons decided to strike out independently, and during the course of one such undertaking they were ambushed near Gaza. Henry of Bar had learned that an Egyptian army under Mameluk Rukn ad-Din was on its way there from the Delta, and made a secret plan to attack it and win all the credit and booty. At nightfall on 12 November he prepared to march out against Gaza with 500 horsemen and over 1,000 foot soldiers. News of the plan leaked out, and Thibaut, with three Grand Masters of the Orders and the count of Brittany, came up and begged, then ordered, them to go back to the camp. Henry refused. He was so confident of success that, when he drew near to Gaza about dawn, he halted his men in a hollow in the dunes of the seashore and told them to rest. The Egyptian army was far larger than he thought, and nearly encircled the Franks. Walter of Jaffa was the first to realise what was happening and rode away northwards with the duke of Burgundy, other knights following as soon as they could. But Henry would not leave the infantry whom he had led into a trap, and his closest friends stayed with him. More than 1,000, including Henry, were killed, and 600 more were captured were carried off to Egypt. The other French crusaders wanted to pursue the enemy and try to free the prisoners, but the Templars and Hospitallers disagreed with this proposal and convinced Thibaut that there was too great a risk of the hostages being put to death.

In his chronicle the *Continuation Rothelin* William of Tyre inserts two Old French songs (RS 164 and 1133) to underpin the events of the narrative. Barbieri observes that the

> rough-and-ready versification and rhetoric of these two songs may be due to their essentially documentary nature, whether they are the result [. . .] of reconstruction through memory by the chronicle's compiler, or whether the text as it is preserved reflects the precarious conditions in which the authors must have found themselves and in which the transmission in any case took place. It is also possible that some allusions to later developments of the episode, closer to the actual events, were woven into the original text during later stages of transmission.[4]

The two pieces present very different points of view. The first (RS 164), uncertainly attributed to a companion of Thibaut de Champagne, Philip II, lord of Nanteuil-le-Haudouin, implicitly adopts that of the barons and bitterly blames the military orders for the decision not to try to rescue the hostages.

> Ha! cuens de Bar, quel souffraite
> de vous li François avront!
> Quant il savront la nouvele
> de vous, grant duel en feront,
> quant France est desheritee
> de si vaillant chevalier.
> Maudite soit la jornee
> dont tant hardi soudoier
> sont esclave et prisonnier.
>
> Se l'Ospitaus et li Temples
> et li frere chevalier
> eüssent donné example
> a noz genz de chevauchier,
> nostre granz chevalerie
> ne fust or pas en prison,
> ne li Sarrazin en vie;
> mais ainsi nel firent mie,
> dont ce fu granz mesprisons
> et samblanz de traïzon.   (vv. 20–38)

Ah, Count of Bar, how the French will miss you! When they hear the news about you they will make a huge lament, when France is deprived of such a valiant knight. A curse on the day when such brave soldiers are slaves and prisoners!

---

4   See Barbieri's notes to RS 164.

If the Hospitallers and the Templars and the brother (Teutonic) knights had given the example to our people to ride in pursuit, our great cavalry would not now be in prison, or the Saracens alive; but this they did not do, and it was a great mistake and virtually treasonable.

The other song (RS 1133), remarkable for the insight it provides into the state of mind of the lesser, poor knights, denounces the barons' rivalries and their imprudent personal initiatives which produced disastrous consequences. It also complains about the prolonged period of inactivity.

> Ne chant pas, que que nuls die,
> de cuer lié ne de joious,
> quant nos baron sont oisous
> en la terre de Surie;
> encor n'i ont envaïe
> cité ne chastiaus ne bours;
> par une fole envaïe
> perdi li cuens de Bar vie.
>
> [...]
>
> S'il euvrent par aatie
> tout iert tourné a rebours:
> trop y a des orgueillous
> qui s'entreportent envie;
> se Diex l'orgueil ne chastie,
> perdu avront leur labors
> et mal leur paine emploïe;
> se ceste voie est perie,
> vilains sera li retours
> et sainte Eglyse abaissie.
>
> Encor n'ont chose esploitie
> dont il soit preus ne hounours,
> ne moustree leur valors
> dont y ait nouvelle oye;
> se Diex l'orgueil ne chastie,
> tout sont cheü en decours;
> si tres haute baronnie,
> quant de France fu partie,
> on disoit que c'ert la flours
> du mont et la seignorie.
>
> Aus bachelers ne tient mie
> ne aus povres vavasours:
> a ceus grieve li sejourz
> qui ont leur terre engagie,

ne n'ont bonté ne aïe
ne confort des granz seignors,
quant leur monnoie est faillie;
il n'i ont mort desservie:
s'il s'en revienent le cours,
d'euls blasmer seroit folie.

Li pueples de France prie,
seigneur prisonnier, pour vous;
trop estiez orgueillous
de moustrer chevalerie,
fole volenté hardie
vous eslonga de secours;
li turc vous ont en baillie:
or en penst li filz Marie,
car ce sera granz dolours
se Diex ne vous en deslie. (vv. 1–50)

Whatever people may say, I do not sing with a happy or joyful heart while our barons are idle in the land of Syria; they have not yet attacked any city or castles or towns; because of a foolish sortie the count of Bar has lost his life.

[...]

If the barons act out of rivalry, everything will go downhill: there are too many arrogant men vying with each other. If God does not punish this pride, they will have wasted their labours and put their efforts to poor use; if this crusade is a failure, the return will be dishonourable and Holy Church humiliated.

They have not yet carried out any exploit producing profit or honour, or demonstrated any valour of which news is heard; if God does not punish this pride, they are heading for total downfall. Such a high company of barons, when it left France, was said to be the finest flower of the world.

It is not the fault of the young knights or poor vavassors: the idle wait weighs heavily on those who have mortgaged their land and have no compassion or aid or comfort from the great lords, when their money has run out. They do not deserve to die there: if they hurry back home, it would be folly to blame them.

The people of France pray, lord prisoners, for you; you were too proud in showing off your valour – a foolish reckless ardour carried you away from help. The Turks hold you in their power; now may the son of Mary give thought to this, for it will be most painful if God does not liberate you from them.

To free the prisoners the French undertook a long and complex series of negotiations and alliances which involved all Christian parties, Syria and Egypt. The negotiations were slow to bear fruit and Thibaut, discouraged and annoyed by the continual internal tensions among the Christians, carried out a swift pilgrimage to Jerusalem and departed for France during September 1240, before being able to establish the hoped-for truce. The negotiations were brought to a conclusion by Richard of Cornwall, who had arrived in the Holy Land after Thibaut's departure, and the prisoners were freed on 23 April 1241.[5]

In his commentary to RS 1133, Barbieri draws attention to

> the realism expressed in these lines which form a sort of caption to the events narrated in the chronicle in which they are set, giving us access to the state of mind and opinions of the participants in the later crusades. Idealistic motives do not seem as clear as they once were, and in any case they are not highlighted; instead, more worldly preoccupations predominate: ambition for personal glory on the part of individual barons, the problems of the high cost of the expeditions and the economic difficulties of the minor knights.[6]

While this may be true of the Gaza pieces, it was noblemen, following in the footsteps of earlier barons such as Thibaut and his companions, who would keep crusading alive up to the end of the thirteenth century.[7] In the meantime, the Albigensian wars would soon erupt again, and the shocking news in 1244 of the sack of Jerusalem would inspire King Louis IX of France to lead not one but eventually two royal crusades.

---

[5] Runciman, *History*, III, pp. 214–15; Barbieri, 'About the text', in his edition of RS 164.
[6] See Barbieri's notes to RS 1133.
[7] Housley, *The Later Crusades*, pp. 12 and 23.

10

The Seventh Crusade, or the First Crusade of Saint Louis

After the defeat at Gaza in November 1239 Thibaut withdrew to Acre. Meanwhile an-Nasir Da-ud of Kerak responded to the attack on the Muslim caravan by marching on Jerusalem, which he was able to occupy without difficulty, as it was almost completely undefended. The soldiers in the citadel held out for twenty-seven days but surrendered on 7 December 1239. An-Nasir destroyed the fortifications, razing the Tower of David to the ground, and retired to Kerak.[1] Four years later, on 11 August 1244, the Khwarismians in turn swept into Jerusalem, sacking the city, slaughtering the Christian population and breaking into the Church of the Holy Sepulchre, where they slew some Latin priests who were celebrating Mass, tore the bones of the kings of Jerusalem from their tombs and set the church itself on fire.[2] The Christian forces of Outremer, allied to Muslim armies under an-Nasir and al-Mansur against a common enemy, gathered to repel the Khwarismians under Baibars, who on October 17 crushed them at the disastrous battle at La Forbie (Harbiyah). 'The Christian army was the largest that Outremer had put into the field since the fatal day of Hattin': 600 knights, 300 Templars and Hospitallers, a contingent from the Teutonic Order, a proportionate number of sergeants and foot soldiers. Within a few hours the whole Frankish army was destroyed. Some 5,000 were dead; 800 prisoners were led off to Egypt. 'Only at Hattin had the losses been greater.'[3] On 27 November the bishop of Beirut sailed from Acre to tell the princes of the West that 'reinforcements must be sent if the whole kingdom were not to perish'.[4]

The Occitan uprising of 1242

Meanwhile, those in the Languedoc suffering the consquences of the Albigensian Crusade had every reason to question the idea of crusading, and had indeed done

---

[1] Runciman, *History*, III, p. 215; see also Wolff and Hazard, *The Later Crusades*, pp. 477–78.
[2] P. Jackson, *The Mongols and The West, 1221–1410* (Harlow, 2005), p. 75; Runciman, *History*, III, p. 225.
[3] Runciman, *History*, III, pp. 225–27.
[4] Runciman, *History*, III, p. 256.

so in the earlier stages of the French invasion. As a result of defeat in the Albigensian crusade, Raymond VII of Toulouse had been forced to accept the humiliating Treaty of Paris of 1229, which stipulated that if he produced no male heir all his lands would revert to the king of France through the marriage of Louis IX's brother Alphonse to Raymond's only daughter, Jeanne. For years the count sought to re-establish his position, hesitantly and unsuccessfully, by asserting his claims on Provence. He appears still to have hoped for support from Frederick II. Two years after his second excommunication Frederick was still at war with the papacy (1240–1241), besieging the north Italian city of Faenza, when the Guelf troubadour Uc de San Circ called on the king of France and the Church to send their crusading army to the aid of the city (BdT 457.42). The emperor wants nothing other than to bring down France and the Church, he declares,

> e la soa crezensa e sa ley far tener;
> don la gleyza e·l reys hi devon pervezer
> que.ns mandon la crosada e·ns venhan mantener. (vv. 36–38)

> and to impose his belief and faith on them; so the Church and the king should see to it that they send the crusade to us and come and support us.

Lambasting the emperor as a cruel, faithless unbeliever, he claims that Frederick is planning not only to restore French territories to England but also to avenge the Toulousain, Béziers and the Carcassès, and warns Raymond not to get involved.

In furtherance of his plans to reclaim his former territories, the count concluded an agreement in 1241 with Raymond Berenguer V of Provence, which saw him betrothed to Sanchia, that count's third daughter and the sister of the queens of France and England. Powicke observes that 'the part played by James of Aragon at this time is very significant of the complicated tugs and strains to which a medieval king might be subjected', and explains why since 1234, despite his claims and titles in the South,

> when war with King Louis of France on behalf of his rights and the rights of his vassals in Languedoc had been imminent, he had preferred a peaceful policy. He felt that a family compact between Raymond of Toulouse and Raymond Berenger of Provence under his and papal auspices would be the best way to check French advance. If Raymond could have a son the treaty of Paris of 1229 would not operate. Hence it was arranged that Raymond's marriage with Sanchia of Aragon, James's aunt, should be annulled on grounds of consanguinity and papal approval be procured also for a new marriage with Sanchia of Provence. The former object was obtained, but Pope Gregory IX died before the second could be reached. Raymond was affianced by proxy at Aix on 11 August 1241, the pope died on 22 August, and during the vacancy in the papal chair Raymond Berenger repudiated the contract.[5]

---

[5] F. M. Powicke, *King Henry III and the Lord Edward*, 2 vols (Oxford, 1947), II, pp. 192–94.

The failure of James' plans led Raymond to align himself with Henry III of England and Count Hugh of La Marche. Henry's attempts to recover Normandy, Brittany, Anjou, Poitou and their satellites had been the central element of Henry's foreign policy since their loss at the beginning of the thirteenth century.[6] On 24 June 1241 the king's brother Alphonse was knighted at Saumur, and at Poitiers in July he was invested with the county of Poitou. Hugh paid him homage with some reluctance, and then regretting it he 'rallied the barons and castellans of Poitou at Parthenay and then, with them, entered into a sworn confederacy with the seneschal, cities, and barons of Gascony'.[7] Henry welcomed the opportunity this offered him and bound himself by oath to go to Gascony and demand his rights of the king of France, sailing there in May 1242, when he was the centre of a widespread alliance of southern princes pledged to support Henry in a war against Louis. After the battles of Taillebourg and Saintes (20–22 July) the count of La Marche submitted humiliatingly to the French king, Henry withdrew, and 'within a few weeks of his arrival, all hope of the restoration of Poitou to himself and his brother was destroyed, and he was thrown back on the southern allies whom Raymond of Toulouse had gathered together'. He seems to have taken no further military action while bogged down in this incoherent alliance, with only limited ability to give unqualified support to the count of Toulouse: in the Bordeaux convention of 28 August Henry said that 'if the Church of Rome attacked Raymond, and the king of France, at the mandate of the pope, moved against him and entered his land in person, he would not desist, at the prayers or admonitions of the Church of Rome, from helping him, unless compelled to do so by sentence of excommunication'. Powicke comments that the French armies 'soon relieved him of any sense of dilemma'. Raymond capitulated on 20 October 1242, and in January 1243 accepted the peace of Lorris, where he undertook to abide by the treaty of Paris of 1229. This put paid to further resistance to French influence in the Languedoc. 'Henry complained bitterly of Raymond's desertion, but could do nothing. In April he made another truce with Louis of France. In September he returned to England.'[8]

Various troubadours speak out about this 1242 uprising, and some choose to make unfavourable comparisons with what is happening in the Midi and crusading efforts elsewhere.[9] Although the circumstances and dating are uncertain, Peire del Vilar seems to anticipate the outbreak of war under Henry III (BdT 365.1), and to blame it as a distraction from the proper use of resources in an oriental crusade.[10]

---

6   S. Lloyd, *English Society and the Crusade, 1216–1307* (Cambridge, 1988), p. 219.
7   Powicke, *King Henry III*, pp. 188–89,
8   Powicke, *King Henry III*, pp. 191–95.
9   Also relating to this uprising is Guillem de Montanhagol's *Bel m'es quan d'armatz aug refrim* (BdT 225.3, P. T. Ricketts, ed., *Les poésies de Guilhem de Montanhagol, troubadour provençal du XIIIe siècle* (Toronto, 1964), IV, p. 60); see A. Jeanroy, 'Le soulèvement de 1242 dans la poésie des troubadours', *AdM*, 16 (1904), 311–29.
10   Since the publication of my article 'Peire del Vilar, *Sendatz vermelhs, endis e ros* (BdT 365.1)', *Lt*, 6 (2013), pp. 1–18, Jonathan Boulton, in a private communication, has indicated

The French fleur-de-lys is 'destined to bloom and spread everywhere if not checked by cold or heat'; but it would have been better, Peire declares, to try and win back the Holy Land.

> Sendatz vermelhs, endis e ros,
> e tendas e traps despleyar,
> elmes et ausbercs flameyar
> e brandir lansas e bordos,
> e cayrels dessarrar espes,
> e ferir de bran demanes
> veirem en breu: que·l lhaupart fenh
> que say per flor culhir s'espenh.
>
> [...]
>
> E fora genser la razos
> que·s coitesso del loc cobrar
> on per Melchion e Gaspar
> fon adzoratz l'altisme tos
> que can l'us a l'autre comes;
> c'ar ses la decima, non es
> us tant caut qu'en arme un lenh
> ni·n bastis trabuquet ni genh.   (vv. 1–8, 33–40)

Soon we shall see banners of scarlet, indigo and red-gold silk and tents and pavilions unfold, helmets and hauberks flash, lances and pikes brandished, bolts fired thickly, and swords struck on the instant: for the leopard [the English king] purposes to leap over here to pick a flower [the French one].

[...]

The cause would have been better were they to hasten to recover the place where the highest Child was worshipped by Melchior and Gaspar, rather than for the one [king] to attack the other; for without the tithe, there is no one keen enough to arm a ship or construct a trebuchet or war machine for this.

---

the existence of the heraldic emblem of a detached winged hand holding a sword that was apparently invented to serve in the role of charge in the quarters of difference in the arms of Don Manuel de Castilla, seventh son of Saint Fernando I (Fernando III of León), first of the continuous line of kings of Castile and León, who lived from 1236 to 1283: see F. Menendez Pidal de Navascués, *Heráldica Medieval Española*, I: *La Casa Real de León y Castilla* (Madrid, 1982), pp. 98–104. If the *ala* were to refer to Don Manuel this would invalidate my dating, since in 1242 he would have been only six years old; however, Professor Boulton also suggests that the 'wing' could have been that of the Hohenstaufen eagle, to which Manuel's probably alluded itself: the fact that 'the author refers to a single pallet in the arms of Aragon suggests a tendency to represent wholes by parts, and that could explain the use of "wing" to represent "eagle".

As hopes of successful resistance fade, the troubadour Duran Sartor de Paernas takes aim against its leaders (BdT 126.1), contemptuously observing that the southern allies are so defeatist they are allowing themselves to be crushed by the French enemy that has proved to be eminently beatable in the East:

> Tant han sufert ll'aut baron lur mescap
> qe·l meill del mon tenon Frances a clap,
> e qar suefron q'aitals gens los atrap
> no·i ha conseilh mas del broc a l'enap
> serva chascus, qe be·os puesc dir ses gap
> qe lai part Sur en la terra d'Alap
> lur feron far Turc mant crit e mant jap,
> e·l croi ric sai no·i sabon penre cap.   (vv. 25–32)

The high-ranking barons have put up with their defeat so long that the French are crushing the world's best. Since they [the barons] let themselves be trapped by such people, the only solution is for each [of the rest of us] to pay them [the French] back in their own coin. It's no exaggeration to say that overseas beyond Tyre, in the land of Aleppo, the Turks have made them [the French)] squeal and yap a lot. But the cowardly nobles over here can't capture a thing from them [the French].

Finally, in what appears to be a hopeless, unrealistic last-ditch attempt to revive the count of Toulouse's claims in the spring of 1243 when Henry is still in France, the troubadour Bernart de Rovenac excoriates the faint-hearts (BdT 66.3), appeals to Henry's self-interest in defending his Gascon possessions and plays on James' name, Jacme (*jac me*, 'I lie down'), linking this to *jazer* ('to lie'), mocking the king of Aragon not only for idleness but also for his well-known womanising. Acknowledging James' successes against the Moors in Spain, he says that the latter are having a hard time of it because the king is inappropriately taking out on them the shame he is suffering in the vicinity of Limoux, where he has lost his seigneurial rights through the treaty of Paris.

> Rey d'Arago ses contenda
> deu ben nom aver
> Jacme, quar trop vol jazer,
> e qui que sa terra·s prenda,
> el es tan flacx e chauzitz
> que sol res no·y contraditz,
> e car ven lai als Sarrazis fellos
> l'anta e·l dan que pren sai vas Limos.   (vv. 17–24)

The King of Aragon should unquestionably bear the name 'Jacme' because he likes lying down [*jazer*] a lot, and if anyone wants to take over his land he is so effete and precious that he hasn't a single thing to say against it, and yet over there he is making the treacherous Saracens pay a high price for the damage he is suffering here near Limoux.

Resistance to French rule probably explains the almost complete silence of troubadours in the Languedoc to the disasters of 1244. The only possible exception is a song by Bernart Alanhan de Narbona of uncertain date (BdT 53.1), who castigates his listeners for forgetting 'the shame and the grievous torment that Jesus endured at the hands of the base, treacherous and cruel Jews' and declares that 'pride brings us low, so we lost / are losing [*perdem*] the holy city'.[11]

Calls for a new crusade

The sack of Jerusalem not unexpectedly aroused deep feelings in the West. In a song probably composed between October and December 1244 the troubadour Lanfranc Cigala speaks of it as an 'abandoned place', and bewails the 'cries and groans and weeping of the sepulchre' and its ruin at Saracen hands (BdT, 282.23). A member of one of the most powerful families in Genoa, in 1241 Lanfranc was sent as an ambassador to the court of Raymond Berenguer V of Provence. In his evocation of 'the knights who have died in Syria' (v. 22) he is almost certainly referring to the huge losses of knights at La Forbie rather than the death of the Christian inhabitants of Jerusalem. He lays the blame for Jerusalem's abandonment on the warring pope Innocent IV and the emperor Frederick II. Scathing about the pope's habitual indecisiveness, he urges the emperor to bring aid to the Holy Land, but to use his great power wisely:

> Jerusalems es luecs desamparatz;
> sabes per que? Car la patz es faillia,
> c'aitan vol dir, per dreich'alegoria,
> Jerusalem com 'vizios de patz';
> mas la guerra dels dos granz coronatz
> a cassada patz d'aqui e d'aillors,
> ni de voler patz no fan entreseingna.
> Eu non dic ges en cui colpa deveingna;
> mas qui mer mal d'aqetz dos granz seingnors,
> Dieus lo meillor o l'aucia de cors!
>
> [...]

---

[11] The verb *perdem* is ambiguous: if it is a preterite, then the reference must be to the fall of Jerusalem to the Turks in 1244, but if a present tense, it could allude to any time after Frederick's retaking of the city in 1229 under the terms of his treaty with al-Kāmil, since Jerusalem's situation continued to remain highly precarious and open to attack. The troubadour could conceivably have composed his song in support of Gregory IX's preaching campaign of 1239 in preparation for the end of the period of the treaty.

> Apostoli, eu crei que si coveigna
> que fassatz patz o guerra qui pro teingna,
> car si totz temps anatz per l'uzat cors,
> per vos non er lo sainz sepulcres sors.   (vv. 11–20, 61–64)

Jerusalem is an abandoned place. Do you know why? Peace has failed, for according to true allegory Jerusalem means 'vision of peace', but the war of the two great crowned potentates has expelled peace here and elsewhere, and they make no sign of desiring peace. I do not say whose fault it is; but whoever of these two great lords is to blame, may God amend him or swiftly put him to death!

[...]

Pope, I think it would be helpful for you to make peace or war, whichever is advantageous, for if you always travel along the well-worn path, the holy sepulchre will not be ressurrected by you.

Attempting to drum up support for a crusade on the part of the English and the Germans, and even the Spanish, he declares that the Reconquista is no excuse for ignoring the Holy Land, since the Iberian Saracens are not the ones who committed the outrage of ruining the holy sepulchre (vv. 43–46). However, he tempers an appeal to the count of Provence by a diplomatic acknowledgment of his host's lack of resources and his need to defend the Church on his home ground:

> Coms Proensals, tost fora deliuratz
> lo sepulcres si vostra manentia
> poges tan aut com lo pretz qui vos guia,
> car amatz Dieu e bonas genz onratz
> e ses biais en totz affars reingnatz
> e per vos es anquer viva valors;
> mas del passar non ai cor que·us destreingna,
> c'obs es que sai vostra valors pro tegna
> a la gleiza d'aitals guerreiadors.
> Ja de lai mar non queiratz Turcs peiors!   (vv. 51–60)

Count of Provence, the sepulchre would be swiftly liberated if your wealth climbed as high as the worth that guides you, for you love God and good honourable people and conduct yourself righteously in all matters; because of you valour is still alive. But I do not feel like pressing you to make the passage, for it is needful that your valour should defend the Church here against such warmongers [in comparison with which] you will never find worse Turks overseas!

The allusion is likely to concern the count's support of the local clergy against widespread attacks on the part of the lay aristocracy in Provence, the massacre of inquisitors at Avignonnet in 1242[12] and his ongoing conflict with Raymond VII of Toulouse, whose military incursions into Provence from the Comtat Venaissin and the lower Rhône valley between 1232 and 1243 had been resisted with the help of the papal legate, Zoën Tencarari.[13]

Louis takes the cross

In December 1244 Louis IX of France lay gravely ill. Joinville records that

> une grant maladie prist le roy a Paris, dont il fu a tel meschief, si comme il disoit, que l'une des dames qui le gardoit li vouloit traire le drap sus le visage et disoit que il estoit mort, et une autre dame qui estoit a l'autre part du lit ne li souffri mie; ançois disoit que il avoit encore l'ame ou cors. Comment que il oïst le descort de ces .ii. dames, Nostre Seigneur ouvra en li et il envoia santé tantost, car il estoit esmuÿs et ne pouoit parler. Il requist que on li donnast la croiz et si fist on.

> the king fell gravely ill in Paris, and he was in such dire straits, as he said, that one of the two ladies who were tending him wanted to draw the sheet over his face, maintaining that he was dead; but another lady, who was on the opposite side of his bed, would not allow it, and said she was sure his soul was still in his body. As the king lay listening to the dispute between the two ladies our Lord worked within him, and quickly brought him back health, for up till then he had not been able to utter a word. He asked for the cross to be given him and this was done.[14]

Louis was the only Western leader in a position to launch another crusade. Preparations began at once, with preachers organised in France, western Germany and the Scandinavian countries.[15] These plans were hampered by a major distraction: the emperor was at war again with the papacy, and Innocent IV had fled from Italy and taken up residence in Lyon, where he summoned a council in the summer of 1245.

---

[12] F. Mazel, *La Noblesse et l'église en Provence, fin Xe–début XIVe siècle. L'exemple des familles d'Agoult-Simiane, de Baux et de Marseille* (Paris, 2002), pp. 405–13 and p. 423; Aurell, *La Vielle et l'épée*, p. 227 (citing R. H. Gere, 'Les Troubadours, Heresy, and the Albigensian Crusade', PhD dissertation, Columbia University (New York, 1956), pp. 111–12), relates that during an inquisitorial trial in February 1243 a witness testified that he had seen a burgher of Castelsarrasin express great delight at the news of the massacre and sang some good *coblas* or a good *sirventes* against one of the victims.
[13] T. Pécout, *L'Invention de la Provence: Raymond Bérenger V (1209–1245)* (Paris, 2004), pp. 189–90 ('1235' on the title page is a misprint), who comments that Raymond Berenguer was still following up his advantage in 1244 with the help of the southern bishops.
[14] Joinville, *Vie de Saint Louis*, ed. J. Monfrin (Paris, 1995), p. 54, §§106–07. For the life of Saint Louis, see J. Le Goff, *Saint Louis* (Paris, 1996), and for his crusades Chapters 1–3.
[15] Wolff and Hazard, *The Later Crusades*, p. 490.

On 17 July he excommunicated Frederick and formally deposed him as emperor. He then caused the dispersal of the crusading effort by authorising the preaching of a crusade against Frederick in Germany and Italy.[16]

When Louis, reviving on his apparent deathbed, took the cross, not everyone was overjoyed. His mother 'mourned as much as if she had seen him lying dead', and Matthew Paris reports that magnates and courtiers severely criticised him for being unwilling to redeem or commute his vow in any way, despite their advice.[17] But two jubilant anonymous Old French songs stir the public to follow his example, no doubt forming part of the programme of preaching launched immediately after the event. The first (RS 1738a) makes a deeply personal and direct appeal, extolling the king's purity of life and telling the moving story of his illness and dramatic recovery, which was evidently entering the mythology of this crusade.

> Ne savey pas le aventure
> pur quey li roys é croysés? [. . .]
>
> [...]
>
> Il out une maladie
> ke lungement li dura,
> par queus reysun se croysa;
> kar ben fu lu e demie
> k'em quidout ke i fu saun vie.
> Auchun dist ke i trepassa [. . .]
>
> [...]
>
> Tusz quiderent vroyement
> ke li roys fu trepassés;
> un drap fu sur li jetés
> e pluroyent durement
> entur li tute se gent:
> un teu doyl ne fu mené.
> Li quens d'Artoys vroyement
> dist au roy mu ducement:
> 'Beaus dusz frere, a moy parlés,
> si Jesu le vus cunsent'.
>
> Adunt li roys suspira:
> 'E, beaus frere, dusz amis,
> u é li veche de Paris?

---

[16] Riley-Smith, *The Crusades. A Short History*, p. 158.
[17] Joinville, *Vie de Saint Louis*, §107; Shaw, *Joinville and Villehardouin*, p. 191; Matthew Paris, *Matthaei Parisiensis Chronica majora*, ed. H. R. Luard, 7 vols (London, 1872–1883), vol. V, 1880), p. 3, trans. by R. Vaughan as *Chronicles of Matthew Paris: Monastic Life in the Thirteenth Century* (Gloucester, 1984), p. 131.

Orę tost si m'en croysiray!
Kar lungement esteya
utre mer mes eprisz,
e li men cors i girra!
Si Deus pleysit conquera
la tere, e susz Saracins
ben eit ke me eydera!'   (vv. 11–12, 21–26, 31–50)

Do you not know what happened to make the king take the cross?

[…]

He had an illness that had affected him for a long time, which was why he took the cross. He had been thought lifeless for over an hour; someone said he was dead.

[…]

All really thought he had died. A sheet was laid over him, and they wept bitterly. All his people went into the room: never was such outpouring of grief. The count of Artois actually said very softly to the king: 'Fair sweet brother, speak to me, if Jesus lets you do so!'

Then the king sighed: 'Ah! fair brother, sweet friend, where is the bishop of Paris? Be quick: I shall take the cross, for my spirit has long been overseas and my body shall go there! God willing, I shall will win back the Holy Land, from the Saracens, and blessed be he who assists me against the Saracens!'

The second song, *Un serventés, plait de deduit et de joie* (RS 1729), also begins on an elated note, recalling the moment of Louis' miraculous resurrection. At the same time it evokes the desolation of the Christian abandonment of Jerusalem and the Saracen destruction of the holy sepulchre, and echoes Urban II's special appeal to the French as a nation:[18]

France, [*bien*] doiz avoir grant seignorie,
sur totes riens te doit en enorer!

---

[18] As reported in Robert the Monk's version of Urban's preaching: 'Gens Francorum, gens transmontana, gens, sicuti in pluribus vestris elucet operibus, a Deo electa et dilecta, tam situ terrarum quam fide catholica, quam honore sancte ecclesie ab universis nationibus segregata: ad vos sermo noster dirigitur, vobisque nostra exhoratio protenditur' ('Frenchmen and men from across the mountains; men chosen by and beloved of God as is clear from your many achievements; men set apart from all other nations as much by geography as by the Catholic faith and by the honour of the Holy Church – it is to you that we address our sermon, to you that we appeal'; see Robert the Monk, *Historia Iherosolimitana*, ed. D. Kempf and M. G. Bull (Woodbridge, 2013), p. 5, and C. Sweetenham, *Robert the Monk's History of the First Crusade. Historia Iherosolimitana* (Aldershot and Burlington, Vt., 2005), p. 79.

> Diex *te requiert* et secors et aïe
> por sun païs de paiens delivrer:
> por ceu a fait le roi resociter.   (vv. 37–41)

France, you ought surely to have great authority; you should be honoured above everything, for God asks assistance and aid of you to deliver His land from pagans: this is why he resuscitated the king.

It ends by urging the king to lead his armies to the East,[19] which he should be able to conquer easily, optimistically looks forward to him baptising the sultan of Turkey and exhorts Louis to make peace between pope and emperor. Then he would conquer Turkey and Persia and go to Babylon (Old Cairo) to be crowned (emperor?).

These anonymous northern French songs unequivocally support Louis' crusading plans. They no doubt formed part of a preaching campaign, reflecting, as well as helping to stimulate, widespread enthusiasm for the new venture, in the North at least. But Occitan comments – preserved in substantially more numerous songs – were more nuanced and reserved, and were seen from regional perspectives.

Regional perspectives: papal–imperial conflict, resistance and burlesque

To judge by the surviving lyrics composed west of the Rhône, no troubadour apart from Bernart Alanhan de Narbona – an uncertain case – shows any support or even interest in Louis' crusade. As far as Provence is concerned, once the king's brother Charles of Anjou became count after Raymond Berenguer V's death on 19 August 1245 and married his daughter Beatrice in 1246, enthusiasm for the crusade was lukewarm at best. Lanfranc Cigala, who in 1244 had written an impassioned song in support of it, later expressed his doubts as to the king's firmness of purpose and the obstacles presented by wars in the West. His song *Quan vei far bon fag plazentier* (BdT 282.20) was composed around 1246–1248, two years or more after Louis' original vow. Bertoni considers it likely to date from the early months of 1248, a year in which he is recorded as being a consul in Genoa and therefore having left Provence.[20] Here Lanfranc is quick to praise the king for taking the cross, but Louis needs to live up to his promise:

> Lau e pres et honor en mier
> lo reis del bon començamen;

---

[19] Bédier is puzzled by the designation *Romanie* (v. 51: see Bédier and Aubry, *Les chansons de croisade*, p. 255). From the age of Saint Louis, *Romanie* or *Romenie* appears to designate not just the Latin empire of Constantinople but all the Latin possessions in the East in general or even an important place of pilgrimage beyond the Alps independently of its geographical position. See Barbieri's online note to RS 1204.

[20] G. Bertoni, *I trovatori d'Italia* (Modena, 1915; repr. Rome, 1967), pp. 98 and 560.

pero dels meillors si n'aten,
q'om li fara lau plus entier.
Doncs so c'a gent començat a cap traia,
car en la fin chant'om lauzor veraia;
e pas de cors la mar, qe granz ops es,
que de lai son crestian mort e pres
e·l sepulcres fondutz e derocatz,
on Dieus pauzet can fon de crotz levatz.   (vv. 21–30)

The king merits praise and renown and honour for this good beginning; yet I hope for [even] better deeds so that people will give him more perfect praise. Therefore let him see through to its conclusion what he has nobly begun, for it is at the end that people sing true praise; and let him swiftly cross the sea, since this is most needful: over there there are dead and imprisoned Christians, and the sepulchre is broken down and ruined, where God rested when he was taken down from the cross.

The rest of the *sirventes* attacks the murderous barons:

Pero si sai la guerra no s'apaia,
crestiantatz greu sera qe non chaia.
Sabes per que? Car el mon non es res
miels puosc'aucir autrui con el metes.   (vv. 35–38)

Yet if the war here continues unabated, Christendom will hardly fail to founder. Do you know why? Because there is no creature in the world that is better at killing his fellow.

If Lanfranc blames Christians in general for waging war among themselves, Bertran Carbonel of Marseille is more specific, blaming the clergy for obstructing the crusade (BdT 82.12). His violent attack was probably composed between 1245 and 1250.

Ai, fals clergue, messongier, traïdor,
perjur, lairo, putanier, descrezen!
Tant faitz de mals cascun jorn a prezen
que tot lo mons avetz mes en error.
Anc sans Peire non tenc captal en Fransa
ni fetz renou, ans tenc drech la balansa
de liautat. No faitz vos pas senblan,
que per argen anatz a tort vedan,
pueys n'absolvetz, pueys no datz empachier,
pueis ses argen no y trob'om deslieurier.

Non crezan pas silh fol entend[ed]or
blasme totz clercx, mas los fals solamen;

ni d'autra part no vazan entenden
c'aiso digua per doptansa de lor,
mais que·m plagra fezessan acordansa
dels reys que an guerr'e desacordansa,
si c'otra mar passessan est autr'an,
e·l pap'ab els, e lay fezesson tan
que crestiantat s'en dones alegrier;
e valgra may, que car son sa guerrier.   (vv. 21–40)

You hypocritical clergy! You liars, traitors, perjurers, thieves, whoremongers, unbelievers! Every day you openly commit so many evil deeds that you have led the whole world astray. St Peter never banked capital in France or practised usury, but acted scrupulously within the law. You do not seem to do so: you wrongly excommunicate people for money, then you lift the interdict, then you offer no impediment, then people have to pay to be granted absolution.

Those foolish listeners should not imagine I blame all clergy, but only the hypocritical ones; on the other hand they should not suppose I speak like this because I fear them (the clergy), but because I would like them to reconcile the kings who are at war and in conflict, so that they might make the passage to the Holy Land this very year, and the pope with them, and to achieve so much that Christendom should have cause to rejoice; and this would be much better, for warriors are expensive here [it's a waste to have men fighting over here when they could be in the East].

The pope's excommunication of Frederick II at the Council of Lyon on 17 July 1245, which sent shock waves throughout Europe, lends topical force to the accusation that the clergy used excommunication unlawfully, though it is also relevant to Bertran's patron, Barral of Baux, most probably the *pus privatz Proensals* ('my undoubtedly closest Provençal friend', v. 51), to whom the *sirventes* is addressed. The situation in Provence was in flux because the great Provençal communes of Arles, Avignon and Marseille were opposing French rule, and in April 1247 they joined together under Barral des Baux in a defensive alliance. Before 1250 Barral vigorously opposed Charles of Anjou and the power of the Church, assuming leadership of the 1247 revolt against them by the Provençal communes. He was excommunicated more than once by Zoën Tencarari, first in 1240 in his capacity as vicar of the legate for Provence, Jacques Pecoraria, and then as bishop of Avignon in 1246–1247. Barral eventually changed sides in 1250 and became a staunch ally of Charles of Anjou,[21] but before that date he would certainly have had a personal reason to appreciate Carbonel's condemnation of clerical abuse of the power of interdict.

The troubadour's rebuke that St Peter did not practise capitalism or usury as the present pope is doing in France relates to Innocent's move to Lyon, from where he

---

[21] Mazel, *La Noblesse*, pp. 409–14.

will have been seeking to raise funds (*captal*, v. 25) for his crusade against Frederick. Occitan towns such as Cahors, Gaillac, Toulouse and Carbonel's home town of Marseille were financially important as the home of bankers and money-lenders. 'Lenders, both lay and ecclesiastical, were numerous in twelfth-century Toulouse. The Church forbade usury but no-one took much notice at this time, and money-lending was a part of everyday life [...] Men from Cahors were particularly successful at money-lending operations and competed with Italians at the fairs of Occitania and Champagne. [...] Money-changers formed a powerful and probably rich corporation in Marseilles, where the Isla dels Cambis was the medieval equivalent of the modern Bourse and business quarter.' Such bankers could supply funds for papal ventures: a rich merchant from Cahors, Raimon de Salvanhac, received all the booty from Lavaur in return for financing the Albigensian Crusade.[22]

Charles was not strong enough to attack the Provençal communes decisively; as a result they paid him no rents in the early years of his rule in Provence, and those who had had no difficulty in recognising him as the legitimate heir to Raymond Berenguer were suffering. Among these was the troubadour Bertran d'Alamanon. A high-level bureaucrat in the count's employ, Bertran certainly accepted Charles's right to rule the county, but wanted him to assert his rights effectively and did not want him sailing off to the Holy Land while there were so many urgent matters at home to contend with. He did not hesitate to criticise publicly, diplomatically but firmly, the count's handling of his Provençal affairs, in particular as they touched him personally. In *Ja de chantar nulh temps no serai mutz* (BdT 76.9) he argues that Charles has been too reluctant and weak in the face of their loud protestations to demand a payment of a thousand marks due to him from the communes. At an early stage of the conflict he, Bertran, had advised Charles not to give in to them, and now that Marseille and Avignon are in league with Arles, instead of reinforcing his claim to his rights, Charles and his supporters have settled for postponing any decisive action. The troubadour professes himself 'bitter and angry' for not being involved in military action, and complains that it is hopeless expecting the count to wake up and do something (vv. 33–40). As far as Louis' crusade is concerned, he suggests that the reason Charles is planning to accompany the king to Syria is actually because he is depressed about the situation at home and unwilling to face it:

> que de Fransa es vengutz lo ressos
> que mos senher se n'es tant irascutz
> que tug dizon qu'el n'a levat la cros
> e vol passar en terra de Suria.
> Guardatz s'o fai ben ni adrechamens,
> que so que pert de sai aunidamens
> vol demandar ad aquels de Turquia.   (vv. 26–32)

---

[22] Paterson, *The World of the Troubadours*, pp. 48, 152, 156.

the rumour has come from France that my lord has become so downhearted about it that everyone says that he has taken the cross as a result and wants to make the passage to the land of Syria. Consider whether he acts well or rightly: what he shamefully loses here he wants to demand from the Turks.

And he concludes on an ironic personal note:

> S'a mon senhor plai qu'ieu en patz n'estia,
> prec li, si·l plai, que mi sia suffrens
> qu'ieu lur deman so de que suy perdens,
> qu'Alamano non es pas en Ongria. (vv. 41–44)

If it pleases my lord that I should remain in peace, I beg him, if it please him, to permit *me* to ask them for what I am losing, for Alamano is not in Hungary.

In other words, if Charles is unwilling for Bertran to resort to arms, he hopes the count will at least let him ask them for compensation for his own personal losses, for Alamo is hardly the land of Eldorado. He is feeling the pinch.

It is uncertain when exactly Charles took the cross, or what gave rise to the rumour he had done so. Joinville's account shows that Louis made his vow in December 1244, but not when precisely his three brothers followed his example, for the chronicler moves swiftly on to events of 1248.[23] Matthew Paris relates that in May 1247 various English nobles took the cross 'encouraged by the example of the king of the French and the nobles of that kingdom', but this does not nail the date of Charles' vow either.[24] The details of Bertran's *sirventes* suggest that it took place between April 1247, when Barral took over leadership of the league of Provençal cities, and before Charles sailed for the Holy Land with his brother Louis IX on 25 August 1248.

Another *sirventes* by this troubadour reflects the same events (BdT 76.15), but also mentions the possibility of Charles of Anjou losing control of the Gapençais. Bertran stresses that Charles, who is away in France, has a small window of opportunity to establish his rights, but needs swiftly to make his presence felt here in Provence (vv. 11–30). He is not afraid to speak out concerning Charles' unfavourable reception by his new subjects. Voicing the anxieties of those who had worked to support his acquisition of Provence, he emphasises that if the count cannot stamp his authority on the region, he can hardly expect to be a successful crusader:

> Tan mala vi sa coindansa
> qi·l mesçai en cest pais,
> qe cil qi la moilheransa
> feron, n'iran am caps clis.

---

[23] Joinville, *Vie de Saint Louis*, §§106–10; Shaw, *Joinville and Villehardouin*, pp. 191–92.
[24] Matthew Paris, *Chronica majora*, IV, pp. 489–90 and 629, and V, p. 3, and Vaughan, *Chronicles*, pp. 110 and 131.

Mas se·l fils del rei de Fransa
pert sai enfre sos vesis,
tart conqerra per semblansa
outramar Turcs ni Colmis,
qar qi mal demanda·l sieu
grieu conqerra l'autrui fieu.

S'en brieu non fai comensansa
le coms, ben sui certz e fis
qe tan l'autra partz s'enansa
q'ar tan sejorn'a Paris.
Per qe pes en la balansa
mas le mals qes hom en dis
no fai le bes ni l'onransa,
se meil çai no s'afortis;
mas tot o revenra lieu,
sol li faig non syon grieu.   (vv. 41–60)

He saw his reception, which is turning out so badly for him in this region, prove so poor that those who arranged the marriage will go hanging their heads in dejection. But if the king of France's son is losing here among the local citizens, it doesn't look as if he will easily conquer Turks or Khwarismians overseas, for anyone who is bad at demanding what belongs to him will hardly conquer someone else's fief.

If the count does not soon make a start, I am perfectly certain that the other side will be gathering momentum commensurate with the time he is now spending in Paris. So the ill spoken of him is outweighing the good or the praise – unless he improves his strength here; but everything can be quickly mended as long as the deeds are not sluggish [he is not slow to act].

These two *sirventes* show acute concern over local, regional events which seem to the new count's supporters to be much more urgent than his brother's crusading venture.

Two other pieces by troubadours at the court of Charles of Anjou suggest a similarly lukewarm, if not cynical, response to the crusade. Referring offhandedly to the bad news from the Holy Land, Granet initiates a *tenso* (BdT 189.5) by demanding of a certain lord Bertran why he continues to love:

Que otramar aug dir que Antecrist renha,
c'ap los seus ve, que totz sels ausiran
que no·s volran covertir prezican.
Per qu'ie·us cosselh que de l'arma·us sovenha,
e partes vos de leys c'amar no·us denha.   (vv. 5–9)

I hear that Antichrist rules overseas, and is coming with his followers who will slaughter all those who are unwilling to convert according to their preaching. Therefore I advise you to give thought to your immortal soul, and separate from the one who disdains to love you.

Bertran replies that he is perfectly happy about the advent of Antichrist since he is so powerful he will be able to force his lady to love him. The debate unfurls along these lines in jocular fashion, with Bertran assuring his interlocutor that God will easily forgive him for placing himself in the order of Antichrist since it was God's fault in the first place for making his lady so lovely.[25]

A more outrageous take on the crusades is found in Sordel's piece *Lai al comte mon segnor voill pregar* (BdT 437.18). Begging Charles of Anjou *not* to take him on crusade with him, the Italian troubadour dextrously interweaves well-worn medieval punning on love (*l'amar*) and the sea (*la mar*) with sexual insinuations around the idea of dying, scatalogical intertextual references to wind and homosexual innuendoes involving the count, Bertran d'Alamanon and himself. Sordel states that rather than make the passage to Outremer, he likes the idea of going to sea with the sailors and staying there, in the middle of the ocean:

> Lai al comte mon segnor voill pregar
> non li plassa q'ab se·m men oltra mar,
> qar ben sapcha qu'eu lai non posc passar
> pero el miez totz temps volri'estar:
> ben volria la gent acompagnar
> e Deus penses de las armas salvar,
> mas fort lo deu nostre segner amar,
> qar dels peccatz vol penedenza far.   (vv. 1–8)

I want to beseech the count my lord not to choose to take me to Outremer [*or* beyond the sea *or* beyond love (*oltr'amar*)] with him, and to be well aware that I can't make the passage there; however I would like to stay in the middle of it all the time: I'd like to go along with the troops and for God to take care of saving souls.

Rather than in the Holy Land, it is in fact on the sea (*la mar*) or in 'love' (*l'amar*) that salvation is to be found:

> Mon seigner prec no li sia plazen
> q'oltra·m fassa passar, part mon talen;
> q'en la mar ven totz hom a perdemen,
> per q'eu non voill passar, al meu viven.   (vv. 25–28)

---

[25] For various attempts to identify references to Antichrist and his imminent arrival with diverse specific persons and events, see Harvey and Paterson, *Tensos*, vol. II, pp. 452–53.

I pray it may not please my lord to make me make the passage, contrary to [*or* beyond] my desire; for on the sea [*or* in love] all men come to salvation, which is why I don't want to pass over during my lifetime.

Apart from the two anonymous northern French texts, all the songs responding to the loss of Jerusalem and the disaster of La Forbie are from Provence. The Genoese ambassador Lanfranc Cigala, even-handed in his blame of the warring pope and emperor for obstructing a military response in the East, concedes that local circumstances make it difficult and indeed inappropriate for Raymond Berenguer of Provence to take part, and later voices his doubts about the likelihood of the crusade's success. The partisan Bertran Carbonel lays the entire blame for impediments to the crusade on the clergy, whose abuse of the power of interdict concerns not only the pope's excommunication of Frederick II but also, probably, the troubadour's patron. Bertran d'Alamanon, for whom local concerns are paramount, has both political and personal reasons to oppose Charles of Anjou's departure on crusade. His negative reactions, and the dismissively burlesque ones of other troubadours at Charles' Provençal court, contrast vividly with the anonymous French trouvères' naïve and tender, and no doubt propagandistic, optimism. In the Languedoc, crusading against Muslims is seen as worthy but compromised by French aggression there. In Provence, Louis' forthcoming crusade – or at least Charles of Anjou's participation in it – meets with resistance and jokes.

The crusade and its aftermath

Louis eventually left Paris on 12 August 1248 and sailed from Aigues-Mortes for Cyprus on the 25th. In September the crusaders all agreed that they should first attack Damietta.[26] A year was wasted in fruitless diplomatic negotiations with the Mongols, and it was only in May 1249 that the army began to embark from Limassol. A storm soon scattered three quarters of the fleet, and the king himself set sail with the remaining quarter on 30 May. In early June the king, together with the knights of Outremer under John of Ibelin, captured Damietta, only to become bogged down in the Nile delta a year later by famine, dystery and typhoid. On April 1250 Louis began to retreat to Damietta, but the crusaders were surrounded. 'The king's own gallantry was beyond all praise. But that night he fell ill, and next morning he could scarcely keep himself on his horse. As the day dragged on, the Moslems closed in round the army and attacked in full force. The sick and weary soldiers scarcely tried to resist them.' The whole army was rounded up and led into captivity. 'The Egyptians were at first embarrassed by the numbers of their prisoners. Finding it impossible to guard them all, those that were too feeble to march were executed at once, and on every evening for a week three hundred were taken out and decapitated.' Louis was lodged in chains in a private house in Mansurah. The

---

[26] Runciman, *History*, III, p. 258.

leading barons were kept together in a larger prison. The king and the greater men were eventually freed in May after the payment of a vast ransom. Leaving many captives behind, Louis set sail for Acre, where he arrived on Sunday 13 May 1250 with his pitifully diminished army. Most of his followers left for France, including his brothers Alphonse of Poitiers and Charles of Anjou, who sailed on 10 August.[27] His men were in a sick and sorry state, and some, including his mother, pressed him to return home, but if he left he would be abandoning the last cities remaining to the Christians, and above all the 2,000 prisoners in Egypt. Others, like Joinville, believed honour and compassion for those still in prison demanded he stay. The chronicler reminds him of what a cousin of his told him as he set out on his crusade:

> Vous en alez outre mer, fist il. Or vous prenés garde au revenir, car nulz chevaliers, ne povres ne richez, ne peut revenir que il ne *soit* honni, se il lesse en la main des Sarrazins le peuple menu Nostre Seigneur en la quel compaingnie il est alé.
>
> You are going overseas, he said. but take care how you come back; for no knight, whether rich or poor, can return without dishonour if he leaves our Lord's humbler servants, in whose company he set out, at the mercy of the Saracens.[28]

On 12 June the king held a preliminary council where he set out the situation. The barons were to give him their advice on the 19th, then he would take a further week to decide. On the 26th he announced his decision to stay. Just at the moment when it was unknown what the king would decide, between 12 and 19 June, an anonymous trouvère composed and disseminated the song *Nus ne poroit de mauvaise raison* (RS 1887) to influence the king's decision and combat the efforts of the 'cowards and flatterers' who were urging him to leave for France.[29]

> Nuns ne poroit de mavaise raison
> bone chanson ne faire ne chanteir,
> por ceu n'i veul mattre m'antansion,
> car j'ai asseis atre chose a panseir;
> et non por cant la terre d'outre meir
> voi an si tres grant balance,
> c'an chantant voil preier lou roi de France
> ke ne croiet cowairt ne losangier
> de la honte nostre Signor vangier.
>
> [...]
>
> Rois, vos savez ke Deus ait poc d'amis,
> nen onkemais n'an ot si boen mestier,

---

[27] Runciman, *History*, III, pp. 261–72.
[28] Joinville, *Vie de Saint Louis*, p. 206, §420.
[29] Bédier and Aubry, *Les chansons de croisade*, pp. 261–62, reporting G. Paris, 'La chanson composée à Acre', *Romania*, 22 (1893), 541–47, p. 545.

car por vos est ces pueples mors et pris,
ne nus for vos ne l'an puet bien aidier;
ke povre sont li atre chivelier,
se criement la demorance,
et s'ans teil point lor feisiez faillance,
saint et martir, apostre et inocentse
plainderoient de vos a jugemant.

[...]

Rois, s'an teil point vos meteis a retour,
France dirait, Chanpagne et toute gent
ke vostre los aveis mis an tristour
et ke gaingniet aveiz moins ke niant;
et des prisons, ke vivent a tormant,
deusiez avoir pesance:
bien deusiez querre lour delivrance;
ke por vos sont et por S'amour occis,
c'est grans pechiez ces i laxiés morir. (vv. 1–9, 19–27, 37–45)

No one could compose or sing a good song on a bad theme; therefore I do not wish to attempt this, having much else to think about; yet I see the land of Outremer so poised on a knife-edge that I wish to beg the king of France not to believe a coward or a flatterer when it is a question of avenging his shame and God's.

[...]

King, you know that God has few friends and never ever had such great need of them; it is through you that his people have been killed and captured, and no one but you could help them, for those other knights are poor and fear remaining here, and if you came to fail them to such an extent, saints and martyrs, apostles and holy innocents would complain of you at the Last Judgement.

[...]

King, if you set out for home at this point, France, Champagne and all people will say that you have turned your back on reputation and gained less than nothing, and that you should have cared about the prisoners living in torment; you certainly should have sought their deliverance: since it is your sake and for Jesus that they are martyrs, it is a great sin if you let them die there.

Touched by the song's elegant style and subtle rhythms, its respect for art in these awful circumstances, Jeanroy praises its beauty, nobility and energy, designed to please connoisseurs and move them to support the cause it is defending.[30] Louis stayed.

---

[30] Bédier and Aubry, *Les chansons de croisade*, p. 263.

Two other Old French songs probably attributable to the period following the defeat at Mansurah refer to the experience of captivity. One of the prisoners was Raoul de Soissons. 'Impulsive, fiery and adventurous in character', he went on three crusades and spent several years in the East. The first expedition was the Barons' Crusade, after which he remained in the Holy Land and married Alice of Champagne to bolster a claim to the kingdom of Jerusalem. Here he found himself involved in a long struggle between the Ibelin family and Frederick II and played a significant rôle in the Ibelins' occupation of Tyre. His pride wounded by the lack of acknowledgment of his aspirations, he decided to return to France, abandoning his consort. He later took part in Louis's first crusade and was taken captive at Mansurah. After his release he once again decided to remain behind in the Holy Land, along with the king, probably returning home at the end of 1253 or the beginning of 1254. Troubled by economic problems (he had already requested a huge loan from Thibaut de Champagne in 1245), he decided to set sail again with Louis's second expedition in 1270.

In a love song probably composed not long after his return to France in 1254 and dedicated to Charles of Anjou, the trouvère refers painfully to the fear he felt daily during his captivity and his illness afterwards in France. As Barbieri remarks, his experience of suffering in the past is compared with the greater suffering provoked by a love relationship in the present (RS 1154).

> Bien m'ait Amors esproveit en Sulie
> et en Egypte, ou je fui meneis pris,
> c'adés i fui en poour de ma vie
> et chascun jour cuidai bien estre ocis;
> n'onkes por ceu mes cuers nen fut partis
> ne decevreis de ma douce anemie,
> ne en France per ma grant maladie,
> ke je cuidai de ma goute morir,
> ne se pooit mes cuers de li partir. (vv. 19–27)

Love has sorely tested me in Syria and in Egypt, where I was taken prisoner, for I was constantly in fear for my life and every day I was sure I would be killed; but despite this my heart was never separated or parted from my sweet enemy, nor in France during my grave illness, when I thought I would die from my gout, was my heart capable of leaving her.

A similar treatment of this theme recurs in his song RS 1204, *Se j'ai lonc tans esté en Romenie*, probably composed in the same period, even if there is nothing in it to pin down the exact date.

In the South, news of the king's defeat at Mansurah met with two very different responses. One is an astonishing *cri du coeur* (BdT 40.1) from the troubadour Austorc d'Aorlhac. Not only does he lament and curse the Christians' misfortune; he also expresses amazement at God's baffling purposes. How could he have let this happen? What a poor reward for his commitment to his cause! God is to blame for giving the Turks the power to destroy such a glorious army, indeed the whole of Christendom; so it makes sense for us to stop believing in him and worship pagan gods!

> Ai Dieus, per qu'as facha tan gran maleza
> de nostre rey frances larc e cortes,
> quan as sufert qu'aital ant'aia preza?
> Qu'elh ponhava cum servir te pogues,
> que·l cor e·l saber hi metia
> en tu servir la nueg e·l dia,
> e cum pogues far e dir tom plazer.
> Mal guizardo l'en as fag eschazer.
>
> Ai, bella gens avinens e corteza
> que oltra mar passetz! Tam belh arnes!
> May no·us veyrem tornar sai, de que·m peza,
> don per lo mon s'en es grans dols empres.
> Mal dicha si'Alexandria,
> e mal dicha tota clercia,
> e mal dig Turc que·us an fach remaner!
> Mal o fetz Dieus quar lor en det poder.
>
> Crestiantat vey del tot a mal meza;
> tan gran perda no cug qu'anc mais fezes.
> Per qu'es razos qu'hom hueymais Dieus descreza,
> e qu'azorem Bafomet lai on es,
> Servagan e sa companhia,
> pus Dieus vol e Sancta Maria
> que nos siam vencutz a non-dever,
> e·ls mescrezens fai honratz remaner.   (vv. 1–24)

Ah God, why have you treated our generous, courtly French king so badly in allowing him to suffer such shame? For he made every effort to serve you, putting heart and mind into this, serving you night and day, and thinking of how he might act and speak according to your pleasure. A poor reward have you granted him.

Alas fair people, gracious and courtly, who sailed to the Holy Land! Such splendid armour! Nevermore shall we see you return again, which grieves me and throws the whole world into deep mourning. A curse on Alexandria, and a curse on all clergy, and a curse on the Turks who have kept you there! God has done ill for he gave them the power to do it.

I see Christendom utterly destroyed; I do not think it ever suffered such an enormous loss. So it makes sense for people to stop believing in God, and for us to worship Mahomet, Tervagan and his company where they are, given that God and Holy Mary want us to be unjustly conquered, and cause the misbelievers to continue to be honoured.

Such apparent blasphemy is explicable as an expression of outrage and incomprehension, and also as a kind of assimilation of God to feudal overlord, not uncommon in the troubadours:[31] if God does not treat his followers properly, they are entitled to switch their allegiance. In fact this seems to reflect a popular idea circulating at the time. The Franciscan Salimbene de Adam relates that the common people 'rose up in anger against the religious Orders – especially the Preachers and the Minorites – because they had preached the Crusade and given men the cross to accompany the king, who had been conquered by the Saracens', and when these friars and preachers asked alms of them, they called over some other poor man and gave him money saying '"Take this in the name of Mohammed who is more powerful than Christ"'![32]

Templars did occasionally apostasise: Malcolm Barber cites an isolated example of a whole garrison that went over to the Saracens in 1268.[33] Austorc himself in fact took the cross two years after composing his song, and his grandson was knighted by Louis in 1266 and accompanied the king on his 1270 crusade.[34] Like other anticlerical troubadours of the period, Austorc heaps obloquy on the pope and the money-loving clergy who 'have killed worth and chivalry, and killed all courtliness, and care little for others' misfortunes as long as they can enjoy resting and sleeping'. He wishes the emperor had taken the cross and left the Empire in the hands of his son (Conrad IV), and appeals to Louis to spend like Alexander, who conquered the whole world, to defeat the Turks. Frederick died on 13 December 1250, so the song was composed before then and after Louis' release in May of that year.

A very different commentary on the French defeat is found in a *sirventes* composed two or three years later, between 1252 and Louis' return on 3 July 1254, by the troubadour Bernart de Rovenac (BdT 66.2). Here reference to crusading is incidental to matters of south-west Occitan politics. Bernart opens by declaring his intention to blame powerful men despite their alleged expectation of praise. The powers concerned prove to be four kings, all of whom merit blame in one way or another: James I of Aragon, Henry III of England, Louis IX of France and Alfonso X of Castile. Bernart heaps sarcasms on the kings of Aragon and England for meekly agreeing not to defend their territories or retaliate against aggressors: more specifically, they are refraining from waging war on Louis IX of France, the king who is 'conquering Syria'. Louis was on crusade, and the reason James and Henry are holding their fire is because of the papal threat of excommunication against any hostile attack on his territory. But after his defeat and capture Louis was certainly

---

[31] Compare Marcabru, BdT 293.22, 55–59, and Daspol, BdT 206.4 *passim*.
[32] Salimbene de Adam, *Chronica*, ed. G. Scalia, 2 vols (Bari, 1966), II, p. 645.
[33] M. Barber, 'Was the Holy Land Betrayed in 1291?', RMS, 34 (2008), 35–52 (p. 46), and see also his *The Crusader States* (New Haven and London, 2012), p. 290.
[34] S. Stroński, 'Notes de littérature provençale', AdM, 25 (1913), 273–97 (pp. 285–87).

not 'conquering Syria'. Bernart's implication is that since he can now hardly be said to be fighting the Turks, nothing justifies the cowardly reluctance on the part of the kings of Aragon and England to pursue their legitimate claims against France, and moreover God is hardly going to be grateful to them for holding off since Louis is doing absolutely nothing to advance the crusading cause. The specific circumstances giving rise to this *sirventes* concerned a complicated dispute between James of Aragon and the commune of Montpellier over the rights to a toll levied at the bridge connecting the town to the port of Lattes. In 1252 the king attempted to take over its revenues and met with armed resistance by the town militia, against the background of numerous claims and counter-claims by Aragon and France over territories under each other's domination. Bernart shows no interest whatever in urging anyone to make good the French failure in Egypt; his concern is for Louis' competitors with a stake in the region of Montpellier to drive the French out.

11

The Eighth Crusade, or the Second Crusade of Saint Louis

After Louis was back in France he continued to send generous assistance to the Holy Land in terms of men and money. His brother Alphonse began planning a new crusade almost as soon as he returned from Syria, but the popes continued to devote their energy and resources to their bitter struggle against the Hohenstaufens. Frederick had died in 1250, leaving the Regno (the kingdom of Sicily and southern Italy) to King Conrad IV, absent in Germany, and appointing his bastard son Manfred regent of both the Regno and North Italy. Excommunicated by Innocent IV, Conrad died on 21 May 1254. In two years Manfred established his rule over the entire Regno, and in August 1258 he succeeded in having himself crowned King of Sicily in Palermo. By the end of 1261 he was a significant threat to the Papal State. In 1262 and 1263 Pope Urban IV authorised negotiations to transfer the Sicilian crown to Charles of Anjou as a papal fief, a project designated from the start as a crusade, and in May 1264 the papal legate Simon of Brie was sent to France to conclude these negotiations and organise the preaching there.[1] He was granted the power to commute the crusading vows of all those in the kingdom of France and the other lands of his legation on condition they instead participate in Charles of Anjou's Sicilian campaign. Charles was crowned on 6 January 1266 at St Peter's in Rome and immediately set out to conquer his fief from Manfred, whom he defeated and killed at the battle of Benevento in 1266. In 1267–1268 young Conradin, the only surviving legitimate grandson of Frederick II, attempted to regain control of the Regno, but was crushed at the battle of Tagliacozzo on 23 August 1268 and then executed.

This overlapped with the period sometimes referred to as the 'Great Interregnum'. After William of Holland's death in 1256 until the election of Rudolf of Habsburg in 1273 there was no established Holy Roman Emperor. The electors were unable to agree on a German prince, and the two initial candidates for the imperial crown were Richard of Cornwall, brother of King Henry III of England, and King Alfonso X of Castile. Richard was crowned at Aachen in May 1257 and obtained partial recognition in Germany, but he never succeeded in gaining papal recognition and coronation in Rome. In 1266 young Conradin also laid claim to

---

[1] For Simon's preaching, see N. Housley, *The Italian Crusades* (Oxford, 1988), pp. 114–15.

this throne. Conradin had been made legally king of Jerusalem as an infant in 1254, and remained so until Charles had him put to death.

These tumultuous events, involving Charles of Anjou as Louis' brother and ruler of Provence, and a papal crusade against the Hohenstaufens, were a powerful distraction from any further expedition to the Holy Land. But during the six years after Louis' first crusade, the Christians of Palestine were not in a critical situation, since the Egyptian Muslims were occupied with fighting the Mongols. The Mongols were sympathetic to Christians and had requested baptism, a request naturally warmly welcomed by Pope Alexander IV. All changed on 3 September of that year at Ain Jalud, when they were defeated by Sultan Qutuz of Egypt at one of the most decisive battles of history. Qutuz returned to Egypt covered in glory, but was assassinated by the Mameluk Baibars who, on 20 October 1260, installed himself in Cairo as the new sultan.[2] Determined to exterminate all enemies of Islam, and with Egypt and Syria united under him, he began a systematic attack on the Christian fortresses, culminating in the sack of Antioch in 1268. The Christian principality of Antioch had lasted for 171 years. Even the Muslim chroniclers were shocked at the carnage. 'Its destruction was a terrible blow to Christian prestige, and it brought the rapid decline of Christianity in northern Syria.'[3]

In 1267 Louis began slowly to make the necessary arrangements for his second crusade, and in 1270 he was ready to leave, though not without being briefly pre-empted by an abortive crusade by James I of Aragon. Why Louis' crusade headed for Tunis is still a mystery. Runciman argues that his 'pious project was twisted out of shape and ruined by the king's brother Charles', but Jean Dunbabin has presented cogent arguments against this point of view.[4] After setting sail on 1 July from Aigues-Mortes the crusaders arrived off Carthage on 18 July, 'in the full heat of the African summer'. There was no fight. Disease spread quickly through the French camp, striking men down in their thousands, and Louis was among the first to succumb. When Charles arrived with his army, on 25 August he learned that his brother had died a few hours before.[5]

---

[2] Runciman, *History*, III, Chapter III, 'The Mongols in Syria', especially pp. 305–14; see also the discussion of BdT 439.1, below, and the notes on <http://www.rialto.unina.it/Templ/439.1Fin.htm>.

[3] Runciman, *History*, III, pp. 325–26.

[4] Runciman, *History*, III, p. 290; J. Dunbabin, *Charles I of Anjou. Power, Kingship and State-Making in Thirteenth-Century Europe* (London and New York, 1998), pp. 195–97. M. Lower, 'Louis IX, Charles of Anjou, and the Tunis Crusade of 1270', in *Crusades – Medieval Worlds in Conflict*, ed. T. F. Madden, J. L. Naus and V. Ryan (Farnham, 2010), pp. 173–93, suggests that he wanted to convert Muslims there.

[5] Runciman, *History*, III, p. 292.

Before Baibars

Until a Templar's desperate plea for help arrived in the West, Old French and Occitan lyrics reflect little interest in a new crusade. The troubadours' attention is focused on the papal–imperial conflict, which provoked a score of *sirventes* between 1250 and 1265.[6] However, in 1250 Henry III of England took the cross, and in 1254 Pope Innocent IV, then his successor Alexander IV, promised him economic support through a new round of ecclesiastical taxes. In 1255 the pope then invited Henry to commute his vow, promising him the throne of Sicily in exchange for military assistance against Manfred. Henry III never officially agreed, and continued to affirm his wish to leave for the Holy Land, but the funds were subsequently diverted to support the Sicilian project. An Anglo-Norman song, the anonymous *Ore est acumplie / par myen escient* (RS 665a) composed in 1256, expresses the protest of an English cleric against these taxes, although unless the statement that the king is off to the Holy Land 'with good intention' is ironic, he does not accuse him of having taken the cross solely to raise money.[7] The text 'opens in a style typical of preaching, with allegorically-interpreted scriptural quotations referring to the present state of the English Church, and goes on to denounce the loss of prestige of the clergy abused by those who ought to support it. The author denounces the injustice of the agreement between king and pope concerning the Church's property, and stigmatises their policies, essentially accusing them of theft at the clergy's expense.'[8] There follow a direct criticism of Henry III's crusading project, in the light of the recent failure of Louis IX's expedition, and a curse on the tax collectors.

> Le rei vet a Surie
> par bon entendement:
> vivẹra de rubberie
> ke la clergiẹ li rent,
> ja ne fẹra bone enprise,
> pur reyndre seynte Glise,
> jo quid certaynement.
> Ke veot aver [semblance]
> regarde·l(e) rei de France
> e sun achiefement.
>
> Grevus est li tallage,
> mes y (nus) cuveynt suffrir;

---

[6] See De Bartholomaeis, *Poesie provenzali*, II, pp. 167–221, poems CXXXIX–CLIX and *L'Italia dei trovatori: repertorio dei componimenti trobadorici relativi alla storia d'Italia*, co-ordinated by P. di Luca, <http://www.idt.unina.it/index.html>, = IDT.

[7] For details of Henry's intentions see S. Lloyd, *Henry III, Edward I, and the Crusade* (Oxford, 1988), pp. 211–19, who rejects the view held by some contemporaries and later historians that Henry took the cross solely for financial reasons (p. 214).

[8] Barbieri, commentary in his online edition.

mes ceous nus funt damage,
ky le deyvent cuillir.
Mes que ke nus [en] die
chescun en sun quer prie,
si Deu le veut oïr,
ke Dampnedeu (les) maudie
(tut) ceous ke mettent aÿe
pur [le] nostre tolir.   (vv. 41–60)

The king goes to Syria with good intentions, [but] he will live on the spoils given him at the clergy's expense, and I certainly believe he will not succeed in his plan to reimburse the holy Church. If anyone wants to have proof let him look at the king of France and what *he* has achieved.

The tax is harsh, but we have to put up with it; but those who have to collect it damage us. Whatever anyone may say, each man prays in his heart – may God hear him – that the Lord will curse all those who collaborate in taking from us what is ours.

Barbieri notes similarities between the tenor and content of the text and protests recorded in chronicles of 1255 and 1256, particularly certain passages of Matthew Paris' *Chronica majora*.[9]

Meanwhile across the Channel and down by the Mediterranean the troubadours occasionally evoke the *Reconquista*. In 1258 the Italian Perseval Doria composes a song in praise of Manfred shortly after his coronation, in which he complains that Alfonso of Castile and James I of Aragon want to conquer Granada from the Moors, but without doing anything about it (BdT 371.1, 40–45). By 1261–1266 James I of Aragon is in fact occupied with crushing a revolt in Murcia by the Mudejars (the subjugated Moors of Andalusia and Murcia) on behalf of Alfonso X, and in 1265 the troubadours Guiraut Riquier and Guillem de Mur are debating whether to follow him there (BdT 248.37). Their interest appears purely mercenary. Guiraut teases his interlocutor, who apparently owned a farm, that he wants a shepherd and a cowherd from the Saracens, and the king will surely give this to him, but he, Guiraut, will stay behind as these are no use to him; Guillem retorts 'as long as the king gives me a good warhorse and nag and packhorse and the other equipment that in my opinion is appropriate, I shall go there to uphold the faith'.

A cry for help

Shortly after the fall of Arsuf to Baibars on 29 April 1265 a Templar knight named Ricaut Bonomel sent out an impassioned cry for help to French barons (BdT 439.1). At the beginning of that year the Mameluk Sultan had led a formidable

---

9   See the Notes in Barbieri's online edition.

army from Egypt to Syria, first intending to confront Mongol aggression in the north, then, on hearing his troops there were in control, moving south to attack the Franks. The town of Caesaria was immediately captured, on 27 February, but the citadel held out for a week, surrendering on 5 March; the garrison was allowed to go free, though castle and town were razed to the ground. Baibars went on to destroy the town and citadel of Haifa and massacre any inhabitants who had not managed to escape, then attacked the great Templar castle at Athlit, burning the village outside the walls but failing to capture the castle. On 21 March he gave up and marched on the Hospitaller fortress of Arsuf, which was garrisoned by 270 Hospitaller knights. Runciman relates that they fought with superb courage, but the lower town fell on 26 April, and three days later the commander of the citadel, who had lost a third of his knights, capitulated in return for a promise that the survivors should go free. 'Baibars broke his word and took them all into captivity.'[10]

Faced with this desperate situation, the troubadour contemplates either suicide or apostasy. The triumph of Islam seems to be what God wants.

> Ir'e dolors s'es e mon cor assiza,
> si c'ab un pauc no m'ausi demanes,
> o meta jus la cros c'avia preza,
> a la honor d'aqel q'en cros fo mes;
> car crotz ni lei no·m val ni guia
> contrals fels turcx cui Dieu maldia;
> anz es semblan, en so c'om pot vezer,
> c'al dan de nos los vol Deus mantener.
>
> Al primier saut an Cesaria conqiza
> e·l fort castel d'Alsuf per forza pres.
> Ai, segner Dieu, a cal via an preza
> tan cavaliers, tan sirven, tan borzes
> con dinz los murs d'Alsuf avia!
> Ailas! lo regne de Suria
> a tant perdut qe, qi·n vol dir lo ver,
> per tostemps mais n'er mermatz de poder.
>
> Doncs ben es fols qi a Turcs mou conteza,
> pois Jhesu Crist non los contrasta res,
> q'il an vencut e venzon, de qe·m peza,
> Francs e Tartres, Erminis e Perses,
> e nos venzon sai chascun dia,
> car Dieus dorm qe veillar solia,
> e Bafometz obra de son poder
> e·n fai obrar lo Melicadefer.

---

[10] Runciman, *History*, III, p. 318.

No m'es semblan qe per tan se recreza,
anz a jurat e dit tot a pales
qe ja nuls hom que en Jhesucrist creza
non remandra, s'el pot, en sest paes;
enan fara bafomaria
del mostier de Sancta Maria,
e·l sieus car fis, q'en degra dol aver,
o vol e·il plaz: ben deu a nos plazer.   (vv. 1–32)

Sorrow and grief have lodged themselves in my heart so that I am tempted to kill myself forthwith, or lay down the cross I had taken up in the honour of him who was set upon the cross; for neither cross nor religion are any help or guide to me against the evil Turks, God curse them! Rather it seems, from the way things appear, that God wishes to support them at our expense.

They have immediately conquered Caesaria and taken the stronghold of Arsuf by force. Ah, my God, to what a road have they taken all the knights, all the sergeants, all the townspeople who were inside the walls of Arsuf! Alas! the kingdom of Syria has lost so many that if truth be told it will be permanently diminished in power.

So anyone who puts up a fight against the Turks is mad, because Jesus Christ opposes them with nothing; for they have defeated, and are [still] defeating – to my grief – Franks and Tartars, Armenians and Persians, and us they defeat every day, as God who used to keep watch is sleeping, and Bafomet works away with all his power and uses it to make the Melicadefer [Baibars] do his work.

In view of this I do not think he will give up. On the contrary, he has sworn and declared quite openly that if he can help it no one who believes in Jesus Christ will remain in this land. Rather, he will make a mosque out of St Mary's church; and her dear Son, who ought to grieve at this, wishes and likes this. We must like it too.

Apostasy was not out of the question, for three years later a whole Templar garrison north of Antioch went over to the Muslims.[11]

Ricaut is particularly bitter about Clement IV granting his legate Simon of Brie the power to commute crusading vows:

Lo papa fai perdon de gran largeza
contr'als Lombartz, a Carl'e als Frances,
e sai ves nos en mostra grant cobeza,
qe nostras crotz perdona per tornes;
e qi vol camjar romavia
per largeza de Lombardia,

---

[11] Compare Chapter 10, n. 33.

nostre legat lor en dara poder,
q'il vendon Deu e·l perdon per aver.

Segnor frances, Alixandria
nos a piegz fait qe Lumbardia
qe sai nos an Turcs sobrat de poder,
pres e vencuz e donatz per aver.   (vv. 33–44)

The Pope is granting a very liberal indulgence to Charles and to the French against the Lombards, and over here he shows great avarice towards us, by commuting our crosses for coins; and if anyone wants to exchange a pilgrimage to the Holy Land for the liberality of Lombardy, our legates will grant them the power to do so, for they sell God and the indulgence [also: they sell God and lose Him] for money.

French lords, Alexandria has treated us worse than Lombardy, for over here the Turks have overcome us in force, captured and defeated us and given us away for money.

The beleaguered military orders had a particular reason to feel aggrieved, for during the collection of the 1264 tenth for Charles of Anjou a controversy about their taxable status ended up with Simon of Brie being the judge of whether the orders had to pay it.

Exhortation and blame

The Templar's cry was not unanswered. By 1267 preaching was under way for Louis' new expedition. An anonymous troubadour reminds listeners of the need for more manpower in the Holy Land (BdT 168.1a):

E si membres a totz la grans amors
que Dieus nos fetz, be fora mielhs gardatz
Jerusalem, e·y agra mais crozatz;
mas era es venguda la sazos
qu'om non a cor mas qu'om sia manen.   (vv. 17–21)

If all remembered the great love that God showed us, Jerusalem would certainly be better protected, and there would be more crusaders there; but now the time has come when people desire nothing but getting rich.

The preaching clergy – perhaps those who were publicising the crusade – should make the passage to 'Outremer beyond Tyre', along with Henry III of England, Richard of Cornwall, James I of Aragon, Louis IX of France, Alfonso X of Castile, and Louis' son Philip (the future Philip III the Bold), and do battle with the pagans: then, he believes, the precious mirror that is the light of salvation, Jerusalem, would be liberated. The *sirventes* ends with praise of Alfonso X of Castile for his humbling of the Saracens in Spain, and urges his listeners to make their way to him, though it is unclear whether the troubadour is urging his listeners to support him in his efforts in Spain or whether he is thinking of him as a leader of an expedition to the Holy Land.[12]

Raimon Gaucelm de Beziers' fervent song of exhortation *Qui vol aver complida amistansa* (BdT 401.8) draws on the customary affective topoi: the desire to have Christ's love, the need to avenge His dishonour and crucifixion, the pains he suffered, accusations of hypocrisy and treachery on the part of those who are reluctant to go. Playing urgently on the forms of *passar*, *passatge* and so on,[13] he details the many excuses people make for not going:

> Mas trop d'omes son qu'eras fan semblansa
> que passaran, e ges no·n an dezire.
> Don se sabran del passar escondire
> ganren d'aquelhs, e diran ses duptansa:
> 'Ieu passera, si·l sout del rei agues',
> l'autre dira·n: 'Ieu no sui benanans',
> l'autre dira·n: 'S'ieu non agues efans,
> tost passera, que sai no·m tengra res'. (vv. 17–24)

There are many men who now pretend they will make the crossing, and have no intention of doing so. A great many of these will know how to get out of travelling, and will not scruple to say 'I would make the passage if the king paid me'; another will say, 'I am not well off'; another will say 'If I didn't have children I wouldn't hesitate to go, for nothing here would hold me back.'

In the *tornada* he asks his friend Miquel – probably a member of a family among the vassals of the viscount of Narbonne, and part of the circle of Guiraut Riquier – to perform the *sirventes* to Aimeric, the eldest son of Amalric IV (1239–1270), who became Viscount Aimeric V on his father's death. The focus on delays and excuses may have a particular application to Aimeric, who made his vow and took the cross on 7 March 1270, but never left for the Holy Land.[14] Was Aimeric held back by his father's death in December 1270, or illness preceding it, and is Raimon Gaucelm warning him against using this as an excuse not to honour his vow?

A more worldly-wise exhortation to support Louis' expedition is found in Bertran d'Alamanon's *D'un sirventes mi ven gran voluntatç* (BdT 76.8). At the time of Louis' first crusade the troubadour had tried to dissuade Charles of Anjou from taking

---

[12] For further details see the online edition and Paterson, 'James the Conqueror', pp. 218–19.
[13] Compare Introduction, p. 4.
[14] For further details see Raimon Gaucelm de Béziers, *Poesie*, ed. A. Radaelli (Florence, 1997), pp. 15–16. The rubric of the single fourteenth-century manuscript in which the song is preserved dates the song to 1268, but this may not be reliable, or may not be reliable for the *tornada*, which could have been added after the initial composition.

part, since he considered that matters in the Angevin's newly acquired county of Provence demanded his more urgent attention. By 1267–1268, when he composed this later *sirventes*, he is so exasperated by the 'state of utter turmoil' in the West that he considers the crusade as a vastly preferable alternative to the chaotic manoeuvres surrounding the succession to the Holy Roman Empire.

> D'un sirventes mi ven gran voluntatç
> ce·l fas'ausir a tutç cominalmen,
> e qu'ieu dirai de las grantç poestatç,
> de cells ques an de l'enperi conten;
> c'al mieu semblan il regnan folamen,
> e·l papa len, car los ten e balansa.
> Be·m meravegll car igll an esperansa
> ques a nengun en fas'autregiamen,
> puois c'el a d'els renda d'aur e d'argien.
>
> Al papa val l'Enperi e·l Regnatç
> mais ce sc'era tut sieu domeniamen,
> car plus monta l'avers c'es presentatç
> per acest plai a lui e a sa gen
> ce li renda ce us emperaires pren,
> e puois d'aver n'a tan gran aondansa,
> no mi sembla ce gia·i met'acordansa,
> ces ell non a en alre son enten,
> per ce lo monç n'es tut e turbamen.   (vv. 1–18)

I feel a strong urge to have everyone listen to a *sirventes*, and to speak out about the great potentates – those who are quarrelling over the Empire; for it seems to me that they are acting foolishly, and the pope tardily, since he is keeping them on tenterhooks. I am amazed they are hoping he will make a commitment to any of them, since they are providing him with rents of gold and silver.

The Empire and the Regno are worth more to the pope than if they completely belonged to him, for the money presented to him and his people as a result of this dispute exceeds the rent that any emperor receives, and since he has such an abundance of wealth, it does not seem to me that he will ever settle the dispute, since he has his mind set on nothing else – which is why the world is in a state of utter turmoil.

Bertran is sceptical about Pope Clement IV's motives, believing him to profit financially by prevaricating over the appointment of the next Holy Roman Emperor. Under the deal finalised with Clement in February 1265, by which Charles accepted the Regno as a papal fief, Charles agreed to give him a one-off payment of 50,000 marks sterling when he acquired the kingdom, followed by an annual rent of 8,000 ounces of gold. As Charles of Anjou's emissary in Italy after 1260, Bertran was in a strong position to be aware of the financial and political situation and, from the point of view of his employer, to have been aghast at the funds channelled to the papacy.[15] He is also sarcastic about the kings who want to parade their martial prowess on the battlefield to settle the matter, and cynically predicts the clerical response. Pope and clergy will immediately accept that might is right, glorify the winner as Jesus Christ Himself if it suits them, then scheme against him once his fortunes change.

> Gia aices platç non er sentençiatç
> puois ce li rei volon abreujamen
> ab cavaliers et ab cavals armatç,
> e ab vasals bons de concerimen
> vegna cascus apoderadamen,
> e en un canp fasa·n un'aital dansa
> c'al departir gasagne l'uns l'onransa.
> Puois decretals no·i nosera·n nien,
> puois trobera·n lo papa bendisen.
>
> Aicell sera fil de Dieu apelatç,
> ce aura faiç al camp lo vensimen;
> per los clerges el er leu coronatç
> car il veran c'auran l'afortimen.
> Adonc seran tutç a sun mandamen,
> car ades an clerges aital uçansa
> ce, can trobon pairo de gran puisança,
> tut cant il vol fan ben e umilmen,
> e puois sun dan quan veison ce deisen.   (vv. 19–36)

This dispute will never end in a formal judgement since the kings want to shorten the process with knights and with armoured horses, and for each one to come in full force with fine conquering warriors, and perform such a dance with them on a battlefield that at the end one will win the office. Then no decretal will be any impediment, as he will find the pope will give his blessing to it.

The one who has secured the victory in the field will be called son of God; he will promptly be crowned by the clergy because they will see their position fortified. Then they will be entirely at his command, for the clergy always behave like this: when they find a very powerful patron they dutifully and humbly do everything he wants, and then work to ruin him when they see he is on the way down.

---

[15] Despite Bertran's castigation of papal greed, the huge unanticipated costs of the conquest plunged Charles into debt, and the pope, raising vast loans from Tuscan bankers, was also in financial difficulties (Dunbabin, *Charles of Anjou*, pp. 4, 57 and 132–33, and see Paterson, 'James the Conqueror', p. 226, n. 28).

These kings are likely to be Charles of Anjou, king of Sicily and Naples, and Conradin, king of Jerusalem since 1254.[16] The young heir to Manfred was another claimant to the throne of the Holy Roman Emperor, and his march through northern Italy to Rome was so little opposed as to suggest that his bid for the throne would be successful. It is interesting that Bertran is ready to criticise both his patron and the pope more specifically than their Ghibelline opponents. The solution to all this upheaval? A crusade to the Holy Land:

> E si als reis so c'ieu lur dic non platç,
> als podon far c'es er miels per un sen
> ce utra mar si pert crestandiatç.
> E s'i pason apoderadamen
> remanra tot so de c'om los repren;
> e autresi pase·s lo rei de Fransa
> el saut primers, ses longia demoransa,
> e·l reis Gaumes, qu'a l'astr'e l'ardimen
> dels Serasis mescregens d'autra gen.   (vv. 37–45)

If the kings dislike what I am telling them, they can do something else which is a hundred times better at present, for in Outremer Christendom is being lost. And if they cross the sea in full force everything that people blamed them for will be set aside; and similarly, let the king of France be the first to cross, promptly, without procrastinating, and King James, who has good fortune and courage as far as the heathen Saracens of a different race are concerned.

But there is no point in counting on the pope for financial support: 'As for the pope, I know he will give generously, with many indulgences and little of his wealth' (vv. 56–57).

England at this time sees the composition of a *tenso* in French (*Sire Gauter, dire vos voil*) between two noblemen about to join the crusade, Count Henry de Lacy of Lincoln and Walter of Bibbsworth, on the traditional conflict between love for a lady and love for Christ.

---

[16] See Paterson, 'James the Conqueror', pp. 13–14 and p. 35: as Gregory IX was making an unprecedented attempt to transform crusading into a universal Christian activity, he appealed to a mass audience, exhorting everyone to swear a crusade vow, including women, the old, the young, the sick and the poor. The vow could then be 'commuted, redeemed, or postponed by apostolic command' (p. 14). Lower (*The Barons' Crusade*, p. 35) comments that Gregory's 'turn to vow redemption proved a watershed not just for papal crusade preaching, but also for papal finance', and that as the association with crusading weakened, vow redemption came to be referred to simply as 'the sale of indulgences'.

Ghibellines

Meanwhile a Genoese cloth merchant, Calega Panzan, was composing a ferocious Ghibelline *sirventes* against the clergy and the French under Charles of Anjou (BdT 107.1), who were 'crusading' against Conradin in northern Italy. The troubadour vengefully anticipates what he sees as Conradin's triumph and the imminent downfall of the papal party, which has neglected the Holy Land to wage crusade in Tuscany and Lombardy.

> Ar es sazos c'om si deu alegrar
> e fals clergue plagner lur caïmen,
> e lur orgueill q'a durat lonjamen,
> e lur enjan e lur fals predicar.
> Ai, deleial! Toscan'e Lombardia
> fais peceiar, e no·us dol de Suria:
> treg'aves lai ab Turcs et ab Persanz
> per aucir sai Frances et Alemanz!
>
> [...]
>
> Qui vol aucir o qi viu de raubar
> e tost e lieu pot aver salvamen,
> sol vengn'aucir de crestians un cen;
> e qi·s volgues d'aucir mil esforzar
> em Paradis en l'auzor luec seria.
> Ai, clergue fals! Laissat aves la via
> e·ls mandamenz qe Dieus fes pur e sanz,
> e Moyzes, cant escrius los comanz.   (vv. 1–8, 17–24)

Now is the time for rejoicing and for false clergy to bewail their decline and their long-standing pride, their deceit and their false preaching. Ah, traitors! You cause Tuscany and Lombardy to be cut to pieces, yet you feel no grief for Syria: over there you have a truce with Turks and Persians so that here you can slaughter French and Germans!

[...]

Anyone who feels like killing or lives by rapine can win salvation quickly and easily as long as he comes to kill a hundred Christians, and if he felt like forcing himself to kill a thousand he would win the highest seat of Paradise. Ah, false clergy! You have left the path and the rules made pure and holy by God, and by Moses when he wrote down the commandments!

Highlighting the Angevin's ruthlessness, he reminds him that when he was in captivity in Egypt he enjoyed better treatment at the hands of the Turks than did the Christian victims of his own atrocities in Italy:

> Al rei Carle degra tostemps membrar
> con el fon prez ab son frair'eisamen
> per Serrazis, e trobet chauzimen
> assas meillor qe non pogro trobar
> a Saint Eler qi forfait non avia
> li Cristian; ailas! q'en un sol dia
> pezeieron Frances petitz e granz
> ni la maire salvet neis sos enfanz.   (vv. 33–40)

King Charles ought always to bear in mind how he was captured by the Saracens along with his brother, and how he was met with much greater clemency than the Christians were able to find at Sant'Ellero, which had committed no crime. Alas! in a single day the French cut great and small to pieces, and mothers could not even save their children.

The French army under Robert de Béthune had been to support Charles' claims in central Italy and had committed numerous atrocities in the land between Bergamo and Mantua. As Conradin approached, nearly all the towns of the province declared themselves on his side. The tactics of Charles' generals, who had insufficient forces to risk pitched battles, was to lay waste the countryside or suburbs of hostile towns, with the worst treatment meted out to the area round Florence, which Guy de Montfort entered on 17 April 1267. Some 800 Ghibellines took refuge in the castle of Sant'Ellero, where nearly all were massacred. Pope Clement IV even wrote to Charles to blame the excesses of the French troops. Calega Panzan also refers to the ill-treatment of two Piedmontese counts who had been captured at the battle of Benevento in 1266:

> Son compaire a laissat perjurar
> l'arcivesqe d'un auzor sagramen,
> e·l senescalc qui juret falsamen
> l'arma del rei per los comtes salvar,
> qi son desfait a tort et a feunia.
> Ai! con es fols qi·s met en sa bailia!
> Per q'eu prec Dieu q'aital rei dezenanz
> qe non tenc fez pos ac passatz vii anz.   (vv. 41–48)

He let his accomplice the archbishop perjure himself in a most solemn oath, and the seneschal too, who swore on the king's soul that the counts would be safeguarded, and they were unjustly and criminally mutilated. Ah! how foolish is anyone who puts himself in his power! I therefore beseech God to confound such a king who has never kept faith since he was seven years old.[17]

---

[17] For the specific accusations levelled at Charles here see L. Paterson, 'Calega Panzan, *Ar es sazos c'om si deu alegrar* (BdT 107.1), *Lt* 5 (2012).

After they had languished in the Provençal fortress of Castellane and tried unsuccessfully to escape by stabbing the guard, Charles had ordered them to be sent to Aix and each have a hand and foot chopped off. When the troubadour speaks of 'counts', everyone knows who he is talking about;: the troubadour is tapping into the contempt and anger their gruesome mutilation will have aroused everywhere, especially since they were captured in honourable combat. He also accuses Charles of favouring his Muslim subjects at the expense of Christians:

> Grecs ni Latis non pot ab lui trobar
> trega ni paz, mas li can descrezen
> de Nucheira l'agron a lur talen,
> e podon be 'Bafumet!' aut cridar;
> q'ar jes de Dieu ni de Sancta Maria
> no·i a mostier, qe non o suffriria
> l'apostolis q'a mes en gran balanz
> la fe de Dieu – don sui meravillianz. (vv. 57–64)

Neither Greek nor Latin can find truce or peace with him, but the heathen dogs of Luchera had it exactly to their liking, and they can happily cry 'Mahomet!' at the tops of their voices for now there is no monastery of God or St Mary there, as the pope, who has placed the faith of God in great jeopardy, would not allow it – which astounds me.

Songs attacking Charles of Anjou were perceived to have a significant propaganda impact and led to some draconian efforts at public censorship. Shortly after the execution of Conradin the authorities in Perugia issued a statute, dated 20 December 1268, ordaining that anyone who composed, recited or sang a song against King Charles, or spoke any insult towards him, should be fined a hundred pounds of *denarii*; and if he could not pay this fine, his tongue was to be cut out, and this would be done to any arguing in favour of Conradin. This prohibition was to be proclaimed once a month in both the city and the suburbs.[18]

Asperti argues that the song in some ways signals the end of the Ghibelline poetic tradition closely linked to Provence and north-west Italy, which expresses similar polemical attacks, in a strongly knightly environment, against the clergy and the Guelf policy of the house of France.[19]

The crusade of James I of Aragon

James the Conqueror was and is mainly known for his successes against the Moors in Spain. Neverthless, he had long harboured the desire to go on crusade in the

---

[18] See Introduction, p. 19.
[19] S. Asperti, *Carlo I d'Angiò e i trovatori. Componenti 'provenzali' e angioine nella tradizione manoscritta della lirica trobadorica* (Ravenna, 1995), pp. 61–62.

Holy Land, and on 16 January 1266, after spending five years suppressing a Muslim uprising in Murcia at the request of King Alfonso X of Castile, he turned his attention eastwards. But in the eyes of the Church he was in a state of sin, being involved in an adulterous and also incestuous relationship with the illegitimate daughter Berengaria of the Castilian king. Clement IV refused to support his plans, admonishing him to stop crucifying Jesus Christ, otherwise neither the Church nor God would be able to help his crusade succeed. Despite this, throughout 1268 James made extensive preparations for an expedition, and seems to have entertained no anxiety about the state of his soul. His autobiography, the *Llibre dels feits*, shows that he believed that he would be forgiven for this liaison because of all his conquests on behalf of God and Christendom, somewhat bullying a dubious Dominican friar to grant him absolution on the eve of battle on the grounds that he was intending from now on to live with her without sin – a declaration with which he signally failed to comply.

James was evidently anxious to pre-empt Louis' departure, which was scheduled to take place in 1270. He set sail from Barcelona on 4 September 1269, at a time of year when travel was already hazardous because of the climate. This was no doubt to protect his commercial interests, to eclipse his rival and to avoid his crusade being subsumed into that of the king of France.[20] Ten days later a violent storm forced him to abandon the voyage. He felt obliged to provide detailed explanations for this failure, insisting that God had clearly not wanted him to pursue his undertaking. After delays because of the continued bad weather, he finally disembarked at Aigues-Mortes, proceeding immediately to Sainte-Marie-de-Vauvert to give thanks to the Virgin for for his safe return. From there he headed for his native town, Montpellier, where he asked the consuls to provide him with some reimbursement for the considerable expenses of his expedition. They offered him the sum of 60,000 sous tournois but, to his great annoyance, only on condition that he re-embark for the Holy Land. The king left the town abruptly for Barcelona, firing off some disparaging remarks about the citizens' lack of love and loyalty towards their overlord.[21]

A song by an otherwise unidentified troubadour named as Olivier the Templar (BdT 312.1) reflects widespread disquiet about James' refusal to re-embark. The troubadour begins by evoking the shocking fate of King Louis and his barons lost at Mansurah, and his pleasure at Louis' determination to claim back the Holy Land as long as there is life in his body. Then carefully indicating an example for others to follow, he points out that the swift abandonment of the ransom and the sepulchre led many noblemen to take the cross. He moves on to address the king of Aragon with respectful and flattering words:

Rey d'Arago, de tot mal non chalen,
c'avetz conqist de Tortos'al Biar

---

[20] For further consideration of James' reasons see E. Marcos, *La croada catalana. L'exèrcit de Jaume I a Terra Santa* (Barcelona, 2007), pp. 198–99.
[21] For further details see Paterson, 'James the Conqueror', pp. 213–15.

> e Malhoga, sovenga·us d'otramar,
> pus qe autre non pot esser tenens
> del sieu Temple qe avetz tan gen servit.
> E car vos es del mon lo pus ardit
> de fag d'armas, ni Roma vo·n covida,
> acorretz lai on tot lo mon vos crida.   (vv. 17–24)

King of Aragon, undaunted by all evil – for you have been victorious from Tortosa to Biar and Mallorca – be mindful of Outremer, since no one else can preserve [?] his Temple which you have served so nobly. And since you are the bravest in the world at deeds of arms and Rome is inviting you to do so, hurry there where everyone is calling out for you.

Pope Clement, who had opposed his crusade, had died on 29 November 1268, nine months before the departure of the Aragonese fleet, and his successor had not yet been elected. Nevertheless, when James left for the Holy Land, he did so still in the absence of papal approval. But when he turned back to France almost immediately, a different ethical framework applied: James had been blamed for undertaking the expedition, but he was also widely blamed for renouncing it. The news of the débâcle was spreading throughout the West, which was an embarrassment to the king's reputation. And popes in the past had not hestitated to excommunicate crusaders who had failed to fulfil their vow for one reason or another. So once the bishop of Maguelone exhorted him to persevere in his enterprise, Olivier could now say that Rome, in the person of the bishop, was inviting James to fulfil his destiny. The troubadour's exhortation does not limit itself to enumerating all the reasons which could have motivated the king to undertake his crusade in the first place – the defence of the Holy Land, the reversal of a shameful Christian defeat, the protection of the Templars' Order, military and political glory – but adds the critical new element of spiritual support. His declaration of Rome's invitation was an important rhetorical ploy to persuade the king that, whatever he may have thought about God's will in impeding his passage, he should not now give up.

Olivier does not seem to be urging him simply to re-embark on the same ship and turn right back towards the East.

> Si·l rey Jacme ab un ters de sa jen
> passes de lay, leu pogra restaurar
> la perd'e·l dan e·l sepulcre cobrar;
> car contra luy Turcx non an garimen,
> qes el del tot ja n'a tans descofitz,
> pres e liatz, mortz, nafratz e delitz
> dins murs e fors en batalha enramida,
> et a conqist so qe tanh a sa vida.   (vv. 25–32)

If King James sailed there with a third of his people, he could easily restore the loss and the damage and recover the sepulchre; for against him the Turks have no protection, as he has already [utterly] discomfited, captured and bound so many of them, slain, wounded and destroyed them within walls and outside in pitched battle, and has conquered what is fitting for his way of life.

The idea that James could restore the losses in the Holy Land if he made the passage with a third of his people suggests that he would have to regroup. Furthermore, the troubadour introduces his song with his satisfaction that Louis is committing himself to claiming back the holy places, so it would seem that Olivier envisages James' conquering rôle as taking place within the context of the French crusade. This was certainly not what James originally had in mind, whether or not the troubadour was aware of it; but the *sirventes* is sufficiently flattering, implying James and his men could alone recover the sepulchre. And with delicate diplomacy the troubadour manages to remind the king that he will one day face God's judgement (vv. 33–40). It is unknown whether this 'Templar' was a propagandist of the Church in general and the Templars in particular, or whether he was simply adding his voice to popular responses to James' débâcle. In that case, it would have been a theatrical masterstroke to present himself as a Templar (whether or not he actually was one), particularly in view of James' lifelong close relations with this order.

The details of a second Occitan lyric (BdT 226.2) suggest that it too is a reponse to these particular circumstances. It was composed by the troubadour Guillem de Mur, an associate of the troubadour Guiraut Riquier, and the significant point here is that he reminds the king to fulfil his vow:

> L'arcivesque prec de cuy es Toleta
> qu'amoneste lo bon rey d'Arago
> que per complir son vot en mar se meta,
> e per tener en pes son bon resso.   (vv. 41–44)

I beseech the archbishop of Toledo to admonish the good king of Aragon to set sail in order to fulfil his vow and to be mindful of his good name.

The song begins by emphasising the need to go on crusade with the right intention:

> E siatz certz, quals que s'en entremeta
> e n'yntr'en mar ab bon'entensio,
> que Jhesu Crist en tan bon luec los meta
> en paradis quon li siey martir so.   (vv. 5–8)

And be sure that whoever undertakes this and sets out on the sea with a good intention, Jesus Christ will place him in as high a place in paradise as his martyrs are.

This admonition certainly reflects preaching commonplaces and can be interpreted in general terms, but in the topical context it has a much more specific force, insinuating that the king has failed to fulfil his vow because of his sins, unconfessed and unrenounced.

Guillem continues in terms that can again be interpreted as both general and specific.

> Pero quascus gart quon ira garnitz,
> quar Dieus no vol qu'ab lautruy garnizo,
> de qu'autre a tort sia despossezitz,
> lai pas nulh hom ses satisfactio
> far, qu'ieu non cre qu'aital home prometa
> Dieus son regne ni qe s'amor li do,
> si ben lai vay ab arc ni ab sageta,
> qu'el sout que pren cobra son gazardo.
>
> Non cre sia per Dieu gent acullitz
> rics hom que pas ab l'autruy messio,
> ni selh qu'a tort n'a los sieus descauzitz,
> ni fai raubar per aquelh ochaizo;
> quar Dieus sap tot que port'en sa maleta,
> e s'ap tortz vay, treballa·s en perdo;
> quar Dieus vol cor fin ab volontat neta
> d'ome que pas mais per luy que per do.   (vv. 9–24)

But let each one take care to go properly equipped, for God does not wish anyone to make the passage there with another's equipment without making reparation, if some man has been wrongly dispossessed of it; I do not believe that God promises such a man his kingdom or gives him his love, even if he does go there with bow and arrow, for he will gain his reward in the pay he receives.

I do not believe that a rich man who makes the journey at another's expense will be graciously welcomed by God, nor will a man who has mistreated his own people or had them robbed for this purpose; for God is well aware of all that he carries in his trunk, and if he goes unjustly, he troubles himself in vain; God wants a pure heart with clean desire in a man who makes this passage for his sake rather than for the sake of a gift.

In the particular context of James' crusade the emphasis on the idea that if a crusader is in a state of sin he is wasting his efforts, and on the need for setting right former wrongs and purifying one's heart, takes on a great deal of topical interest. It suggests some pointed admonitions to the king himself, whose reputation for immorality was considerable. One may also wonder whether the remarks about a 'rich man who makes the journey at another's expense' hint at local resentment at James' demands for money to pay for his failed crusade, and at his angry disdain for their offer conditional upon his resuming it. The need to fulfil his vow (*complir son vot*) in the historical context can be seen as implying not simply following up on his crusading vow but bringing it to proper completion and not abandoning it half-way.

Celebration and mourning

After Louis set out from the north of France for Africa on 16 March 1270 the troubadour Bertolome Zorzi composed a song to celebrate his departure (BdT 74.11). The great king Louis, he declares, is off to avenge the shameful decline of the Holy Land; he has paid no heed to cost, and failure is unthinkable! – 'for he sets out with such vast forces that there is no reason whatever to entertain doubts about it'. Praising Louis' companions, King Thibaut of Navarre and Louis' brother Alphonse of Poitiers, he anticipates the arrival of the English king from across the Channel to join the French:

> Mas ges non taing qu'om l'engles rei reprenda
> s'un petit es per non-poder tarsatz,
> quar ben sa cor que sa promez'atenda
> e·n faza mais tan q'en sia lauzatz;
> ni no·s cuj'on qu'el fassa tal tarsansa
> q'us n'ai'asaut qu'el no·i sia prezenz,
> qu'estiers com val non valg d'utra·ls presatz,
> pois Deu acor ab tal poder de genz
> qu'autre socors al sieu non sobravanza.   (vv. 55–63)

But the English king should not be reproached if he has delayed a little because of inability [to go any earlier], for he is definitely hastening here in order to fulfil his promise and do so much more that he may be praised for it; and let it not be thought that he will delay so long that anyone will launch an attack without him being present, for he has never been more valued than he is now, above those who are prized, since he comes to the aid of God with such a power of men that no other help surpasses his.

A Venetian merchant, Zorzi was a prisoner in Genoa at the time, and may not have been well informed about the events he describes; the English 'king' to whom he refers is probably the Lord Edward rather than his father Henry III. His idea that 'the king' was to be accompanied by an unsurpassably powerful army is based on poetic licence, misinformation and/or wishful thinking, since English recruitment to his crusading army was poor.

Louis' death at Tunis on 25 August 1270 inspired two surviving *planhs*, or funeral laments, both Occitan. Raimon Gaucelm de Beziers (BdT 401.1) briefly praises the king: 'He was valiant above all the valiant, for he bravely set out from his own land against the treacherous wicked Turks for the sake of Jesus Christ.' He even insinuates a certain criticism of God for what has happened: 'God has taken him and called him from this life, even though he will not be greatly thanked for this death.' The troubadour's reponse to this desperate loss is to urge people to step up their crusading efforts in order to try to repair the damage, 'at least in part'. What the Church needs to do is preach everywhere and grant the kind of indulgence that would energise people to follow the French, but it 'is so torpid that it rouses none to make the passage'; moreover many Church authorities persuade people to commute their vows for cash and fail to galvanise them with their preaching:

> Ans vos dirai que fan cominalmens
> selhs que la crotz solian far levar:
> elhs per deniers, la fan a moutz laissar,
> e degron mielhs prezicar a las gens!
> Quar moutz n'estan sai flacx et adurmitz?
> Quar del crozar nulhs prezicx no·i 's auzitz!
> E del prezic degra·s movre tals crida
> per que·s crozes la gens pus afortida.   (vv. 25–32)

But I'll tell you what is generally done by those who once used to make people take the cross: they convince many of them abandon it in exchange for money, when they ought instead to be preaching to the people! Why do so many stay here, flabby and inert? Because no preaching of the crusade is heard! But preaching ought to provoke such an outcry as to fire people up to take the cross more fervently.

If only the Christian world were in harmony it would be easy to crush the Turks! At the end of the song the troubadour's hopes turn to Louis' son and heir Philip III the Bold, but these hopes would be disappointed. In 1275, following the Council of Lyon in 1274, Philip would take the cross but not make the passage.

The second *planh*, by Daspol (or Guillem d'Autpol; BdT 206.2), is a more moving tribute to the king, full of an affective lexis of heart-broken sorrow, loss and death, reiterated in a quasi-liturgical fashion in a refrain at the end of each stanza. The poet can only explain this death by God's desire to have Louis with him rather than his people:

> Fortz tristors es e salvaj'a retraire
> qu'ieu chant am joy de tan coral dolor
> con n'es li mort del rei nostre seinhor
> francs de Fransa, de fin pres emperaire;
> e per so chant ieu marrit e joyos
> car Dieus lo volc mais a si que a nos
> car el s'era tost datz a luy servir –
> qu'estiers sa mort Dieus no·s volgra sufrir,
> per qu'es maiers le dans e·l desconort,
> c'ar ieu aug dir que·l rey de Fransa es mort.
> *Ai Dieus, cal dans es!*
>
> [...]
>
> Le mal ni·l dan non pot lengua retraire,
> per que cascus devem viure am paor,
> c'ades pren mort del mont so qu'es milhor,

que·ns a sostrah li francs reys de bon ayre,
car si visques l'onrat reys corayos,
tost foron mortz Sarazins ergulhos,
c'a tostz fera terras e fieus giquir
e Baffomet reneguar e grepir,
e·ns obrira totz los camins e·ls portz.
Guardas de quan nos a mermat sa mortz
Ay Dieus, cals dans es! (vv. 1–11, 34–44)

It is a sadness harsh and cruel to tell that I sing with joy of such heart-breaking grief as is the death of the king, our noble lord of France, emperor of perfect worth; and I sing in sorrow and in joy since God wished him more to be with him than with us because he had given himself promptly to serve him – otherwise God would not have allowed his death, so that the harm and desolation are [all the?] greater, now that I hear tell that the king of France is dead. *Ah God, what a loss it is!*

[...]

Tongue cannot tell the damage and the loss, which is why each of us must live in fear, since death constantly takes away what is best in the world, for it has stolen from us the gracious high-born king. If the honoured, brave king were living, the proud Saracens would soon be dead, for he would swiftly make them abandon lands and fiefs and deny and abandon Mahomet, and would open up the highways and passes for us. Look how much his death has diminished us! *Ah God, what a loss it is!*

In his magisterial study of Louis, the historian Jacques Le Goff sums up the pious king's crusades, from a modern perspective, as 'the lethal defining moment of the crusades, the aggressive phase of penitential and self-sacrificing Christianity. At its final, high point it embodied the egoism of a faith which at the cost of sacrificing the believer for the sake of his salvation, to the detriment of the "other", generates intolerance and death.' But he adds that in the medieval world, where crusading ideals continue to arouse profound admiration even among those such as Rutebeuf or Joinville who no longer believe in them, Saint Louis' image emerges magnified by these catastrophic crusades, 'illuminated by the "beauty of the dead man", and begins a process of "Death and transfiguration". From this perspective the crusade of Tunis will, in its dazzling and mortal brevity, be a form of coronation.'[22]

---

[22] Le Goff, *Saint Louis*, p. 207: 'le point d'orgue mortel de la croisade, de cette phase agressive d'une Chrétienté pénitentielle et auto-sacrificielle. Il a incarné, à son ultime et plus haut point, cet égoïsme de la foi qui, au prix du sacrifice du croyant, mais pour son salut au détriment de l'«autre», porte intolérance et la mort. [...] Elle est illuminée par «la beauté du mort» et entame un processus de «Mort et transfiguration». Dans cette perspective, la croisade de Tunis sera, dans sa fulgurante et mortelle brièveté, une manière de couronnement.'

If so, this is not reflected in the lyrics of the trouvères. In fact there is not a single surviving lyric response from northern France to Louis' second crusade. For this we must look to other genres, such as, precisely, Joinville's chronicle, which pleads for Louis' sanctification, and the *dits* of Rutebeuf.[23] It needs to be borne in mind that the latter were commissioned works, contributing to propaganda for the Sicilian crusade as well as the crusade of Tunis.[24]

The absence of lyric responses may be attributable to the Old French manuscript tradition, which favours the preservation of songs celebrating courtly love.[25] What the troubadour lyrics show is that, first, before 1265 the Reconquista continues to be present in people's minds, unsurprisingly given the proximity of Occitania and Spain and patronage of troubadours by Spanish kings. Second, the papal–imperial conflict colours attitudes to Louis' crusade. Anticlerical troubadours inveigh against the papal diversion of funds to Charles of Anjou's Sicilian campaign, and their virulent attacks on Charles of Anjou are met by attempts at censorship and counter-propaganda. Even a solid supporter of Charles, Bertran d'Alamanon, is sceptical about papal motives, sarcastic about the Western rulers and the clergy, and prepared to present the crusade as an expedient to put paid to the 'state of utter turmoil' in the West. Third, some troubadours and their audiences are clearly moved by the prospect of Louis' expedition, and disturbed when James of Aragon, lord of Monpellier, fails to fulfil his vow. And finally, some are deeply troubled at the difficulty of reconciling the triumphs of Islam, and the king's death, with God's purposes.

---

[23] From Louis IX's majority all sorts of works termed 'dits' proliferate, the term being given to all poems in verse, narrative or otherwise, generally having moralising or satirical tendencies, of no more than 2,000 lines (P. Zumthor, *Histoire littéraire de la France médiévale, VIe–XIVe siècles* (Paris, 1954), p. 261).

[24] For the Sicilian crusade see the *Chanson de Pouille* (May 1264) and the *Dit de Pouille* (July 1265), and for Louis' crusade, *La Complainte d'Outremer* (1265–66), *La Voie de Tunis* (summer 1267) and *La Disputaison du croisé et du décroisé* (1268), in Rutebeuf, *Oeuvres complètes*, ed. Zink, pp. 827–57 and 875–917. See also Adam de la Halle's unfinished *chanson de geste* in Charles' honour: Adam de la Halle, *Oeuvres complètes*, ed. P.-Y. Badel (Paris, 1995), pp. 376–93, and J. Dunbabin, 'Charles of Anjou, Crusaders and Poets', in Parsons and Paterson, *The Crusades*, pp. 150–58 (pp. 151–55).

[25] See Introduction, p. 11.

12

After Saint Louis

Two days after the death of Louis IX at Tunis on 25 August 1270, his brother Charles of Anjou arrived from Sicily. Two months later, on 30 October, as Dunbabin records, 'he made an agreement with the emir of Tunis which clearly benefited the king of Sicily if no-one else; on the following day the crusade was abandoned. The bulk of the army, including the new king Philip III, retreated with Charles to Sicily, and from there made its way back to France. Vast amounts of money and manpower had been expended for no gain to Christendom.' Charles was widely blamed, both for the abandonment of the crusade and for the decision to head for Tunis in the first place. His treaty with the emir brought him an annual tribute in gold, some trading privileges and the banishment from Tunis of some major figures of Ghibelline sympathies who had fled there after the battle of Tagliacozzo in 1268, and he was accused of diverting the crusade for his own purposes. Dunbabin argues that the second instance the case against him is weak; but 'the total abandonment of any expedition to the Holy Land or to Egypt can be fairly laid at Charles's door'. This, she reports, 'evoked sharp criticism in some quarters, most vociferously in the entourage of the English prince Edward who appeared to take his agreed part in the crusade just after the army arrived back in Sicily'.[1] Charles continued to figure in the crusading context for nearly another twenty years in criticisms of his conduct, both by the Catalan troubadour Cerverí de Girona in the aftermath of the Council of Lyon in 1274 and by an unknown troubadour just before the outbreak of the War of the Sicilian Vespers (Easter 1282). The latter war would then spark off a political, internecine crusade against Christians in Spain, the so-called Aragonese crusade.

Charles of Anjou

Criticism of Charles of Anjou in the entourage of the English prince Edward is borne out by a particularly vitriolic *sirventes* composed by the troubadour Austorc de Segret and sent through a jongleur to Viscount Arnaud-Othon II of Lomagne

---

[1] Dunbabin, *Charles I of Anjou*, pp. 195–96.

and Auvillars in Gascony (BdT 41.1).[2] It probably dates from 1273 or the earlier part of 1274, when Edward, now king of England, travelled to that region in order to put down a rebellion by Gaston of Béarn. Austorc's purpose was to whip up anti-French sentiment and urge Edward to wage war on the French, but he approached this indirectly, via the failure of Louis' crusade. He begins by declaring himself to be at an utter loss to understand how the catastrophe could have occurred: was it brought about by God or the Devil?

> No sai qui·m so tan suy desconoyssens,
> ni say don venh, ni sai on dey anar,
> ni re no sai que·m dey dire ni far,
> ni re no sai on fo mos nayssemens,
> ni re no say tan fort suy esbaÿtz:
> si Dieus nos a o dïables marritz,
> que Crestïas e la ley vey perida,
> e Sarrazis an trobada guandida.   (vv. 1–8)

I am at such a loss I cannot tell who I am, or where I come from, or where I ought to go, I know nothing of what I ought to say or do, or anything about my birth: I know nothing, I am so bewildered: God or a devil has so afflicted us that I see Christians and the Christian religion destroyed, and Saracens have found safe haven.

The fault is soon, however, attributed to the ineffective new French king, Philip III, and above all his powerful uncle, Charles of Anjou. Charles, instead of opposing the Muslims, has actually become their leader!

> Yeu vey gueritz los paguas mescrezens:
> e·ls Sarrazis e·ls Turcx d'outra la mar,
> e·ls Arabitz, que no·n cal un gardar
> del rey Felips dont es grans marrimens,
> ni d'en Karle, qu'elh lur es caps e guitz!
> No sai dont es vengutz tals esperitz
> que tanta gens n'es morta e perida,
> e·l reys Loïx n'a perduda la vida.   (vv. 9–16)

I see the false-believing pagans left in peace: the Saracens, and the Turks of Outremer, and the Arabs too, for none of them needs pay regard to King Philip, most sad to say, or Lord Charles, for *he* is their captain and leader! I cannot tell what place has brought forth such a spirit that has caused so many people to die and perish, but King Louis has lost his life from it.

---

[2] Despite the impassioned tone there is no need to suppose, as does the DBT (pp. 74–75), that Austorc was present at the distaster of Tunis.

With his military capability Charles could easily have done something to defend Christendom; but because of him it has suffered the worst failure in its history.

> Anc mais no vim del rey que fos perdens:
> ans l'avem vist ab armas guazanhar
> tot quant anc volc aver ni conquistar.
> Mas eras l'es vengutz abaissamens,
> et es ben dreitz quar es a Dieu falhitz:
> qui falh a Dieu en remanh escarnitz,
> qu'anc mais no fo mas per Karl'escarnida
> crestïantatz, ni pres tan gran falhida. (vv. 17–24)

Never before have we seen the king [Charles] defeated: instead we have seen him win by force of arms all that he ever wished to own or conquer. But now he has been humbled, and this is right, because he has failed God: anyone who fails God ends up in ignominy, for never before, except through Charles, has Christendom been mocked or suffered such a failure.

The *sirventes* first presents itself as a sort of *devinalh* or riddle song, where spiritual confusion is attributed to the Muslim triumph at the behest of some unknown force, which might conceivably be God himself: a seemingly blasphemous idea previously expressed by Austorc d'Aorlhac after Louis' failed first crusade in 1250, and by Ricaut Bonomel after Baibars' capture of Arsuf in 1265.[3] The riddle form allows the troubadour to hint that the devil that has led the Christians astray is Charles himself. He further attempts to goad the English king into action by reminding him of the need to avenge his kinsman Henry. It is uncertan whether this refers to Henry of Almain assassinated while he was attending Mass in Viterbo on 13 March 1271 by Charles' cousins Guy and Simon de Montfort, or to Henry of Castile, whom Charles imprisoned and put in a cage after the battle of Tagliacozzo, but in either case it serves to fuel anti-French sentiment and focus on the 'devilish' Charles.[4]

After the death of Louis IX at Tunis on 25 August 1270 hope had briefly persisted in some quarters that new leaders might make their way to the Holy Land to

---

[3] See above, pp. 206–08. More or less contemporaneously with Austorc de Segret's *sirventes*, a mock *tenso* with God by Daspol (BdT 206.4) treats this idea comically: see below.

[4] I have argued elsewhere in favour of Henry of Almain: See L. Paterson, 'Austorc de Segret, *[No s]ai qui·m so tan suy [des]conoyssens* (BdT 41.1)', *LT*, 5, 2012, < http://www.lt.unina.it/Paterson-2012.pdf>. Margaret Bent (*Magister Jacobus de Ispania, Author of the 'Speculum Musicae'* (Farnham and Burlington, Vt., 2015), pp. 101–02 and 183–85) has recently presented new arguments in favour of the identification with Henry of Castile, emphasising that Edward had a 'close and long-standing friendship with his brother-in-law and kinsman Henry of Castile', and indicating that Edward and Eleanor had rescued and raised that prince's son (p. 185). I. de Riquer Permayer, *Historia literaria del infante Enrique de Castilla (1230–1303)* (Barcelona, 2016), pp. 89–93, also presents strong arguments in favour of Henry of Castile.

avenge the loss. One of the *tornadas* to a *sirventes* of Peire Cardenal (BdT 335.62), probably composed when the Lord Edward of England was on his way there in 1271, had prayed for his success and for Louis' son Philip's support.

> A trastotz prec qe pregon coralmen
> Dieu Ihesu Crist que don lai alegransa
> a n'Audoard, qar es la meilher lansa
> de tot lo mon, e don cor e talen
> al rei Phelipp qe.l secorra breumen.   (vv. 46–50, MS M)

> I beseech all to pray sincerely to God, Jesus Christ, that he may grant joy to Lord Edward over there [in the Holy Land], as he is the best lance in the whole world, and grant to King Philip the heart and desire to assist him soon.

This was a futile hope, as except for Edward all the crusade leaders, including Philip, had agreed to postpone further expeditions for three years.[5] In 1272–1273 Folquet de Lunel had urged Pope Gregory X to settle the matter of the vacancy to the throne of Holy Roman Emperor so that then all the Christian kings might go to avenge Christ in Syria. Both of these texts reflect on Charles in some way. Folquet blamed him for imprisoning of Henry of Castile, who ought to be freed so that he could join forces with the hoped-for crusaders.

The *tornada* to Peire Cardenal's song is different. Both Asperti and Vatteroni see it as apocryphal, since the body of this piece is a tirade against both clerical and lay wickedness and hypocrisy, and the reference to the king of France is puzzling on the part of a troubadour well known for his strongly anticlerical and anti-French compositions. Vatteroni argues that the song serves a subtly propagandistic purpose, and was composed in an act of cultural politics designed to recuperate to the Angevin or more generically French cause a politically 'heretic', yet popular, troubadour.

The Council of Lyon

As soon as he became pope in 1271, Gregory X bent his mind to the task of reviving the crusading spirit. He sent appeals throughout Europe as far as Finland and Iceland – even perhaps Greenland and the North American coast – but without response. When he summoned the Council of Lyon in 1274, he hoped to give impetus to his desire for a new crusade. James I of Aragon was the only European monarch to attend, and discussions ground to a halt in the absence of support from

---

5 Edward had reached North Africa just before the crusaders left on 11 November, and with Charles of Anjou and Philip of France sailed to Sicily, where he spent the winter. He voyaged to the Holy Land at the end of April 1271, arriving in Acre on 9 May, and eventually left for home on 22 September. The *tornada* seems likely to have been composed when he was wintering in Sicily on his way to the Holy Land.

the other European monarchs. Troubadours voice various criticisms of the lack of support for God's cause.

It was probably after James' return that the Catalan troubadour Cerverí de Girona composed the intricate and allusive *sirventes En breu sazo aura·l jorn pretentori* (BdT 434a.20). In this he warns of the coming Day of Judgment, and urges James to prepare to attack the Turks who threaten to overwhelm the Christian religion, rather than take the easy route of doing deals with them. James himself should take the lead and confound the foot-draggers, but he needs the support of Rome, and Rome's arrogance is an impediment.

> En breu sazo   aura·l jorn pretentori,
>   mas hom
> quera baratz, car tal son sey contrari.
>   Mel que·l
> reys [En] Jacmes, ab mans, crey, que·s plevischa
> pel lo[c] de Deu cobrar, e pels Turcs tondre,
> sol Roma·ls prest,   que·s fay tan seynoriv[a]
>   que·n paron li layc pech.   (vv. 1–8)

The day of reckoning is almost upon us, but some people will look to do deals, for this is what their enemies are like. Better, I think, that the king, lord James, with summonses [*also* many others], should pledge himself to recover God's place and thrash the Turks, as long as they [the summons etc.] are supported by Rome, which behaves so arrogantly that it makes the laymen look like fools.

The reference to 'Rome's arrogance' is explained by what happened before James left for home. In his *Llibre dels feits*, James relates that in the absence of either a crusade or a crown he wanted at least papal blessing, so as not to embody the proverb 'qui fol va a Roma pech se'n torna' ('whoever goes to Rome as a fool comes back as a dimwit'). He had trumpeted his support for the proposed crusade, but after it became clear that none would take place, he asked for a papal coronation. Gregory agreed as long as James paid a tribute he owed him relating to the kingdom of Aragon, and when James bridled at what he considered an entirely unreasonable demand in the circumstances of his unique support, the pope excused himself, saying that some of his cardinals had refused to overlook the debt.

Cerverí goes on to urge 'the king of Aragon to equip himself and pass over the sea to confound all the laggards' (vv. 13–14), and then to attack on base barons, among whom one in particular, unnamed, has been acting like a pirate:

> No temen so   ara pel porgatori
>   c'un – c'om
> vey c'a pres pretz, com sol veser corsari –
>   qu'isnel
> no vey un rich de dar que no·y gandischa.   (vv. 33–37)

Now they have no fear of purgatory: I see not one – for I can see someone who has taken payment just as I commonly see pirates [behave] – not one single rich man who does not avoid giving.

Miriam Cabré explains this as an allusion to James' arch-enemy Charles of Anjou, condemned, yet again, for his supposed deflection of the crusade to Tunis for commercial profit. When he had arrived there immediately after Louis' death, he entered at once into negotiations with the caliph, obtaining a double tribute to himself as king of Sicily, indemnification in coin, the expulsion of anti-Angevin Sicilian exiles from Tunis with its profitable commercial port, and free trade for Christians, and returned forthwith to Sicily. From the Catalan point of view he went there in a ship, gained booty and left. James, on the other hand, had prohibited Catalan pirate activity in Tunis in order not to damage commerce. The Catalans held mercantile colonies and a consulate there, and took part in the town militia. If Charles was harming Catalan economic interests, Cabré argues, this could clearly contribute to the formation of the image of him as a pirate, not to mention other events which could have contributed to this image, such as the looting after Charles' victories at Benevento and Tagliacozzo, constant accusations of greed made against him, denunciations of robberies on part of his officials and his capture of the Infant Henry of Castile. At this time piracy was also a current theme in relation to crusade: the Council of Lyon, among other economic arrangements, prohibited trade with Saracens, specified that pirates were enemies of the crusade because they impeded the journeys of crusaders, and anathematised those who had been 'knowingly associating with them in any contract of sale or purchase' or who 'exercise command in piratical ships of the Saracens, and who give them counsel or assistance on equipment or anything else at the expense of the Christians, particularly in the Holy Land'.[6]

When Charles' enemy James dies (26 July 1276), Matieu de Caerci composes a conventional eulogy of the king of Aragon, praising his unsurpassed record against the Saracens 'here or over the sea' (BdT 299.1, 26). Certainly James had an impressive record of successes in the Reconquista. As far as crusades 'over the sea' are concerned, Matieu glosses over James' failed expedition of 1269; but his unique support of Gregory's 1274 council may have been thought to mitigate it.

Probably dating from the same time is a fictive *tenso* (BdT 206.4) with God by Daspol (Guilhem d'Autpol), in which the troubadour mockingly condemns the kings, princes, prelates and religious orders for ignoring the plight of Palestine. He makes James the sole exception to this, and his blame of apathetic princes may include implicit criticism of Philip III of France (1270–1285), whom in his *planh* for Philip's father, Louis, he had warned not to heed false counsellors steering

---

[6] M. Cabré, '*En breu sazo aura·l jorn pretentori* (BDT 434a,20): Jaume I i Cerverí interpreten els fets de 1274', in *Actes del X Col·loqui de l'Associació Hispànica de Literatura Medieval, Alaicant 2003* (Valencia, 2005), pp. 453–68, and Paterson, 'James the Conqueror', pp. 245–49.

him away from doing good (BdT 206.2, vv. 56–65). But the most interesting part of the *tenso* is the comic rôle he ascribes to God. Daspol is not the first to have invented a humorous dialogue with the Divinity,[7] but here he provocatively – even blasphemously – argues against God's ordering of the world: in his omnipotence, he could so easily arrange matters so that there would be no need for a crusade and the cruel suffering it entails. The exchange begins with God accusing his Christian subjects of disloyalty.

> Seinhos, aujas, c'aves saber e sen,
> que m'esdevenc l'autre ser can dormia.
> Sus el sel fuy on Dieu tenc parlament,
> es entorn si saria·l compainhia;
> e dir vos ai la clamor que tenia
> de crestïans: com reinhon falsament,
> car non claman lo sieu sant moniment
> comte ni duc ni prinse ni clersia.　　　(vv. 1–8)

Lords, you who have knowledge and sense, listen to what happened to me the other night when I was asleep. I was up in Heaven where God was holding assembly, and people were crowding all around here; and I'll tell you about the charge he was making against Christians: that they behave falsely, since neither counts nor dukes nor princes nor clerics are claiming back his holy sepulchre.

Comically demonstrating his rhetorical know-how, Daspol offers an instant rebuttal. God himself is to blame for giving power and wealth to the wrong people who make feeble excuses not to fight.

> Et ieu leviei, que respos sapchament:
> 'Tort n'aves, Dieus, e prendes autra via,
> car vos donas poder a falsa jent
> que·n fan quex jorn erguell e vilania;
> qu'il non crezon ni fan ren que bon sia,
> e vos das lor sobras d'aur e d'argent,
> tant que n'estan crestïans recrezen –
> car combatre no·s pot hom cascun dia!'　　　(vv. 9–16)

And I stood up and spoke wisely in refutation: 'You are in the wrong here, God, and you should take a different approach: you give power to false people who commit the sin of pride and villainy with it every day, for they neither believe nor do anything that is good; and you give them heaps of gold and silver, so that Christians are spineless – for after all, people can't be fighting all the time!'

7　See Gouiran, '*Os meum replebo increpationibus*, pp. 77–98, and Chapter 4, p. 82.

God caves in at once, submissively promising to shower the clergy with misfortune, deprive the orders of their property and make them seriously ill so that the princes will lose their tax revenues. But Daspol is not satisfied and returns to the charge: God is both powerful and comfortably safe, and yet honours the Saracens who destroy his strongholds (in other words lets them win). So why, exactly, should Christians fight for him?

> 'Bel seinher Dieus, ben par qu'est poderos,
> qu'en luoc segur estag ez en autura.
> Per que·us pensas que·ns combatam per vos?
> Que sarazins onretz e jent tafura
> que no·s laison fort castel ni clauzura,
> e·l bastiment volvon de sus en jos.' (vv. 25–30)

> 'Dear lord God, you're obviously powerful, since you live in a safe place and on high. Why do you think we should fight for you, since you honour Saracens and vicious people who leave you no stronghold or stockade, and raze the buildings to the ground?'

God tries to defend himself by resorting to one of the standard thirteenth-century preaching commonplaces, a reminder of his sacrifice on the cross to redeem mankind.

> 'Seinher Daspol, si·l prinse ni·l prelat
> m'agueson jes d'amor en lur corage,
> que·ls sovengues ab vera caritat
> com fuy en cros mes per l'uman linhage,
> cascus fora volontos del passaje,
> si lur membres mon sanc c'ai escampat,
> e s'il moron can si son trebailhat;
> e nus non pren guarda d'aquel viage.' (vv. 33–40)

> 'Lord Daspol, if the princes and prelates had any love for me in their hearts, they ought to remember with true charity how I was put on the cross for the human race; each of them would willingly take part in the passage if they recalled the spilling of my blood, even if they died after such a hard endeavour; but none of them pays any attention to that journey.'

But the troubadour scoffs at this facile appeal to the emotions. God is omnipotent, is he not? So why not simply make the Saracens recognise the error of their beliefs? Why does he make his own subjects pay for the sins of others and land them in a bloodbath?

> 'Bel seinher Dieus, ben mot aures parlat,
> e pogras ben revenir sest damnage
> s'als Sarazins donases volontat

cascus per si conoges son follage;
pueis non calgra negus annar arage,
pueis que cascus conogra sa foudat;
car nos prendem mort per lur viell peccat –
e vos es leu que·ns gites a carnage.' (vv. 41–48)

'Dear lord God, you've talked a great deal, but you could easily repair this damage if you made each Saracen want to acknowledge his sin of his own accord; then no one would need to go astray, since each would recognise his error. For we suffer death for their ancient sin – and you think nothing of pitching us into a massacre.'

God deflects this onto blame of the military orders for their pride and greed, but Daspol stubbornly continues to question the Divinity's societal arrangements. Why does God let the religious orders carry on in their vile ways? What he needs to do is share out wealth equally (a good idea from the troubadour's point of view, obviously) and then everyone will be noble, in both birth and spirit. It is easy to imagine the audience's cynical laughter at this point – the phrase 'dream on' comes to mind.[8] In fact the fictional dream comes to an end, though the troubadour still prays for God 'to ordain that the kings and cardinals, prelates and princes have a change of heart'. The final *envoi*, serious in tone, is to James, 'father and son of prowess, castle of worth, fount of what makes a man worthy'.

In this period following the failure of the Council of Lyon to kick-start another crusade to the East, Guiraut Riquier returns repeatedly to the collapse of Christendom through the sins of its rulers. In January 1276 he urges leaders to stop warring among themselves and treating the Holy Land as a matter of trade (BdT 248.48): if they did so, 'the Saracens would soon be vanquished through either fighting or preaching' (vv. 55–56);[9] in March 1276 he singles out his patron Alfonso X of Castile as the one exception (BdT 248.87). More positively, at the end of December 1280, when he was probably at the court of Henry II of Rodez, he appears hopeful that the longed-for peace among the rulers has arrived (BdT 248.79). On 26 November a conflict between Alfonso X of Castile and Philip II of France had been resolved.[10] Guiraut indicates that Charles of Anjou ('the prince who is lord of the Provençals') had been instrumental in the agreement, which should please the English king (Edward I, Alfonso's brother-in-law), and that Alfonso should now be able to take

---

[8] For ecclesiastical attempts to explain God's purposes behind crusading defeat, see Cole, *The Preaching of the Crusades*, pp. 56 and 178–84.
[9] The conversion of Muslims had apparently been an avowed aim of prominent Europeans from the 1070s and had gathered momentum from the twelfth century on: see B. Kedar, *Crusade and Mission. European Approaches towards the Muslims* (Princeton and Oxford, 1984), pp. 44–45, 51, 61–62, 65.
[10] It concerned Sancho of Castile's usurpation of the right to inherit the throne after the death of Alfonso X's eldest son, Ferdinand, at the expense of Ferdinand's sons.

Granada rapidly by storm. The troubadour expresses pleasure at seeing Christians prepared to serve the Saviour, 'as long as they go for love of Him to recover the Holy Land' (vv. 47–50).

The Sicilian Vespers

This positive view of Charles of Anjou, rare among the troubadours, appears to have been short-lived. The War of the Sicilian Vespers (Easter 1282) was looming, and the following piece, wrongly attributed to Giraut de Borneil in the single manuscript P, is in all probability a ferocious attack on the king and his papal ally, Martin IV (BdT 242.77).

> Tals qeir d'enperi corona
> qui nostra fe mal defen,
> e·l pap'entre terz'e nona
> s'endorm aissi planamen,
> q'encontra sarrazina gen
> non vei baron qi s'opona;
> anz an per lur malvolen
> qi d'aiso mot lor sona.
>
> Jesu-Crists, per salvar la gen,
> portet d'espinas corona,
> e·l papa so monimen
> malamen abandona.
>
> L'Antecrists, cug, venra breumen,
> tan aonda gens fellona;
> car tostemps vei c'om aten
> la ploia, qant fort trona.   (vv. 33–48)

One man seeks the imperial crown when he ill defends our faith, and the pope sleeps so sweetly between terce and none that no nobleman is to be seen fighting the Saracens; instead they treat with hostility anyone who breathes to them a word of this.

Jesus Christ bore a crown of thorns to save mankind, but the pope wickedly forsakes His sepulchre.

The Antichrist will soon be here, I think, so vast is the evil horde; for in my experience rain is always on its way when the thunder rolls.

For a number of reasons the *sirventes* must be dated to a much later period than that hitherto proposed, and, as Asperti has suggested, the one who is seeking the imperial crown but bad at defending the Christian faith could certainly be Charles of Anjou. The troubadour Luquet Gatelus clearly alludes to his imperial aims, and

Gregory X granted Charles the office of Senator of Rome which traditionally lay with the emperors, this then being confirmed by the popes Innocent V, John XXI and Martin IV. Charles was also king of Jerusalem, having bought the rights to it from Maria of Antioch in 1277, and so was at least the nominal head of the Franks in the Holy Land; but because of this new position he had a poor reputation in the West, since he had been patently uninterested in the most recent crusading projects. In the case of the one organised by his brother Louis IX in 1270, Charles had given priority to his plans for expanding his personal domains in both the East and the Mediterranean. So he could certainly have been presented as an extremely bad defender of the Christian faith. For his part, Martin IV must have appeared highly indolent and subject to the Angevin's interests, especially in comparison with his predecessor Nicholas III. He was primarily remembered for his excessive fondness for eels, and the accusation by the author of our *sirventes* that the pope sleeps during the middle hours of the day would fit him perfectly.

The Aragonese crusade

After Charles of Anjou returned from Tunis he concentrated on his ambitions to build a Mediterranean empire. Invested with the throne of Sicily in 1262 by a papacy desperate to counter the threat posed by the heirs of Frederick II, he took possession of the island in 1266. But he paid scant attention to his new subjects, who were harshly taxed by his French deputies. At Easter 1282 they rebelled against his rule and offered the throne to James' son, Peter III of Aragon, sparking off the twenty-year war of the Sicilian Vespers: 'a big war', as Housley puts it.[11] This also triggered a new political crusade against Christians. In January 1283 Martin IV granted crusade indulgences against the rebels, and in response, a month later, the Aragonese crossed the Straits of Messina and took the war into Italy. Martin in turn offered the throne of Aragon to Philip III of France's younger son, Charles of Valois, which Philip accepted on his behalf in February 1284, agreeing to invade and occupy Aragon. In this he was supported by Peter's own jealous brother, King James of Mallorca, who resented being in a position of vassalage to his sibling. James opened the campaign by landing troops in Roussillon and sacking Elne on the road from Perpignan to the Pyrenees. With the way clear, Philip crossed the Pyrenees in the spring of 1285 with a crusading army of some 8,000 men. Peter wisely avoided battle, using guerrilla tactics to harass the French army, which then spent more than two months besieging the fortress of Gerona. It eventually fell on 5 September, but after a hot summer on malarial plains half the French army was ill. Then came news that Roger of Luria, Peter's brilliant admiral, had wiped out much of the French fleet, landed troops at Rosas and cut off Philip's supply route, whereupon Philip ordered his army to withdraw. Runciman observes that 'with the Almogavar guerillas striking from all sides the retreat soon became a panic-stricken flight. The whole crusade

---

[11] Housley, *The Later Crusades*, p. 239.

proved a humiliating fiasco.' On 5 October Philip himself died of fever at Perpignan; meanwhile Charles of Anjou had suffered reverses in Italy and had abandoned the province of Calabria, before dying at Foggia in early 1285.[12]

While Philip was mustering his vast army in the Narbonne region during 1284, not all the locals were overjoyed. Memories of French massacres during the Albigensian Crusade and continued French occupation can hardly have led them to welcome the presence of Capetian forces, and a new crusade against Christians stirred up long-standing indignation against the diversion of crusading ideals and resources towards purely political ends. During the French preparations in the region the troubadour Guillem Fabre castigates the great princes who feud among themselves whilst the pagans in Palestine are left in peace (BdT 216.2). He provides an interesting insight into the manner of the propaganda war that accompanied the forthcoming invasion, referring to the mustering and public addresses (*prezicx*) that the warring kings directed brutally at each other instead of the heathens.

> Pus dels maiors
> princeps auzem conten
> say entre nos, enquer tenran a frau
> li menscrezen, meyns de guerra, suau,
> lo sancte loc on Dieus pres nayssemen,
> per que salvamen
> det a sos amicx;
> don penran destricx
> tug li amador
> de nostre senhor,
> si·n desamor ven la fe
> don ys saus paguanesme.
>
> La desamors
> s'aferma e ss'empren,
> si que l'us reys cuyda tener la clau
> d'afortimen, e l'autr'a·l contraclau,
> que a poder e ric cor d'ardimen;
> mas l'ajustamen
> que fan e·ls prezicx
> degran als mendicx
> que son en error
> virar, ad honor
> d'aquelh senhor que nos fe,
> per guazanhar sa merce.   (vv. 1–24)

Since we hear the greatest princes feuding among us over here, the infidels will fraudulently continue, without war, nice and quietly, to hold the holy place

---

[12] Runciman, *Sicilian Vespers*, pp. 241–57; Housley, *The Later Crusades*, pp. 238–40.

where God was born, through which he gave salvation to his friends. As a consequence all lovers of Our Lord will be racked with anguish if the faith comes to be unloved and paganism emerges safe and sound.

The hostility grows stronger and more deep-rooted, so that the one king thinks he holds the key to gaining the upper hand, and the other has the duplicate key, for he is powerful and full of driving ambition; but they ought to direct their mustering and public addresses at the dastardly heathens, to the honour of that Lord who created us, in order to deserve his grace.

The troubadour goes on to evoke the horror of civil war, where families tear each other apart:

Ar em el cors
on veyrem man paren
l'us vas l'autre encaussar per esclau,
pueys al colpar ab felh cor mal e brau,
et esvazir veyrem maynt guarnimen,
si Dieus doncx no·y pren,
qu'es nostres abricx,
tal cosselh que·ls ricx
torn totz en amor;
pueys do entre lhor
sen e voler que desse
passon lay, si quo·s cove.   (vv. 25–36)

Now we are on course to see many kinsmen hunting one another down, then wounding each other with a deadly, wicked, ruthless heart, and we shall see many pieces of armour pierced, unless God who is our refuge then finds a way to convert the men of power wholly to love; afterwards may he give them the intention and desire immediately to make the passage overseas, just as they ought to do.

He blames the pope for not first declaring a crusade against the Turks, which he believes would have pre-empted the present hostilities. And yet again, along with the pope (Martin IV), the hated Charles resurfaces, as 'the best-known man in the world'.

Selh qu'es rectors
pauzatz en regimen
de nostra fe n'a d'aitan gran deslau,
quar, pus lo mielhs del mon que hom mentau
li obezis, no mandet crozamen,
ans qu'est mesclamen
fos ni·l segl'enicx,
sobre·ls fals mendicx

que teno·l sanctor;
quar tug li melhor
per que l'ira se mante
crey qu'er foran lai em be.   (vv. 49–60)

The one who is ruler established to govern our faith deserves equally heavy blame because, given that the best-known man in the world obeys him, he did not declare a crusade against the false ruffians who hold the holy sepulchre, before these hostilities broke out and the world was filled with enmity; for I believe that all the best of them who are the cause of this continuing anger would now be willingly over there [in the Holy Land].

A second song by this troubadour (BdT 216.1) similarly inveighs against the lay and eccelsiastical rulers that misdirect their powers.

Among the *prezicx* to which Guillem refers is a cycle of five pieces in Occitan, which offer a special insight into the use of vernacular songs for war propaganda. The first was composed by Bernart d'Auriac in the spring of 1285 as Philip III was about to cross the Pyrenees and invade Aragon (BdT 57.3). Riquer suggests that it was designed to inspire the French 'crusaders', and that they were sung by jongleurs attached to the French king and disseminated through the invading army until they were heard by the enemy during its advance into Spain.[13] While he may be right, it is noticeable that the song is in Occitan, not French, so the emphasis would seem to be on intimidating the Catalans, in the language of culture adopted by their king's court.

> Nostre reys qu'es d'onor ses par,
>   vol desplegar
>   son gomfano,
> don veyrem per terra e per mar
>   las flors anar;
>   e sap mi bo,
> qu'aras sabran Aragones
>   qui son Frances,
> e·ls Catalas estregz cortes
> veyran las flors, flors d'onrada semensa,
> et auziran dire per Arago
> 'oï noni' en luec d''oc' e de 'no'.
>
>   E qui vol culhir ni trencar
>   las flors, be·m par
>   no sap quals so
>   li ortola, que per gardar

---

[13] M. de Riquer, 'Un trovador valenciano: Pedro el Grande de Aragón', *Revista valenciana de filologia*, 1 (1951), 273–311 (p. 299).

>   fan ajustar
>   tan ric baro;
>   quar li ortola son tals tres
>   que quascus es
>   reys plus ricx que·l Barsalones;
>   e Dieus e fes es ab lur, e crezensa.
>   Donc quan seran outra Mon Canego
>   no·y laisson tor ni palays ni maizo.
>
>   Catala, no·us desplassa ges
>   si·l reys frances
>   vos vai vezer ab bels arnes,
>   qu'apenre vol de vostra captenensa,
>   et absolver ab lans'et ab bordo,
>   quar trop estaitz en l'escominio.   (vv. 1–30)

Our king, whose honour is unrivalled, intends to unfurl his banner, so we shall see the flowers [the fleurs-de-lys of France] advancing across land and sea; and I am pleased that the Aragonese will now realise who the French are; and the Catalans, tight-fistedly courtly, will see the flowers, flowers of glorious seed, and hear *oï noni* spoken throughout Aragon, instead of *oc* and *no* [Old French and Occitan respectively for 'yes' and 'no'].

But it seems to me that anyone who wants to pick or cut the flowers [capture or kill the French] does not know what the gardeners are like who are assembling such high barons to guard them. There are three gardeners, and each is a king richer and more powerful than the one from Barcelona, and God and faith and true belief are on their side. So when they are beyond Mount Canigou, let them leave not a tower or palace or house standing.

Catalans, be not displeased if the French king is coming to see you with splendid armour, for he wants to find out about your conduct and absolve you with lance and rod, because for a long time you have been excommunicate.

King Peter of Aragon responded to these *coblas* himself (BdT 325.1) in the same poetic and musical form, as a rebuttal of the enemy's propaganda. Riquer argues that he would have heard them in the Ampurdán when he was organising the defence of his lands, and composed his riposte in 1285, when the French army had already crossed the Pyrenees. At this time Peter was in Barcelona and had given orders for peasants in Vallés and the Llobregat to take wheat to the city in preparation for a possible siege.[14] He first addresses his song to the troubadour Peire Salvatge.

>   Peire Salvagg', en greu pessar
>   me fan estar

---

[14] Riquer, 'Un trovador valenciano', pp. 297–98.

> dins ma maizo
> las flors que say volon passar
> senes gardar
> dreg ni razo;
> don prec a sselhs de Carcasses
> e d'Ajanes
> et als Guascos prec que lor pes
> si flors mi fan mermar de ma tenensa.
> Mas tals cuja sai gazanhar perdo
> que·l perdos l'er de gran perdecio.
>
> E mos neps, que sol flors portar,
> vol cambiar,
> don no·m sap bo,
> son senhal, et auzem comtar
> que·s fai nomnar
> rey d'Arago.
> Mas cuy que plass'o cuy que pes,
> los mieus jaques
> si mesclaran ab los tornes:
> e plass'a Dieu que·l plus dreyturiers vensa,
> qu'ieu ja nulh temps per bocelh de Breto
> no layssarai lo senhal del basto.
>
> Si midons qu'es ab cors cortes
> ples de totz bes,
> Salvagge, valer mi volgues,
> e del sieu cors me fes qualque valensa,
> per enemicx no·m calgra garnizo,
> ab sol qu'ieu vis la sua plazen faisso.   (vv. 1–30)

Peire Salvatge, the flowers that intend to come over here without right or reason are seriously disturbing me in my own home; so I beg those of the Carcassès and the Agenais, and I beg the Gascons, to show concern if flowers cause me loss of territory. But there are those who think to win an indulgence here when the indulgence will bring them great perdition.

And my nephew, who usually wears flowers, intends to change his emblem, to my displeasure, and we hear it said that he is having himself called King of Aragon. But whether anyone likes it or not, my *jaques* [Aragonese coins *or* weapons] will mix [do battle] with the *tornes* [coins from Tours]. Please God let the more just man win, for I will never renounce the emblem of the staff [part of the arms of Aragon] for a Breton wine cup.

> Salvatge, if my lady, who with a courtly heart is full of all good qualities, desired to help me and wished to grant me some personal favour, I would need no armour against enemies, as long as I could see her lovely face.

Peter clothes his defiance of the French, and his courteous appeal to his Occitan allies beyond the Pyrenees, in elaborate wordplay and a reminder of his familiarity with Occitan courtly culture, part of the propaganda effect being to outshine his opponent in courtly accomplishment and take the moral high ground. He also reminds his listeners that they would do well not to rely for their spiritual salvation on a papal indulgence issued in a false cause. His final words of courtly love are taken up by other poets of the sequence.

Peter had in fact hired Peire Salvatge to compose a song as part of his propaganda drive. On 13 July, during a general mobilisation, he arranged for various knights and Peire Salvatge to come together in a specified place to plan their campaign against the invaders. Salvatge composed a third piece, of which only one *cobla* has survived, with the same poetic form (BdT 357.1).

> Senher, reys qu'enamoratz par
>   non deu estar
>   ab cor felo
> contra flors, ans deu arbirar
>   cum puesca far
>   ab bon resso
> culhir las flors en aissel mes
>   on l'estius es,
> e las flors naysson plus espes,
> els culhidors sian d'aital valensa
> qu'en pueg ni en pla, en serra ni·n boysso,
> no laisson flors de sai Monbaulo.   (vv. 1–12)

> My Lord, a king who appears to be in love should not dwell on his anger against flowers, but should rather take thought as to how he should gloriously pick the flowers during that summer month when the flowers grow most abundantly, and [how] the pickers should be so valiant that in hill and plain, mountains and woods they leave no flowers from here to Montbolò.

In other words a king, however courtly, needs to translate words into action. Peire was rewarded for his verses on 30 July, in Barcelona, when the king granted him a salary for the upkeep of his family.

Shortly afterwards, possibly between mid-July and mid-August, two other composers, Count Roger Bernat III of Foix and an anonymous troubadour, also intervened in the cycle on the side of the French invaders: their chronological order is not known. The count of Foix was also viscount of Castelbó from 1265 until his death in 1302, and was son of the brother-in-law of the James II of Mallorca who was claiming the throne of Sicily. He had taken an active part in a rebellion of nobles against the king of Aragon in July 1280, which ended in their surrender in 1281. The count was the only one who did not obtain a royal pardon, 'because he did not wish to comply with anything he had promised the king and because he spoke haughtily and gave the king to understand that if he left prison he would do more damage to the king than he had already done'. He was kept in chains and only freed in December 1283 by giving his daughter Constanza as a hostage. On liberating him Peter demanded that he hand over the viscounty of Castelbó, giving him certain lands in exchange, but Roger Bernat induced the inhabitants of the viscounty to refuse to comply with this order under various pretexts, including the one that the king had been excommunicated by the pope. He appears to have had a close relationship with the king of France during the crusade, supplying advice and information about the Aragonese and negotiating with them on his behalf.

His *coblas* (BdT 182.2) are a sneering reply to those of Peire Salvatge, in which the count of Foix's personal territorial concerns weigh as heavily as his interest in the French cause.

> Salvatz[e], tuitz ausem cantar
>   e'namorar
>   reis d'Arragon.
> Digatz me se poria tant far;
>   c'a mi no par
>   ses lo lion
> que si asemble en tot ar[n]es
>   contra·l Frances,
> si que·l sieu afar sia ges.
> E car el dis que·l plus dreiturier vensa,
> de faillir tort a cascun lai raison:
> per o sapchatz qu'eu deteing Castelbon.
>
>   Mas qui a flor se vol mesclar
>   ben deu gardar
>   lo sieu baston,
>   car Frances sabon grans colps dar,
>   et albirar
>   ab lor bordon.
>   E no·us fizes en Carcases,
>   ni·n Agenes,
>   ni·n Gascon, car no l'amon de res
> depos vas mi a faita la faillenza;
> e·n breu de temps veirem nos Brogoingnon
> cridar 'Monjoi!', e·l crid'en Arragon.   (vv. 1–24)

Salvatge, we can all hear the king of Aragon singing and falling in love. Tell me whether he will be able to achieve so much, for it does not seem to me that without the lion he will appear in full armour against the French, so that his enterprise will amount to anything. And because he says that the more righteous man should win, everyone there [in Aragon] is right to desert wrong; you should know this is why I retain Castellbó.

But anyone who wants to mix [*or* do battle] with flowers should guard his staff, as the French know how to give mighty blows and aim straight with their lance; don't rely on the Carcassès or the Agenais or a Gascon, for they have no love for him whatever since he committed the injustice against me; but in a short while we shall be seeing the Burgundian cry 'Monjoie!' for us, and may he cry it in Aragon.

Riquer suggests that the *coblas* of the king and Peire Salvatge spread very rapidly through Catalonia and soon arrived at the fighting frontier, and argues convincingly that the count of Foix was writing at the time when the invasion of Catalonia was not far advanced, very soon after their compositions.

The fifth, anonymous, song (BdT 182.1) is a nasty piece, full of vindictive threats. The text is corrupt and has been emended, though its overall thrust is clear enough.

> Frances c'al mon non a par,
>   degran forzar,
>   e Bergoingnon,
>   les patarins a romevar;
>   e qui clamar
>   s'an d'Arragon
>   al gran foc seran menatz pres,
>   com rason es,
>   e gitad'al vent lor cenes.
> E quan seran de vostra obediensa.
> faran tal fin qu'al mar per lo sablon
> saviaran, com l'arma a perdison.
>
>   L'escaran veirem empinhar,
>   n'i plus scampar
>   poir'a saison,
>   e sieu seingner veirem ligar
>   et aforcar
>   come laron.
>   Non i sera lo premier mes;
>   e·l trait que fes
>   cridar, don destrui nostra fes,
> nos chalzer'on per aucir soa semenza,
> e pois veirem chascun de soa maison
> e de son sen morir en la preison.   (vv. 1–24)

The French, unrivalled in courage, and the Burgundians, ought to force the Patarins to go on a pilgrimage [?], and anyone who complains to Aragon [claims to be from Aragon?] should be taken captive to the great fire and their ashes thrown

to the wind, as is right and proper; and when they are in your power they will
die in such a manner that they will make their way through the sand to the sea,
like the soul to perdition.

We shall see the brigand seized [?] and be unable to escape from this in time;
and we shall see his lord [the king of Aragon?] bound and hanged on the gibbet
like a thief. He will not be the first to be strung up there; and the crossbow bolt
he announced, whereby he is destroying our faith, will be reloaded for us to kill
his seed, and then we shall see everyone of his house and mind die in prison.

The reference to Patarins is intriguing and may mean the French were persuaded by
emissaries from Rome to qualify the Aragonese as heretics, though this is uncertain.

The fall of Acre

In 1291 Acre fell to the Muslims, and the Christians were expelled from Syria. Tony
Hunt records that it was followed by a proliferation of writings variously known
as 'proposals, memoranda, treatises, propaganda pamphlets, tracts, advisory documents, intelligence reports, missionary treatises, itineraries, for the recovery of the
Holy Land'.[15] Despite this evidence of crusading aspirations, the remaining songs
in which troubadours addressed the subject exude an atmosphere of pessimism,
the military orders being singled out for blame. Crusading vows by Philip IV and
Philip VI of France briefly revive hopes on the part of a few singers, but these come
to nothing, and the poets fall silent. Guiraut Riquier returns to the plight of the
Holy Land (1292) in what is perhaps his most pessimistic view of both his personal
condition and the state of the world (BdT 248.17). Famously declaring that he was
'born too late', like some earlier troubadours he thinks God has turned His face
away from his Christian subjects.

> Per erguelh e per malvestat
> de cristias ditz, luenh d'amor
> e dels mans de nostre Senhor,
> em del sieu sant loc discipat
> ab massa d'autres encombriers;
> don par quelh nos es aversiers
> per desadordenat voler
> e per outracuiat poder.
>
> Lo greu perilh devem temer
> de dobla mort, qu'es prezentiers:
> que·ns sentam Sarrazis sobriers,
> e Dieus que·ns giet a nonchaler.
> Ez entre nos qu'em azirat,

---

[15] A. B. Hunt, 'An Old French Crusade Proposal', *RMS*, 34 (2008), 123–36 (pp. 123–24).

tost serem del tot aterrat;
e no·s cossiran la part lor,
segon que·m par, nostre rector.   (vv. 25–40)

Because of the pride and wickedness of so-called Christians, far removed from the love and commandments of Our Lord, we have been chased from his holy place and [have suffered] a mass of other reverses. It is clear from this that he is against us because of our unbridled will and overweening power.

We should fear the grave peril of double death which is upon us: that we may find the Saracens triumphing over us, and God casting us away in his indifference. Moreover those of us who are hated will soon be completely annihilated; and it seems to me our [Church?] leaders do not think of their responsibility.

In 1299 or early 1300 Rostaing Berenguier de Marseilla accuses the military orders for failing to win back the holy sepulchre (BdT 427.1). Rostaing was in contact with a member, albeit illegitimate, of the ruling house of Aragon: Lo Bort del Rey d'Arago. He is particularly scornful of the Templars, accusing them of indolence, vanity and arrogance, and of wasting the resources supplied to them for crusading purposes, but he also includes the Hospitallers in blame for the sorry state of the Holy Land.

Pos de sa mar man cavalier del Temple,
man cavall gris cavalcant, si solombran
e, lurs cabeils saurs remiran, s'enombran,
mostran soven al mont malvays eysemple,
ez es tan grieus e tan fers lur ergueilhs
c'om non los pot esguardar de dregz hueilhs,
diguas mi Bort: per que·l Papa los sufre
pos sap e ves qu'ehn mans pratz, sotz vers sims,
– don lur ressort deshonors e grieus crims –,
guastan lo ben que hom per Dieu lur hufre?

Car pos ho an per cobrar lo sepulcre
e guastan ho menan rumor al segle,
ez enguanan lo pobol d'aquest segle
contrafasen Guolias e Sahul, cre
que desplassa a Dieu; car tan lonc tems
hill, ez aquill de l'Espital emsemps,
han sufertat que li falsa gens turgua
haya tengut Jherusalem ez Acre;
car son, fugen, plus fort que falcon sacre:
per que·m par tort qui.l segle non en purgua!   (vv. 1–20)

Since on this side of the sea many Knights Templar, mounted on their various grey horses, rest in the shade and, admiring their golden locks, take their ease, often showing the world a bad example, and their arrogance is so harsh and so cruel that one dare not look them in the eye, tell me, Bort: why does the pope endure them since he knows and sees that in many a meadow, beneath a canopy of green – and dishonour and grievous crimes result from this – they waste the goods that people offer them for God's benefit?

Since they have them for the purpose of winning back the sepulchre, and they waste them, giving rise to widespread protests, and cheating the people of this world on the model of Goliath and Saul, I think this is displeasing to God; for both they and the Hospitallers have allowed the false Turkish people to hold Jerusalem and Acre for such a long time; for they are stronger – when they take to flight – than a saker falcon. So it seems wrong to me if someone does not purge the world of them!

Fabio Barberini rejects Meyer's view that the text was composed in c.April 1310, just before the final phase of the trial of the Templars. Instead he links the piece to difficulties encountered by the military orders in Cyprus after 1291. He interprets Rostainh's attack as an act of sincere devotion to the Hospitallers and to the family of the Villarets (the recently elected Master was Guillaume de Villaret), whose protection he enjoyed and felt honoured by: the song would be conveying a discreet hint to those directly concerned that, if they were losing interest in the armed struggle for Christendom in order to fight among themselves, they could be liable to the accusation that were no better than the Templars.[16]

However, the attack on the Templars may be more than generic: the particular accusation of wasting the resources supplied to them for crusading purposes resonates strikingly with the Grand Master Molay's determined and successful efforts to maintain and increase the Templars' supplies of men, food and clothing from the West around this time, when he travelled to the West to make a personal appeal to key rulers, including James II of Aragon, brother of Rostainh's interlocutor Bort. This resulted in, among other things, numerous important export privileges for the order. The Templars owned considerable property and wealth in any case, but their resources may then have been particularly conspicuous and been a source of resentment on the part of people who naïvely believed that the Templars should therefore have been putting more effort into oriental crusading rather than fleeing westwards (v. 19). Moreover Bort had a particular reason for hostility towards any actions of his brother, including any support for the supposed extravagances of the Templars, which would make these *coblas* addressed to him especially pointed.

The particular emphasis on the Templars as knights may relate to discussions at this time over a possible merger of military orders, seriously mooted at the Council of Lyon in 1274, though not carried through since the Spanish kings wished to retain their Iberian orders. The proposal was revived by Pope Nicholas IV in 1291

---

[16] F. Barberini, 'Rostainh Berenguier de Marseilha e l'*affaire* dell'Ospedale (BdT 427.4)', *RLM*, 12 (2011), 43–69.

but opposed by the Templar grand master, James of Molay, on the grounds that with the Hospitallers charitable work took precedence, while the Templars 'were founded especially as a knighthood'. Barber describes the discussions about a union as 'lively and persistent'.[17]

Philip IV and Philip VI of France

Among the books and pamphlets in favour of a new crusade written after the fall of Acre and the expulsion of the Franks from Syria was a memorandum presented to the pope in about 1295 by the Majorcan Raymond Llull. When he published his *Liber de Fine* on the subject in 1305, it seemed that one might indeed take place.[18] Philip IV of France had announced his wish to launch an expedition, and Pope Clement V was a Frenchman who collected memoranda for his own and the king's advice. But Philip faced difficulties in Flanders, and the only military activity to materialise in the first decade of the fourteenth century was directed not by a secular power but by the Knights of Saint John. In 1306 the Provençal Fulk of Villaret, grand master of the Hospitallers in 1305–1319, wrote a tract arguing for the reconquest of the Holy Land, which proposed the organisation of an expedition under Clement's direction and led by the Hospitallers. After a series of similar instances in which the order advocated the crusade project and the conquest of Rhodes, in September 1307 the pope conceded the investiture of the island to the grand master Fulk of Villaret. On 11 August 1308 Fulk saw his diplomatic efforts crowned with the bull *Exsurgat Deus*, in which the pope announced an expedition to Rhodes under Hospitaller leadership. The fleet left Marseille in mid-September 1309 with twenty-five crusader galleys and ten Genoese boats. Rhodes was conquered on 15 August 1310, establishing a state of the Knights of Saint John. In 1311, Fulk wrote to Philip to tell him of the preparations that his order had made and could make for the crusade to the Holy Land. At first Philip IV showed interest in an advance party under the Hospitallers to pave the way for a general passage he would then lead, and in 1313 he took the cross during 'one of the greatest ceremonies of the French monarchy', agreeing to lead such a general expedition in 1319.[19] Nothing came of it: Clement V and Philip died in 1314. Housley observes that while no crusade set sail, 'the Vienne tenth was slowly collected and disappeared into the coffers of the pope and the secular rulers of Christendom', and 'the original suspicions of many that crusading plans had become a pretext for massive fraud were confirmed'. But recent scholarship, he argues, has been more sympathetic to the rulers of their time, for

---

[17] M. Barber, *The New Knighthood* (Cambridge, 1994), pp. 283–85.
[18] Runciman, *History*, III, p. 432.
[19] Housley, *The Later Crusades*, pp. 24 and 27, and Radaelli's comments in her online edition to RS 1656b.

discussions and planning for a crusade had continued in a very active way during the reigns of the last Capetian kings of France and the first Valois king, Philip VI.[20]

During the time of Raymond Llull's activities, in 1303–1305, the Catalan poet known as the 'Father of Raimon de Cornet' blames corruption throughout all levels of society for the fall of Acre in 1291, and prays for a new crusade (BPP 557.1). The departure of the Hospitaller expedition to Rhodes in 1309 saw the production of a French *chanson d'ami*, a short composition in the form of a Florentine *ballete* in which a girl reproaches the 'Master of Rhodes' for taking away her lover, 'the handsomest of all who wear the cross' (RS 1656b). Meanwhile an anonymous French song *Seigniurs, oiez, pur Dieu le grant* (RS 344a) on the death of Edward I of England (7 July 1307), composed or modified after the coronation of Edward II on 25 February 1308, blames the king of France for preventing Edward from going on crusade to the Holy Land.

> Le rei de Fraunce grant pecché fist
> le passage a desturber,
> qe rei Edward pur Dieu enprist,
> sur Sarazins l'ewe passer.
> Sun tresour fust outre la mer(e),
> ordiné sa purveaunce
> seint Eglise pur sustenir(e):
> ore est la tere en desperaunce.
>
> Jerusalem, tu as perdu
> la flour de ta chivalerie,
> rey Edward le viel chanu,
> qe tant ama ta seignurie.   (vv. 19–30)

The king of France committed a great wrong in obstructing the crusade that Edward undertook for God, to cross the sea against the Saracens. His treasure was overseas, and his decisions aimed at the support of the holy Church: now the Holy Land is in despair.

Jerusalem, you have lost the flower of your chivalry, King Edward the old and hoary, who so loved your nobility.

Five years before the fall of Acre, in June 1287, Edward had taken the cross. Numerous factors prevented his departure, and by 1294 he was at war with France.[21]

Philip V of France (1316–1322) also took the cross, but died without fulfilling his vow. Philip VI had been *crucesignatus* since 1313; at first he had been interested in Granada, but in 1330 the patriarch of Jerusalem, Peter of La Palud, deliv-

---

[20] Housley, *The Later Crusades*, p. 30. See also C. J. Tyerman, 'Philip VI and the Recovery of the Holy Land', *EHR*, 100 (1985), 25–52.
[21] See Powicke, *King Henry III and the Lord Edward*, p. 728, and M. Prestwich, *Edward I* (London, 1988), p. 332.

ered a rousing sermon at court for a crusade to the Holy Land. Philip responded enthusiastically and persuaded Pope John XXII to initiate preaching at the end of 1331. He planned to lead a *passagium* beginning in August 1336. But by 1336 the state of finances meant that this deadline could not be met, and he cancelled the project. Housley argues that 'Since Philip stood to gain nothing from failure but public obloquy, this sequence of events cannot be explained in terms of deliberate duplicity, at least not on the king's part.'[22]

Three Occitan songs by Catalan troubadours responded to the king's plans. It was probably around the time when Philip formally announced his determination to go on crusade (2 October 1332), that Raimon de Cornet expressed himself cautiously about Philip's leadership qualities (BPP 558.31, vv. 5, 19, 53–54), but presented Edward I of England as 'valiant and worthy' (*pros e valen*, v. 29) and Alfonso IV of Aragon as 'certainly one of the principal men in whom merit and worth are born' (*certamens es / dels prencipals on nays pretz e valors*, vv. 39–40). As for those who refused to finance the crusade, the troubadour proposed they should simply be dispossessed:

> Si de passar ha nostre reys talan,
> mande sas gens: comtes, dux e marques
> e dels baros e dels autres sosmes
> tro n'aja pro dels que veyra melhors.
> E mercadiers, borgues e grans senhors
> que no voldran ab el far lo viatge,
> merme d'aver ab que fassa·l passatge,
> e dels prelatz que·s damno per boban
> aja·l tezaur, si lay per [Dieu] no van.   (vv. 19–27)

If our king intends to make the passage, let him summon his people: counts, dukes and marquises, and barons and other subjects, until he has enough of those he judges the best. And as for merchants, burghers and great lords who will not wish to make the voyage with him, let him confiscate resources with which to pay for the crusade, and let him have the treasure of the prelates who damn themselves through their pomp, if they do not go there for God's sake.

As the time for departure approached, possibly 1334, the troubadour Joan de Castelnou rejected such disparagement of Philip's valour. In a philosophical *vers* (BPP 518.10) he declared that he had 'clearly proved, through true reason, through the Holy Scriptures and through arguments of natural philosophy, that every creature should follow the path of his superior', and that all ought therefore to follow the French king (vv. 65–77), whom the Holy Father had made leader of the crusade because 'he has more strength and courage than other kings – and let no man question this' (*car ha forç'e coratge / mais qu'autres reys*, vv. 75–76).

---

[22] Housley, *The Later Crusades*, pp. 34–35.

However, by 1336 Philip's failure to carry out his crusade provoked two final, bitter songs of reproach on the part of the troubadours. The first is by the disappointed Raimon de Cornet (BPP 558.4). The troubadour accuses him of being a pillaging oath-breaker who has perverted nature of crusading and aroused discontent among his people.

> Tan cobes es d'aver
> nostre reys malapres
> que leyaltatz ni fes
> no pot en el caber.
> Ges no vey son capduelh
> franc ni leyal cum suelh,
> don soy fels e dolens,
> quar may pilha fortmens
> que no fan renoyer.
> Passatge fay costier,
> lo qual tenh per estranh,
> quar ab lo rey que·l tanh
> d'Anglaterra vol far
> guerra, ses dreg gardar,
> e·ls payas orgolhos
> layssa viure joyos.   (vv. 17–32)

Our boorish king is so greedy for riches that neither loyalty nor faith can be found in him. I do not see his leadership as noble or loyal, as it used to be; this makes me angry and sad, for he pillages more determinedly than usurers. He perverts the crusade [*also:* he leaves the crusade aside], which seems strange to me, because he wants to wage war illegally against his kinsman the king of England, and he leaves the arrogant pagans to live in happiness.

The king would be more worthy if he left the English and went overseas to the Turks, instead of using the crusade tenth in his campaign against Edward (vv. 35–48). He provokes popular discontent, yet is fierce in its repression (vv. 49–64), and is more interested in impoverishing Christians than in subduing the enemies of Christ:

> El vol, so·m cug, el banh
> de cobeytat negar
> e vol dezeretar
> humils crestias bos
> mays que pay[a]s felos.   (vv. 92–96)

In my opinion he wants to drown in the bath of greed and wants to disinherit good humble Christians more than treacherous pagans.

The second disappointed critic is Peire de Lunel, otherwise known as Cavalier Lunel de Montech. Peire reiterates age-old complaints against kings who seek their own wealth and comfort rather than going on the holy passage (v. 16). He himself appears to be planning to go: 'if we take the cross, and once we have left riches behind, we shall make the crossing to the Holy Land without much delay' (vv. 57–60). But he ends with a curious piece of misogyny:

Molhers nos fan mudar cor,
per que mal nos combatrem,
e.ns fan so que promezem
passar, tan fort las crezem.   (vv. 61–64)

Women make us change our minds so that we shall fight poorly, and they make us abandon what we promise, so strong is our belief in them.

This general comment is in fact a barb aimed at Philip's wife, Jeanne de Bourgogne, an intelligent, educated, pious and strong-willed women who ruled as regent when her husband was away on military campaigns. Her opponents dubbed her *la male royne boiteuse* ('the lame evil queen'), her deformity being considered by some as a mark of evil; they spread the belief that she was wicked and dangerous, behaved like a king (!) and had those who thwarted her destroyed.[23]

---

[23] See A. Vallé-Karcher, 'Jeanne de Bourgogne, épouse de Philippe VI de Valois : une reine maudite?', *BEC*, 138 (1980), 94–96; P. S. Lewis, *Later Medieval France: The Polity* (London, 1968), pp. 110–11; R. J. Knecht, *The Valois Kings of France 1328–1589* (London and New York, 2004), p. 11.

Conclusion

This book has been written in the belief that it is possible, by carefully re-examining the manuscript versions of lyric texts that have come down to us and the historical circumstances in which they were originally composed, to tease out fresh historical information and insights into lay views of the crusades. These texts speak to us in a variety of voices. Their hundred or more composers may express their own individual concerns and opinions, but they also, and more often, speak for others, for they need to please and be meaningful to at least part of their audience: a powerful member of the high nobility, a group of local aristocracy with its aspirations and discontents, other poets, a settled court imbued with courtly and knightly ideology, a court in transit to a crusading expedition, an army camp, people under siege.

The troubadours and trouvères were composing songs for oral performance at particular times and places, in front of particular audiences. Their contemporaries and successors did not see their songs as ephemeral, occasional pieces, for they preserved them through a long process of oral and written transmission. We have seen how political songs could be passed on orally and still resonate seventy years later as the voice of lasting political dissidence.[1] At the oral stage of performance and transmission, memorable, memorised and repeatable songs could be a powerful medium for putting pressure on leaders and others conscious of their reputation and for reinforcing socially accepted values. For us the songs survive in written form, arranged in medieval anthologies compiled from the thirteenth century onwards, sometimes a hundred years or more after their original composition. The various purposes of these anthologies are still to be fully explored. Some evidently sought to create prestigious cultural objects for their aristocratic patrons, as was the case for a number of Italian manuscripts and the French aristocratic songbooks. The latter, as we have seen, generally excluded political and other material which surfaces in marginal sources or collections.[2] Other, all-inclusive, compilations represent a retrospective, all-encompassing, symbolic monument designed to preserve the poetic and cultural baggage of a tradition. As Marisa Galvez has observed, the collecting and ordering of lyric texts into a codex 'was a fluid, often ad hoc process' reflecting 'the shifting horizons of the songbook's medieval public'.[3] But the value

---

[1] See p. 17.
[2] See p. 11.
[3] M. Galvez, *Songbook. How Lyrics Became Poetry in Medieval Europe* (Chicago and London, 2012), p. 4; see also S. Asperti, 'La tradizione occitanica', in *Lo spazio letterario del*

of these texts at all phases of their transmission clearly lay in both their artistry and their ideology: the high status accorded to their poetic and musical craft, their courtly and knightly ideals, and to a certain extent their political beliefs, especially in the form of resistance to foreign, ecclesiastical or seigneurial control. Our view of troubadour and trouvère responses to the crusades does of course depend on what has survived. Texts preserved in a single manuscript or loose-leaf folio, or cited within a narrative text, suggest the disappearance of many more songs that do not conform to a mainstream literary canon.

The individual pieces in our corpus have revealed many particular details of potential relevance to historians. If we view the corpus from a broader perspective, one of the most striking features to emerge is the difference between north and south. The manuscripts have preserved three times as many Occitan as Old French lyrics. Troubadour texts appear earlier: only one or two Old French songs precede the Third Crusade, in comparison with twenty-one in the South. The earlier emergence of the Occitan songs is partly due to troubadour interest in the Spanish Reconquista, an interest not shared by the northern poets and their audiences. In general, troubadours fervently support crusades to the Holy Land, but in particular, in contrast to their northern counterparts, they show hostility, criticism, scepticism or indifference to oriental crusades led by French royalty. Whereas troubadours are mesmerised by Richard the Lionheart, no lyric trouvères show any interest in either his crusading or his imprisonment. Troubadour attitudes are deeply coloured by crusades against Christians and by the clashes between pope and emperor; the Albigensian Crusade, unsurprisingly, provokes anger and bitterness, leading troubadours to declare crusades to the Holy Land compromised and the very notion of crusade corrupted by clerical apathy, greed and deviousness. There is some sympathy for this on the part of the northerner Thibaut de Champagne, a kinsman and ally of Raymond VII of Toulouse, while regional politics produce some differences in the South: a Provençal troubadour mocks Raymond's (forced) crusading vow. As well as attacking the Albigensian 'false crusade' troubadours also denounce the Aragonese crusade as a corruption of the crusading idea, and the clergy for their attacks on Frederick II and his crusade. Only one trouvère, Philippe de Novare, comments on the emperor's expedition: his stance is a personal one, affected by his connection to the Ibelins in Cyprus. If trouvères unequivocally back Louis IX's plans for his first crusade, there is only one, uncertain, case of troubadour support, while Bertran d'Alamanon, the pragmatic employee of Charles of Anjou, opposes Charles' interest in his brother's venture because it is harmful to Provençal interests. Troubadours otherwise revile the Angevin for his political crusading against the Hohenstaufen, and blame him for what they see as his role in Louis IX's death.

Hostility to Charles of Anjou coincides with the development of a particular feature of the Occitan lyrics, namely humour. The twelfth century saw troubadours such as Peire Vidal and Giraut de Borneil associating crusading with the playfulness typical of the southern courts; by the time of Charles of Anjou, exam-

---

medioevo, 2. Il medioevo volgare (Rome, 2002), pp. 521–54 (547–48).

ples of burlesque are more barbed and cynical. Only one Old French lyric poet treats crusading themes humorously: Philippe of Novare, who satirically depicts his enemies in Cyprus as figures from the *Roman de Renart*. Songs most explicitly challenging the idea of crusading, some humorous, others bitter, are Occitan, reflecting what others have noticed to be a more general phenomenon, namely the contestatory nature of Occitan culture.[4]

While many of these differences between North and South are due to political geography and events, poetic developments and manuscript transmission are also likely to have affected our perceptions. The Old French corpus includes many *chansons de départie*, a type of crusade song emphasising the emotional conflict between serving God and the beloved lady and often giving little space to crusading as such. There is no real equivalent in the Occitan tradition. Close in mood, form and status to the courtly love song, the *chanson de départie* occupies a privileged place in the aristocratic group of French manuscripts, and may have developed as a result of the close contact of certain noblemen during the Third and Fourth Crusades and the expedition led by Thibaut de Champagne. While there are some *sirventes*-type verse texts in Old French, these are generally confined to peripheral manuscript traditions, and other such texts may simply not have been preserved. The poetry found in the more inclusive Occitan manuscript tradition sees the lively proliferation of non-*canso* genres referring to crusading themes, such as the *tenso* and especially the *sirventes*, which expanded as a result of the rise of vernacular anticlerical poetry and the political situations behind it.

Songs exhorting men to fight in God's cause appear before the Second Crusade and continue until the first third of the fourteenth century. If the trouvères virtually ignore the Reconquista, the troubadours promote it from the 1130s through to the 1280s. Tensions and variations in emphasis surface from time to time between support for the Spanish crusade and the claims of the East. In the early years Marcabru denigrates French crusading efforts and promotes those of the Spanish *lavador*; the Muslim triumph at Alarcos generates alarm across the Pyrenees and concentrates the minds of troubadours and their public on Iberia; that of Christians at Las Navas de Tolosa fills them with confidence in the Spanish rulers' courage and abilities, and successes in Spain often provoke unfavourable comparisons with lack of attention to the holy places. Major Christian losses in the East, however, galvanise the poets to promote crusades to Outremer. From Saladin's victory at the Horns of Hattin until the end of the Third Crusade, the Reconquista is forgotten. After the sack of Jerusalem in 1244, a troubadour remarks that participation in the Reconquista is no excuse for failing to go to the Holy Land.

From the Third Crusade, poets from both North and South often mix their crusading appeals with love themes, the trouvères through their particular development of *chansons de départie*. As the plight of the Holy Land occupies the poets' minds, troubadours also reveal a growing disquiet at a new, sober, climate at odds with the traditional values of a secular courtly society. Perhaps the *chansons de*

---

4   G. Gouiran, '*Os meum replebo increpationibus*'.

départie of the aristocratic trouvères are not simply an elaboration of established courtly values but also a response to a perceived threat from clerical power.

The lyric poets continue to promote crusading expeditions well into the fourteenth century, but their support is interspersed with a variety of misgivings and is overshadowed by a gradually darkening cloud. Songs from the Fourth Crusade present examples of anxiety over the deviation from the crusade's original goal. Initial enthusiasm for the Fifth Crusade gives way to reservations and, once the Albigensian Crusade is under way, to anger and cynicism. Trouvères start to complain of the sanctioning and practice of commuting vows: a concern later voiced by an English cleric in 1256 criticising Henry III's plans for a crusade, and in the 1260s by troubadours bitter that Clement IV had granted the power of commutation to his hated legate Simon of Brie.

Trouvères show no interest in Frederick II's crusade. Troubadour exhortations on the other hand feed into his propaganda drive, though some have a separate agenda involving the politics of the Latin empire in Greece. Louis IX's first crusade stimulates particularly moving French songs of exhortation, as well as an emotional plea to Louis to stay on in the Holy Land after his release from captivity. Some troubadours and their audiences are clearly moved by the prospect of Louis' expedition, and disturbed when James of Aragon, lord of Montpellier, fails to fulfil his vow; but the papal–imperial conflict colours Southern attitudes to Louis' crusade, and anticlerical troubadours inveigh against the papal diversion of funds to Charles of Anjou's Sicilian campaign. To Louis' second crusade the trouvères make no lyric response. Some troubadours promote it, one remarking somewhat cynically that the crusade would be preferable to the political manoeuvres surrounding the succession to the Holy Roman Empire. The failures of the French king's two crusades lead troubadours to question God's inscrutable purposes and think of apostasy and suicide. Daspol makes a joke of God's reasons for failing to support his subjects: blaming his ordering of the world, he remarks that in his omnipotence he could so easily arrange matters so that there would be no need for a crusade and the cruel suffering it entails. Hope revives briefly after the fall of Acre. Raimon de Cornet even offers financial advice to Philip VI of France: those who refuse to finance the crusade should simply be dispossessed. But when Philip's plans come to nothing, he and his wife are reproached for perverting the crusade. The rest is silence.

During a period of three centuries the songs in our corpus reflect many twists and turns in public or individual support for different expeditions, individuals and groups, and shifts of mood in the face of crusading fortunes. They also offer insights into activities in the Crusader States, personal experiences, particular incidents and events, and the point of view of ordinary combatants. Before the shock of Saladin's triumph at Hattin, Peire Vidal's sojourn in Tripoli gives the impression of a settled feeling in Syria. At the time of the Fourth Crusade troubadours evoke their own vows, their preparation and parting from loved ones, their journeys and homecoming. The Fifth Crusade marks the earliest lyric concern for the lot of Christians taken prisoner by the Saracens. This seems to have been a mark of changing times, since such captivity was formerly regarded as shameful, the result of cowardice or incompetence. Raoul de Soissons is later able to evoke his experiences as a prisoner and his consequent illness in France, and a trouvère urges Louis to stay in Egypt to negotiate the release of those imprisoned after Mansurah. Describing his personal involvement in the war in Cyprus, Philippe de Novare evokes the sufferings of the common soldier; responding to events in Gaza during the Barons' Crusade, a trouvère blames the military orders for preventing a rescue attempt of Christian captives, while another depicts the poor condition of lesser knights who have mortgaged their lands to take part in the expedition, and are waiting in enforced idleness with no opportunity for compensation. Guillem Fabre reports on the mustering and public addresses taking place in the propaganda war that accompanied the Aragonese crusade, and the horror of civil war where families tear each other apart. Such details offer a fresh and welcome perspective on the predominant courtly and knightly ethos of these nevertheless many-sided lyric witnesses.

Appendix A

The Words To Say It: The Crusading Rhetoric of the Troubadours and Trouvères[1]

Introduction

Following Aristotle, I understand the rhetoric of Old French and Occitan crusade songs to comprise their stylistic devices and ideological content.[2] If, as I believe, literary and philological studies ought to make use of the discipline of discourse analysis,[3] this is particularly important for a crusading text, which is essentially a rhetorical appeal for action. It is from the perspective of analysis of literary discourse that I shall examine the chief characteristics of the argumentation elaborated by the authors of crusade songs, and I shall also attempt to assess the extent to which they can be regarded as an echo of crusade preaching.[4]

In the context of the present project a crusade song is understood as any lyric text linked to the phenomenon of crusading and to the political, religious or social

---

[1] My thanks go to Martin Aurell, the director of the Centre d'études supérieures de civilisation médiévale (UMR 7302 CNRS-Université de Poitiers), for accepting me as an invited researcher during the writing of this chapter. I also warmly thank Linda Paterson for having made this stay possible through the support of the project *Troubadours, Trouvères and Crusades*, which she has been directing at the University of Warwick.

[2] The basis of this approach is C. Perelman and L. Olbrechts-Tyteca, 'Logique et Rhétorique', *Revue philosophique de la France et de l'étranger*, 140 (January–March 1950), 1–35, reprinted in C. Perelman, *Rhétoriques* (Brussels, 1989), pp. 63–107. See also R. Amossy and R. Koren, 'Rhétorique et argumentation: approches croisées', *AAD*, 2, 2009, <http://aad.revues.org/561> [accessed 8 December 2015].

[3] See, for example, D. Maingueneau, 'Analyse du discours et littérature: problèmes épistémologiques et institutionnels', *AAD*, 1 (2008), <http://aad.revues.org/351> [accessed 9 December 2015], and R. Amossy, 'Faut-il intégrer l'argumentation dans l'analyse du discours? Problématiques et enjeux', *AAD*, 9 (2012), <http://aad.revues.org/1346> [accessed 11 January 2016].

[4] Crusading sermons use the same vocabulary, images and themes as our lyrics, particularly the directly hortatory ones: see *infra*.

history of the expeditions.⁵ This study will attempt to describe the art of writing associated with crusading: in other words, the art of writing the crusade. I shall not therefore address the question of the typology of the genre, but proceed via themes rather than sub-genres. The crusade song is a thematically based poetic genre and includes texts linked to other genres such as the *canso* or *sirventes*, and it presents an emblematic case of the interference of registers.⁶

The great majority of pieces include a crusading appeal urging the listener to follow the poet's example. Many of the texts are ideological – political or religious – and are assimilable to the *sirventes*. They therefore very often constitute a reasoned argument based on the idea of proof of the need to take the cross or correct the conduct of the crusade, whether or not this 'proof' is rational. But there are perceptible changes in the articulation of this discourse, and hence the argumentation underpinning it, as it aims to convince and sway the audience. Such changes are bound up with the chronological development of the genre and hence, for political reasons, its renewal, as well as with the events of the crusades and its individual authors.

Poets do not write the same things and in the same way when they are in love, in prison, after or at the point of departure or when they shrink at committing themselves to a voyage overseas; when they are on the side of war or peace; when they consider the clergy worthy or unworthy; when they are young or old, rich or poor, men or women, in the service of a lay or ecclesiastical lord, or writing from their own individual point of view; or, sometimes, whether they are writing in Occitan or French. In short, the crusade song as poetry of action is particularly tied to the circumstances affecting its author: the history of ideas, theology, preaching, lay education and culture.

Salvation and edification

Unsurprisingly, the themes linked to the religious content of crusading – piety, the path to salvation, and edification – constitute the ideological nub of these texts.

Salvation

These songs contain two affirmations concerning redemption. The first and most important is that the Christian's salvation is made possible by the Son of God's sacrifice on the cross for mankind. Linked to a particular eschatology, salvation is not an automatic right but a promise which must be deserved. The second is that of the salvation granted in exchange for a man's commitment to serve God in the Holy Land, which corresponds directly with the love he feels for him. In both cases, the salvation is the same. Christ's gift of his person for mankind, a perpetual

---

⁵ See p. 7.
⁶ Bec, *La lyrique française*, vol. I, p. 151.

gift emanating from the one who is alpha et omega,[7] is the promised reward for those who must make themselves worthy of it in the here and now. The ideology of crusading and its economy of salvation relies on this double tension of gift and desert.

It is to attain this salvation, to give proof of this love, that one takes the cross. This is based on a strong logic of remuneration. But the texts refer little to *salvament* or *garison*,[8] and instead their discourse primarily refers to entering paradise, along with a cluster of images: Jesus, Mary[9] and the angels welcoming the Christian into heaven.[10] Our authors prefer to instruct through images[11] and *exempla*[12] rather than theological concepts. In their concern for the efficacy of their discourse they rely largely on affective rather than intellectual resources. Heaven and hell and the iconography surrounding the medieval Christian (sculptures, paintings, stained-glass windows) offer extremely effective mental images for such instruction. We find the same affective aspect of persuasion in the innumerable types of discourse linked to Christ and his sacrifice; medieval Church iconography is certainly related to this phenomenon.[13]

---

[7] Acts 1.8, 17; 22.13.

[8] For example, CtProv/Arn BdT 184.1=25.1, v. 7 and Anon RS 227b, v. 17.

[9] For example, TbChamp RS 6, vv. 36–38: 'Douce dame, roïne coronee, / priez por nos, vierge bone eüree, / et puis aprés ne nos puet mescheoir' ('Sweet Lady, crowned queen, pray for us, blessed Virgin, and then no harm can befall us').

[10] See the early song Anon RS 1548a, whose refrain states that the crusader 'ja mar d'Enfern avarat povur, / char s'alme en iert en Pareïs / od les angles nostre Segnor' ('will never have fear of hell, for his soul will be in Paradise with the angels of our Lord').

[11] Christ is presented not simply as the son of God but also the one who was nailed to the cross, bled, and so on. The visual aspects of his attributes and descriptions suggest a series of images in the audience's mind: for example, 'ves la terra on Deus volc morir / e mes son cors en gage; / per nos en fo en croiz levaz / et es totz hom desesperaz / qi no·i a ferm corage / qi ve com el fo clavellaz / per nos e battuz e nafraz' (FqRom BdT 156.11, vv. 44–50, 'towards the land where God chose to die, and pledged His body for our sake; He was raised on the cross, and anyone who sees how He was nailed and beaten and wounded for our sake and has not a firm heart in this affair is a man without hope of salvation').

[12] The use of an *exemplum* is common in preaching, including crusade preaching: see C. T. Maier, *Crusade Propaganda and Ideology, Model Sermons for the Preaching of the Cross* (Cambridge, 2000), p. 6, and the sermons of Jacques de Vitry (*Thema sumptum ex Apoc.* [sermo I, §21 and 22], in Iacobus de Vitriaco, *Sermones vulgares vel ad status I*, ed. J. Longère, Corpus Christianorum Continuatio Mediaevalis (CCCM 255) (Turnhout, 2013), p. 99. On the *exemplum* sce M. G. Briscoe and B. H. Jaye, *Artes Praedicandi, Artes Orandi.* (Turnhout, 1992), pp. 9–76. For preaching see also N. Bériou, *L'avènement des maîtres de la Parole. La prédication à Paris au XIIIe siècle*, 2 vols (Paris, 1998), and 'Les sermons latins après 1200' in B. M. Kienzle, ed., *The Sermon* (Turnhout, 2000), pp. 363–447, as well as J. Flori, *Prêcher la croisade XIe–XIIIe siècle. Communication et propagande* (Paris, 2012).

[13] See J. Baschet, *L'iconographie médiévale* (Paris, 2008) and *L'image médiévale: fonctions dans l'espace sacré et structuration de l'espace cultuel*, dir. C. Voyer, E. Sparhubert (Turnhout, 2011).

Abandoning the sins of the world

Risking one's life for the sake of the good, and abandoning the evil dominating the world through the fault of man, is the crusader's ontological choice. As an anonymous trouvère declares, to take the cross means to abandon sin and devote oneself to the good, in order to assist God because he requires it and because he himself died on the cross for mankind in the person of his son:

> Parti de mal e a bien aturné
> voil ma chançun a la gent fere oïr,
> k'a sun besuing nus ad Deus apelé
> si ne li deit nul prosdome faillir
> kar en la cruiz deignat pur nus murir.
> Mult li doit bien estre gueredoné
> kar par sa mort sumes tuz rachaté.   (Anon RS 401, vv. 1–7)

Having renounced evil and turned back to goodness, I wish to make the people hear my song, since God has called on us to assist him and so no worthy man should fail him, for he deigned to die upon the cross for our sake. We should be deeply grateful to him because with his death he has redeemed us.

Emphasis lies here on man's thankfulness to Christ or God. The address to the audience in the second line is typical of these exhortations, often formulated as a rhetorical question or through the use of the second person plural.

Pilgrimage

The Christian departs on crusade in order to complete a pilgrimage overseas. The idea of his 'passage',[14] his sea crossing, may be linked to the crusader's pilgrim staff.[15] The use of the words *pelerinage*,[16] *voie*,[17] *pelerin*[18] and *viage*[19] is a key feature of our songs[20] and indicates devotion to Christ through commitment to crusading which, notwithstanding the presence of invective in a number of pieces, is at the heart of this poetry. There may be several such references in a single piece, emphasising its devotional aspect or the distance to be travelled by the crusader.[21] Troubadours such as Gaucelm Faidit speak of *romeria* and *peleris*, or of *romieu* with its etymological link to Rome.[22]

---

[14] For example, FqRom BdT 156.11, v. 18 *passage*, v. 57 *croçaz*, v. 58 *viage*.
[15] CtFoix BdT 182.2, v. 18.
[16] RlSoiss (?) RS 1204, v. 2; GuDij RS 21, v. 15.
[17] ChCoucy RS 679, v. 37.
[18] PhNov RS 184a, v. 10.
[19] HgBerzé RS 37a, v. 19.
[20] See Introduction, pp. 3–4.
[21] CnBéth RS 1125, vv. 27 and 32, 'pelerinaige' and 'voiaige'.
[22] GcFaid BdT 167.9, vv. 27 and 76; AimPeg BdT 10.11, v. 4.

Judgement

The judgement awaiting each man will take place on the basis of his sins. Crusading is a definitive step towards goodness and Christ's service. The crusading indulgence allows the crusader to be sure of his salvation. However, rather than the indulgence's logic of repayment, the authors stress the crusader's personal commitment to Christ, in and through crusading.[23] If theologians emphasise that nothing can definitively assure man of his salvation, the lyric authors, like many preachers, free themselves from such precautions. Everyone will be judged according to his sins:

> e sabem cert que totz serem jutgatz,
> e bos e mals, segon nostres peccatzs
> davant l'aut Rey, al jorn del jutgamen.   (Anon BdT 168.1a, vv. 22–24)

> Yet we know for sure that we shall all be judged, good and evil, according to our sins, before the high king, on the Day of Judgement.

The interest of this discourse on judgement lies not so much in its constant repetitions as in the way in which the authors issue warnings to the Christian. Jesus may be the Saviour but he has nevertheless taught man how to make a good end (in other words be saved) through the secure path of penitence.

> Jhezus Cristz, que·ns a prezicatz
> per que fos bona nostra fis,
> nos demostra qu'es dregz camis:
> qu'ab penedens'er perdonatz
> lo peccatz que d'Adam se moc.   (Gav BdT 174.10, vv. 37–41)

> Jesus Christ, who has preached to us so that our end should be a good one, shows us which is the right path: for the sin that came from Adam will be pardoned with penitence.

This also means supporting the idea of the unrepentant sinner's responsibility. The crusade lyric, understood as this kind of warning, resorts to a type of salvation discourse; and in using the same devices as crusade preaching it is itself a form of preaching. The crusading indulgence and its benefits do not excuse man from

---

[23] See M. Raguin, 'Remarques sur le serment et l'engagement personnel dans les chansons de croisade lyriques françaises et occitanes', *Le sacré et la parole: le serment au Moyen Âge*, ed. M. Herrero and J. Aurell (Paris, 2018, in press).

sincere repentance and confession,[24] so the returning crusader may risk losing the benefits he obtained for his salvation.[25]

The cross of Christ and the cross of men

The cross of Christ 'ki pur nus fut en croiz pen<e>t' ('who was tormented on the Cross for our sake'), on which He suffered to redeem mankind, is the cross that inspires the crusader, and which he in turn is invited to take in order to leave on crusade.[26] He takes it to amend his life: 'Pris a la croiz por amender sa vie' ('He took the cross to purify his life'), the anonymous French author of a *serventés* (v. 1) declares of Louis IX.[27] Such expressions are common. Jesus died on the True Cross in Jerusalem, therefore Christians should commit themselves to go and liberate the city, where Jesus 'fon liatz / e receup mort sus en la vera cros' ('was bound and received death upon the true cross'), or 'por nos fu en la vraie croiz mis' ('who was set on the True Cross for our sake').[28] The cross, qualified as 'true' and sometimes

---

[24] ThChamp RS 1152, vv. 10–14, 'Li royaumez de Surie / nous dist et crie a haut ton, / se nouz ne nouz amendon, pour Dieu que n'i alons mie: / n'i feriemes se mal non' ('The kingdom of Syria tells us and cries aloud that if we do not amend our lives, it is better for God if we not go there: we shall do nothing but harm'). For the need for confession and contrition, see Jacques de Vitry, author of the first collection of sermons *ad status* on crusading and crusaders: 'Unde et crucesignati qui vere contriti et confessi ad Dei servitium accinguntur, dum in Christi servitio moriuntur, vere martires reputantur, liberati a peccatis venialibus simul et mortalibus, ab omni penitentia sibi iniuncta, absoluti a pena peccatorum in hoc seculo, a pena purgatorii in alio, securi a tormentis gehenne, gloria et honore coronandi in eterna beatitudine' ('Because of this, those crusaders who prepare themselves for the service of God, truly confessed and contrite, are considered true martyrs while they are in the service of Christ, freed from venial and also mortal sins, from all the penitence enjoined upon them, absolved from the punishment for their sins in this world and the punishment of purgatory in the next, safe from the tortures of hell, in the glory and honour of being crowned in eternal beatitude'), Jacques de Vitry, sermon II, §18, in Maier, *Crusade Propaganda and Ideology*, pp. 112–13.

[25] ChCoucy RS 679, vv. 33–40.

[26] Anon RS 1548a, v. 32; Anon RS 1020a=1022, v. 3–4: 'souviegne vous de la mort angoiseuse / que li fiex Dieu soufri au premerain!' ('remember the painful death which the son of God first suffered!'); AustAur BdT 40.1, v. 25.

[27] Anon RS 1729, v. 42. The poet begins by announcing that he is composing at God's command: 'Un serventés, plait de deduit, de joie, / comencerai au Dieu comandement, / qu'il nos enseint le chemin et la voie / a li aler sanz nul encombrement' (vv. 1–4, 'At God's command I shall begin a *sirventes*, a discourse of happiness and joy, so that he may teach us the way and the path to go to him without impediment'). It is both God and the *serventés* (and hence its author) which show man the right path. Here we see the hortatory and didactic function of these compositions aiming to instruct the Christian.

[28] Anon BdT 168.1a, vv. 11–12 (see also *crozatz*, v. 19); ThChamp RS 6, v. 14.

'holy', is found in both French and Occitan texts.[29] The crusader's commitment to God is that of a man to his lord: he must 'Dieu servir crozatz' ('serve God having taken the cross').[30] If the words *Dieu* and *Christ*, in their various forms, are the most widespread, the poets also speak of 'nostre Creator'('our Creator').[31]

The Holy Land

The crusader commits himself to liberate the holy places, Jerusalem and Christ's tomb,[32] as well as some locations whose designation does not correspond exactly to their modern equivalent: Egypt, *Surie* (which in the Middle Ages designates the Holy Land), Romania and important towns such as Acre, Damietta, Edessa and Bethlehem. It is here in the 'terre de promission' ('promised land') that are situated the holy places where God was served: Jerusalem and the holy sepulcre, 'lou vrai sepulcre ou Dieu fut mis, / et ke li saint leu son desert / ou Nostre Sire estoit servis!'('the true sepulchre where God was laid and for the holy places where Our Lord was served to be abandoned').[33] An anonymous song about the Second Crusade contains the most biblical, historicising description, aimed at appealing to the Christian through the antiquity of God's possession of the Holy Land which is the basis for the doctrine of God's heritage:

> Alum conquere Moïses,
> ki gist el munt de Sinaï;
> a Saragins ne·l laisum mais,
> ne la verge dunt il partid
> la Roge Mer tut ad un fais,
> quant le grant pople le seguit,
> e Pharaon revint apro<e>f
> il e li suon furent perit!   (Anon RS 1548a, vv. 73–80)

---

[29] AimBel BdT 9.10, vv. 22–23, 'e·ill cros sanct'on Dieus pres dolor / e mort – e·i fo per nos levatz!' ('the holy cross where God suffered pain and death – and was placed there for our sake!')'; BtBorn BdT 80.30, v. 5 (the *vera crotz*); Anon. RS 1967, vv. 21–30, 'Cil ki por nos fut an creus mis, / ne nos amait pais faintemant, / ains nos amat com fins amins, / et por nos, honorablemant, / la Sainte Crox mult doucemant / antre ces bras, an mi son pis, / com agnials dous, simples et pis, / et l'astraing angoisousemant. / Puis i fut a trois clos clofis / per piez, per mains, estroitemant' ('The one who was set upon the cross for us did not love us dissemblingly but did so as a perfect lover, and for our sakes, with dignity, [He took] the holy cross most sweetly in his arms, holding it tightly in anguish across his chest, like a gentle, innocent and pious lamb. Then he was nailed fast with three nails through feet and hands').

[30] AimPeg BdT 9.10, v. 5.

[31] Anon RS 1020a=RS 1022, v. 13.

[32] ThChamp RS 1152, v. 18; see also the note to this line on the identification of the *maison* with the holy sepulchre in *Thibaud de Champagne, Recueil de Chansons*, ed. A. Micha (Paris, 1991), p. 136, n. 3.

[33] Renas RS 886, v. 38 and vv. 22–24.

Let us go and win back Moses, who lies on Mount Sinai! Let us not leave him to the Saracens any longer, or the staff with which he parted the Red Sea at one go, when the great people was following him, and Pharoah followed him closely and his men were drowned!

It is as the heirs to the spiritual and temporal patrimony of Moses, through the Christian Old Testament line of descent, that Christians are under an obligation to recover the land. These few lines could stir up so many different levels of reception in the public's mind. The listener is prompted to think, *inter alia*, of the line of descent from Moses to Jesus, of the identification of the Saracens of Egypt at the time of Moses with those faced by the crusaders – and the corollary, the idea that the miracles performed for Moses will be performed for his sons – and of the insistence on the holiness of the Holy Land as a whole and not one particular place in it. The tomb of Moses in the Old Testament is a lost place somewhere in Sinai defining the identity of those who see themselves as the chosen people, among whom Christians then include themselves. The fact that its locality is unknown, in contrast to the tomb of Christ clearly identified with Jerusalem, helps to sanctify the whole of the Holy Land, and not simply Jerusalem.

Jerusalem is one of the key place names in our corpus. Linked to God and his royal dominion, it is common in the Occitan texts but in fact rare in the French ones. In French it is, like the Holy Land, designated above all by elliptical expressions such as 'en cele terre ou Dix fu traveilliés' ('to that land where God was tortured').[34] As this poetry deals with current events, it often mentions towns and the personified 'païs'('land'),[35] especially to denounce the tribulations to which they are condemned after being abandoned by the crusaders: for example 'cant vos volés laisier / Jherusalem estre an chativeson' ('if you are prepared to leave Jerusalem in captivity').[36] Huon de Saint-Quentin's piece (RS 1576) encapusulates French criticism of crusading, and the words 'Jerusalem se plaint' ('Jerusalem laments') occupy the key position at the beginning of the line, stanza and song. In the Occitan corpus Jerusalem is often named but also qualified, essentially as the place of Christ's capture and torture.[37]

Much commoner is the use of *Surie* or *Suria*, occurring very frequently in both French and Occitan texts to designate the Holy Land and its Christian kingdom.

---

[34] ChArr RS 140, v. 2.
[35] HuStQuen RS 1576, v. 1. Huon is also the author of the *Complainte de Jerusalem contre Rome*, whose incipit, encapsulating the essence of the song *Rome, Jherusalem se plaint*, in some ways echoes the *sirventes* GlFig BdT 217.2 of Guillem Figueira. See Serper, *Huon de Saint-Quentin*, pp. 87–114.
[36] Anon RS 1887, vv. 12b–13.
[37] Anon BdT 168.1a, vv. 11–12.

Heaven v. hell : to leave or stay is to live or die for eternity

The poet's hortatory discourse, directly inspired by ecclesiastical preaching and qualifiable as popular preaching,[38] is strongly marked by millenarianism and is essentially a discourse of conversion anticipating the Last Judgement. Here the emphasis is on gaining paradise through crusading, sometimes to the exclusion of any other means:

> Seignor, sachiez, qui or ne s'an ira
> en cele terre ou Diex fu mors et vis
> et qui la croiz d'outremer ne penra
> a painnes mais ira en paradis.   (TbChamp RS 6, vv. 1–4)

> Lords, know this: whoever will not now go to that land where God died and rose again, and whoever will not take the cross to Outremer will find it hard ever to go to heaven.

The crusader's death is praised as the ultimate sign of devotion to Christ and to the liberation of his heritage. Paradise promised and won ('pur voir avrad paraïs conquesté', 'he will certainly have conquered paradise') and its cohorts of angels welcoming the faithful soldier of Christ who has borne his cross with him and humbly shared his suffering ('Vos qui m'a croiz m'aidastes a porter, / vos en irez la ou mi angle sont', 'You who helped me carry my cross, you will go to where my angels are') are contrasted with hell, the certain destiny of anyone lacking Christian faith: 'et vos par cui je n'oi onques aïe / descendrez tuit en anfer le parfont' ('and you from whom I had no help will all descend into the depths of hell').[39] The damnation promised to those who do not go on crusade is evoked in the song *Oiés, seigneur perceus par oiseuses*, where the trouvère threatens the reluctant French Christians, 'Souviegne vous de la mort doleureuse / ki ert sans fins et tous jours iert poiours!' ('Call to mind the painful death which will be everlasting and will be ever worse!').[40] Possible death in this world is presented as a small sacrifice to make in comparison with the risk of eternal damnation for not going on crusade. To die in God's service means one can say at the Last Judgement that one has died for him, as he has died for us: 'E poiran dir selhs que morran crozat: / "E nos, Senher, mort pe vos eyssamen!"'('But then those who die on crusade will be able to say: "And we, Lord, died in the same way for You!"').[41]

---

[38] For example Huon d'Oisy reproaches Conon de Béthune for not going on crusade after all 'ses preechemans' (his preaching, HuOisy RS 1030, v. 3), and being constantly occupied 'de sermoner et de gent preechier' ('in giving sermons and preaching to people', v. 16).
[39] Anon RS 401, v. 35; TbChamp RS 6, vv. 24–25; TbChamp RS 6, vv. 27–28.
[40] Anon RS 1020a=RS 1022, vv. 10–12.
[41] FqRom BdT 156.12, vv. 39–40.

The urgency of departure, the guilt of those who refuse to go

As well as the lover's lament at parting from his beloved, crusading songs voice the laments of God, or those of a man over the conduct of his co-religionists. Notable is the emphasis on the Christians' great guilt, which lends penitential value to the pilgrimage. These are guilty of not taking the cross (they typically choose to *demorer*, to remain behind), guilty of being bad (unworthy) crusaders and, above all, of having abandoned the heritage which God bequeathed to his Church, of allowing its loss and therefore having neglected Christ's tomb:

> Outre la mer, en cele sainte ter<r>e
> ou Dieus fu nés et ou fu mors et vis,
> devons aler nostre iretaje qerre,
> car a grant tort en fu pour nous hors mis.[42]   (Anon RS 1020a=RS 1022, vv. 25–28)

Overseas, in that holy land where God was born and where he died and lived again, we should go to claim our inheritance.

This abandonment of the Holy Land is in itself a sin which is added to others :

> Senhors, per los nostres peccatz
> creys la forsa dels Sarrazis:
> Jherusalem pres Saladis
> et encaras non es cobratz.   (Gav BdT 174.10, vv. 1–4)

Lords, because of our sins the Saracens' strength increases: Saladin captured Jerusalem and it is still not reconquered.

Christ's coming at the end of time, longed for and linked to the Last Judgement ('Au pesme jour coureçous et plain d'ire / que li fieus Dieu venra fiers et iriés', 'On the dread dark day of wrath, when the Son of God will come, terrible and wrathful'),[43] summons each man to hasten ardently to reconquer the Holy Land. The martyrdom of Christ which is extolled in the poets' songs, like that of the Christian, is the martyrdom implied by its etymology: the bearing of witness (in terms of faithfulness, love and renunciation of the world for the other world).

Finally, edificatory discourse, the call to conversion and departure on crusade, may also be modelled on the biblical parables characteristic of New Testament writing. The song *Pour lou pueple resconforteir* uses the same methods as the Gospel: the telling of the parable followed by the explanation of a sense at first veiled to the one receiving instruction and in this case being exhorted:

---

[42] Compare the two songs of exhortation HuStQuen RS 1576 and Renas RS 886 lamenting the crusaders' abandonment of the crusade and hence Jerusalem.

[43] Anon RS 1020a=RS 1022, vv. 17–18.

Encontre l'Espous en aleis,
et si porteis oille en vaixiaulz!
S'en vos lampes est feus troveis
li gueridons en iert molt biauls.

...

Elais, ne cognoissent lor sen!
Ke sont lampes, oile desus?
Lampes se sont les bone gens
dont Deus est ameis et cremus,
ke son servixe font tous tens.
Lai est bien alumeis li feus.
Cil irait o les Innocens
ki en bone oevre iert conxeüs.   (Renas RS 886, vv. 65–68, 71–77)

Go to meet the Spouse and carry with you jars of oil! If the light is found in your lamps, the reward will be most wonderful. [...] Alas, they do not understand their meaning! What are the lamps, the oil just mentioned? The lamps are the good people who love and fear God, who are always at His service. In them the light is well lit. The one who is intent on performing good deeds (when Christ arrives) will go to where the Innocents are.

This recalls the New Testament parable of the wise and foolish virgins in Matthew 25, with the oil lamps, the bridegroom and the question of salvation.[44] The use of parables and *exempla* is typical of preaching and of moral and didactic literature.[45]

The honour of men for the glory of God

Our corpus also develops a type of discourse about the glory of God to be restored by the honour of men.

'Pretz', or the sense of honour

Bertran de Born's poetry exemplifies this, with its key emphasis on *pretz*, the merit or honour acquired through crusading or one's crusading vow. 'Ara parra de prez

---

[44] The reuse of biblical parables and texts from the Psalms is recurrent in this corpus: see also the foolish virgins of Renas RS 886, the pelican of ThChamp RS 273, the rich man of HgBerzé RS 37a or the paraphrase of Psalm 79 (heritage, CnBéth RS 1125, v. 17) and Psalm 137 (the loss of Jerusalem and its lamentations, HuStQuen RS 1576).
[45] Briscoe and Jaye, *Artes praedicandi. Artes orandi*; C. Brémond, J. Le Goff and J.-C. Schmitt, *L'exemplum* (Turnhout, 1982); and Kienzle, ed., *The Sermon*.

qals l'a plus gran'('Now it will be clear who has the greatest merit')[46] clearly signals that *pretz* is what is at stake in crusading.

Through their merit as warriors believers are called upon to avenge Christ's dispossession: 'Qui a en soi pitié ne remembrance, / au haut Seignor doit querre sa vanjance / et delivrer sa terre et son païs' ('Whoever has pity and good remembrance in his heart must seek to avenge the Highest Lord and liberate his land and his country').[47] A recurring theme is revenge for the shame endured by God due to the Saracens' capture of the Eastern territories.[48] The worthiness of those who depart are contrasted with the idleness of those who remain behind : 'Oiés, seigneur, pereceus par oiseuses' ('Listen, Lords, idling in indolence').[49]

God expects help from mankind for whom he sacrificed himself in Jerusalem in the person of his son. Exhortation may be based on faith or on more human or even political considerations bringing in the addressee's pride. His dignity as a king, lord or simply man is measured against his readiness to depart on crusade: 'Deus ! qel dolor, qeu perda et qeu dampnage / D'ome qui vaut quant ill no se chastie!' ('God, what grief, what loss and what damage [comes about] when a man of worth fails to correct himself!').[50] The Saracens' capture of the Holy Land is an offence against God, for which men are responsible if they fail to respond. Since the tenets of Christian faith are believed to be true and certain, exhortation is always based on apparently rational argument; a prerequisite of the crusade song is that it speaks to those sharing Christianity as a common heritage and basis for their faith. But the primary way of appealing to the public is through the emotions.

---

[46] BtBorn BdT 80.17, v. 15; compare also BtBorn BdT 80.30, vv. 10–18: 'Cel qui es coms e ducs e sera reis / s'es mes enan, per q'es ses prez doblatz, / q'el vol mais prez q'om de las doas leis: / dels cristians ni dels non-bateiatz. / E s'el vol prez, a las obras pareis; / q'el vol tan prez e tan bon'aventura, / – per que sos prez creis ades et meillura –, / q'el vol lo prez del mal e·l prez del be; / tant ama prez q'ambedos los rete' ('The one who is count and duke and will be king has stepped forward, which doubles his honour, for he loves honour more than anyone of the two religions, the Christians and the unbaptised. And his love of honour can be seen in his deeds, for he so loves honour and happiness – so his honour constantly grows greater and more perfect – that he wishes the honour of evil and the honour of good, and he loves honour so much that he retains both'). The king is Richard the Lionheart, count of Poitou, duke of Aquitaine and future king of England.

[47] TbChamp RS 6, vv. 5–7. For this notion of vengeance, or restoring the honour of Christ and the Christians through crusading, see S. Throop, *Crusading as an Act of Vengeance, 1095–1216* (Farnham, 2011).

[48] See for example CnBéth RS 1125 or Anon RS 1887, vv. 14–15, 'kar cant Deus fist de vos election / et signor de sa vanjance' ('once that God has chosen you to champion His vengeance').

[49] Anon RS 1020a=1022, v. 1.

[50] HgBerzé RS 37a, vv. 9–10.

Supporting poor crusaders

Coming to God's assistance in his Holy Land also means, for powerful men, aiding his defenders materially. The French king must assist poor crusaders, otherwise he risks rebuke on the Day of Judgement:

> ke povre sont li altre chivelier,
> se criement la demorance
> et s'ans teil point lor feisiez faillance,
> saint et martir, apostre et inocent
> se plainderoient de vos a jugemant.[51] (Anon RS 1887, vv. 23–27)

since the other knights are poor, and they fear a long stay, and if you were to abandon them at this point, saints and martyrs, apostles and innocents would complain of you on the Day of Judgement.

Louis is therefore asked to donate his wealth and throw himself personally into the crusade: 'si an doveis doneir plus largemant / et demoreir por gardeir cest pais' ('and so you ought to spend more liberally and stay to defend this land'). Thus, after the loss of territory following his Egyptian defeat in 1250, he can hope to reconquer it and restore the honour of France, 'tant ke France ait recovree s'onour' ('until France has recovered her honour').[52]

Crusading for all

The Christian's crusading effort – and its concomitant indulgence – is also expected of, and by, those unable to leave for reasons of age, health or family obligations. Mostly they are expected to make a financial contribution to the war effort. Conon de Béthune is clearest: all clerics and old men who stay behind and are generous (towards the Church), through their alms and good works, will have their part in the pilgrimage and hence its spiritual rewards.[53] The same applies to women under conditions relating to their chastity.

---

[51] On crusaders' poverty see also Anon RS 1133, which mentions *bachelers* and *povres vavasours* (vv. 31–32), poor because of their crusading commitment and neglected by the rich lords.

[52] Anon RS 1887, vv. 30–31 and 36.

[53] CnBéth RS 1125, vv. 25–27: 'Tous li clergiés et li home d'eaige / qui ens ausmogne et ens biens fais manront / partiront tot a cest pelerinaige' ('All the clergy and the old men who stay behind performing deeds of charity and good works will have their share in this pilgrimage').

Criticism

The issue of criticism of crusading in the lyric corpus is complicated because of disparities between the Occitan and French corpus, and between these texts and criticisms expressed in ecclesiastical texts, chronicles and other non-lyric literary sources.

The great majority of critical texts are by Occitan and not French poets. The few French pieces preserved criticising the crusades concern the diversion of expeditions to the Holy Land and the conduct of certain crusaders and clerics. Their attacks are not so much *ad hominem* as *ad rem*. They contain traces of anticlericalism or invective designed to bring the sinful believer to repentance, but do not call into question any crusade as a path to salvation.

Occitan poetry is very different. This can be explained by a lively practice of the *sirventes*, and by the fact that the poets are primarily concerned with events in the Languedoc. There are numerous critical pieces against the Albigensian and Byzantine crusades. If the troubadours denounce these false crusades, it is in order to emphasise that the Christian's true duty is to crusade in the Orient, where it is possible to win salvation.

Crusading criticism in the French and Occitan lyrics differs substantially from that of twelfth-century ecclesiastical writings,[54] even if thirteenth-century Occitan lyric criticism is closer to it in its virulence and the diversity of its arguments.

Criticism of, or challenges to, crusading to the Holy Land as an institution of salvation is virtually absent from our corpus. All forms of criticism concern people who pervert the true nature of the crusade: Christians, clergy, laymen. The Albigensian and Byzantine crusades are a very different matter, both in their aims and in the criticisms they provoke. If the poets here blame people for their conduct, they above all deny the possibility of being saved by taking part in these false crusades. The Holy Sepulcre, the Holy Land itself, and hence Christ's legitimate heritage entrusted to the Christians overseas, make crusades to the Holy Land unique.

In both French and Occitan we find criticism of the perversion of expeditions through the fault of both clergy and knights: the lure of gain, massacres, the abandonment of the ministry of preaching. The crusaders' sinfulness means that God turns aside from his people and can even end up favouring the Muslims. Rome, representing the Catholic Church, can both be betrayed by the Christian and may itself have betrayed God, according to the author's point of view. The most extreme figure of this betrayal is undoubtedly the Antichrist. Whilst our corpus does not voice the challenge to crusading as formulated by certain ecclesiastics such as Ralph Niger, Walter Map or Isaac of L'Etoile,[55] a good number of similar rebukes are

---

[54] The main works on this are: Throop, *Criticism of the Crusade*; E. Siberry, *Criticism of Crusading, 1095–1274* (Oxford, 1985); and M. Aurell, *Des chrétiens contre les croisades, XIIe–XIIIe siècle* (Paris, 2013). See also Kedar, *Crusade and Mission*.

[55] See the works cited in note 53.

nonetheless found in both the vernacular lyrics and ecclesiastic literature, albeit in different periods.

Crusades to the Holy Land

The denunciation of abuses by the clergy always concerns simony, greed and consequently the abandonment of its flock to the forces of evil. Huon de Saint-Quentin's song *Jerusalem se plaint et li païs* is the most virulent of the French lyrics. Huon took part in the Fifth Crusade. A detractor of the legate Pelagius and his abuses, he considers the amorality of the expedition's spiritual guides as having caused the fall of Damietta. Strongly anticlerical in tone, this text focuses particularly on the tenth and the clergy's abandonment of the Holy Land and Jerusalem: 'Nostre pastour gardent mal leur berbis / quant pour deniers cascuns al leu les vent, / mais li pechiés les a si tous souspris / k'il ont mis Dieu en oubli pour l'argent' ('Our shepherds take little care of their sheep when each of them sells them to the wolf for money, but sin has so taken hold of them that they have forgotten God for the sake of silver').[56] The poet accuses these bad shepherds of taking no care of their flock's salvation, which would be assured by the crusade, and instead selling them to the wolf, in other words giving their soul to the Devil – whose agents they therefore are. What is targeted here is, first, the sale of the crusade indulgence, which would allow a man capable of fighting to stay at or return home, and second, the taxation of crusaders to the Holy Land, which prevents them from devoting this money to God, together with clerical simony which misuses taxes and alms.[57] The poet is outraged that the product of this bought indulgence serves not the crusade but the enrichment of the clergy. This also naturally means the absence of effective assistance to the Lord since money cannot replace physical service. 'Que devenront li riche garniment / k'il aquierent assés vilainement / des faus loiers k'il ont des croisiés pris?' ('What will become of the rich ornaments they acquire most shamefully with the fraudulent payment they have taken from the crusaders?').[58] Huon castigates sermons which summon the faithful to go on crusade when in fact nothing is really done to recover the land where God paid for our sins with His blood: 'Ki osera jamais en nul sermon / de Dieu parler em place n'em moustier, / ne anoncier ne bien fait ne pardon, / [one-line lacuna], / chose qui puist Nostre Segneur aidier / a la terre conquerre et gaaignier / u de son sanc paia no räençon?' ('Who will dare to preach and speak of God any more in square or cloister, and

---

[56] HuStQuen RS 1576, vv. 12–15. Huon de Saint-Quentin's *Complainte contre Rome* is even more virulent towards the legate.

[57] The Saladin tenth in France and heavy taxation in England provoke many criticisms in the twelfth and thirteenth centuries. Compare similar complaints by the Cistercian abbot Adam de Perseigne, a preacher of the Fourth Crusade (Aurell, *Des chrétiens contre la croisade*, pp. 124–38; A. Andrea, 'Adam of Perseigne and the Fourth Crusade', *Cîteaux*, 36 (1985), 21–37, on p. 6).

[58] HuStQuen RS 1576, vv. 16–18.

announce benefits and indulgences, [when no one is disposed to perform] anything which can assist Our Lord to conquer and win back the land where He paid our ransom with His blood?).[59] God's enemy in all this is the prelate, who replaces the Saracen from a historical point of view, and Ganelon from a mythical one: 'Segneur prelat, ce n'est ne bel ne bon / que son secors faites tant detriier: /vos avés fait, ce poet on tesmoignier, / de Deu Rolant et de vos Guenelon' ('Lord prelates, it is neither good nor just that you so delay helping Him: you, this can certainly be said, have made Roland of God and Ganelon of yourselves').[60]

The accusation contrasting wolf and shepherds, biblical in origin, is reminiscent of reformist or anti-heretical preaching exploiting images of wolf and sheep.[61] Peire Cardenal and Guilhem Figueira make this their key charge against clerical abuses in the context of the Albigensian Crusade.[62]

Accusations against the Templars and Hospitallers are marginal. The author of *En chantant vueil mon dueil faire* accuses them of not having tried to rescue the men taken captive during the defeat at Gaza.[63]

The main charges against the nobility are greed, idleness and the commutation of vows. Certain nobles are accused of not taking the cross in order to be able to extort money out of the people placed under their authority. The crusading tenth raised on the lord's lands provided financial support for his expedition. Conon de Béthune bluntly declares that 'plus en croisa covoitiés que creance' ('greed more than faith has made them take the cross').[64] The well-deserved consequence of these abuses would be divine punishment: 'a teus croisiés sera Dieus mout soffrans / se ne s'en venge a peu de demorance' ('and God will certainly prove very patient with such crusaders if He does not swiftly take vengeance on them').[65] The tenth should be used for the crusade, in a fair way; otherwise, the Christian would risk divine wrath.[66] God's vengeance against his sons who have taken the cross but are lost in sin is shown in Saracen victories and for some crusaders, the bad death they will find in the combat.

Anyone who chooses the act of *descroisier*, the commutation or abandonment of his vow, counts among the 'recreans'.[67] This is how Huon d'Oisy qualifies the trou-

---

[59] HuStQuen RS 1576, vv. 23–29.
[60] HuStQuen RS 1576, vv. 30–33.
[61] See Matthew 7. 15 and John 10. 12; for Bernard of Clairvaux's intensive use of the figure of the *lupus rapax* in his preaching (sermons and letters) against the heretics see particularly letter 241 and sermon 66.1 in *Sancti Bernardi Opera*, ed. J. Leclercq, H.-M. Rochais and C. H. Talbot, 8 vols (Rome, 1957–1977). See also B. M. Kienzle, *Cistercians, Heresy and Crusade in Occitania, 1145–1229. Preaching in the Lord's Vineyard* (York, 2001), pp. 87 and 93.
[62] PCard BdT 335.31; GlFig BdT 217.2.
[63] PhNant RS 164, vv. 29–38 (37–38).
[64] CnBéth RS 1314, v. 29.
[65] CnBéth RS 1314, vv. 31–32.
[66] CnBéth RS 1314, vv. 17–24.
[67] HuOisy RS RS 1030, v. 11.

vère Conon de Béthune, who, after exhorting Christians to take the cross, returns home without fulfilling his vow. Huon de Saint-Quentin devotes the first stanza of his song *Jerusalem se plaint et li païs* to these oath-breakers, declaring:

> S'il sovenist cascun del jugement
> et del saint liu u il souffri torment
> quant il pardon fist de sa mort Longis,
> le descroisier fesissent mout envis;
> car ki pour Dieu prent le crois purement,
> il Le renie au jor que il le rent,
> et com Judas faura a paradis.   (HuStQuen RS 1576, vv. 5–11)

If each one remembered the judgement [the Last Judgement] and the holy place where he suffered torture when he forgave Longinus for his death, he would not readily renounce his crusading vow; for whoever takes the cross with full consent for God's sake denies him on the day he gives it back, and like Judas will lose paradise.

To give back one's cross, to return home, and therefore to abandon Christ, is for these authors the surest way of closing the gates of Paradise to oneself. The piece *Nus ne poroit de mauvaise raison*[68] denounces the shame that would ensue if Louis IX of France commuted his vow. Issuing this warning has two advantages for the author: what applies to the king rebounds on his whole people, and once he is chastised in this way, Louis cannot withdraw without shame.

One cause for recrimination is the idleness of the crusaders in the Holy Land, or those in France who do not take the cross. *Oiés, seigneur, pereceus par oiseuse* is the clearest example. *Ne chant pas, que que nuls die* denounces the conduct of the crusaders in Syria, particularly the most high-ranking: the poet cannot sing with a joyful heart 'quant nos baron sont oisous / en la terre de Surie' ('while our barons are idle in the land of Syria').[69] Pride and rivalry drive the great lords to disorganisation, causing death, the loss of territory or the capture of prisoners, as well as as a certain apathy in the face of disaster.[70]

Finally, the poets complain of the absence of assistance to others. Prisoners are abandoned, and whereas rich crusaders ought to support the poorest, the poet of RS 1133 considers that it would be mad to reproach poor crusaders for returning home when the great lords pay no heed to supporting them financially, and that those who have pawned all their goods for Christ's service did not take the cross in order to lead a life of idleness overseas.[71]

---

[68] Anon RS 1887.
[69] Anon RS 1133, vv. 3–4.
[70] Anon RS 1133, vv. 27–30, 'si tres haute baronnie, / quant de France fut partie, / on disoit que c'ert la flours / du mont et la seignorie' ('Such a high company of barons, when it left France, was said to be the finest flower of the world').
[71] Anon RS 1133, vv. 31–40.

Crusades elsewhere

Neither lyric nor epic poetry denouncing the Albigensian Crusade expresses support for heterodoxy.[72] However, by attacking unworthy clergy, poets undeniably not only denounce the interference of the clergy in temporal affairs but also the effect of their unworthiness on the sacraments : if a priest sleeps with a prostitute in the evening, the next day the sacrament he administers has little value. The public may have seen in this not just political dissidence, which it certainly is, but also possible religious dissent. Crusades taking place elsewhere than in the Holy Land become for their detractors wars of conquest masquerading as crusades, corrupting the crusading spirit and promulgating fraud under the nose of the whole of Christendom. This fraud naturally entails material consequences for the conquered but also, much more seriously, spiritual consequences for false crusaders massacring Christians and neglecting the defence of Christ's heritage.[73]

Criticism of the diversion of the Fourth Crusade found in troubadours such as Raimbaut de Vaqueiras and Guilhem Figueira[74] is not echoed in Old French texts. However, the ageing trouvère Hugues de Berzé, like his companion the chronicler Geoffrey of Villehardouin, beats his breast, recalling that the abuses and pleasures indulged in by the crusaders have led them astray.[75] Once again we encounter the idea of going astray, common to all compositions criticising crusading.

The case of the emperor Frederick II is extremely interesting. He is situated at the convergence of two types of crusade and two types of troubadour composition. On the one hand there is the crusade the clergy launches against him, and on the other, the more or less unauthorised one he himself successfully launches for the reconquest of the Holy Land. In both cases an unworthy clergy is blamed for

---

[72] For the epic, see Martin-Chabot, *La Chanson de la Croisade albigeoise*; see especially M. Raguin, 'Propagande politique et religieuse dans la *Chanson de la Croisade albigeoise*, texte de l'Anonyme' (unpublished Thèse de Doctorat, Études occitanes, Université Paul-Valéry - Montpellier III, 2011); M. Raguin, *Lorsque la poésie fait le souverain. Étude sur la 'Chanson de la Croisade albigeoise'* (Paris, 2015).

[73] For the deviation of the crusade and ensuing criticisms see Aurell, *Des chrétiens contre la croisade*, pp. 203–98.

[74] RbVaq BdT 392.9a, vv. 41–45: 'Q'el e nos em tuig pecchador / dels mostiers ars e dels palais, / on vei pecar los clercs e·ls lais; / e se·l sepulchre non secor, / serem vas Dieu plus pechaire' ('For he and we are all guilty of burning monasteries and palaces, and I see both clergy and laymen sin in this; and if he does not assist the sepulchre, and if our conquest does not make progress, our sin against God will be all the greater'; composed just after the sack of Constantinople, the text deplores the conduct of the crusaders and the clergy); GlFig BdT 217.2.

[75] See Hugues de Berzé, *La Bible au seigneur de Berzé. Edition critique d'après tous les manuscrits connus*, ed. F. Lecoy (Paris, 1938), vv. 463–94, GV, §303, and Aurell, *Des chrétiens contre la croisade*, pp. 210–11.

preferring to attack the emperor for political reasons, rather than unite Christian forces or take part in the victorious expedition overseas.[76]

Amongst the many Occitan lyrics critical of crusading, two texts by Peire Cardenal and Guillem Figueira merit special attention.[77] Two Old French texts, one outside our lyric corpus, are also important for similar themes: Thibaut de Champagne's *Diex est ausis conme li pellicans*[78] and Huon de Saint-Quentin's *Complainte contre Rome*.[79]

Peire Cardenal's *Li clerc si fan pastor* is primarily anticlerical. In the context of the conflict between the emperor Frederick II and the papacy, it denounces the perversion of rapacious and simoniacal clerics who interfere in the affairs of the world instead of preaching the reconquest of the Holy Land. Stanza III, by a double process of anaphora, highlights the author's complaints through a play of contraries:

Aissi com son maior
son ab meins de valor
et ab mais de follor
et ab meins de ver dir
et ab mais de mentir
et ab meins de clersia
et ab mais de failhir
et ab meins de paria;
dels fals clergues ho dic,
c'anc mais tant enemic
hieu a Dieu non auzic
de sai lo temps antic.   (PCard BdT 335.31, vv. 25–36)

The more senior they are the less worthy they are, with more folly and less truthfulness, more lying and less learning, more sin and less friendliness; I say this about the false clergy because I have never come across so many enemies of God since ancient times.

The violence of Guillem Figueira's attack on the clergy and the crusade is all the more powerful because of its exceptional length (twenty-three stanzas). Guillem too plays on anaphora, and uses the word 'Roma' forty-six times.[80] He is well

---

76 FqRom BdT 156.11.
77 PCard BdT 335.31 and GlFig BdT 217.2.
78 ThChamp RS 273 (see Chapter 8, p. 156). In this text, unique in the French corpus and written by a man of the stature of the future king of Navarre, the author censures the clergy and adopts a pro-imperial position which is close to the themes and opinions of contemporary Occitan *sirventes*.
79 Serper, *Huon de Saint-Quentin*, vv. 82–83.
80 Forty-six occurrences plus the derivative *Romans* (v. 99), all of which, bar the first (v. 9), constitute an attack at the beginning of the line.

aware that his *sirventes* will attract the clergy's ill-will: Rome is the supreme place of degeneracy, annihilating goodness (st. 1), Rome is deceitful (st. 2) and causes blood to be spilt, it is treacherous even to kings, and fleeces its sheep (st. 3) in the West and the Latin Orient; Rome sells indulgences and leads its followers into the abyss (st. 4); it cares nothing for the Holy Land and has caused the loss of Damietta (st. 5); it has promised a false pardon to the French who have come to fight in the Albigeois (st. 6); it abandons the struggle against the Saracens in order to massacre Christians in the Albigeois and Constantinople (st. 7); it is a bad guide, leading its followers to Hell (st. 8), and has Christians massacred despite the Scriptures (str. 9); it has launched false crusades (*perdons trafans*, v. 102) against Toulouse, and the Midi should soon take revenge for it, and France will suffer from this (st. 10). God and his saints are forgotten by Rome, which is concerned with worldly affairs, especially the Albigensian Crusade (st. 11), and the poet beseeches God to remember the count of Toulouse, Raymond VII, and support him against the French and Rome (st. 12). If the emperor achieves his ends, Rome will soon fall, and Guillem implores the true Saviour to let him see it (st. 13); despite God and his commandments, Rome loves worldly rule and money, and damns itself for it (st. 14). Rome, like a raptor, holds the world in its grip and destroys merit: these are its miracles (st. 15). The troubadour prays that the one who is the light of the world should punish Rome, promising it hell (st. 16); Rome's preachers, particularly its cardinals, are an abomination, selling compromises with the faith to the highest bidder (st. 17). Through its cheating pastors Rome's power grows, when it is the source of shame and deceit (st. 18), and its pope acts wrongfully in disputing the crown with the emperor (st. 19). Rome, swollen with greed, has its heart bent on possession, and always wants a full purse (st. 20), and its word is venom poisoning the world (st. 21); from being shaved its head is empty, and it would be just to remove its brains after the massacre it caused at Béziers with the support of Cîteaux (st. 22).[81] The poem ends magisterially: 'Roma, ab fals sembel / tendetz vostra tezura, / e man mal morsel / manjatz, qui que l'endura. / Car'avetz d'anhel / ab simpla guardadura, / dedins lops rabatz, / serpens coronatz / de vibr'engenratz, / per que·l diable·us cura / coma·ls sieus privatz' ('Rome, with a cunning lure you set your trap, and eat many an evil mouthful, whoever suffers for it. You have the face of a lamb with an innocent look, [but] inside [you are] a ravening wolf, a crowned serpent sired by a viper, which is why the Devil looks after you like one of his close friends').[82] The attack is exceptionally violent, even for Occitan anticlerical literature dating from the Albigensian Crusade or the ensuing wars of revolt. Ravening wolves, crowned serpents and those engendered by a viper,[83] the figure of evil, remind the listener that it is Rome that is the anti-Church and a distortion of Christianity. The author

---

[81] Arnaud Amaury, abbé de Cîteaux, was the papal legate at the time of the 1209 massacre of Béziers, when the crusaders slew the population and burned the inhabitants who had taken refuge in the church of la Madeleine.
[82] GlFig BdT 217.2, vv. 243–53 (st. 23).
[83] Matthew 3. 7 and 23. 33.

is supporting not heresy as such, but disobedience to Rome. The mentions of hell, the infernal fire and the promises made to the Romans (standing for Christendom) that they will burn in the eternal flames (vv. 85, 174, 175) are another twist. It is not the Church that is criticised, but rather Rome, as it is made by the men of the time, which has perverted God's Church. In addition, as Guillem denounces the false crusade and the papal war against Frederick II, he is careful to recall that Damietta and the Saracens are forgotten, as he refocuses attention on the crusade to the Holy Land.

Love: to love and to part in a higher cause

A time for love and a time to part

The crusader's great hardship is to abandon an earthly love for a divine promise. Many love songs with crusading elements adopt the *topos* of the nature opening and introduce the theme of the lovers' parting. As the Châtelain de Coucy declares:

> Li noveaus tans et mais et vïolete
> et roussignols me semont de chanter,
> et mes fins cuers me fait d'une amourete
> si douç present ke ne l'os refuser;
> or me laist Diex en tel honor monter
> ke cele ou j'ai mon cuer et mon penser
> tiegne une fois entre mes bras nuete
> ains ke aille outremer.   (ChCoucy RS 985=986, vv. 1–8)

The new season and May and violet and nightingale invite me to sing, and my courtly heart makes me such a sweet gift of a new love that I dare not refuse it; now may God allow me to rise to such honour as to hold naked in my arms the one in whom I have my heart and thoughts, before I go overseas.

The main thrust of this *chanson de departie* is its final line, an imprecation against those who have betrayed the secret of the crusading lover: 'ja n'aient il pardon!' ('may they never receive pardon!').[84] The use of *pardon* in this crusading context resonates with fertile ambivalence: it means pardon for their betrayal of the secret, but especially pardon for their sins and hence salvation.

The inversion of the spring opening with that other half-way season, autumn, is a motif used to denounce the sinful world, including true lovers, in a state of perdition, which they escape thanks to crusading.[85] This is the case of Cercamon's song BdT 112.3a:

---

[84] ChCoucy RS 985=986, v. 48.
[85] I interpret this text somewhat differently from Linda Paterson: see p. 31–32.

Puois nostre temps comens'a brunezir
e li verjan son de la fuelha blos
e del solelh vey tant bayssar los rays,
per que·l jorn son escur e tenebros
et homs no·i a d'auzel ni chant ni lays,
per joy d'amor nos devem esbaudir.

[...]

Ves manhtas partz vey lo segle faillir

[...]

Ara·s pot hom lavar et esclarzir
de gran blasme, silh q'en son encombros;
e s'i es pros, yssira ves Roays,
e gurpira lo segle perilhos.[86] (Cercam BdT 112.3a, vv. 1–6, 31, 43–46)

Since our season begins to darken and the orchards are stripped of leaves, and I see the sun sink so low that the days are gloomy and obscure, and songs and lays of birds have fallen silent, we should gladden ourselves with the joy of love. [...] In many places I see the world fall into decline [...]. Now a man can cleanse and purify himself of great guilt, if he is burdened with it; and if he is brave, he will set out for Edessa.

Notable here are the force of the verbal infinitives at the rhyme in the first lines of these stanzas: *brunezir*, *faillir* (referring to the world), everything that man needs to *esclarzir* himself (literally 'grow bright and clear) by going on crusade,[87] and the rhyming of *Roays* (v. 45) with *fays* (v. 47). It is on crusade that one frees oneself from the burden of sin (v. 48).

Painful departure

Thibaut de Champagne's words encapsulate the sorrow with which the crusader bewails, even to God himself, the very existence of the Holy Land. This has caused so many lovers to part: 'Dex! pour quoi fu la terre d'outremer, / qui tant amant avra fait dessevrer?' ('God, why did the Holy Land ever exist? It will have separated so many lovers').[88] The deep religious feeling and the desire for salvation are what drive the crusader's departure: 'Desoremaix ai talent de bien faire: / aleir m'en veul a glorïous tornoi / outre la meir, ou la gent sont sens foi, / ke Jhesu Crist firent

---

[86] The song was composed after Christmas 1144 and the fall of Edessa to Zengi, and before Louis VII's departure in 1147 on the Second Crusade.
[87] The versification enhances the force of the infinitives in *-ir* in rhyme position in the first and last line of each stanza, with a variation in the *tornada*, in themselves conveying the ideological content of the composition.
[88] ThChamp RS 757, vv. 5–6.

tant de mal traire' ('Henceforth I have the desire to do what is good: I wish to go away to the glorious tourney overseas, where live the faithless people who brought Jesus Christ so much suffering'),[89] and bring him face to face with the hardship of separation. These French love songs retain elements of classic exhortation which over time develops the strand of *chansons de départie*, and are concentrated at the time of the Third and more clearly the Fourth Crusade and that of Thibaut de Champagne.[90] Developing the motif of a farewell with no certainty of return,[91] they share a common stock of motifs and formulae designating the poet's departure and feelings.[92] Hence the expression of the crusader's duty: *m'estuet* or *me covient*,[93] sometimes twisted to indicate the resolution to die in the absence of the beloved.[94] Yet more emblematic is the noun *départie* together with the infinitive *départir* often used as a noun.[95] This lamented *départie* from the lady gives rise to several developments, such as sorrow,[96] or the motif of the body leaving and the heart staying behind.[97] But this sorrow can turn to the joy of serving Christ, as the crusading knight goes 'por Damlediu servir, mon criator' ('to serve the Lord God my creator').[98] God, in the person of Jesus Christ, is his supreme lord, and he declares that 'cil que vos sert ne puet estre traïz' ('the one who serves you cannot be betrayed');[99] and he affirms that his lady of flesh and blood should be replaced by love for another lady, the Virgin Mary: 'Quant dame per, dame me soit aidanz' ('When I lose a lady, may a lady be my aid').[100] To leave on crusade and leave the beloved behind is to accept separation in a holy cause which transcends the crusader and his understanding of the world, even if this is hard: 'Mult a croissiés amourous a

---

[89] Anon RS 1659, vv. 5–8.

[90] Dijkstra, *La chanson de croisade*, p. 164.

[91] ChCoucy RS 679, v. 43, 'ne sai je se ja verrés mais mon retor' ('and I know not if you will ever see my return').

[92] Songs of ThChamp, GtDarg, HgBerzé, Char Crois, ChCoucy and some anonymous ones.

[93] ChArr RS 140, v. 1; ChCoucy RS 679, v. 3; TbChamp RS 1469, v. 39; CharCrois RS 499, vv. 3, 10 and 22; HgBerzé RS 1126, vv. 35 and 42.

[94] In a *chanson de départie* with a masculine subject: RlSoiss RS 1154, or a *chanson d'ami* with a feminine subject: Anon RS 191.

[95] ThChamp RS 757, v. 2; CharCrois RS 499, vv. 1, 22 and 41; HgBerzé RS 1126, v. 1; CnBéth RS 1125, v. 1.

[96] HgBerzé RS 1126, vv. 7–8, 'mais il n'est nuns congiés, que que nuns die, / si dolerous com d'amin e d'amie' ('there is no parting as painful as that between lover and beloved').

[97] CharCrois RS 499, vv. 6–8, 'car tot li lez mon cuer et ma pensee: / se mes cors va servir Nostre Seignor / por ce n'ai pas fine amor oubliee' ('since I leave it all my heart and my thoughts: if my body goes to serve Our Lord, I have not forgotten true love on this account').

[98] CharCrois RS 499, v. 4.

[99] ThChamp RS 757, v. 32.

[100] ThChamp RS 757, v. 44. This is the last line, which began by addressing the poet's 'Dame' and ends with the 'Dame des ciels' (v. 41).

contendre / d'aller a Dieu ou de remanoir ci' ('A crusader in love must well ponder whether to go towards God or to remain here').[101]

An incidental but significant case involving a very powerful Catholic queen who sets an example is that of Blanche of Castile, who embraces her son and encourages him to leave on crusade after she thinks him dead: a death which was the only real 'dure departie'.[102]

Total commitment

The listener, as envisaged by the author, certainly partly in his own image, is called to commit himself whole-heartedly. He should not be concerned about returning home and if he does return he will take it as a further mark of grace: 'Mult iert celui en cest siecle honuré / ki Deus donrat ke li puisse revenir' ('A man to whom God grants that he may return will be greatly honoured in this world').[103] Even if he has no guarantee of returning, he can leave without fear by taking the beloved everywhere in his heart: 'Ki bien avrad en sun païs amé / par tut l'en deit menbrer e suvenir' ('Whoever has loved well in his country should preserve the memory of it wherever he goes').[104]

A lady who is truly pious and wise

An anonymous poet stages an interesting encounter between lover and lady in which the man says he will go off to God's tournament and the woman says she will eagerly await his return. Each of them prays: he to her, she to the Mother of God. At the end the man declares that any Christian worthy of the name will take the cross:

> Maix nuls ne puet trop por Damedeu faire:
> quant me menbre ke il morit por moi,
> tant ai en lui de pitiet et de foi,
> riens que je laisse ne me poroit mal faire.   (RS 1659, vv. 21–24)

> But no one can do too much for the Lord God: when I remember that he died for me, I have so much compassion and faith in him that nothing I leave behind could hurt me.

As reassurance for the potential crusader it is stated that the lady or the wife will be virtuous and chaste during his absence, as she is so in love that she will preserve

---

[101] HgBerzé RS 1126, vv. 25–26.
[102] See Anon RS 1738a, v. 30, and vv. 51–60. This role of the mother, Blanche, echoes that of the Mother of God found in the final lines, reminding the listener that 'la Deus nacquit de l'auncele' (v. 70, 'where God was born from [His] handmaid').
[103] Anon RS 401, vv. 36–37.
[104] Anon RS 401, vv. 38–39.

her heart and body for him.[105] A lady confesses that, when she misses her lover at night, as she lies in bed she holds next to her naked body the shirt he wore and then gave her before he left:

> Sa chemise qu'ot vestue
> M'envoia por embracier:
> La nuit, quant s'amor m'aigue,
> La met delez moi couchier
> Mout estroit a ma char nue
> Por mes malz assoagier.   (RS 21, vv. 51–56)

I deeply regret not having been in his convoy; he sent me the shirt he had been wearing, for me to embrace. At night, when I feel the pangs of love for him, I place it beside me in my bed, next to my naked flesh, all night long, to alleviate my suffering.

Despite protestations of virtue, the erotic nature of the situation is unmistakable. The man will depart freer in spirit, yet still fearing 'li faus losengeor' ('the false slanderers').[106] This prompting to chastity represents a form of women's active participation in the holiness of the crusades: to remain chaste and modest in the absence of one's legitimate spouse on crusade is their own crusading effort. By taking part in the institution they can hope for favours from it and contribute to its success: they will have their part in this pilgrimage. These are

> … les dames ki chastement vivront
> se loiauté font a ceus qui i vont;
> et s'eles font par mal consel folaige,
> as lasques gens et mauvais le feront,
> car tot li boin iront en cest voiaige.   (CnBéth RS 1125, vv. 27b, 28–32)

… the ladies who live chastely and remain faithful to those who go there; but if they ill-advisedly commit folly, they will be doing so with cowardly wicked people, for all the good ones will go on this voyage.

The same logic should demand that the crusaders also act with restraint and chastity, as they are urged to do; but as we have seen, this is questionable.

---

[105] The question 'Ma feme, que fera?' ('What will my wife do?'), is asked by the future crusader in TbChamp RS 6, v. 10. If the obvious sense is 'how will my wife manage without me', what most concerns the crusader is with whom this weak-natured female creature may deceive him and place his lineage in danger.
[106] ChCoucy RS 679, v. 33.

Conclusion: service and love

The title of this appendix refers to 'the words to say it'. In the crusading literature of these lyric poets it is critical to observe the words they choose. These texts are rooted in a strongly warrior ideology and mainly formulated as a spur to action, and the choice of words is essential.

The key vocabulary here draws on two registers: the religious and the courtly/feudal. Politics as such are barely relevant: mentions of kings or leaders, or considerations of secular politics, are almost incidental. What only really matters is the believer, the person to whom the text is addressed, whatever his social status. The value system deployed adopts a cultural background conceived of as that of the addressee, which allows the text to work effectively. This involves first of all postulating a public that is Christian, usually fairly educated, and imbued with a political culture of feudal values and courtly love – these two elements merging in its value system. This is what I see as the ideal crusading framework as it should be postulated in our corpus. In the case of the majority of these texts, in other words those referring to crusading to the Holy Land, this is complemented by the address to listeners who have had no experience of crusading and who are personally ignorant of the realities of Outremer. Once this postulate does not apply, when the author or his audience has voyaged overseas or experienced war in the Albigeois or Greece, the possibility emerges of a discourse of protest. Someone familiar with the Languedociens, the Saracens and the turpitudes of the Latin East has considerable difficulty in seeing the divine hand in these affairs. While these crusading songs do not resort to an inherently political discourse, it is through their effects on believers that they entail political consequences.

Crusading is a matter for Christians, the custodians of God's heritage. The way these songs speak is not to give an account of the expeditions as such. Any events they mention are there essentially as themes or reference points in the text's account of its own concerns. The main concern of these texts is to elaborate a hortatory discourse and to criticise the way in which the expeditions are run: a criticism which mostly generates a new kind of exhortation, by calling on people to do better or to do more. There is no trace, outside of criticism of the Albigensian Crusade, of any discourse such as that of the cleric Raoul le Noir, Thomas Becket's supporter against Henry II, who vehemently opposes the Third Crusade on the grounds of corruption in the Holy Land.[107]

I have signalled the preeminence of vocabulary linked to Christian religious sentiment and faith in salvation through Christ. These texts are imbued with innumerable occurrences of words designating God, salvation, the Passion, the Cross, angels, paradise, the Holy Land and so on. At the same time the crusader is also a

---

[107] See Aurell, *Des chrétiens*, pp. 139–59; also G. B. Flahiff, '*Deus non vult*: A Critic of the Third Crusade', *MS*, 9 (1947), 162–88, and 'Ralph Niger: an introduction to his life and works', *MS*, 2 (1940), 140–26; Radulfus Niger, *De re militari et triplici via peregrinationis Ierosolimitane (1187/88)*, ed. L. Schmugge (Berlin, 1977).

lover, and the lady, his beloved or perhaps his wife, is at the heart of the concerns of the crusader or the man who envisages being one. The lady, earthly love, the *departie*, the anguish of absence clash with the higher cause of recovering God's overseas territories and, in the end, the need to be worthy of the love of both the lady and of God.

Whether we are faced with crusading exhortation or criticism, praise or denunciation of the clergy and the war being waged, one aspect of this vocabulary is key: its semantic slippage from the earthly, feudal and hence courtly world into that of a divine power drawing men and women into its ambit and calling for standards of conduct surpassing all others. Two words and their derivations are the key elements of this: service and love. This literature is one of the service demanded of men for God's sake, and of the love which moves one towards the other. It is also the literature of love for the lady by which one's love for the Creator will be measured.

Modelled on earthly feudo-vassalic relations and those reproduced in the bond between Lady and her lover within the conceptual framework of courtly love, this service and love are referred to innumerable times.[108] But there is no mistaking the fact that this love is above all the love dedicated to the lady which has to be transferred to God. This transfer always takes place within the epistemological framework of the service which is now no longer that of the lady or even the temporal lord, but of God himself. If I were to highlight just two words from these songs, they would be these: service and commitment.

Marjolaine Raguin-Barthelmebs

[108] For the idea of dying for the love of God see Anon RS 1887, v. 18; on God giving birth to true love see BnAlanh BdT 53.1, v. 37; for God's suffering out of love for mankind see FqRom BdT 156.11 , v. 53.

Appendix B

Chronology of events and texts

Year	Date	Event	Text
1101		*Crusade of William IX of Aquitaine*	
1120		*Battle of Cutanda*	
1137		*Death of William X of Aquitaine*	
1137–1138			Cercamon, BdT 112.a
1144			Marcabru, BdT 293.22
1145	31 March	*Zengi captures Edessa*	
1146		*St Bernard preaches at Vézelay*	
1146–1148			Anon, RS 1548a
1147			Jaufre Rudel, BdT 262.6
1148			Marcabru, BdT 293.1
			Marcabru, BdT 293.15
			Marcabru, BdT 293.21
	July	*Siege of Damascus*	
	December	*Christian conquest of Tortosa*	
1148–1149			Marcabru, BdT 293.7
1149			Cercamon, BdT 112.3a
			Marcabru, BdT 293.35

1125–1150		Marcabru, BdT 293.12a
1157–1158		Peire d'Alvernhe, BdT 323.7
1175–1177		Peire Bremon lo Tort, BdT 331.2
		Peire Bremon lo Tort, BdT 331.1
1167	Cathar assembly at Saint-Félix-de-Caraman	
1177–1178		Peire Vidal, BdT 364.11, st VI 1187–88
1179–1180, or 1190		Giraut de Borneil, BdT 242.24
		Giraut de Borneil, BdT 242.30
1182–1183, or 1188		Peire Vidal, BdT 364.36
1182 (*terminus post quem*)		Conon de Béthune, RS 1325
1183, or 1186?		Giraut de Borneil, BdT 242.28
1184	Death of Pons de Mataplana	
1184–1185		Guillem de Berguedà, BdT 210.9
1187		Peire Vidal, BdT 364.2
1187?		Peire Vidal, BdT 364.9
1187 3 July	Battle of Hattin	
2 October	Jerusalem surrenders to Saladin	
1187, Oct.	Gregory VIII, 'Audita tremendi'	
	Richard the Lionheart takes the cross	
1187–1188		Conon de Béthune, RS 1125

1187–1189		Bertran de Born, BdT 80.30
1187–1189		Peirol, BdT 366.29
1187–1190		Peire Vidal, BdT 364.4
1187–1190		Peire Vidal, BdT 364.43
1187–1190?		Anon, BdT 323.5
1188	*Henry II and Philip Augustus take the cross*	
mid-January		Conon de Béthune, RS 1314
March/October		Anon, RS 401
		Bertran de Born, BdT 80.17
		Giraut de Borneil, BdT 242.6
		Giraut de Borneil, BdT 242.18
1188–1189		Conon de Béthune, RS 1314
1188–1190		Giraut de Borneil, BdT 242.33
		Giraut de Borneil, BdT 242.41
1188–1190, or 1200		Châtelain de Coucy, RS 985
1189	*Coronation of Richard I*	
3 September		
1189		Huon d'Oisy, RS 1030
1189–1190		Bertran de Born, BdT 80.4
		Bertran de Born, BdT 80.3
1190	*Death of Frederick Barbarossa*	
10 June		
July	*Philip and Richard set out from Vézelay*	

Date	Event	Poet
1190, or 1202		Folquet de Marselha, BdT 155.3
		Châtelain de Coucy, RS 697
1191	Accession of Pope Celestine III	
1191–1194		Giraut de Borneil, BdT 242.15
		Guiraut del Luc, BdT 245.1
		Guiraut del Luc, BdT 245.2
1191 12 July	Acre recaptured from Saladin	
1192 December	Richard imprisoned by Leopold of Austria	
1193		Roi Richard, RS 1891
1193–1194		Peire Vidal, BdT 364.35
1194 4 February	Richard released from captivity	
13 March	Richard lands in England and is crowned again	
12 May	Richard sails for Normandy	
December	Death of Raymond V of Toulouse	
1194–1195		Monge de Montaudo, BdT 305.12
early 1190s?		Aimeric de Pegulhan, BdT 10.37
		Elias d'Ussel, BdT 136.5
c.1190–1236		Gautier de Dargies, RS 795
		Gautier de Dargies, RS 1575
Third or Fourth Crusade		Gontier de Soignies, RS 1404

1195	19 July — Battle of Alarcos	Gavaudan, BdT 174.10
1195–1196		Folquet de Marselha, BdT 155.7
		Folquet de Marselha, BdT 155.15
1196		Giraut de Borneil, BdT 242.74
1198	Accession of Pope Innocent III	Perdigon, BdT 370.5
1199	Death of Richard I	
	20 November — Tournament of Ecry	
1199–1202		Gaucelm Faidit, 167.22
		Giraut de Borneil, BdT 242.73
		Giraut de Borneil, BdT 242.56
1201		Gaucelm Faidit, BdT 167.36
		Gaucelm Faidit, BdT 167.58
1201–1202		Raimbaut de Vaqueiras, BdT 392.3
		Gaucelm Faidit, BdT 167.9
		Gaucelm Faidit, BdT 167.14
		Peire Vidal, BdT 364.8
1202	after 8 June — French crusaders set out for Italy	Gaucelm Faidit, BdT 167.15
	October/November — Crusaders sail from Venice	

	24 November	Sack of Zara	Hugues de Berzé, RS 1126
1202–1203			Gaucelm Faidit, BdT 167.33
1203	April	Crusaders sail from Zara	
	May/June	The Châtelain de Coucy dies at sea	Gaucelm Faidit, BdT 167.50
		Crusaders land at Galata	Gaucelm Faidit, BdT 167.13
			Gaucelm Faidit, BdT 167.3a
			Gaucelm Faidit, BdT 167.19
			Elias d'Ussel, BdT 136.2
			Elias d'Ussel, BdT 136.3
			Vidame de Chartres, RS 421
			Vidame de Chartres, RS 502
1204	12 April	Conquest and sack of Constantinople	
	16 May	Baldwin of Flanders crowned emperor of Romania	
1204	summer	Revolt of Boniface of Monferrat	Raimbaut de Vaqueiras, BdT 392.9a
1205		Baldwin captured by Johanitza at Adrianople	
1206	August	Henry of Flanders crowned emperor	
1205			Raimbaut de Vaqueiras, BdT 392.24

1207	4 September	Death of Boniface of Monferrat	
1208		Innocent III launches the Albigensian Crusade	
1208?			Elias Cairel, BdT 133.9
1208	winter	Henry travels to Thessalonica	
1209		Lombards submit to Henry	
		Otto IV crowned Holy Roman Emperor	
1211		Innocent III proclaims new crusade in Spain	
1211–1212		Frederick II lays claim to Empire	
			Peire d'Alvernhe?, BdT 323.22
1211–1213			Guillem Ademar, BdT 202.9
1212		Christian victory at Las Navas de Tolosa	
		Beginning of five-year truce with Sultan al-Adil	
1213		Crusade encyclical 'Quia major'	
	12 September	Battle of Muret	
c.1213			Anon, RS 1967
1213			Aimeric de Pegulhan, BdT 10.11
			Raimon de Miraval, BdT 406.12
			Pons de Capdoill, BdT 375.2
			Pons de Capdoill, BdT 375.8
1213–1214			Pons de Capdoill, BdT 375.22
1213–1217			Châtelain d'Arras, RS 140

Date	Event	Author
1213(1220?)–1221		Hughes de Berzé, RS 37a
1214	Battle of Bouvines	
1214–1216		Maistre Renas
1215	Lateran Council sentences Raymond VI of Toulouse	
1215	Frederick II takes the cross	
1215–1220		Guillem Figueira, BdT 217.7
1216	Accession of Pope Honorius III	
First third of thirteenth century		Tomier and Palaizi, BdT 442.2
		Audefroi le Bastart, RS 1616
		Guiot de Dijon (?), RS 21
1217, or 1221		Huon de Saint–Quentin, RS 1576
After 1217 or after 1249–1250		Anon, RS 1229a
1218 August	Crusaders take Damietta	
1219–1245		Arnaut, BdT 25.1
1220 November	Honorius crowns Frederick Emperor	
1220–1227		Coms de Proensa, BdT 184.1
1220–1228		Falquet de Romans, BdT 156.12
1221 7 September	Final loss of Damietta	Falquet de Romans, BdT 156.2

1221–1222		Peirol, BdT 366.28
1222		Anon, RS 640
1224	Fall of the kingdom of Thessalonica	
1225	Honorius excommunicates Rayond VII of Toulouse	Elias Cairel, 133.13
1225–1227		Elias Cairel, 133.11
1226	Louis VIII marches south to Avignon	Eias de Barjols, BdT 132.4
	Easter	Tomier and Palaizi, BdT 442.1
1226–1228, or 1236–1239	Diet of Cremona	Thibaut de Champagne, RS 273
1227	Accession of Pope Gregory IX	
	8 September Frederick embarks from and returns to Brindisi	Blacatz, BdT 97.2
	29 September Frederick excommunicated	
1227–1228		Falquet de Romans, BdT 156.4
1227–1229		Falquet de Romans, BdT 156.11
		Guillem Figueira, 217.2
1228	28 June Frederick sails again from Brindisi	Gormonda de Monpeslier, BdT 177.1

1228?	21 July	Frederick lands in Cyprus	
	7 September	Frederick arrives in Acre	Peire Cardenal, BdT 335.18
1228–1229			Guillem Figueira, 217.1
1228–1239?			Uc de Pena, BdT 456.1
			Anon, RS 191
1229	18 February	Frederick II and al-Kāmil sign ten-year peace treaty	
	12 April	Treaty of Paris	
	June	Frederick arrives home	
	14 July	Battle of Nicosia	
1229			Philippe de Novare, Verse letter
1229–1230			Philippe de Novare, RS 184a
			Philippe de Novare, RS190a
			Philippe de Novare, RS 199oa
1229, or 1244–1254			Peire Cardenal, BdT 335.51
1229–1230, or 1245–1246			Peire Cardenal, BdT 335.31
1229–1244			Bernart Alanhan de Narbona, BdT 53.1
1230	23 July	Treaty of San Germano	
First half of thirteenth century			Anon (Nompar?), BdT 461.122
			Anon, RS 227b

Second quarter of thirteenth century (1239?)		Anon, RS 1020a
Second half of thirteenth century		Anon, BdT 461.67a
1230–1234, or 1234–1239		Aimeric de Belenoi, BdT 9.10
1232–1233		Bertran d'Alamanon, BdT 76.16
1236–1237		Peire Bremon Ricas Novas, BdT 330.14
1236–1240?		Peire Cardenal, BdT 335.54
1235		Thibaut de Champagne, RS 6
1235–1239?		Anon, RS 1582
1239	27 March	*Gregory excommunicates Frederick again*
		End of truce between Frederick II and al-Kāmil
		Anon, BdT 217.4a
		Chardon de Croisilles, RS 499
		Thibaut de Champagne, RS 757
		Thibaut de Champagne, RS 1152
1239?	September	*Crusaders land in Acre*
1239	13 November	*Barons ambushed at Gaza*
		Philippe de Nanteuil?, RS 164
1239?		Anon, RS 1133

1239	7 December	Jerusalem surrendered to an-Nasir Da-ud of Kerak	
1239–1240			Thibaut de Champagne, RS 1469
1240			Guillem Figueira, BdT 217.8
1240?			Anon, BdT 80.42
1240–1241			Uc de Saint Circ, BdT 457.42
1242		The southern uprising	
			Duran sartor de Paernas, BdT 126.1
			Peire del Vilar, BdT 365.1
1243			Bernart de Rovenac, BdT 66.3
1243, or after			Raoul de Soissons, RS 1204
1253–1254			
1244	11 August	Khuarizmians sack Jerusalem	
	17 October	Baibars' victory at the battle of La Forbie	
			Lanfranc Cigala, BdT 282.23
	December	Louis IX takes the cross	
1245			Anon, RS 1738a
	17 July	Innocent IV deposes Frederick as emperor	
	August	Death of Raymond Berenguer V of Provence	
		Charles of Anjou becomes count of Provence	
1245–1248			Anon, RS 1729
1245–1250?			Bertran Carbonel, BdT 82.12

1246–1248		Lanfranc Cigala, BdT 282.20
1247	April	
1247–1248	Southern cities rebel against French rule	Bertran d'Alamanon, BdT 76.9
		Bertran d'Alamanon, BdT 76.15
Mid-thirteenth century		Bertran d'Alamanon, BdT 76.14
1248		Granet, BdT 189.5 = 76.14
		Sordel, BdT 437.18
1248	25 August	Louis IX sails from Aigues-Mortes
1250	12–19 June	Louis IX imprisoned at Mansurah
	10 August	Charles of Anjou sails for France
		Anon, RS 1887
1252–1254		Austor d'Aorlhac, BdT 10.1
1254–1265		Anon, RS 1887
		Bernart de Rovenac, BdT 66.2
		Raoul de Soissons, RS 1154
1256		Anon, RS 665a
1258–1261		Perseval Doria, BdT 371.1
1261		End of Frankish rule in Constantinople
1265		Guiraut Riquier, BdT 248.37
		Guillem de Mur, BdT 226.4

Date	Event	Author
1265–1270		Templier (Ricaut Bonomel), BdT 439.1
1267?		Gauceran de Saint Leidier, BdT 168.1a
1267–1268		Bertran d'Alamanon, BdT 76.8
1268	Battle of Tagliacozzo	
		Raimon Gauc. de Beziers, BdT 401.8
		Calega Panzan, BdT 107.1
1269	September James of Aragon's crusade	Guillem de Mur, BdT 226.2
		Olivier lo Templier, BdT 312.1
1269–1270	Second crusade of Louis IX	
1270	25 August Death of Louis IX at Tunis	Bertolome Zorzi, BdT 74.11
		Bertolome Zorzi, BdT 74.12
		Daspol (Guillem d'Autpol), BdT 206.2
		Raimon Gauc. de Beziers, BdT 401.1
		Peire Cardenal, BdT 335.62 (*tornada*)
1270–1271	Accession of Pope Gregory X	
1271		
1272–1273		Folquet de Lunel, BdT 154.1
1273–1274		Austorc de Segret, BdT 41.1
1274	Council of Lyon	Cerveri de Girona, BdT 434a.20

1276	26 July	Death of James I of Aragon	Daspol (Guillem d'Autpol), BdT 206.4
1280	January		Matieu de Caerci, BT 299.1
	March		Guiraut Riquier, BdT 248.48
	end of December		Guiraut Riquier, BdT 248.87
1280–1282?			Guiraut Riquier, BdT 248.79
1282	Easter	The Sicilian Vespers	Anon, 242.77
1284			Guillem Fabre, BdT 216.2
			Guillem Fabre, BdT 216.1
1285		The Aragonese crusade	Bernart d'Auriac, BdT 57.3
			Peire III d'Arago, BdT 325.1
			Peire Salvarge, BdT 375.1
			Lo coms de Foix, BdT 182.2
1285?			Anon, BdT 182.1
1291		The fall of Acre	
1292			Guiraut Riquier, BdT 248.17
1299–1300			Rostaing Ber. de Marseilla, BdT 427.4
1304–1305			Paire de Raimon de Cornet, BPP 557.1
1307	7 July	Death of Edward II of England	

1307–1308		Anon, RS 344a
1308	Death of Edward III of England	
1309		Anon, RS 1656a
1310	Capture of Rhodes	
1313	Philip IV of France takes the cross	
1314	Death of Philip IV of France	
1332–1333		Raimon de Cornet, BPP 558.31
1333–1336 (1334)		Joan de Castelnou, BPP 518.10
1336	Philip VI of France's planned crusade cancelled	
		Cavalier Lunel de Monteg, BdT 289.1
1336–1337		Raimon de Cornet, BPP 558.4
		Anon, RS 1636
Unknown		Anon, 1659

Where more than one date is possible, the text is placed according to the earliest.

Appendix C

Melodies attested in the MSS

RS	author	incipit	MSS with melody
1616	AudBast	*Bele Yzabeaus, pucele bien aprise*	MT (2/3)
499	ChardCrois	*Li departirs de la douce contree*	KNPTX (5/5)
140	ChArras	*Aler m'estuet la u je trairai paine*	KNPTX (5/5)
679	ChCoucy	*A vous amant, plus k'a nul'autre gent*	AKMOPRTUVX (10/11)
985	ChCoucy	*Li nouveaus tans et mais et violete*	AKMOPRXUTVa (11/14)
1125	CnBéth	*Ahi! Amors, com dure departie*	KMNOPRTVXa (10/15)
1325	CnBéth	*Bele douce dame chiere*	MTO (3/5)
1314	CnBéth	*Bien me deüsse targier*	KMNOTX (6/7)
795	GtDarg	*Bien me cuidai de chanter*	MT (2/2)
1575	GtDarg	*Se j'ai esté lonc tanz hors du païs*	KMNPRTVX (8/10)
21	GuDijon	*Chanterai por mon corage*	KMOTX (5/7)
1576	HueStQuen	*Jerusalem se plaint et le païs*	MT(2/3)
1030	HueOisy	*Maugré tous sains et maugré Diu ausi*	MT (2/2)
1126	HgBerzé	*S'onques nuns hons por dure departie*	ADKOPRTVXa (10/17)
1154	RlSoiss	*E! coens d'Anjo, on dit per felonnie*	O (1/2)

	author	incipit	MSS with melody
1204	RlSoiss(?)	Se j'ai lonc tans esté en Romenie	NV (2/4)
1891	Roi Richart	Ja nus homs pris ne dira sa raison	CKNOX (5/10)
1152	TbChamp	Au temps plain de fellonie	KMORVX (6/7)
757	TbChamp	Dame, ensint est qu'il m'en covient aler	KMOPVX (6/9)
273	TbChamp	Diex est ausis conme li pellicans	KMOVX (5/9)
1469	TbChamp	Li douz pensers et li douz sovenir	KMOR(R¹ & R³)TVXa (9/9)
6	TbChamp	Seignor, sachiez qui or ne s'an ira	KMNOVX (6/8)
421	VdChar	Conbien que j'aie demoré	AKMNPRTUa (9/10)
502	VdChar	Tant com je fusse hors de ma contree	AKMNPʹTUXa (9/9)
1548a	Anon	Chevalier, mult estes guariz	Erfurt, n° 32 (1/1)
1229	Anon	Ja de chanter en ma vie	MO+KNPX (6/10)
1887	Anon	Nuns ne poroit de mavaise raison	V (= RS 700) (1/2)
1020a	Anon	Oiés seigneur, pereceus par oiseuses	a (= RS 1125) (1/1)
401	Anon	Parti de mal e a bien aturné	Harley 1717 (1/1)
BdT			
155.3	FqMars	Ai! quan gen vens et ab quan pauc d'afan	GR (2/22)
167.15	GcFaid	Chant e deport, ioy, domney e solatz	GRX (3/22)
167.22	GcFaid	Fortz cauza es que tot lo maior dan	GWXh (4/18)
189.5	Gran/Bertr	Pos anc no·us valc amors, senhe·N Bertran	R (1/2)
248.48	GrRiq	Karitatz ez amors e fes	R (1/2)
248.79	GrRiq	S'ieu ja trobat non agues	R (1/2)

	author	incipit	MSS with melody
248.87	GrRiq	Cristias vey perilhar	R (1/2)
262.6	JfrRud	Quan lo rossinhols el folhos	R (1/13)
293.35	Mbru	Pax in nomine Domini	W (1/8)
364.4	PVid	Anc no mori per amor ni per al	GRX (3/21)
364.11	PVid	Be·m pac d'ivern e d'estiu	GRX (3/18)
364.36	PVid	Plus que·l paubres, quan jai el ric ostal	R (1/22)
366.29	Peirol	Qant Amors trobet partit	G (1/14)
392.3	RbVaq	Ara pot hom conoisser e proar	R (1/12)
392.24	RbVaq	No m'agrad'iverns ni pascors	R (1/15)
406.12	RmMirav	Bel m'es q'ieu chant e coindei	R (1/20)
461.122	Anon	Finament	Wd (French MT) (2/2)

French manuscripts

A	Arras, Municipal library 657
C	Bern, Municipal library 389
D	Frankfurt-am-Main, Municipal library no. 29
K	Paris, Arsenal 5198
M	Paris, Bibliothèque Nationale 844
N	Paris, Bibliothèque Nationale 845
O	Paris, Bibliothèque Nationale 846
P	Paris, Bibliothèque Nationale 847
R	Paris, Bibliothèque Nationale 1591
S	Paris, Bibliothèque Nationale 12581
T	Paris, Bibliothèque Nationale 12615
U	Paris, Bibliothèque Nationale 20050
V	Paris, Bibliothèque Nationale 24406
X	Paris, Bibliothèque Nationale, Nouv. acq. fr. 1050
a	Rome, Vatican Library Reg. 1490
Erfurt	Erfurt, CA. 8° 32
Harley	London, British Museum, Harl. 1717

Occitan manuscripts

G	Milan, Biblioteca Ambrosiana, S.P.4
R	Paris, Bibliothèque Nationale, f.f. 22543
W	Paris, Bibliothèque Nationale, f.f. 844
X	Paris, Bibliothèque Nationale, f.f. 20050
d	Modena, Biblioteca Estense, annex to D (Modena, Biblioteca Estense, a, R.4.4)
	Quotations in Terramagnino of Pisa: see BdT, p. xxxv

The numbers in brackets in the column 'MSS with melody' show the number of MSS preserving music and text respectively.

Bibliography

Further bibliography for each of the individual texts, and for all the Old French texts together, are found through the website <http://warwick.ac.uk/crusadelyrics/texts>.

Abulafia, D., *Frederick II: A Medieval Emperor* (London, 1988)
Adam de la Halle, *Oeuvres complètes*, ed. P.-Y. Badel (Paris, 1995)
Alvira Cabrer, M., 'Del *Sepulcro* y los *sarracenos meridionales* a los *herejes occidentales*. Apuntes sobre tres "guerras santas" en las fuentes del sur de Francia (siglos XI–XIII)', in *Regards croisés sur la guerre sainte. Guerre, idéologie et religion dans l'espace méditerranéen latin (XIe–XIIIe siècle)*, Actes du Colloque international tenu à la Casa de Velásquez (Madrid) du 11 au 13 avril 2005 (Toulouse, 2006), pp. 187–229
Amossy, R., 'Faut-il intégrer l'argumentation dans l'analyse du discours ? Problématiques et enjeux', *AAD*, 9 (2012), http://aad.revues.org/1346
—, and R. Koren, 'Rhétorique et argumentation: approches croisées', *AAD*, 2, 2009, <http://aad.revues.org/561>
Andrea, A., 'Adam of Perseigne and the Fourth Crusade', *Cîteaux*, 36 (1985), 21–37
Anglade, J., 'Le troubadour Guiraut Riquier de Narbonne et les Catalans', *Institut d'Estudis Catalans, Anuari*, 1–2 (1909–1910), 571–87
Annunziata, F. S., 'Tomier e Palaizi, *Si co.l flacs molins torneia* (BdT 442.2)', *Lt*, 6 (2013), 1–23 (http://www.lt.unina.it/Annunziata-2013)
Asbridge, T., *The Crusades. The War for the Holy Land* (London, 2010)
Asperti, S., *Carlo I d'Angiò e i trovatori. Componenti 'provenzali' e angioine nella tradizione manoscritta della lirica trobadorica* (Ravenna, 1995)
— 'Testi poetici volgari di propaganda politica (secoli XII e XIII)', in *Propaganda politica del basso medioevo*, Atti del XXXVIII Convegno storico internazionale, Todi, *14–17 ottobre 2001* (Spoleto, 2002), pp. 533–59
— 'La tradizione occitanica', in *Lo spazio letterario del medioevo, 2. Il medioevo volgare* (Rome, 2002), pp. 521–54
— 'Generic poetici di Cerveri de Girona', in *Trobadors a la península ibèrica. Homenatge al Dr. Martí de Riquer*, ed. V. Beltran, M. Simó and E. Roig (Barcelona, 2006), pp. 29–71
Aurell, M., *La vielle et l'épée. Troubadours et politique en Provence au XIIie siècle* (Montaigne, 1989)

— 'Chanson et propagande politique: les troubadours gibelins (1255–1285)', in *Forme della propaganda politica nel Due e nel trecento*, ed. P. Cammarosano (Rome, 1994), pp. 183–202

— *Des chrétiens contre les croisades, XIIe–XIIIe siècle* (Paris, 2013)

Barachini, G., *Il trovatore Elias de Barjols* (Rome, 2015)

Barber, M., *The New Knighthood* (Cambridge, 1994)

— 'Was the Holy Land Betrayed in 1291?', *RMS*, 34 (2008), 35–52

— *The Crusader States* (New Haven and London, 2012)

Barberini, F., 'Rostainh Berenguier de Marseilha e l'*affaire* dell'Ospedale (BdT 427.4)', *RLM*, 12 (2011), 43–69

Barbero, A., *Il mito angioino nella cultura italiana e provenzale fra Duecento e Trecento* (Turin, 1983)

Barbieri, L., 'Note sul Liederbuch di Thibaut de Champagne', *MR*, 23 (1999), 388–416

— '*A mon Ynsombart part Troia*: une polémique anti-courtoise dans le dialogue entre trouvères et troubadours', *MR*, 37 (2013), 264–95

— 'Un sirventese religioso di Thibaut de Champagne: *Diex est ausis conme li pellicans* (RS 273)', *CN*, 73 (2013), 301–46

— 'Le canzoni di crociata e il canone lirico oitanico', *Medioevi*, 1 (2015), 45–74

Baschet, J., *L'iconographie médiévale* (Paris, 2008)

— *L'image médiévale: fonctions dans l'espace sacré et structuration de l'espace cultuel*, ed. C. Voyer and E. Sparhubert (Turnhout, 2011)

Bec, P., *La lyrique française au moyen âge (XIIe–XIIIe siècles)*, 2 vols (Paris, 1977–1978)

Bédier, J., and P. Aubry, *Les chansons de croisade avec leurs mélodies* (Paris, 1909; repr. Geneva, 2011)

Beggiato, F., '"Belha m'es la flors d'aguilen"', *CN*, 48 (1988), 85–112

Belperron, P., *La croisade contre les Albigeois et l'union du Languedoc à la France, 1209–1249* (Paris, 1961)

Bent, Margaret, *Magister Jacobus de Ispania, author of the 'Speculum Musicae'* (Farnham and Burlington, Vt., 2015)

Bériou, N., *L'avènement des maîtres de la Parole. La prédication à Paris au XIIIe siècle*, 2 vols (Paris, 1998)

— 'Les sermons latins après 1200', in B. M. Kienzle, *The Sermon*, pp. 363–447

Bertoni, G., 'Un serventese di Guilhem Figueira', *ZRP*, 35 (1911), 489–91

— *I trovatori d'Italia* (Modena, 1915; repr. Rome, 1967)

Biddlecombe, S., *The Historia Jerosolimitana of Baldric of Bourgueil* (Woodbridge, 2014)

Billy, D., *L'Architecture lyrique médiévale: analyse métrique et modélisation des structures interstrophiques dans la poésie lyrique des troubadours et des trouvères* (Montpellier, 1989)

Biographies des troubadours: textes provençaux des XIIIe et XIVe siècles, ed. J. Boutière and A. H. Schutz, second edition by J. Boutière and I.-M. Cluzel (Paris, 1973)

Brémond, C., J. Le Goff and J.-.C. Schmitt, *L'exemplum* (Turnhout, 1982)

Briscoe, M. G., and B. H. Jaye, *Artes Praedicandi, Artes Orandi* (Turnhout, 1992)

Bruckner, M., 'Marcabru et la chanson de croisade: d'un centre à l'autre', *CCM*, 53 (2010), 219–36

Cabré, M., 'Italian and Catalan troubadours', in Gaunt and Kay, *The Troubadours*, pp. 127–40

—'*En breu sazo aura·l jorn pretentori* (BDT 434a,20): Jaume I i Cerverí interpreten els fets de 1274', in *Actes del X Col·loqui de l'Associació Hispànica de Literatura Medieval, Alaicant 2003* (Valencia, 2005), pp. 453–68

Chibnall, M., ed., *The Ecclesiastical History of Orderic Vitalis*, 6 vols (Oxford 1969–1975)

Chrissis, N. G., *Crusading in Frankish Greece: A Study of Byzantine–Western Relations and Attitudes, 1204–1282* (Turnhout, 2012)

Cole, P. J., *The Preaching of the Crusades to the Holy Land, 1095–1270* (Cambridge, Mass., 1991)

Constable, G., 'The Historiography of the Crusades', in *The Crusades from the Perspective of Byzantium and the Muslim World*, ed. E. Laiou (Washington, 2001)

Cosgrove, W. R., '*Crucesignatus*: A Refinement or Merely One More Term among Many?', in *Crusades – Medieval Worlds in Conflict*, ed. T. F. Madden, J. L. Naus and V. Ryan (Farnham, 2010), pp. 95–107

Costen, M., *The Cathars and the Albigensian Crusade* (Manchester and New York, 1997)

Dante, *De vulgari eloquentia*, ed. S. Botterill (Cambridge, 1996, repr. 2006)

De Barthomolaeis, V., 'Osservazioni sulle poesie provenzali relative a Federico II', *Memorie della Real Accademia delle scienze dell'Isituto di Bologna*. Classe di scienze morali, sezione storico-filologica, serie 1, vol. 6, 1911–1912, pp. 97–124

— *Poesie provenzali storiche relative all'Italia*, 2 vols (Rome, 1931)

De Sainte Leocade: au tans que Sainz Hyldefons estbit arcevesques de Tholete cui Nostre Dame donna l'aube de prelaz: miracle versifié, ed. E. Vilamo-Pentti (Helsinki, 1950)

Dijkstra, C. T. J., *La chanson de croisade: étude thématique d'un genre hybride* (Amsterdam, 1995)

Dizionario Biografico degli Italiani, ed. A. M. Ghisalberti and M. Pavan (Rome, 1960–), vol. 60 (2003)

Dunbabin, J., *Charles I of Anjou. Power, Kingship and State-Making in Thirteenth-Century Europe* (London and New York, 1998)

— 'Charles of Anjou, Crusaders and Poets', in Parsons and Paterson, *Literature of the Crusades*, pp. 150–57

Ernst, W., 'Die Lieder des provenzalischen Trobadors Guiraut von Calanso', *RF*, 44, 2 (1930), 255–406

Flahiff, G. B., 'Ralph Niger: An Introduction to His Life and Works', *MS*, 2 (1940), 104–26

— '*Deus non vult*: A Critic of the Third Crusade', *MS*, 9 (1947), 162–88

Fletcher, R. A., 'Reconquest and Crusade in Spain, c. 1050–1150', *Transactions of the Royal Historical Society*, 37 (1987), 31–47

Flori, J., *Prêcher la croisade XIe–XIIIe siècle. Communication et propagande* (Paris, 2012)

Formisano, L., 'Un nou sirventes ses tardar: l'emploi du français entre pertinence linguistique et pertinence culturelle', in *O Cantar dos Trobadores: actas do congreso celebrado en Santiago de Compostela entre os días 26 e 29 de abril de 1993* (Santiago de Compostela, 1993), pp. 137–54

Frank, I., *Répertoire métrique de la poésie des troubadours*, 2 vols (Paris, 1953–1957)

Frappier, J., *La poésie lyrique française aux XIIe et XIIIe siècles: les auteurs et les genres* (Paris, 1966),

Galvez, M., *Songbook. How Lyrics Became Poetry in Medieval Europe* (Chicago and London, 2012)

Garcia Larragueta, S. A., *El gran priorado de Navarra de la orden de san Juan de Jerusalen: Siglos XII-XIII*, 2 vols (Pamplona, 1957)

Gatien-Arnoult, M., *Monuments de la littérature romane depuis le quatorzième siècle* (Toulouse, 1843)

Gaunt, S., and S. Kay, *The Troubadours. An Introduction* (Cambridge, 1999)

—, R. Harvey and L. Paterson, *Marcabru: A Critical Edition* (Cambridge, 2000)

Gelzer, H., 'Zum altfranzösischen Kreuzugslied, *Chevalier, mult estes guariz*', ZRP, 48 (1928), 438–48

Gere, R. H., 'Les Troubadours, Heresy, and the Albigensian Crusade', PhD dissertation, Columbia University (New York, 1956)

Ghil, E. M., *L'Age de Parage: Essai sur le poétique et le politique en Occitanie au XIIIe siècle* (New York, Bern, Frankfurt am Main and Paris, 1989)

Gillingham, J., *Richard I* (New Haven and London, 1999)

— 'The Kidnapped King: Richard I in Germany, 1192–1194', *German Historical Institute London Bulletin*, 30 (2008), 5–34

Gillingham, J. and R. Harvey, 'Le troubadour Giraut de Borneil et la troisième croisade', RST, 5 (2003), 51–72

Gouiran, G., *L'Amour et la guerre: l'œuvre de Bertran de Born*, 2 vols (Aix-en-Provence, 1985)

— 'Os meum replebo increpationibus (Job, XXIII, 4). Comment parler à Dieu sans prier, ou la contestation contre Dieu dans les lyriques occitane et galaïco-portuguaise', in *O cantar dos trobadores. Actas do Congreso celebrado en Santiago de Compostela entre os días 26 e 29 de abril de 1993* (Santiago de Compostela, 1993), pp. 77–98

Griffe, E., *Le Languedoc cathare de 1190 à 1210* (Paris, 1971)

Grimaldi, M., 'Il sirventese di Peire de la Caravana (BdT 334,1)', CN, 73 (2013), 25–72

Guibert de Nogent, *Historia quae dicitur Gesta Dei per Francos*, in RHC Oc, IV

Guida, S., 'L'attività poetica di Gui de Cavaillon durante la crociata albigese', CN, 3 (1973), 235–71

— *Canzoni di crociata* (Parma, 1992)

Harvey, R., *The Troubadour Marcabru and Love* (London, 1989)

— 'À propos de la date de la première "chanson de croisade": *Emperaire, per mi mezeis* de Marcabru (PC 292.22)', *Cahiers de civilisation médiévale*, 42 (1999), 55–60

— 'On the Date of Gaucelm Faidit's Dialogue with Albertet (BdT 16,16), with a Note on *Ara nos sia guitz*', *CN*, 71 (2011), 9–21

Harvey, R., and L. Paterson, *The Troubadour Tensos and Partimens: A Critical Edition*, 3 vols (Cambridge, 2010)

Hoch, M., 'The Price of Failure', in *The Second Crusade. Scope and Consequences*, ed. J. Phillips and M. Hoch (Manchester, 2001), pp. 183–85

Hölzle, P., *Die Kreuzzüge in der okzitanischen und deutschen Lyrik des 12. Jahrhunderts* (Göppingen, 1980)

Housley, N., Crusades against Christians: Their Origins and Early Developments, c. 1000–1216', in *Crusade and Settlement. Papers Read at the First Conference of the Society for the Study of the Crusades and the Latin East Presented to R. C. Smail*, ed. P. Edbury (Cardiff, 1985)

— *The Italian Crusades* (Oxford, 1988)

— *The Later Crusades* (Oxford, 1992)

— *Contesting the Crusades* (Oxford, 2006)

Hugues de Berzé, *La Bible au seigneur de Berzé. Edition critique d'après tous les manuscrits connus*, ed. F. Lecoy (Paris, 1938)

Hunt, A. B., 'An Old French Crusade Proposal', *RMS*, 34 (2008), 123–36

Huon de Saint-Quentin, poète satirique et lyrique, étude historique et édition de textes, ed. A. Serper (Madrid, 1983)

Iacobus de Vitriaco, *Sermones vulgares vel ad status I*, ed. J. Longère, Corpus Christianorum Continuatio Mediaevalis (CCCM 255) (Turnhout, 2013)

Jackson, P., *The Mongols and the West, 1221–1410* (Harlow, 2005)

Jeanroy, A., 'Le soulèvement de 1242 dans la poésie des troubadours', *AdM*, 16 (1904), 311–29

Joinville, *Vie de Saint Louis*, ed. J. Monfrin (Paris, 1995)

Kedar, B. Z., *Crusade and Mission: European Approaches toward the Muslims* (Princeton, 1984)

Kienzle, B. M., ed., *The Sermon* (Turnhout, 2000)

— *Cistercians, Heresy and Crusade in Occitania, 1145–1229. Preaching in the Lord's Vineyard* (York, 2001)

Knecht, R. J., *The Valois Kings of France 1328–1589* (London and New York, 2004)

Lachin, J., *Il trovatore Elias Cairel* (Modena, 2004)

Lambert, M., *The Cathars* (Oxford, 1998)

Lambert, S., and H. Nicholson, eds, *Languages of Love and Hate. Conflict, Communication, and Identity in the Medieval Mediterranean* (Turnhout, 2012)

LaMonte, J. L., with M. J. Hubert, *The Wars of Frederick II against the Ibelines in Syria and Cyprus* (New York, 1936)

Larson, P., 'Primordi della ballata politica italiana', in *Comunicazione e propaganda nei secoli XII e XIII. Atti del convegno internazionale (Messina, 24–26 maggio 2007)*, ed. R. Castano, F. Latella and T. Sorrenti (Rome, 2007), pp. 413–29

Lazzerini, L., *Les Troubadours et la sagesse* (Ventadour, 2013)
Le Besant de Dieu de Guillaume le Clerc de Normandie, ed. P. Ruelle (Brussels, 1973)
Lee, C., 'Richard the Lionheart: The Background to *Ja nus homs pris*', in Parsons and Paterson, *Literature of the Crusades*, pp. 00–00
Léglu, C., 'Defamation in the Troubadour *sirventes*', *MAe*, 66 (1997), 28–24
— 'Vernacular Poems and Inquisitors in Languedoc and Champagne', *Viator*, 33 (2002), 117–32
Le Goff, J., *Saint Louis* (Paris, 1996)
Le Vot, G.,'Les chants courtois relatifs aux croisades dans le chansonnier de Saint-Germain-des-Prés (Paris, BnFr. 20050)', in *Lettres, musique et société en Lorraine médiévale. Autour du 'Tournoi de Chauvency'*, ed. M. Chazan and N. F. Regalado (Geneva, 2012), pp. 487–519
Lewent, K., 'Das altprovenzalische Kreuzlied', *RF*, 21 (1905), 321–448
Lewis, P. S., *Later Medieval France: The Polity* (London, 1968)
Linskill, J., ed., *The Poems of the Troubadour Raimbaut de Vaqueiras* (The Hague, 1964)
Lloyd, S., *English Society and the Crusade, 1216–1307* (Cambridge, 1988)
— *Henry III, Edward I, and the Crusade* (Oxford, 1988)
Lower, M., *The Barons' Crusade: A Call to Arms and Its Consequences* (Philadelphia, 2005)
— 'Louis IX, Charles of Anjou, and the Tunis Crusade of 1270', in *Crusades – Medieval Worlds in Conflict*, ed. T. F. Madden, J. L. Naus and V. Ryan (Farnham, 2010), pp. 173–93
Lug, R., 'Chevaliers chantant à cheval. Nouvelles observations sur la rythmique des troubadours', in *Toulouse à la croisée des cultures. Actes du Ve Congrès international de l'Association Internationale d'Etudes Occitanes, Toulouse, 19–24 août 1996*, ed. J. Gourc and F. Pic, 2 vols (Pau 1998), vol. 1, pp. 337–47
Madden, T. F., 'The Latin Empire of Constantinople's Fractured Foundation: The Rift between Boniface of Montferrat and Baldwin of Flanders', in *The Fourth Crusade: Event, Aftermath, and Perceptions, Papers from the Sixth Conference of the Society for the Study of the Crusades and the Latin East, Istanbul, Turkey, 25–29 August 2004*, ed. T. F. Madden (Aldershot, 2008), pp. 45–52
Maier, C. T., *Crusade Propaganda and Ideology, Model Sermons for the Preaching of the Cross* (Cambridge, 2000)
Marcos, E., *La croada catalana. L'exèrcit de Jaume I a Terra Santa* (Barcelona, 2007)
Markowski, M., '*Crucesignatus*. Its Origins and and Early Usage', *JMH*, 10 (1984), 157–65
Martin-Chabot, E., ed., *Chanson de la croisade contre les Albigeois*, 3 vols (Paris, 1931–1961)
Martindale, J., '*Cavalaria et orgueill*', in C. Harper-Bill and R. Harvey, eds, *The Ideals and Practice of Medieval Knighthood II: Papers from the Third Strawberry Hill Conference* (Woodbridge, 1988), pp. 87–116

'Succession and Politics in the Romance-Speaking World, c. 1000–1140', in *England and Her Neighbours, 1066–1453. Essays in Honour of Pierre Chaplais*, ed. M. Jones and M. Vale (London, 1989)

Marvin, W., *The Occitan War: A Military and Political History of the Albigensian Crusade, 1209–1218* (Cambridge, 2008)

Matthew Paris, *Matthaei Parisiensis Chronica majora*, ed. H. R. Luard, 7 vols (London, 1872–1883, vol. V, 1880)

Mayer, H. E., *The Crusades*, translated by J. Gillingham (Oxford, 1988, first published in German, Stuttgart, 1965)

Mazel, F., *La Noblesse et l'église en Provence, fin Xe–début XIVe siècle. L'exemple des familles d'Agoult-Simiane, de Baux et de Marseille* (Paris, 2002)

Melani, S., *Guerra di Federico II in Oriente (1223–1242)* (Naples, 1995)

— 'Aimeric de Belenoi, Thibaut de Champagne e le crociate', in *RST* 1 (1999), 137–57

— 'Il cammino della croce e gli artigli della lussuria: ipotesi sulle "perdute" *cantilenae* composte da Guglielmo IX in occasione della sua crociata', in *Le letterature romanze del Medioevo: testi, storia, intersezioni. Atti del V Convegno Nazionale della SIFR*, ed. P. Antonio (Soveria Mannelli, 2000), pp. 281–93

Meliga, W., 'L'Aquitaine des premiers troubadours. Géographie et histoire des origines troubadouresques', in *L'Aquitaine des littératures médiévales (XIe–XIIIe siècle)*, ed. J.-Y. Casanova and V. Fasseur (Paris, 2011), pp. 45–58

— 'Gaucelm Faidit et la (les) croisade(s)', in *Gaucelm Faidit: amours, voyages et débats. Trobada tenue à Uzerche les 25 et 26 juin 2010* (Ventadour, 2011), pp. 25–36

— '*Pos de chantar m'es pres talenz*: l'adieu au monde du comte-duc', in *Guilhem de Peitieus, duc d'Aquitaine, prince du* trobar (Ventadour, 2015), pp. 193–203

Meneghetti, M.-L., 'Uc de Saint Circ tra filologia e divulgazione', in *Il medioevo nella Marca: trovatori, giullari, letterati a Treviso. Atti del Convegno, Treviso 28–29 settembre 1990*, ed. M.-L. Meneghetti and F. Zambon (Dosson, 1991), pp. 115–28

Menéndez Pidal de Navascués, F., *Heráldica medieval española*, I: *la casa real de León y Castilla* (Madrid, 1982)

Meyer, R., *Das Leben des Trobadors Gaucelm Faidit* (Heidelberg, 1876)

Mölk, U., *Das älteste französische Kreuzlied und der Erfurter Codex Amplonianus 8°* (Göttingen, 2001)

Mouzat, J., *Les poèmes de Gaucelm Faidit* (Paris, 1965)

Nichols, S. G., 'Urgent Voices: The Vengeance of Images in Medieval Poetry', in *France and the Holy Land. Frankish Culture at the End of the Crusades*, ed. D. H. Weiss and L. Mahoney (Baltimore and London, 2004), pp. 22–42

—, J. A. Galm et al., eds, *Bernart de Ventadorn: The Songs of Bernart de Ventadorn* (Chapel Hill, 1962)

Noble, P., '1204, The Crusade without Epic Heroes', in *Epic & Crusade. Proceedings of the Colloquium of the Société Rencesvals British Branch Held at Lucy Cavendish College, Cambridge, 27–28 March 2004*, ed. P. E. Bennett, A. E. Cobby and J. E. Everson (Cambridge and Edinburgh, 2006), pp. 89–104

Oeding, F., *Das altfranzösische Kreuzlied, Inaugural-Dissertation zur Erlangung der Doctorwürde bei der hohen philosophischen Facultät der Universität Rostock* (Brunswick, 1910)
Parsons, S., and L. Paterson, eds, *Literature of the Crusades* (Cambridge, 2018)
Paterson, L., *Troubadours and Eloquence* (Oxford, 1975)
— *The World of the Troubadours* (Cambridge, 1993)
— 'Marcabru's Rhetoric and the Dialectics of *trobar*: Ans que.l terminis verdei (PC 293.7) and Jaufre Rudel', in *Conjunctures: Medieval Studies in Honor of Douglas Kelly*, ed. K. Busby and N. Lacy (Amsterdam and Atlanta, 1994), pp. 407–23
— 'Occitan Literature and the Holy Land', in *The World of Eleanor of Aquitaine: Literature and Society in Southern France between the Eleventh and Thirteenth Centuries*, ed. M. Bull and C. Léglu (Woodbridge, 2005), pp. 83–99
— 'James the Conqueror, the Holy Land and the Troubadours', *CN*, 71 (2011), 211–86
— 'Greeks and Latins at the Time of the Fourth Crusade: Patriarch John X Kamateros and a Troubadour *tenso*', in Lambert and Nicholson, eds, *Languages of Love and Hate*, pp. 119–39
— 'Austorc de Segret, *[No s]ai qui·m so tan suy [des]conoyssens* (BdT 41.1)', *Lt*, 5 (2012), <http://www.lt.unina.it/Paterson-2012.pdf>
— 'Calega Panzan, *Ar es sazos c'om si deu alegrar* (BdT 107.1)', *Lt* 5 (2012), <http://www.lt.unina.it/Paterson-2012b.pdf>
—'Peire del Vilar, *Sendatz vermelhs, endis e ros* (BdT 365.1)', *Lt*, 6 (2013), <http://www.lt.unina.it/Paterson-2013b.pdf>
— 'Anonymous (Nompar de Caumont?). *Finament* (BdT 461.122)', *Lt*, 23 (December 2014), <http://www.lt.unina.it/Paterson-2014.pdf>
—'Troubadour Responses to the Reconquista', *RPh*, 70 (2016), 181–201
Paul, N. L., *To Follow in Their Footsteps. The Crusades and Family Memory in the High Middle Ages* (Ithaca, NY, 2012)
Pécout, T., *L'Invention de la Provence: Raymond Bérenger V (1209–1245)* (Paris, 2004)
Pegg, M. G., *A Most Holy War: The Albigensian Crusade and the Battle for Christendom* (Oxford, 2008)
Peire Vidal, *Poesie*, ed. A. S. Avalle, 2 vols (Milan and Naples, 1960)
Perelman, C., and L. Olbrechts-Tyteca, 'Logique et rhétorique', *Revue philosophique de la France et de l'étranger*, 140 (January-March 1950), 1–35 (repr. C. Perelman, *Rhétoriques* (Brussels, 1989), pp. 63–107)
Philippe de Novare, *Mémoires*, ed. C. Kohler (Paris, 1913)
Phillips, J., *The Fourth Crusade and the Sack of Constantinople* (London, 2005)
— *The Second Crusade: Extending the Frontiers of Christendom* (New Haven and London, 2007)
Pollina, V., '*Si cum Marcabrus declina*': Studies in the Poetics of the Troubadour Marcabru* (Modena, 1991)
— 'Les mélodies du troubadour Marcabru: questions de style et de genre', in *Atti del Secondo Congresso Internazionale della 'Association Internationale d'Etudes Occitanes'*, ed. G. Gasca Queirazza (Turin, 1993), pp. 289–306

Powicke, F. M., *King Henry III and the Lord Edward*, 2 vols (Oxford, 1947)
Prestwich, M., *Edward I* (London, 1988)
Radaelli, A., '*voil ma chançun a la gent fere oïr*: un appello anglonormanno alla crociata (London, BL Harley 1717, c. 251v)', *CN*, 73 (2013), 361–99
— '*Voil ma chançun a la gent fere oïr*: an Anglo-Norman Crusade Appeal', in Parsons and Paterson, *Literature of the Crusades*, pp. 109–33
Radulfus Niger, *De re militari et triplici via peregrinationis Ierosolimitane (1187/88)*, ed. L. Schmugge (Berlin, 1977)
Raguin, M., 'Propagande politique et religieuse dans la *Chanson de la Croisade albigeoise*, texte de l'Anonyme' (unpublished PhD thesis, Études occitanes, Université Paul-Valéry – Montpellier III, 2011)
— 'Remarques sur le serment et l'engagement personnel dans les chansons de croisade lyriques françaises et occitanes', *Le sacré et la parole: le serment au Moyen Âge*, ed. M. Herrero and J. Aurell (Turnhout, 2016, in press)
— *Lorsque la poésie fait le souverain. Étude sur la 'Chanson de la Croisade albigeoise'* (Paris, 2015)
Raimon Gaucelm de Béziers, *Poesie*, ed. A. Radaelli (Florence, 1997)
Raugei, A. M., *Gautier de Dargies, Poesie* (Florence, 1981)
Ricketts, P. T., ed., *Les poésies de Guilhem de Montanhagol, troubadour provençal du XIIIe siècle* (Toronto, 1964)
Riley-Smith, J., *The Crusades. A Short History* (New Haven and London, 1987)
Riley-Smith, L., and J. Riley-Smith, *The Crusades: Idea and Reality* (London, 1981)
Riquer, M. de, 'Un trovador valenciano: Pedro el Grande de Aragón', *Revista valenciana de filologia*, 1 (1951), 273–311
— 'El trovador Giraut del Luc y sus poesías contra Alfonso II de Aragón', *Boletín de la Real Academia de Buenas Letras de Barcelona*, 23 (1950), 209–48
— *Los trovadores: historia literaria y textos*, 3 vols (Barcelona, 1975)
Riquer Permayer, I. de, *Historia literaria del infante Enrique de Castilla (1230–1303)* (Barcelona, 2016)
Robert de Clari, *La Conquête de Constantinople, edition bilingue*, ed. and trans. J. Dufournet (Paris, 2004)
Robert the Monk, *Historia Iherosolimitana*, ed. D. Kempf and M. G. Bull (Woodbridge, 2013)
Roncaglia, A., 'Marcabruno: *Lo vers comens quan vei del fau* (BdT 239.33)', *CN*, 9 (1951), 25–48
Runciman, S., *A History of the Crusades*, 3 vols (Harmondsworth, 1971; first published Cambridge 1951–1954)
Rutebeuf, *Oeuvres complètes*, ed. M. Zink (Paris, 1989–1990)
Salimbene de Adam, *Chronica*, ed. G. Scalia, 2 vols (Bari, 1966)
Sancti Bernardi Opera, ed. J. Leclercq, H.-M. Rochais and C. H. Talbot, 8 vols (Rome, 1957–1977)
Schöber, S., *Die altfranzösische Kreuzzugslyrik des 12. Jahrhunderts, 'Temporalibus aeterna ... praeponenda'* (Vienna, 1976)

Setton, K. M., ed., *A History of the Crusades*, 6 vols (Madison and London, 1969–1989)

Sharman, R. V., ed., *The Cansos and Sirventes of the Troubadour Giraut de Borneil* (Cambridge, 1989)

Shaw, M. R. B., *Joinville and Villehardouin, Chronicles of the Crusades* (Harmondsworth, 1963, repr. 1970)

Shepard, W. P., and F. M. Chambers, *The Poems of Aimeric de Peguilhan* (Evanston, Ill., 1950)

Siberry, E., *Criticism of Crusading 1095–1274* (Oxford, 1985)

Squillacioti, P., *Le poesie di Folchetto di Marsiglia* (Pisa, 1999)

Strayer, J. R., *The Albigensian Crusades* (New York, 1971)

Stroński, S., *Le Troubadour Folquet de Marseille* (Kraków, 1910)

— 'Notes de littérature provençale', *AdM*, 25 (1913), 273–97

Sumption, J., *The Albigensian Crusade* (London, 1978)

Sweetenham, C., *Robert the Monk's History of the First Crusade. Historia Iherosolimitana* (Aldershot and Burlington, Vt., 2005)

—'Reflecting and Refracting Reality: The Use of Poetic Sources in Latin Accounts of the First Crusade', in Parsons and Paterson, *Literature of the Crusades*, pp. 25–40

—, and L. M. Paterson, *The 'Canso d'Antioca'. An Occitan Epic Chronicle of the First Crusade* (Aldershot, 2003)

Switten, M., *Songs of the Troubadours and Trouvères: an Anthology of Poems and Melodies* (New York and London, 1998)

— 'Music and Versification', in Gaunt and Kay, *The Troubadours*, pp. 141–63

Thibaud de Champagne, Recueil de Chansons, ed. A. Micha (Paris, 1991)

Throop, P. A., *Criticism of the Crusade: A Study of Public Opinion and Crusade Propaganda* (Philadelphia, 1940)

Throop, S., *Crusading as an Act of Vengeance, 1095–1216* (Farnham, 2011)

Trotter, D. A., *Medieval French Literature and the Crusades (1100–1300)* (Geneva, 1988)

Tyerman, C. J., 'Philip VI and the Recovery of the Holy Land', *EHR*, 100, n. 394 (1985), 25–52

— 'Were There Any Crusades in the Twelfth Century?', *EHR*, 110 (1995), 553–77

Vallé-Karcher, A., 'Jeanne de Bourgogne, épouse de Philippe VI de Valois: une reine maudite?', *BEC*, 138 (1980), 94–96

Van Cleve, T. C., *The Emperor Frederick II of Hohenstaufen, immutator mundi* (Oxford, 1972)

Vatteroni, S., *Falsa clercia. La poesia anticlerical dei trovatori* (Alessandria, 1999)

— *Il trovatore Peire Cardenal*, 2 vols (Modena, 2013)

Vaughan, R., *Chronicles of Matthew Paris: Monastic Life in the Thirteenth Century* (Gloucester, 1984)

Villehardouin, *La Conquête de Constantinople*, ed. E. Faral, 2 vols (Paris, 1938)

Vincent, N., 'A Letter to King Henry I from Toulouse', *JEH*, 63 (2012), 331–45

Weber, B., 'Nouveau mot ou nouvelle réalité? Le terme *cruciata* et son utilisation dans les textes pontificaux', in *La papauté et les croisades / The papacy and the*

Crusades. Actes du VIIe Congrès de la Society for the Study of the Crusades and the Latin East/ Proceedings of the VIIth Conference of the Society for the Study of the Crusades and the Latin East, ed. M. Balard (Farnham and Burlington, Vt., 1988), pp. 11–25

Wolff, R. L., and H. W. Hazard, *The Later Crusades, 1189–1311*, in Setton, ed., *A History of the Crusades*, vol. II

Zambon, F., 'Una nuova ipotesi sull'autore della seconda parte della *Canzone della Crociata Albigese*', *RPh*, 70 (2016), 267–81

Zufferey, F., 'Nouvelle approche de l'amour de loin', *CN*, 69 (2009), 7–58

Zumthor, P., *Histoire littéraire de la France médiévale, VIe–XIVe siècles* (Paris, 1954)

Index

Aachen 136, 203
abbots 121, 157, 273
Abû-Jûsûf Ya'qub al-Mansur, Almohad caliph of Morocco 81, 89, 179
Achaea 121–22
Acre 32, 129, 133, 137, 265
   Third Crusade 48, 66–67 n.21, 80, 82–83, 289
   Fifth Crusade 124
   Sixth Crusade 142, 144–45, 146, 294
   Barons' Crusade 167, 174, 296
   Seventh Crusade 179, 197
   the Lord Edward at 228
   fall 244–48, 256, 300
Adam de la Halle 224, 307
Adam de Perseigne, preacher 273
Adrianople 113, 116, 118, 120, 291
afar (Dieu?) 38, 71, 93, 95–96, 242
Africa 14, 84, 98, 104, 115, 139, 204, 221, 228
Agen, Agenais 79, 240, 242
Ager Sanguinis (Field of Blood) 26
Aigues-Mortes 196, 204, 217, 298
Aimar V, viscount of Limoges 1, 42, 62, 67, 91, 94-96
Aimaric V, viscount of Narbonne 210
Aimeri (of Narbonne), chanson de geste hero 119
Aimeric de Belenoi (AimBel) 3, 12, 62, 155, 168, 265, 296, 313
Aimeric de Peguilhan (AimPeg) 4, 11, 12, 74, 125, 262, 265
Aimery Barlais 144, 147
Ain Jalud, battle 204
Aix–en–Provence 180, 216
al-Adil, sultan 124, 292
al-Kãmil, sultan 124, 142, 152, 153, 164, 167, 170, 184, 295, 296
Alarcos 82, 84, 87–88, 90, 96, 255, 289

Albertino of Canossa 120
Albi 79
Albigensian Crusade 1, 4, 5 n.17, 6, 8, 192, 236, 254, 256, 272, 274, 278, 284
   wars of 1224–1233 3, 22, 123 and n.1, 124, 127, 132–35, 154–66, 291
   1242 uprising 22, 178, 179, 186 n.12
   heterodoxy 276
   see also Guilhem de Tudela; Anonymous Continuator
alcaydes 157
Aleppo 60, 183
Alexander IV, pope 204, 205
Alexander the Great 72, 119, 201
Alexandria 200, 209
Alexius (young) 98–99
Alexius III 98
Alexius V (Murzuphlus) 99
Alfonso I the Battler, king of Aragon 86
Alfonso II, king of Aragon 42–43, 84–86, 87 n.17, 315
Alfonso IV, king of Aragon 249
Alfonso VII, king of Castile-Leon 26, 40
Alfonso VIII, king of Castile 16, 81, 84, 88, 90–91, 134, 143
Alfonso X, king of Castile 201, 203, 206, 209, 210, 217, 233 and n.10
Alfonso IX, king of León 90
Alice of Champagne 144, 199
almansors 157
Almogavars 235
Almohads 81, 84, 89
Almoravids 27–28, 30
Alphonse, count of Poitiers 180, 181, 197, 203, 221
Alps 102, 141, 143, 189 n.19
Amalric IV, viscount of Narbonne 210
Amaury of Bethsan 147
Ampurdán 239

an-Nasir Da-ud of Kerak 179, 296
Anatolia 25
Andalusia 206
Andalusians 89
Angevins 54, 77–78, 91, 211, 214, 228, 230, 235, 254
  see also Charles of Anjou
Anglo-Norman 12, 205
Angoulême 78, 81, 87
Anjou 78, 181
  see also Angevins; Charles of Anjou
Anonymous Continuator 5–6
Ansel of Brie 148
Antichrist 195, 234, 272
Antioch 66
  see also Raymond of Antioch; Bohemond of Antioch; Maria of Antioch
apostasy 207–08, 256
Apulia 138 n.5, 142
Aquitaine 3 n.7, 60-61, 81, 270
  see also William IX; William X; Eleanor of Aquitaine; Richard the Lionheart
Arabs 74, 85, 89, 119, 162, 226
Aragon 7, 14, 91, 155, 201–02, 229, 235, 238
  Aragonese 90
  arms of 182, 202
  see also Aragonese Crusade; James I, king of Aragon; Crown of Aragon
Aragonese Crusade 16, 225–44, 257, 300
Arles 45, 79, 154–55, 157, 191-96
Armenians 208
Arnaud Amaury, abbot of Cîteaux, papal legate 278 n.81
Arnaud-Othon II, viscount of Lomagne and Auvillars 226
Arnaut de Mareuil 87 n.17
Arnaut joglar 86–87 n.17
Arsuf 144, 206-08, 227
Ascalon 67 n.21, 152
Asia Minor 47, 112
Athlit 207
Audfroi le Bastart (AudBast) 12 n.48, 302
audiences 7, 14–17, 20, 31, 65, 110, 126, 132, 213, 224, 233, 284
  courtly 171, 253
  French audience for troubadour 108
  lay audience and sermons 126
  mass 213 n.16
  means of swaying 260, 261 n.11, 262
  northern 254
  Provençal 143
  troubadour 256
  see also public
Austorc d'Aorlhac (AustAur) 2, 12 n.47, 199–201, 223. 227 and nn.3–4, 264 n.26
Austorc de Segret (AustSegr) 12 n.47, 225–26 and n.1, 299
Austria 48, 76, 289
Auvergne 12, 125, 127, 132
Avignon 154–55, 160, 164, 191–92, 294
Avignonnet 18, 186
Aytona 85-86

Babylon 116, 189
Bafomet 90-91, 200, 207–08
  see also Mahomet
Baibars 179, 204–08, 227, 297
baillis 144
  see also Aimery Barlais; Amaury of Bethsan; Gauvain of Chenichy; Hugh of Gibelet; William of Rivet
Baldric of Bourgueil 36 n.20
Baldwin of Ibelin 144
Baldwin I, king of Jerusalem 26
Baldwin II, emperor of Constantinople 122
Baldwin IX, count of Flanders 107
  emperor of Constantinople 112–116, 118 n.42, 291
Balian of Ibelin 144–46
ballete 248
bankers 192, 212 n.15
Barbary 85
Barcelona 26 n.4, 37, 217, 239, 241,
Barfleur 81
Barral of Baux 191, 193
Bearn 91
  see also Gaston of Bearn
Beatrice of Provence 189
Beirut 144–45, 151–52, 179
Bel 69–70
Benevento, battle 203, 215, 230
Benoît de Sainte-Maure 54
Berbers 89
Berbezilh 85
Berengaria, illegitimate daughter of Alfonso X of Castile 217
Bergamo 215

INDEX

Bernard of Clairvaux 30, 274 n.61, 286
Bernart Alanhan de Narbona (BnAlanh) 184, 189, 285 n.108, 295
Bernart d'Argentau, jongleur 131
Bernart d'Auriac (BnAur) 12 n.50, 238, 300
Bernart de Rovenac (BnRov) 10 n.37, 183, 201, 297–98
Bernart de Ventadorn 46 n.9
Bernart de Venzac 54 n.7
Bernart Raimon Baranhon 17
Berry 3 n.8, 28, 70, 81
Berta, daughter of Ravano and Isabella delle Carceri 121
Bertolome Zorzi (BertZorzi) 10 n.41, 12 n.49, 221, 299
Bertran Carbonel de Marseilla (BtCarb) 2 n.6, 12, 190–92, 196, 297
Bertran d'Alamanon (BtAlam) 10 n.37, 12 n.47, 296, 297, 298
   Seventh Crusade 13, 195–96, 210, 224, 254
   attacks Raymond VII of Toulouse 164
   revolt of southern communes 192–93
Bertran de Born (BtBorn) 4 and n.10, 10 n.37, 12 n.47, 51, 82, 83, 265 n.29, 269, 270 n.46, 287, 288
   connections with other poets 3, 46
   reflects public opinion 13–14
   Third Crusade 55–61, 125
Bethlehem 32, 127, 129, 265
Béziers 123, 132, 162, 180,
   see also Raimon Gaucelm de Béziers
Biar 217-18
Blacatz (Blacst) 12 n.47, 294
Blanche of Castile 157, 282
Blaye 85–86
Bohemond III, prince of Antioch 66
Bohemond IV, prince of Antioch 144
Boniface I, marquis of Monferrat 12, 100–01, 103–04, 107 and n. 27, 119–21, 138, 291
   elected leader of Fourth Crusade 20, 98, 100
   claim to Thessalonica 3 n.7, 15, 112–13, 116, 118 n.42
Bordeaux 181
Bosphorus 119
Botona, river Boutonne 86–87
Bourges 30, 154
Bouvines, battle 123, 292

Bretons 91
Brindisi 60, 119, 142, 158, 294
Bristol 61
Brittany, loss of 3 n.8, 55, 123, 174, 181
Buffavento, Cyprus 147
burghers 13, 51, 249
Burgundians 122, 243
Burgundy 103 n.15, 174
burlesque 10, 134, 189, 196, 255
Byzantines 99

Caen 61
Caesaria 207–08
Cahors 192
Cairo 116, 139, 189, 204
Calabria 138 n.5, 236
Calega Panzan (CalPanz) 10 n.37, 12 n.49, 214–15, 298
Cambresians 91
Campania 138 n.5
Canaanites 70
Canigou, mount 239
Canso d'Antioca 14, 25 n.1
Carcassonne 79, 123, 132
cardinals 126, 158 n.6, 161, 229, 233, 278
Carhaix 61
Carthage 204
Castelbó 241–42
Castellane, Provençal fortress 216
Castelsarrasin 186 n.12
Castile 90–91, 182 n.10
   see also Alfonso VII; Sancho III; Alfonso VIII; Alfonso X; Blanche; Henry
Castilians 67 n.21
Catalans 3 n.6, 238–39
Catalonia 79, 155, 243
Cathars 8, 79, 287
Cavalier Lunel de Monteg (CavLun) 12 n.51, 301
Celestine III, pope 79, 289
Cercamon (Cercam) 4 n.10, 18 n.70, 28–29, 31, 34 n.19, 37–38, 279–80, 286
Cerdagne 91
Cerverí de Girona (Cerv) 12, 18 n.70, 21 n.77, 225, 229–30 and n.6, 299
Champagne 17 n.66, 100–01, 118, 192, 198
   see also Thibaut, Alice
Chanson de Pouille 224 n.24
chansons de départie 9-12, 18, 42, 131, 255–

56, 279, 281
   primary audience 15
   of Conon de Béthune 48–50, 58, 125,
      103, 171, 281 n.95
   of Châtelain de Coucy 52–53, 103, 172,
      279, 281 nn.91–93
   of Thibaut de Champagne 171–73
Chardon de Croisilles (CharCrois) 2, 11
   n.46, 171, 281 n.93, n.95, n.97, n.98, 296
Charente 40, 61, 87
Charlemagne 56, 94, 119
Charles of Anjou 122, 210, 233, 236–37
   Seventh Crusade 13, 189, 192–93, 197,
      199, 209–10, 298
   Eighth Crusade and aftermath 225–28,
      230
   Aragonese Crusade 16, 235
   burlesque songs 135, 194–96, 254–5
   censorship of songs 194
   Provençal rebellion against 191–93, 254,
      297
   and Sicily 203, 211, 212 n.15, 224,
      234–36, 256
   war against Frederick II 203–04, 209, 211,
      212 n.15, 213–16, 224 and n. 24
   see also Angevins
Charles of Valois 235
Châtelain d'Arras (ChArr) 2, 11 n. 46, 131,
   266 n.34, 281 n.93, 292, 302
Châtelain de Coucy (ChCoucy) 4 nn.10–11,
   11 n.46, 102, 262 n.17, 264 n.25, 283
   n.106, 288, 291, 302
   on crusade 2, 102
   see also chansons de départie
Châtelaine de Vergi 53
Chef-Boutonne 87 n.17
Choriatis 120
Chronica majora *see* Matthew Paris
Chronique des Ducs de Normandie *see* Benoît
   de Sainte-Maure
Chronique de St-Maixent 26
Cistercians 162, 274 n.61
Cîteaux 121, 278
Clement IV, pope 208, 211, 215, 217, 218,
   256
Clement V, pope 247
Cluny 121
Compiègne 97
Complainte de Jérusalem contre Rome 130,

166, 266 n.35, 273 n.56, 277
Complainte d'Outremer 224 n.14
Coms de Foix (CtFoix, Count Roger Bernat
   of Foix) 12 n.47, 241–43, 262 n.15, 300
Coms de Proensa (CtProv) 11 n.43, 12 n.47,
   185, 261 n.8, 293
Comtat Venaissin 186
Conon de Béthune (CnBéth) 4 nn.10–11
   and n.13, 11 n.46, 45, 103, 127 n.9, 171,
   262 n.21, 275, 95, 283, 287–88, 302
   Fourth Crusade 2, 97, 102, 113–14, 116,
      120, 122,
   connections with other poets 3 and n.7,
      46, 51–52, 56, 58, 125, 267 n.38,
   exhortation arguments 269 n.44, 270 n.48,
      271 n.53, 274 nn.64–66, 283
   see also chansons de départie
Conrad III, king of Germany 54 n.7
Conrad IV Hohenstaufen, king of Sicily 161
   n.8, 201, 203
Conrad of Montferrat 47, 57–60, 74, 125
Conrad, archbishop of Mainz 76
Conradin 19, 203–04, 213–16
Constance, empress, wife of Frederick II 136
Constantine the African 14 n.58
Constantinople 79, 102–03, 118, 120, 189,
   276, 278, 291
   council to decide Boniface's claim to
      Thessalonica 3, 15, 112–13
   deviation of the crusading army 98–99,
      104, 111–12
   William IV of Montferrat's claim to 120
   end of Frankish rule 122, 298
Constanza, daughter of Roger Bernat III,
   count of Foix 242
Continuation Rothelin 171, 175
Corfu 102 n.13, 108, 111–12
Corrosana 7, 36
councils:
   Acre 197
   Bourges 154
   Greece 3 n.7, 15, 113–14
   1215 Lateran council 123–24, 132, 160,
      292
   Lyon in 1245 158 n.6, 186, 191
   Lyon in 1274 222, 225, 228, 230, 233,
      246, 299
Cremona 140–41, 151–52, 294
criticism of crusading 10, 13 n.55, 166, 205,

221, 254, 266, 272, 284–85
crozada, crosada 4–6, 180
crucesignatus 5 n.17, 248
Crusader States 29, 39, 40, 46, 134, 201 n.33, 257
Crusader Kingdom 142, 164
crusading terminology 3–7
crusading vows 25, 100, 104, 106, 122, 244, 257
   commutation of 129, 135, 203, 208, 222, 256, 274
Cutanda, battle 26, 286
Cyprus 1, 7, 162, 196, 246, 254–55, 257, 294
   Richard the Lonheart in 48, 66, 142
   war for the control of 144–53
   see also Ibelins

Dalfi of Auvergne 127
Damascus 33 n.18, 37–39, 73, 119, 286
Damietta 138, 145, 155, 161, 166, 265, 273, 278–79, 293
   Fifth Crusade 123–24, 130, 135–36
   Seventh Crusade 196
Daniel, Old Testament figure 69–70
Dante 56, 64
Daron 45
Daspol (Dasp, Guillem d'Autpol) 10 n.42, 82 n.11, 201 n.31, 222, 227 n.3, 230–33, 256, 299
Dauphiné 42
Delta *see* Nile
Demetrius, son of Boniface of Montferrat and Margaret of Hungary 120, 138–39
Demotica 113, 116
descort 46, 134
Devil 159, 162, 226–27, 273, 278
devinalh 227
Dieu d'Amour 144–45, 147, 149
disease *see* illness
Dit de Pouille see Chanson de Pouille
dits 224
Dominicans 165
Dordogne 61
Drogobites 118
Duran Sartor de Paernas (DurSartr) 10 n.37, 12 n.47, 22, 183, 297

Edessa 7–8, 30–31, 60, 93–94, 116, 265,
280 and n.86, 286
Edward I, king of of England 226, 227 n.4, 233, 248–50, 312
   see also Lord Edward
Edward II, king of of England 300
Egypt 66 n.20, 98, 136, 160, 202, 204, 207, 225, 265–66, 271
   Christian prisoners 15, 175, 177, 179, 196–97, 199, 214, 257
   Fifth Crusade 124, 130–31
   Barons' Crusade 174–75, 177
Eleanor of Aquitaine 28–29, 33 and n.18
Eleanor of Castile, wife of Edward I of England 227 n.4
Eleanor of England 88
Elias Cairel (ElCair) 2, 3, 9 n.30, 12, 121, 138–39 and nn.9–10, 291, 293–94
Elias d'Ussel (ElUss) 4 n.11, 12 n.47, 74, 111, 289, 291
Elias de Barjols (ElBarj) 12 n.49, 18 n.70, 141, 294
Empire:
   Angevin 78
   Byzantine 99
   Eastern 101
   Holy Roman 124, 155, 158, 201, 211, 292
   Latin in Greece 9, 116, 118–20, 122–24, 189 n.19, 256, 312
   Mediterranean 235
   see also Holy Roman Emperor
England 14, 48, 57, 97, 122, 167, 180, 201–02, 213, 273 n.57
   see also Edward I; Edward II; Eleanor of; Henry II; Henry III; John I; Richard the Lionheart
English 82–83, 85–86, 105, 181 n.6, 185, 193, 205, 250, 256
   wars between English and French 54, 82
   loss of Brittany and Normandy 123
   see also Edward I; Henry III; Richard the Lionheart
Enrico Dandolo, doge of Venice 113, 116
Eracles 145
Eudoxia of Constantinople 10 n.38
Eugenius III, pope 30
exempla 261 and n.12, 269

Faenza 180
Falquet de Romans (FqRom) 18 n.70, 162,

INDEX

261 n.11, 62 n.14, 143, 267 n.41, 277 n.76, 285 n.108, 293–94
  connected to other poets 2–3, 131, 156, 160
  Ghibelline sympathies 10 n.33, 140–43
Father of Raimon de Cornet (FrRmCorn) 248
Ferdinand of Castile 233 n.10
Finland 228
Flanders 101, 247
  see also Baldwin IX; Henry of Flanders
Flemish 101, 122
Florence 215
folly *see foudat*
Folquet de Lunel (FqLun) 11 n.43, 228, 299
Folquet de Marseilla (FqMars) 4 nn.12–13, 12 n.49, 18 n.70, 20 n.76, 83–84, 87, 288–90, 303
  see also Richard the Lionheart
foot soldiers 174, 179
foudat (playful folly) 65–66, 71–72, 95, 233
Fraga 85–86
Franks 90, 144, 174, 179, 207–08, 235, 247
Frederick Barbarossa 47, 54 n.7, 67 n.21, 288
Frederick II Hohenstaufen 2, 10, 17 and n.17, 123–24, 126, 131, 292–97
  and Barons' Crusade 171, 180
  crown of Jerusalem 158, 161
  crusade against 187, 192, 279
  death 201, 203
  departure on crusade 142, 148
  Empire 123–24
  excommunicated 158, 160, 162, 187, 191, 196
  illness 142, 162
  King of the Romans 130–31, 135
  papacy 10, 138, 141–42, 153, 156–64, 170–71, 180, 184, 189, 205, 224, 234, 254, 256, 276–77
  propaganda 140
  ruler of Arles 154–55, 157, 164
  Sixth Crusade 136–153
  treaty with al-Kāmil 167, 170
  see also Cyprus, war for the control of; Sicilian Vespers
Fulk of Villaret, grand master of the Hospitallers 247

Gace Brulé 53 n.7

Gaeta 158
Gaillac 192
Galata 99, 291
Galicia 91
Ganelon 129, 274
Gascons 240
Gascony 91, 181, 226
Gaspar 182
Gaston of Béarn 226
Gaucelm Faidit (GcFaid) 2–3, 4 n.11, 10 nn.38–39 and 42, 12 n.49, 15 n.59, 18 n.70, 91, 101, 262 n.22, 290–91, 303
  and Limousin court 15
  did not go on Third Crusade 102 n.10
  movements on Fourth Crusade 104–12
  composed in Old French 108
  versification and music 20 n.76, 21
Gauceran de Saint Leidier 12 n.47, 298
Gautier de Dargies (GtDarg) 2, 9, 11 n.46, 53 n.7, 75 n.25, 281 n.92, 289, 302
Gauvain of Chenichy 147
Gavaudan (Gav) 89, 91, 263, 268, 289
Gaza 174, 178–79, 257, 274, 296
Genoa 10, 60, 184, 189, 221
Genoese 12 n.49, 196, 214, 247
Geoffrey of Perche 78
Geoffrey of Vigeois 13–14, 25 n.1
Geoffroy of Villehardouin, chronicler (GV) 97, 99, 102, 105 n.22, 106, 120, 276
  a leader of the Fourth Crusade 97, 111
  deserters of the expedition 98, 102, 112 n.33
  see also councils: Greece
Geoffroy of Villehardouin, nephew of GV 121–22
Gerbert de Montreuil *see Roman de la Violette*
Germans 67, 91, 158, 185, 214
Germany 15, 47, 76 n.1, 104, 107 n.27, 124, 136, 158, 186–87, 203
Gerold of Lausanne, patriarch of Jerusalem 142
Gerona 29 n.9, 235
Ghibellines 17, 141, 142, 152–53, 160–61, 213-16, 225
  see also Frederick II Hohenstaufen
Giraut de Borneil (GrBorn) 4 nn.10 and 12, 10 nn.32 and 39, 12, 18 n.70, 51, 64 n.18, 80 n.7, 234, 255, 287–90

324

connections with other poets 3, 51
performance 22 n.85
pilgrimage with Aimar V of Limoges 1, 42, 62, 67, 95
Reconquista 2, 86, 91
Third Crusade 2, 42, 66–71, 96
see also Richard the Lionheart; *foudat*
Gisors 47
Gloucester 55
Gontier de Soignies (GoSoig) 4 n.12, 9, 75 n.25, 135 n.17, 289
Gormonda (Gorm) 163, 294
Goths 89
Gouffier of Lastours 14
Goulet 102
Granada 206, 234, 248
Granet (Gran) 194, 298, 303
Great Interregnum 203
Greece xvii, 1, 2, 3, 7, 9, 10, 98, 102, 112, 120–23, 256, 284
see also Boniface I; councils: Greece; Elias Cairel; Geoffroy of Villehardouin
Greenland 228
Gregory Bechada 14, 25 n.1
Gregory VIII, pope 47, 287
Gregory IX, pope 122, 145, 167, 180, 184, 213 n.16, 294, 296
and Frederick II 142–43, 149, 157, 158, 162, 170
Gregory X, pope 228–30, 235, 299
Guelfs 17, 180, 216
Guerau III de Cabrera 29 n.9
Gui de Cavaillon 2
Gui IV, count of Forez 2
Guibert de Nogent 36 n. 20
Guido Pelavicino 120
Guilhem Anelier de Tolosa 5
Guilhem de Tudela 4, 6
Guillaume de Dole 53
Guillaume de Villaret, master of the Hospitallers 246
Guillaume le Clerc *see Le Besant de Dieu*
Guillelmi 28 n.7
Guillem Ademar (GlAdem) 10 n.42, 12 n.47, 134, 292
Guillem d'Autpol *see* Daspol
Guillem de Berguedan (GlBerg) 12 n.47, 40, 287
Guillem de Montanhagol (GlMont) 181 n.9

Guillem de Mur (GlMur) 2, 12 n.49, 19, 219, 298, 299
Guillem Fabre de Narbona (GlFabre) 12 n.49, 16, 236, 257, 300
Guillem Figueira (GlFig) 10 n.41, 12, 17, 149, 276 n.74, 293, 294, 296
and Frederick II 10 n.33, 130, 152–53
anticlerical *sirventes* 17, 161–63, 266 n.35, 274 n.62, 277 and n.77, 278 n.83
Guillem Montanhagol *see* Guillem de Montanhagol
Guiot de Dijon (GuDij) 36 n.22, 103, 131, 262 n.16, 293, 302
Guiraut de Calanson 134
Guiraut de Luc (GrLuc) 12 n.47, 22 n.84, 84, 96, 289
Guiraut Riquier (GrRiq) 10 nn.38 and 42, 12 n.49, 20 n.76, 21, 210, 219, 298, 299, 300, 303, 304
and Spain 2, 206
after the Council of Lyon (1275) 233, 244
Guy de Montfort 215, 227
Guy of Auvergne 127
Guy of Lusignan, king of Jerusalem 47
Guy, marquis 121
Guyenne 19, 38

Haifa 207
Harbiyah *see* La Forbie
Hattin, battle 43, 47, 84, 179, 255, 257, 287
Henry I, king of Cyprus 144–47
Henry I, king of England 19 n.74
Henry II, king of England 12–14, 47, 54–55, 73, 284, 288
Henry III, king of England 180–81, 183, 201, 203, 205, 209, 221, 256
Henry II, count of Rodez 233
Henry IV, duke of Limburg 142
Henry de Lacy 11 n.46, 213
Henry of Almain 227
Henry of Bar 174
Henry of Castile 227–28, 230
Henry, count of Flanders 118–20, 122, 291, 292
Henry VI, Holy Roman Emperor 76, 80–81, 83
Henry, the 'Young King' 13–14, 55
heresy 5 n.16, 17, 79, 81, 126–27, 279
holy fire 56

Holy Roman Emperor 76, 80, 123–24, 203, 211, 213, 228, 256, 292
  see also Frederick II; Henry VI; Otto IV
Honorius III, pope 124, 142, 293, 294
Hospitallers *see* military orders
Hugh VII le Brun, lord of Lusignan 3, n.8
Hugh IX, lord of Lusignan 106
Hugh of Gibelet 147
Hugh of Lusignan, king of Cyprus 144
Hugh, count of La Marche 181
Hughes de Berzé (HgBerzé) 11 n.46, 262 n.19, 269 n.44, 270 n.50, 276, 281 nn. 92-93 and 95-96, 282 n.101, 290, 292, 302
  connections with other poets 2, 131
  Fourth Crusade 102–03
Hungary 98, 111, 112 n.33, 113, 120, 138, 139, 193
Huon d'Oisy (HuOisy) 4 n.10, 11 n.46, 51–62, 267 n.38, 274 n.67, 288, 302
Huon de Saint-Quentin (HStQuen) 12, 129–30, 166, 266 n.35, 268 n.42, 269 n.44, 273 nn.56 and 58, 274 nn.59–60, 275, 277, 293, 302

Ibelin 45
Ibelins 144–49, 152–53, 199, 254
  see also John of; Balian of; Philip of; Baldwin of
Iberia xvi, 1, 6, 25–26, 37, 86, 89, 185, 246, 255
Iceland 228
illness 140 n.11, 142, 162, 187–88, 199, 210, 257
Imbert = Uberto II, count of Biandrate? 2 n.2
Innocent III, pope 5, 136, 290, 291, 292
  Albigensian Crusade 79, 127, 132, 134
  and Frederick II 158 n.6
  Third Crusade 91, 93, 97, 123–25, 129
Innocent IV, pope 158 n.6, 184, 186, 191, 203, 294
Innocent V, pope 235
Ireland 55 n.8
Irene Angelus, wife of Philip of Swabia 98
Isaac II Angelus, emperor of Greece 99
Isaac II Comnenus 113
Isaac of L'Etoile 272
Isabella delle Carceri 121–22, 138
Isla dels Cambis 192
Islam 27, 204, 207, 224

Italy xvii, 1, 7, 139, 144, 167, 186, 187, 203, 216, 235–36, 290
  conflicts in northern Italy 17, 141, 213–15
  courts 125, 139, 143,
  crusaders pass through 102–04, 107–08, 112, 158
  see also Charles of Anjou; Frederick II Hohenstaufen; Guillem Figueira

Jacques de Vitry 261 n.12, 264 n.24
Jacques Pecoraria 191
James I, king of Aragon 2, 180–81, 183, 201-02, 206, 209, 213, 299
  crusade 19, 204, 216–20, 224, 298
  at the 1174 Council of Lyon 228–230, 233, 256
James II, king of Mallorca 16, 235, 241
James II, king of of Aragon 246
James of Vitry *see* Jacques de Vitry
Jaufre Rudel (JfreRud) 1, 3 n.8, 31 n.14, 32–34, 38, 286
Jean Renart *see Guillaume de Dole*
Jeanne de Bourgogne 251
Jeanne, daughter of Raymond VII of Toulouse 180
Jerusalem 14, 98, 111, 119, 129, 139, 209, 246, 248, 264–66, 268 n.42, 270, 273, 275, 296, 302
  fall to Saladin 1, 38, 42, 43 n.6, 47–48, 63, 69, 269 n.44, 287
  kingdom of 1, 13, 42, 46, 47, 199
  pilgrimages to 10, 111, 136, 178
  returned by al-Kāmil to Frederick II 142, 144, 152–53 n.32, 160, 164
  sack of 1244 178–79, 184–85, 188, 196, 255, 297
  via Jerusalem 25–26
  see also Charles of Anjou; Conradin; Frederick II Hohenstaufen; John of Brienne; Joscelin III (or IV); Odo of Montbéliard
Jews 184
Jewish women 85–86, 88
Joan de Castelnou 249, 300
Johannitz, tsar of the Wallacho-Bulgarians 116
John I, king of England 55, 78, 97 n.3, 97, 123, 124, 126
John of Brienne 124, 139, 157 n.5, 158, 166

John of Ibelin 10, 144–49, 151, 152–53, 196
John XXI, pope 235
John XXII, pope 249
Joinville 186, 193, 197, 223, 224
Jordan, river 8, 36–37, 137
Joscelin III (or IV), seneschal of Jerusalem 125

Kantara (La Candare), Cyprus 145, 147–48
Kerak *see* an-Nasir Da-ud of Kerak
Khwarismians 179, 194
Knights of St John *see* military orders
Kyrenia, Cyprus 145

La Castrie, Cyprus 147
La Disputaison du croisé et du décroisé 224 n.24
La Forbie 179, 184, 196, 297
La Voie de Tunis 224 n.24
Lanfranc Cigala (LanfrCig) 12 n.51, 184, 189–90, 196, 297
Languedoc 70, 79, 132, 134, 154, 179–81, 184, 196, 272, 284
Las Navas de Tolosa, battle 123, 127, 143, 255, 292
Lateran council of 1215 123, 132, 292
Latins 117–18, 122, 153 n.32, 161,
Lattes 202
Lavaur 192
Le Besant de Dieu 166
Le Puy 90, 127
León 26, 90, 91, 182 n.10
Leopold V, duke of Austria 48, 76, 289
Leys d'Amors 22
Liguria 140, 143
Limassol 144, 196
Limousin 13-14, 15, 43, 83, 106, 109
Limoux 183–84
Llibre dels feits 217, 229
Llobregat 239
Lo Bort del Rey d'Arago 245-46
Lombards 145, 147, 157, 158, 214
 in Thessalonica 120–22, 138, 292
Lombardy 79, 103, 107, 131, 140 n.11, 208–09
 Lombard League against Frederick II 141, 150–52, 158
London 61
Lord Edward 221, 225–28; *see also* Edward I, king of England
Lorris, peace of 181
Louis VI, king of France 29
Louis VII, king of France 28–30, 33 n.18, 34–36 and n. 22, 37, 38, 54 n.7, 101
Louis VIII, king of France 154–55, 161, 294
Louis IX, king of France 10, 122, 178, 264, 271, 275
 captivity in Egypt 2, 15, 217
 'death' and 'resurrection' 186–89
 Seventh Crusade 13, 158 n.6, 160, 179, 180–81, 192–93, 196–99, 201–02, 254, 256, 257, 297–98
 Eighth Crusade 203–05, 209–10, 217, 219, 221–27, 235, 256, 299
 death 221–23, 225–27, 230, 254
Louis, count of Blois 97, 113
Louis, hero of the epic cycle of Charlemagne 119
Luc de la Barre 19
Luchera 216
Luquet Gatelus 234
Lyon 60, 171, 186
 see also councils

Ma'arrat-an-Nu'man 14
Maguelone 218
Mahomet 91, 200, 201, 216, 223
 see also Bafomet
Mainz 69
Malaspina 15, 125
Mameluks 174, 204, 206
Manfred 203, 205, 206, 213
Mansurah 2, 196, 199, 217, 257, 298
Mantes 60
Mantua 215
Manuel I Comnenus 112–13
Marabouts 90
Marcabru (Mbru) 4 n.10, 10 n.32, 19, 20 n. 76, 22, 31 n.14, 53–54 n.7, 79 n.7, 201 n.31, 286, 287, 304
 Reconquista 2, 20, 26, 27, 29, 255
 Second Crusade 3, 20, 26–29, 32–39, 255
Marchesopulo of Parma 120
Margaret (Maria) of Hungary 113, 120, 138
Maria de Ventadorn 107
Maria of Antiochv235
Marseille 104, 105, 136, 137, 164, 171, 191–92, 247

Richard the Lionheart in 20, 60, 62
Martin IV, pope v16, 234, 235, 237
Masmudes 89
Matieu de Caerci (MatQuercy) 2 n.6, 230, 299
Matthew Paris 187, 193, 206
Meaux 155
Melchior 182
Melicadefer *see* Baibars
merchants 249
Messina 108, 235
Michael Comnenus Ducas 139
Milan 151
military orders 29 n.8, 175, 209, 233, 244–46, 257
   Hospitallers 54 n.7, 146, 175–76, 179, 245–47, 274
   Templars 2, 9, 12 n.50, 37, 42, 84–86, 135, 144, 175–76, 179, 201, 205, 207–09, 217–19, 245–47, 274
   Teutonic knights 176, 179
Milon of Brabant 116
Minorites 201
Modon 118
Mohammed *see* Mahomet
Molay, grand master of the Templars 246-47
money-lenders *see* bankers
Monferrat *see* Boniface I; Conrad of Monferrat; William VI
Monge de (Monk of) Montaudo (MoMont) 10 n.42, 12 n.50, 82–83 n.12, 87, 289
Mongols 196, 204
Moniot d'Arras 166
Mont-Aimé, Champagne 167
Mont-Cénis 102, 146
Montagut, castle 132
Montbolò 241
Montpellier 202, 217
Moors 40, 66, 81, 89, 101, 123, 140, 183, 206, 216
Morea 112
Morocco 16, 40, 81, 89
Moses 214, 266
Mudejars 206
Murcia 2, 206, 217
Muret 123, 292
Murol 60
music 12, 20-22, 23, 63, 239, 254, 302-05

mustering 16, 236–37, 257

Naples 143, 157, 213
Narbonne 16-17, 79. 210, 236
Navarrese 4
Névelon 116
Nicetas, Cathar bishop of Constantinople 79
Nicholas III, pope 235
Nicholas IV, pope 246
Nicosia, Cyprus 145, 146-47, 149, 295
Nile 85, 122, 174, 196
Nompar de Caumont 11, 131–32, 295
Normandy 61, 78, 81, 101–02, 123, 166, 181, 289
Normans 29
North America 228
Northampton 61

Odo of Montbéliard, constable of Jerusalem 147
Oléron 82
Olivier lo Templier 19, 217–19, 299
Orderic Vitalis 19 n.74, 25
Othon del Carret 140, 143
Otranto 142
Otto IV of Brunswick, Holy Roman Emperor 123–24, 126, 292
Otto von Bolentauben, count of Hennenberg and Anhalt 124

Padua 149, 151
Palaizi *see* Tomier and Palaizi
Palermo 203
Palestine 39, 66 n.20, 98, 130, 144, 158, 204, 230, 236
Palma 151-52
papal bulls 9, 16, 79
   Quia major 123–29, 127, 129, 292
   Exsurgat Deus 247
papal-imperial hostilities *see* Frederick II Hohenstaufen, papacy
Papiol 59–61
Paris 101, 102, 122, 155–57, 160, 163–64, 180–83, 185, 186, 188, 194, 196, 295
Parthenay 181
Patarins 243–44
Peire Bremon lo Tort (PBremTort) 1, 4 n.10, 12 n.47, 40, 287
Peire Bremon Ricas Novas (PBrem) 2, 296

INDEX

Peire Cardenal (PCard) 3, 10 nn.32–33 and 36, 12 n.47, 17, 143, 160, 165, 228, 274, 294–96, 299
  Albigensian Crusade 3, 274
  connections with other poets 156
  pro-imperial songs 156, 160, 277
Peire d'Alvernhe (PAlv) 4 n.10, 10 n.32, 12 n.49, 22 n.85, 39, 287, 292
Peire de la Caravana 17
Peire de Lunel *see* Cavalier Lunel de Montech
Peire del Vilar (PVilar) 181, 297
Peire III d'Arago (PArag) *see* Peter III, king of Aragon
Peire Salvatage 239–43, 300
Peire Vidal (PVid) 4 and nn. 10–12, 10 n.32, n.63, n.38, n.42, 20 n.76, 78, 254, 287–89, 304
  Reconquista 40, 120 n.44
  at court of Tripoli 43–46, 62, 69
  Third Crusade 70–73
  Fourth Crusade 101
Peirol 12, 73–74, 138, 288, 293, 304
  pilgrimage to Jerusalem 2, 10, 136
Pelagius, papal legate 166, 2273
Peleponnese 112, 116, 118 n.42, 122
Perdigon 91, 290
performance of songs 15–16, 20–23, 253
Périgord 87 n. 17
Perpignan 235-36
Perseval Doria (PersDor) 10 n. 36, 12 n. 51, 206, 298
Persians 60, 92–93, 115, 165, 208, 214
Perugia 19, 216
Peter II, king of Aragon 91, 120, 123, 127, 132
Peter III, king of Aragon 16, 235, 239–42
Peter of Blois 51, 76
Peter of La Palud, patriarch of Jerusalem 248
Peter the Deacon 14 n.58
Philip Augustus, king of France 54 n.7, 84, 97 n.3, 101–02, 123–24, 126, 288
  and Richard the Lionheart 47–48, 56, 58–60, 62, 78, 80, 81, 91
Philip II, king of France 233
Philip III the Bold, king of France 16, 209, 222, 225, 228, 230, 235–36, 238
Philip IV, king of France 244, 247, 300
Philip V, king of France 248
Philip VI, king of of France Philip II, lord of Nanteuil-le-Haudouin 175 244, 247–51, 256, 300
Philip II, lord of Nanteuil-le-Haudouin 175
Philip of Beauvais 76
Philip of Ibelin 144
Philip of Montreal 40, 42
Philip of Swabia 98
Philip the Chancellor 128
Philippe de Nanteuil (PhNant) 296
Philippe de Novare (PhNov) 2, 10 n.41, 11 and n.43, n.46, 145–49, 153, 254, 255, 257, 262 n.18, 295
Piedmont 140
Piedmontese 215
pirates 108, 229–30
planh 21, 28, 40, 91, 93–94, 221–22, 230
Plantagenets 54, 62, 102 n.10
Poitevins 31 n.12, 77
Poitiers 70–71, 181, 197, 221
Poitou 3 n.8, 26, 28–29, 38, 40, 91, 181, 270 n.46
Polpís del Mastrazgo 84–86
Pons de Capdoill (PoCapd) 2, 9 n.31, 12 n.47, 125–27, 132, 292
Pons de Mataplana 40, 287
Pons II, lord of Gerona 29 n.9
Portugal 91
Pozzuoli 142
priors 157
prisoners 110, 15, 26, 130, 142, 175, 177–79, 196–99, 275
Provençals 91, 233
Provence 45, 70, 90, 104, 137, 141, 143, 164, 186, 189, 191–93, 196, 211, 216, 297
  see also Charles of Anjou; Raimon Berenguer, count of Provence; Sanchia of Provence
public 1, 13, 16–19, 38, 96, 128, 187, 216, 236–37, 254, 255, 257, 266, 270, 276, 284
  opinion 10 n. 34, 13, 18, 47, 63, 158
  bourgeois 15
  ritual 56, 81, 105 n.20, 167
  see also audiences
purgatory 230, 264

Quia major see papal bulls
Qutuz of Egypt, sultan 204

Raimbaut de Vaqueiras (RbVaq) 2, 3, 9 n.30,

10 and n.38, 12 n.47, 15, 20 n.76, 276, 290–91, 304
  connection with other poets 46
  on Fourth Crusade 98, 100, 103, 113–20
Raimon de Cornet (RmCorn) 10 n.36, 12 n.50, 249, 250, 256, 300, 301
Raimon of Baux 164
Raimon de Miraval (RmMirav) 12 n.47, 132, 292, 304
Raimon Gaucelm de Beziers (RmGauc) 9 n.31, 210, 221, 299
Ralph Niger 272, 284 n.107
Ramón Berenguer IV, count of Barcelona 37, 86
Raoul de Soissons (RlSoiss) 2, 9, 11 n.46, 199, 257, 262 n.16, 281 n.94, 297, 298, 302, 303
Raoul le Noir, supporter of Thomas Becket 284
Ravano dalle Carceri of Verona 120–22, 138
Ravennika 120
Raymond, prince of Antioch 33
Raymond Berenguer V, count of Provence 134, 164, 180, 184, 186 n.13, 189, 192, 196, 297
Raymond II, count of Tripoli 1, 43, 62, 69
Raymond IV, count of Saint-Gilles 25
Raymond V, count of Toulouse 79, 289
Raymond VI, count of Toulouse 124, 132, 134, 292
Raymond VII, count of Toulouse 8, 154–57, 161, 163–65, 180–81, 186, 254, 278
Raymond Llull 247–48
Raymond-Roger, count of Foix 124, 133
Reconquista 2, 10, 29, 37–40, 43, 75, 81, 87, 96, 185, 206, 230, 254, 255–56
Regno 158, 203, 211
Renas 12 n.48, 265 n.33, 269 and n.44, 292
Renaud de Montmirail 102
renegade Christians 73, 90–91
Renier, brother of Boniface of Monferrat 112
Rhodes 247, 248, 300
Rhône, river 154, 164, 186, 189
Ricaut Bonomel 2, 206–08, 227, 298
Richard de Fournival 169
Richard Filangieri 145
Richard of Cornwall 178, 203, 209
Richard the Lionheart (RoiRich) 11 n.46, 13–14, 20, 54 n.7, 54–55, 62, 87, 169, 288–90
  captivity 2, 76–84
  death and reputation 21, 91–94, 96, 97, 254
  Third Crusade 47–48, 63, 66–67, 70, 75, 287
  see also Bertran de Born
Robert, bishop of Clermont 127
Robert de Béthune 215
Robert de Clari 99
Robert of Mehun, bishop of Le Puy 127
Robert the Monk 188
Rodez 54 n.7 233
Roger Bernat III, count of Foix see Coms de Foix
Roger of Howden 80
Roger of Luria, admiral 235
Roland, chanson de geste hero 119, 129, 137, 274
Rolandino of Canossa 120
Romain de Saint-Ange, papal legate 154
Roman de la Violette 53
Roman de Renart 11, 146–48, 157, 255
Romania 112, 265, 291
Romanie, Romenie 189 n.19, 199, 303
Rome 17, 79, 98, 99, 112, 140, 157, 181, 203, 213, 218, 229, 235, 244, 272
  Guillem Figueira's invective against 17, 151 n.28, 161–63, 277–79
  see also *Complainte de Jérusalem contre Rome*
Rostaing Berenguier de Marseilla (RostBer) 10 n.36, 245, 300
rotrouenge 16
Rouen 61
Roussillon 235
Rudolf of Habsburg 203
Rukn ad-Din 174
Rutebeuf 223, 224

Safadin 101, 111
Saint Denis 101–02
Saint-Céré 43
Saint-Félix-de-Caraman 79, 287
Saint Hilarion see Dieu d'Amour
Saint-Romain 165
Saint-Sernin 54 n.7
Sainte-Marie-de-Vauvert 217
Saintes, battle 181
Saladin 38, 43, 47, 48, 51, 57–58, 67, 69,

75, 89
Salimbene de Adam 201
San Germano 140, 145, 153, 157, 295
San Gimignano 17
Sanchia of Aragon 180
Sanchia of Provence 180
Sancho III, king of Castile 40
Sancho IV, king of Castile 233 n.10
Sancho VII, king of Navarre 40
Sancho VIII, king of Navarre 90
Sancta Maria d'Orien 53–54 n.7
Sant'Ellero 215
Saumur 181
Savoy 60
Sea of Galilee 47
sergeants 51, 105 n.22, 148, 179, 208
sermons 16, 52, 159, 165, 267 n.38, 274 n.61
   crusade 136, 188 n.18, 249, 259 n.4, 261 n.12, 264 n.24, 273
   musical 63, 128–29
   vernacular 126
Sicar 118
Sicilian Vespers, war of 225, 234–36, 299
Sicilians 158
Sicily 203, 205, 224, 230, 256
Sidon 42
Simon de Montfort, leader of the Albigensian Crusade 5, 112 n.33, 123, 132
Simon de Montfort, cousin of Charles of Anjou 227
Simon of Brie, papal legate 203, 208–09, 256
Soissons 100, 103, 107
Song of the Albigensian Crusade 4
songs of departure see *chansons de départie*
Sordel (Sord) 10 n.42, 12 n.47, 13, 135, 195, 298
Spain 4 n.10, 9, 26–29, 54 n.7, 84, 89, 91, 101, 120 n.44, 123, 224, 255, 292
   criticism of Spanish kings 40, 81, 86, 96
   troubadours in 2, 26, 139
   war against Muslims in Spain compared with war in Holy Land 8, 27, 37–38, 87
   see also Alfonso X of Castile; Aragonese crusade; James I of Aragon; Reconquista
Spaniards 91
Speyer 80
St George's straits 119
Sussex 61

Tagliacozzo, battlev203, 255, 227, 230, 298
Taillebourg, battle 181
Tarascon 164
Tarragona 26 n.4
Tartars 208
taxation 51, 97, 206, 209, 232, 235, 273
Templars see military orders
Temple 38, 137, 175, 218, 245
Templier see Ricaut Bonomel
tenso 20, 28, 73, 82–83, 121, 138, 194, 213, 227 n.3, 230–31, 255
Tervagan 60, 200
Teutonic knights see military orders
Thessalonica 122, 138–39, 292, 293
   see also Boniface of Monferrat; Lombards; William IV, marquis of Montferrat
Thibaut III, count of Champagne 9, 97–98
Thibaut IV, count of Champagne, king of Navarre from 1234 (TbChamp) 3, 154–56, 166, 199, 254, 280–81, 294, 296
   Barons' Crusade 2, 167–79
   connection with other poets 3, 255, 277
   Liederbuch 11
Thibaut V, count of Champagne, king of Navarre 221
Thierry of Loos, seneschal 113
Thouars 61
Tiberias 47, 73
Tillières 81
Titgrave 61
Toledo 88, 219
Tomier and Palaizi (TomPal) 5, 10 n.37, 12 n.47, 133, 154, 293, 294
Toron 45
Tortosa 37, 218, 286
Toulon 45
Toulousain 90, 155, 180
Toulouse 12 n.49, 17, 45, 78, 79, 133, 154, 160, 162–65, 192, 278
   see also Raymond V, Raymond VI and Raymond VII, counts of Toulouse
Touraine 78, 81
Tours 70, 240
Tower of David 74, 179
Trifels 76
Tripoli 45, 66, 137, 257
   see also Raymond II, count of Tripoli
True Cross 47, 56, 70, 101, 264,
Tunis 204, 221, 223–27, 230, 235, 299

INDEX

Turkey 189
Tuscany 214
typology 9, 260
Tyre 74, 124, 137, 183, 199, 209
   defended by Conrad of Monferrat 47, 57, 59, 125
   see also Continuation Rothelin

Uc of Baux 104
Uc de Pena (UcPenn) 2, 12 n.49, 294
Uc de saint Circ (UcStC) 180, 296
Urban II, pope 26 n.4, 36 n.20, 188
Urban III, pope 47
Urban IV, pope 184

Valencia 85
Vallés 239
Velay 127
Venetians 97–99. 106. 112. 115. 122
Venice 98, 102, 104, 107–08 n.17, 113, 290
versification 18, 20, 22, 46, 132, 175, 280 n.87
Vertaizon 127
Vézelay 30, 48, 54 n.7, 59, 286, 288
Vidame de Chartres (VdChar) 2, 9, 102, 291
Vienne tenth 247
Vigneri 120
Villarets 246
   see also Guillaume de Villaret
Villehardouin *see* Geoffroy of Villehardouin
Virgin Mary 8, 54 n.7, 107, 124, 200, 216, 217, 261 n. 9, 281
Viterbo 227

Vlachs 115, 118

Wallacho-Bulgarians 15, 116
Walter de Bibbesworth 11 n.46, 213
Walter Map 272
Walter of Jaffa 174
William IX, duke of Aquitaine 25–26, 286
William X, duke of Aquitaine 26, 28, 29, 79 n.7, 286
William Longsword, marquis of Montferrat 41–42
William VI, marquis of Montferrat 120–21, 131, 138–40
William Malaspina 125
William of Baux 133
William of Cayeux 78
William of Champlitte 118 n.42
William of Holland 203
William of Longchamp 76
William of Newburgh 76
William of Rivet 147
William of Tyre *see* Continuation Rothelin
Winchester 81
women 33, 48, 85, 147, 213 n.16, 251, 271, 283, 285

Yolanda (Isabella), queen of Jerusalem 139, 140 n.11, 161 n.8

Zara (Zadar) 98–99, 102, 104, 108, 111–12, 290, 291
Zengi 30, 280 n.86, 286
Zoën Tencarari, papal legate 186, 191

www.ingramcontent.com/pod-product-compliance
Lightning Source LLC
Chambersburg PA
CBHW051557230426
43668CB00013B/1884